Crossings 29

The Transplants

The Transplants

Giuseppe Prezzolini

Edited and translated by
Fabio Girelli Carasi

BORDIGHERA PRESS

Cover photo by Pamkoner, CC BY-SA 4.0, via Wikimedia Commons

Library of Congress Cataloging-in-Publication Data
Names: Prezzolini, Giuseppe, 1882-1982, author. | Girelli Carasi, Fabio, translator.
Title: The transplants / Giuseppe Prezzolini ; edited and translated by Fabio Girelli Carasi.
Other titles: Trapiantati. English
Description: New York, NY : Bordighera Press, [2021] | Series: Crossings; 29 | Includes bibliographical references and index. | Summary: "This collection of writings from Giuseppe Prezzolini is about the Italians who migrated to North America. Compiled here, they contain observations that differ from other, more conventional approaches and analyses. Most of those who have come to know and have written about these migrants and their descendants have been impressed by their economic success. While a large portion have triumphed over the trials of migration, they have done so at the cost of becoming mutilated in language and, therefore, in spirit. The Transplants attempts to trace this journey."-- Provided by publisher.

Identifiers: LCCN 2020050101 | ISBN 9781599541372 (trade paperback)
Subjects: LCSH: Italian Americans--Social life and customs--20th century. | Italian Americans--History--20th century.
Classification: LCC E184.I8 P8413 2021 | DDC 973/.0451--dc23
LC record available at https://lccn.loc.gov/2020050101

Printed in the United States.

Published by
BORDIGHERA PRESS
John D. Calandra Italian American Institute
25 W. 43rd Street, 17th Floor
New York, NY 10036

CROSSINGS 29
ISBN 978-1-59954-137-2

TABLE OF CONTENTS

Coelum non animum mutant qui trans mare currunt.

HORACE

FOREWORD

In this volume I collected some of my writings about the Italians who migrated to North America. I decided to compile them here for I believe they contain observations that differ from other more conventional approaches and analyses. Most of those who have come to know and have written about these migrants and their descendants have been impressed by their economic success. I certainly do not deny the end result, and I am happy for it. However, I have been struck mostly by the price they had to pay to achieve it. A large portion of them has triumphed over the trials of migration, but at the cost of becoming mutilated in the language and, therefore, the spirit. At the same time, their vanity has been enlarged by the newly acquired economic status that, in their eyes, is higher than what they would have ever achieved in yesterday's Italy, a country that doesn't exist anymore and in whose recent development they have not taken part.

I also believe that the term *Italo-americani* does not reflect their true nature in that they are not the children of a mixing of races and cultures. Rather, they are the product of adaptation. In this process they have simultaneously lost touch with the people they originated from without melting with the people who took them in. The result, therefore, is not the fusion of Italian and American qualities; it is instead the confusion of different habits and the smoothening of sharp edges by two cultures that are complete strangers to each other. In other words, they are not the sum of two wholes, but, rather, the remainder of two subtractions. The migrants have not preserved Italy inside nor have they added America. They are like a seed that, planted in the soil, decomposes in order to give birth to a new plant. I have no doubt that something new and important will be born of them, as several examples already suggest, but in this moment the Italian seed is only in the process of decaying.

When I am asked for a definition of the term Italian American, I don't indulge in the lawyerly and superficial criterion of citizenship, according to which Italian Americans are people who were born in Italy, or children of Italian-born parents who were in turn born in this country. To me, Italian Americans are those who cannot speak well any of the two languages, either Italian or English, and are satisfied with a vernacular of a few hundred words dealing with the daily material existence, with no nuances or emotions, often pronounced with a brutish accent, unappealing both to Italian and to American ears.

The majority of Italian Americans, after leaving an ungrateful nation and finding an even harsher one, could no longer keep up with the events and the transformations of the country of origin, and often not even with those of their new home. Nothing had prepared them for the new land. They shared no common ideals with it; no moral, religious or political perspectives and not even similar customs in sports, food or religion. Their economic status improved mostly because America was growing and becoming richer, carrying along on its drive for wealth and power those who could survive; the very same ones who had contributed as raw material to fuel its rise.

Freedom, the most precious legacy left by the Founding Fathers and of which America is enormously proud, was an alien concept to their minds. It was a kind of freedom that had nothing positive to offer to the newly arrived. It was a vacuum. In this vacuum they had to keep going, under the strain of hunger and poverty. The fact that only a few of them, often the most courageous ones, ended up choosing crime is truly admirable. As I wrote in several occasions, any Italian who migrated to the United States and did not become insane or turned out a criminal, or did not get killed as a young man, is truly worthy of admiration.

Those who did survive, even if they were good people, still carry the scars of the trials they had to face. First of all, let me say that all the *Transplants* (my definition) are—to a certain degree—a little strange, touchy, almost paranoid and always defensive in front of every criticism. They are also very insecure, as is typical of those who speak a poorly-learned language; or use unfamiliar instruments; or walk along an unknown path they had never seen before. Mine is more a feeling than clinical, demonstrable observations, but I happened to notice these aspects many times in the course of my contacts with them. Only someone who has lived in an Italian American environment without becoming one of them and without their language and behavior can be aware of it.

Another aspect that was noticed as far back as last century is a sort of arrogant nationalism displayed especially by the children of migrants. Edmondo De Amicis[1] observed this phenomenon in the Italians that had migrated to Argentina but the same holds true also for those who came to North America. This is probably the response to the fear of being considered foreigners, a perfectly reasonable fear in that, despite the protestations of equality by the American ruling class, the immigrants; their descendants; whoever else belongs to a race other than the Anglo-Saxon or has a foreign accent and does not belong to one of the Protestant denominations, has always been considered a second-class citizen.

The premise of my writings is that I consider emigration to be a tragedy. (Probably it is also the first time that anyone has stated this fact unequivocally.) There are many reasons, both intrinsic and historical, that make the condition of being a migrant a tragic one. Certainly, this doesn't reflect the impression of the non-migrant Italians who visited America between 1880 and 1930. In this volume I discuss some examples of how Italian travelers and journalists have described the experience of migrants, in a mixture of comments, reporting and, sometimes, caricatures.

I also denounce Italy's official policies which, in my opinion, are at odds with Italy's interests in her relation with the United States. These policies have been limited to securing the easy loyalty of the *Transplants* who, as I already said, are insecure representatives both of Italy and the United States. I have said and reported all this without a hidden agenda; with no desire to attack anyone; without rancor and with a bit of sadness. I would have been happier to report only success stories (and some instances of success indeed appear in these pages). But that is a subject that has already been covered by many others.

Notice to the Reader: Many of my observations on Italian Americans also apply to other ethnic groups in the United States, the so-called

---

1   Edmondo De Amicis (1846-1908). Novelist, essayist and journalist. He is best known for the international bestseller *Cuore* (Milano, Fratelli Treves, 1886) [*Heart: A School-Boy's Journal*]; and numerous travelogues including *Sull'oceano* [*On the Ocean*] (Milano, Fratelli Treves, 1889), a reportage on his journey to Argentina with Italian emigrants.

hyphenated.[2] There are two partial exceptions to this generalization: Jews and Irish. European Jews came to America in conditions that were completely different from those of rural populations from other countries. Most of them were modest merchants with a greater respect for intellectual life and with an understanding of how important education was for survival. The Irish came to American with the ability to speak English and with centuries-long experience in politics, an experience gained in the struggle against England.

* * *

I have often been asked by Italians: "Who are these Italian Americans? Why don't they speak Italian like us? Why don't they read the same books we read? Why don't they behave like us? Why do they serve a lunch of spaghetti with meat balls as if it were an Italian dish instead of the sorry marriage of a Swedish recipe with an Italian one?" As I said earlier, Italian Americans bear the wrong name. They are not a mixture of Italy and America: they are Italians lost in America. With the exception of very rare instances, there is no trace of Anglo-Saxon blood in them, just a veneer of learned behaviors applied over an Italian way of life. Millions of Italian migrants, although tossed in and mixed in the American salad, are actually a barrier or a geological fault between the two countries. For a long time they have prevented Americans from learning what Italy really is. Between 1880 and 1922 Italy sent to the United States and into the world millions of people who did not represent Italy as a cultivated country; rich in monuments and noble traditions; endowed with an intellectual élite that was on a par with the French; with industries, railroads, universities and social mores equal to those of the rest of Europe. The migrants were called *Italian* but they weren't *Italian*. They weren't the product of a national educational system that later transformed rural populations, saddled with a parochial or provincial perspective, into citizens of a country with a unique place in the world and with the legacy of a great civilization.

---

2   For a comprehensive discussion about the issue of hyphenation, see Anthony Tamburri's *To Hyphenate or Not to Hyphenate?: The Italian/American Writer: An Other America.* Montreal, Guernica, 1991.

The poor farmhands that left southern Italy (and often also central and northern Italy) were completely ignorant of this civilization. They only knew their little villages and their only aspiration was to escape hunger. Each one of them only felt a connection with the *paesani*. The only form of social life that elevated them above those almost sheep-like forms of group identity was the Catholic religion, although its ministers were not particularly well educated and often did not live up to the ideals of a Christian life. And let's not talk, please, about the Italian diplomatic and consular authorities who, with few exceptions, from the height of their sophistication regarded this mass of migrants as an annoyance to be kept as distant as possible.

These things need to be said, albeit without hostility toward the migrants who were often good and courageous people. Italy sent these people to the United States almost like an afterthought, without thinking that in fifty years they would become the equivalent of commercial samples, used by the American ruling class to form a judgment on today's Italy! It is not these immigrants' fault if today they speak a broken Italian and their children don't speak it at all. I have long maintained that if an Italian immigrant didn't end up in an insane asylum or didn't become a gangster it was a miracle; and these miracles are millions. Their overriding goal was to escape the poverty of their forbearers and achieve positions that fulfilled the ambition to be relevant in their communities. The first generation is still present today and has shaped the Italian model in the collective mind of Americans who don't travel much abroad. Hence, the widespread representation in America of the Italian as an insignificant man with earth-tone complexion, short, poorly dressed, with huge handlebar mustache, with an organ grinder on his back in the company of a small monkey, begging for money while playing querulous Neapolitan songs. Out of the need for survival and because of lack of education, in the largest cities the first generation of Italian immigrants had to resign to jobs that Americans regarded as humiliating, such as rag picker, waiter, barber or shoeshine. Relegated to the same jobs were also people of color such as Blacks and Chinese. Only those Italians who—by luck or wisdom—settled down in the countryside were able to achieve human respectability in addition to a dignified economical position. The second generation, which in general no longer speaks the parents' dialects, was educated in American schools. In its midst some leaders emerged who established connections with the Republican or, more frequently, the Democratic party and became de-facto representatives of electoral clienteles identified as the Italian vote. In the last few decades the interests of Italian Americans have been represented in general by discredited individuals who stand in low esteem in the community. Their power in the Italian communities was not the result of respect or affection. Rather, it comes from the privileges and recognition the Italian government bestows on them. In fact, the Italian government has embraced these individuals with honors and rewards, giving them the kind of legitimacy and relevance that they could not achieve by their own merit. All Italian governments and political regimes, from the pre-Fascist liberal to the Fascist and finally the Christian Democrat[3] have persevered in the same error.

In all major American metropolises that have been invaded by foreign peoples, with their differences in culture, language, religion and political customs, even those where the Italian vote is irrelevant, there are numerous ties between politicians and organized crime. Often these secret connections are denounced by the media and have thus become a sort of legend, in all likelihood darker than reality. The word Mafia today has taken the place of what was once called racket. These were loose associations of criminals who extorted illicit gains by offering protection to all sort of activities—some illegal themselves. The protection, in turn, was obtained by bribing the police, politicians and political groups and associations that benefited from those profits. This form of criminal system was not brought to America by Italians. They found it here. They simply trained at this school and perfected it.

Thus, when people ask me: "What kind of people are these Italian Americans," my answer is: "They are what you made them: America enlarged them and the Italian government legitimized them as representatives of America."

New York, 19 dicembre 1958

---

3   Pre-Fascist liberal: the so-called *Giolitti Era* from 1892 to 1921 during which Giovanni Giolitti was prime minister in five different governments.

   • Fascist: the Mussolini regime lasted from 1922 to 1943.

   • Christian Democrat: the largest party in every coalition government from the end of World War II (1946) until the party dissolved in 1992.

LAMENT ON THE DESTINY OF THE EXILED[1]

It is hard
to remove one's roots and
rip them up from the ground
where our dead lie.

Ah, scrawny tree.
You are not
like the wildflower in a meadow
or the cherry tree that at ripening
blushes with red pearls:
always there,
to die and be reborn.

It goes
from land to land
from sea to sea
and, at each rip
it leaves a piece of its roots…
and carries away
the naked weight of what remains
until it dies, shriveled up,

never to be reborn.
In all places abandoned:
It is the destiny of the exiled
on the sand of the shore.

ANTONIO BAROLINI[2]

---

1 *Poesie alla Madre*, Venezia, Neri Pozza Ed., pp. 60, 1960

2 Author's note: This beautiful poem by Antonio Barolini, an Italian writer who now resides in the United States, opens my book. It is, in a way, the summary of my ideas and feelings. I thank the author for his kind permission to print it here.

Part One

*The Italian American Electorate
and the Elected*

NEW YORK'S *EMINENCE GRISE*

The long, ongoing fight in New York's political world to dethrone Carmine De Sapio[1] from the leadership of the Democratic Party, and consequently from the city's secret government, got nastier. The fight is now involving Mayor Robert Wagner[2] who is wrapping himself in the mantle of honorable causes, both ethical and political. But the true prize is the distribution of positions in the administration, or, to use the local term, *patronage*. The maelstrom created by the contenders has sucked in even President [John F.] Kennedy[3] who is trying to stay as much as possible above the fray while at the same time keeping an eye on what is going on between his party's factions. In European countries, where the populations have been stable for centuries and national unity is a done deal, political fights tend to have a *regional* character (and Italians know this pretty well.) In America, instead, racial unity has not been reached yet. Thus, the stocks of European bodies, removed from native lands, are caught in *racial* wars, rather than *regional* ones. The current fight in New York fits this pattern: De Sapio's base is composed of Italians while the competitors are generally Irish, Jews and Anglo-Saxons.

It doesn't matter that the propaganda themes discussed in public by the political bosses are morality, democracy, the electoral systems and hegemony. The only thing that matters is the spoil system, which means jobs and prestigious posts. Something similar also happens in some European countries where the state is not the product of a true national unity. This is the case of Belgium, for instance, where political fighting often boils down to the reciprocal animosity of two races forced to live under the same roof.

Twenty years after Fiorello La Guardia[4] had defeated it, Tammany

---

1   Carmine De Sapio (1908-2004). Last boss of the Tammany Hall political machine that dominated municipal politics in New York.

2   Robert Wagner, Jr. (1910-1991). Mayor of New York City for three terms, from 1954 to 1965.

3   John F. Kennedy (1917-1963). Senator from Massachusetts and 35th President of the United States from January 1961 until his assassination in November 1963.

4   Fiorello La Guardia (1882-1947). Mayor of New York City for three terms,

Hall[5] came back thanks to the efforts of the suave persuader Carmine De Sapio. In 1953 he supported Robert Wagner and managed to get him elected city mayor. The following year he did the same with the millionaire Averell Harriman[6] for the governorship of the State of New York. It was an enormous success. From then on, he was considered the most powerful boss of the Democratic Party in New York and, consequently, one of the most powerful in the entire country. Tammany Hall is the common name of the Democratic political organization in New York County. Similar to Lorenzo de' Medici[7] (no offense to Lorenzo is intended,) De Sapio doesn't care about being mayor, governor, senator or congressman. All he wants is to be the boss. He doesn't care about being popular, but he wants congressmen, senators, mayors and others to take orders from him, regardless of their political orientation, right or left. Tammany Hall has always included people with reputations for being socialists as well as reactionaries. For De Sapio it suffices that when he wants something done, the thing gets done without too much fuss. When he talks about the *organization*, it sounds like he is talking about the sacrament of the Eucharist.

He speaks in velvet tones, walks with a gliding stride and bows with curial deference. These, at least, are the personal impressions I recently gathered when I attended a ceremonial banquet. After the usual speeches were over, De Sapio came to our table to greet the big wigs. He glided around the table and it felt as if his velour-lined wings cast a reassuring shadow over us. Ostensibly, he was coming to pay homage to the people at the table, but it was rather clear that he was like the shepherd who keeps an eye on his flock. He couldn't

---

from 1934 to 1945.

5   Tammany Hall, founded in 1789 as the Tammany Society, was the Democratic Party's political machine that played a major role in controlling New York City's politics and promoting immigrant involvement, predominantly Irish, in New York politics from the 1790s to the 1960s.

6   Averell Harriman (1891–1986). He served as secretary of commerce under President Harry Truman and later became governor of New York (1954 to 1958).

7   Lorenzo de' Medici (1449–1492). The de-facto ruler of Florence at the peak of the Renaissance is known as *Lorenzo il Magnifico* [Lorenzo the Magnificent]. He was a politician and patron of the period's greatest artists, poets, philosophers and intellectuals.

understand exactly what I was doing among those powerful people but nevertheless he paid homage to me too. Then he moved on to the next table, to review his troops, weighing precisely the smiles, the handshakes, the words and their sincerity.

Tall, with a handsome Italian face (he shows resolve, in comparison to the faces of Irish, Anglo-Saxons and Jews in circulation,) he sports gray hair and a pair of big dark eye glasses. Given my suspicious disposition toward politicians, I thought they were a screen to hide his *window to the soul* and to prevent his true feelings from transpiring. I later discovered that he suffers from a condition that causes the irritation of the iris, called iritis. This is also the reason why his office is the only one among all New York politicians' not to be filled with smoke—like those that appear in political cartoons portraying the bosses of American democracy. De Sapio dresses like a British gentleman, smartly, without ostentation and without the histrionics of Fiorello La Guardia with his cowboy hat and Italian-anarchist cravat. Apparently, he does not own a car and lives on a modest salary from the party. He has the good taste of living on Washington Square which in my opinion is the most beautiful and poetic square in New York. Nobody has ever challenged his personal honesty. There is a curious anecdote, however. It so happened that one day a taxi driver went to the police to report that a client had left on the back seat an envelope with $40,000 in five and ten dollar bills. Sums of cash of this entity usually pertain to illicit transactions, so this aroused some interest. This is the way gangsters and extortionists handle their accounts, since larger-denomination bills are marked by banks. Moreover, the taxi driver said he *thought* De Sapio was the client who forgot the money. De Sapio denied it and the thing died there. I don't know if anybody else came forth to claim the money or if the taxi driver ended up keeping it.

De Sapio is said to be tough when it's necessary for the good of the party. But he is also said not to harbor rancor and to be a master in the art of compromise. Like all politicians active in democratic systems, he has an excellent memory and remembers every single person he met even for a few minutes; and he remembers if they are married and have children. If he were an opera singer his natural role would be the caricature Don Basilio.[8] He is sharp, intelligent, a quick study and a hard worker. His usual workday lasts fourteen hours between office, meetings, visits and events. He has no days off, as is the case for all top leaders in business and politics (who are even more dedicated as workers than Marcus Aurelius[9]). His greatest passion, he claims—and it's hard to deny it—is people. He likes people. He likes to meet people. Among the various ways to meet people are lectures and speeches he gives to colleges or clubs, despite the fact that he doesn't even have an undergraduate degree. Some mean-spirited commentators alluded to the possibility that those speeches may be written by someone else. First of all, having a speechwriter compose a speech is standard operating procedure for American politicians, presidents included. Second, speeches and lectures by De Sapio on *good government* don't stray much from the usual string of boilerplate rhetoric about the ideals of democracy (as opposed to the reality of democracy, as denounced by Vilfredo Pareto, Gaetano Mosca, Robert Michels,[10] and others).

He became the head of the Democratic organization in 1949, after it suffered a severe loss at the hand of Fiorello La Guardia in 1934 and after the election of William O'Dwyer,[11] a non-Tammanist independent Democrat. De Sapio knew how to move comfortably behind the scenes in the hallways of power and in the local clubs. He was totally devoted to politics and struggled to get to the top. In

---

8   Character in Gioacchino Rossini's opera *Il barbiere di Siviglia*.

9   Marcus Aurelius Antoninus Augustus (121–180). Emperor of Rome from 161 until his death in 180. He is regarded as one of the most important stoic philosophers. His work, *Meditations*, written in Greek, is still revered as a great literary achievement and a tribute to duty and public service.

10   Vilfredo Pareto (1848-1923). Italian industrialist, sociologist, economist, and philosopher. He made several important contributions to the study of economics, particularly income distribution and analysis of individual choices.
   • Gaetano Mosca (1858-1941). Italian political scientist and journalist. He is credited with developing the theory of elitism and the doctrine of the political class.
   • Robert Michels (1876-1936). German sociologist. He wrote about the political behavior of intellectual elites and contributed to the theory of elitism. He is best known for the book *Political Parties* (1911), which contains a description of the "iron law of oligarchy."

11   William O'Dwyer (1890-1964). One-hundredth mayor of New York City, he held office from 1946 to 1950.

some circumstances he wasn't helped by his principles, or by luck. He supported the election to mayor of Judge Ferdinand Pecora who was defeated by Vincent Impellitteri,[12] an absolute zero whose only skill was to move to tears the hearts of New Yorkers playing the part of the poor victim. De Sapio had his revenge when he mastered the victory of Robert Wagner, thus interrupting the Irish domination of the city administration. The first one who had succeeded against the Irish political machine was La Guardia, who clearly had both ambition and abilities far in excess of what was needed to be the head of New York City. His election, however, was a huge disappointment for Italians. For the longest time, Italians had complained about the distribution of perks and offices in the spoil system, and in particular there had always been bad blood between them and the Irish (which is curious, since they are both Catholic). With La Guardia's election things didn't improve much for Italians, at least if we pay heed to their complaints. La Guardia wanted to choose people on the basis of their abilities and not their race. In the end, though, it was the Irish and the Jews that came out ahead.

With De Sapio the Italian faction felt protected. The unjust wheel of fortune that assigns favors to the winners (in every country in the world, Russia included) stopped by the Italian houses for the first time. Today this supremacy is once again under attack and the recent election of President Kennedy strengthens the faction dominated by the Irish. In the following chapters we will see how this has come to pass.

New York, February 5, 1961

---

12   Ferdinand Pecora (1882-1971). Born in Sicily, he was a lawyer and judge who became famous in the 1930s as chief counsel to the senate's banking committee during the investigation of Wall Street's banking and stock-brokerage practices.

• Vincent Impellitteri (1900–1987). Born in Sicily, he was elected mayor in 1950, serving one term.

FOR THE FIRST TIME DE SAPIO LOSES A BATTLE

The first battle, or, should we say, the first skirmish between the Irish and the Italian factions ended on February 1, 1961, with the defeat of Carmine De Sapio. It is not a final defeat, but it is a red flag. Defections among his allies indicate that the rats are sensing that the ship may be in danger of sinking and are hurrying to jump onto another boat. The skirmish did not directly involve De Sapio and the faction that wants to get rid of him; rather, it was between De Sapio and New York's Mayor Robert Wagner. Wagner has distanced himself from De Sapio (to whom he owes his election) only recently and, as is his style, after a long hesitation. The clash did not happen in the name of De Sapio's adversaries, the so-called Reformists, but as a show of force between the mayor and De Sapio. It was a little like two fighters who, before a match, sit down at a table and, almost as a game, start arm wrestling. They clasp their hands together, place the elbows on the table and, both smiling and clenching their jaws, try to win the opponent's resistance. Naturally, around the table there gathers a small crowd of experts and friends, quiet and fully vested in the outcome. When the match is over, they spread the news. And now the news is out: Carmine De Sapio did not prevail in choosing the Manhattan deputy mayor. He was sure he had the votes, but, surprisingly, he lost. Rumors have it that De Sapio was betrayed by Daniel Weiss.[1] I don't know this individual personally, but it seems to me he is equipped with very long antennas and sensitive political radar. Carmine De Sapio is the secretary of Tammany Hall, the Democratic Organization of New York County. Basically he is the party's puppeteer in New York while Wagner is the city's mayor. Now, the Democratic system in America presents some feudal characteristics, namely loyalty to the leaders by the subordinates and protection of the subordinates by their leaders. These relationships are not codified by law but by culture and tradition and as such they are even more relevant. Elected officials have the power of appointment for several positions. President Kennedy, for instance, will have six thousand positions to fill, many of which are

---

1   Daniel Weiss (1910-1996). Elected city councilman in 1953, he was appointed judge in 1965.

THE TRANSPLANTS • 27

highly coveted. If Kennedy were to anoint De Sapio as his representative in New York, the latter would have at least some say in the president's local appointments. Again, this is not a codified role, but all presidents, with few exceptions, would be careful not to appoint anyone who has not been *approved* or *proposed* by his representative in the New York area. But now that the power of patronage is no longer in De Sapio's hands there is no reason to fear him and, consequently, De Sapio might disappear from the map of power. A boss is a boss only as long as he can dole out appointments and command obedience. (Usually he bestows onto his under-bosses the privilege of choosing or approving second-tier appointments, just like in Charlemagne's[2] era.) It so happened recently that Mayor Wagner revolted against De Sapio and wanted it to be known that he, not De Sapio, is the boss in charge of patronage. Apparently, the move succeeded. Politics is a cruel and cynical activity and even President Kennedy in several recent cases showed that powerful allies can be used and later dumped without second thoughts, providing examples worthy of Machiavelli's[3] best pages. Before the presidential election, Kennedy came to New York and sent his brother [Robert] to mend the rip between De Sapio (and other Italian American bosses) on one side, and the Reformist faction (Irish-Anglo Saxon, Jewish) on the other. Nobody knows what kind of promises he was instructed to make on behalf of the president. What is known is that, as soon as Kennedy won the primary election, he threw De Sapio overboard (in a classy way, of course). The margin of Kennedy's win in New York took everybody by surprise. The victory was due to De Sapio's support, in opposition to the Reformists who endorsed Adlai Stevenson[4] in the primary election. Nobody can be

---

2   Charlemagne (c.742-814). King of the Franks. He unified most of Western Europe under his rule and was consecrated Emperor of the Romans by Pontiff Leo III in 800 C.E.

3   Niccolò Machiavelli (1469-1527). Renaissance politician, writer, historian and philosopher. He is considered the founder of modern political science. His masterpiece is the treatise *Il principe* [*The Prince*] (1532).

4   Adlai Stevenson (1900-1965). He served one term as governor of Illinois and was the Democratic Party's nominee for president in 1952 and 1956. Both times he was defeated by Eisenhower. He sought the Democratic presidential nomination for a third time in 1960, but was defeated by John Kennedy.

certain, but it is arguable that without De Sapio's machine Kennedy would not have won the nomination. But electoral gratitude only lasts until Election Day. Once on shore, we pray no more.[5]

The Reformists have now been fighting De Sapio for the last two years. Their leaders are Senator Herbert Lehman (Jewish, highly respected), Ms. [Eleanor] Roosevelt (Anglo Saxon) and Thomas Finletter,[6] a lawyer (probably Irish). What are their accusations against De Sapio? That he is a *boss* and a dictator; that he does not use democratic methods; that he chooses unworthy people based not on merit but on their loyalty in dirty-politics affairs. That is exactly De Sapio's idea of politics: forget about the character and competence of the candidates to be elected and protected. What matters is that they act like foot soldiers, obedient and loyal servants of the organization. Until recently the Reformist faction did not have what it takes to attract a majority of party members and elect its members to positions of leadership at the precinct level. De Sapio used to laugh at the Reformist agenda, but with the election of President Kennedy the situation has changed. Soon after he took office, Kennedy clearly indicated his preference for the Anglo-Saxon, Jewish and Irish reformist faction. Among the various appointments one was particularly significant: Thomas Finletter, one of the leaders of the De Sapio's opposition, was appointed Ambassador to NATO, a plum job that was given out without even bothering to notify De Sapio. The mayor, who until that moment had maintained a balanced distance between the two factions despite the fact that he owed his election to De Sapio, when he saw this, took a decisive position against one of De Sapio's candidates and managed to get his own man elected. Among those who control the elections in the electoral clubs in New York as well as in other parts of the United States where the Italian vote dominates, there is widespread suspicion that Kennedy does not like Italians. Many have

---

5   The original Italian proverb is: *Passata la festa, gabbato lo santo.*

6   Herbert Lehman (1878-1963). Governor of New York from 1933 to 1942; U.S. senator from 1949 to 1957.

   • Eleanor Roosevelt (1884-1962). Politician, diplomat and activist. She was very influential in Democratic Party's affairs and actively participated in the nation's political life. She was the wife of President Franklyn D. Roosevelt.

   • Thomas Finletter (1893-1980). Lawyer, politician and statesman.

complained that Kennedy has not appointed a single Italian American to a high-level position. (Several years ago I asked a Catholic bishop how come Italian American clergymen were excluded from the top echelons of the American church. He answered: "Do you know any who are actually able and worthy of being bishops?") In a report from Washington published by *Il Progresso Italo-Americano*[7] on January 8, the rabble-rouser Drew Pearson[8] wrote: "People begin to notice that President-elect Kennedy has yet to nominate an Italian American to a high position. This is causing resentment among the Italian American leaders who have worked tirelessly for the Kennedy-Johnson[9] ticket. Among them are Mike De Salle[10] [sic], Governor of Ohio, one of the first politicians to endorse Kennedy; Tommy D'Alessandro [sic], the former mayor of Baltimore who convinced Maryland Governor Millard Tawes to withdraw his candidature and bow to Kennedy; Cleveland's mayor Anthony Celebrezze, credited with the landslide victory for Kennedy in his city; and Louis Mariani [sic], mayor of Detroit, who contributed to Kennedy's victory in Michigan. In addition, in

---

7 *Il Progresso Italo-Americano.* Daily newspaper published from 1880 to 1988. In the early 20th century it was the most popular of New York's Italian language newspapers, selling between 90,000 and 100,000 copies daily. Generoso Pope bought the newspaper in 1928 and assumed the direction. Shut down after a union dispute in 1989, most journalists united to found the new Italian daily *America Oggi.*

8 Andrew Pearson (1897-1969). Syndicated columnist.

9 Lyndon B. Johnson (1908-1973). U.S. senator from Texas, senate majority leader, vice president in the Kennedy administration. He became president after the assassination of John Kennedy and was later elected president in 1964.

10 Michael DiSalle (1908-1981). Democratic politician, served as governor of Ohio from 1959 to 1963.
• Thomas D'Alesandro (1903–1987). U.S. representative from Maryland from 1939 to 1947, he subsequently was mayor of Baltimore from 1947 to 1959. His daughter, Nancy Pelosi, is the first woman and first Italian American to become speaker of the House of Representatives, elected in 2008.
• John Tawes (1894-1979). Governor of Maryland from 1959 to 1967.
• Anthony Celebrezze (1910-1998). Mayor of Cleveland from 1953 to 1962. In the Kennedy and Johnson administrations he was secretary of Health, Education, and Welfare (now Department of Health and Human Services). In 1965 he was appointed judge to the U.S. court of appeals where he served until 1980.
• Louis Miriani (1897-1987). Mayor of Detroit from 1957 to 1961.

New York there is Carmine De Sapio, the boss of Tammany Hall, who worked hard—at least during the campaign—for the Kennedy-Johnson ticket alongside former Governor Lehman and Tom Finletter. De Sapio buried the hatchet but rumors circulating in Kennedy's headquarters are sending the message that he should be ignored. The issue has been discussed recently when Carl Soresi (a Washington-based Italian American journalist with an important role in the office of ethnic minorities in Kennedy's electoral committee) was mentioned as a possible candidate for head of the consular division of the State Department. The position, which is far from being the most desirable, deals with all the U.S. consular offices abroad and the issuing of entry visas. Years ago, during the Eisenhower administration, the Republican Edward Corsi, former labor commissioner of the state of New York, was appointed assistant to Scott McLeod, who was director of the consular division. Several Italian American congressmen, including Peter Rodino[11] of Newark, N.J., have come out in favor of Soresi. However, it is reported that the Kennedy clan holds the opinion that all Italian Americans are "Appalachig [sic]."[12]

A very authoritative Boston weekly, the *Gazzetta del Massachusetts*[13] (despite the Italian name the publication is written primarily in English) attributed Kennedy's negative attitude toward Italian Americans to his political fight against Governor John Furcolo[14] (January 13). "It is not a secret that Italian Americans have voiced their criticism of President Kennedy for the exclusion of representatives of this powerful

11 Edward Corsi (1896-1965). Republican candidate in the 1950 New York City mayoral election. In 1954 he became special assistant to the U.S. secretary of state for refugee and migration problems.

• Peter Rodino (1909-2005). Congressman from New Jersey from 1949 to 1989. He was the chairman of the House judiciary committee in the impeachment hearings of President Richard Nixon.

12 Reference to the town of Apalachin in upstate New York where in 1957 a meeting of several dozen Mafia bosses took place.

13 Published continuously since 1896, its name was recently changed to *Post Gazette*. The original name was spelled *Gazetta*. In 1905 it was bought by James Donnarumma who turned it into the most successful and authoritative Italian American newspaper in Boston and surrounding region.

14 John Furcolo (1911–1995). U.S. representative from 1949 to 1952; governor of Massachusetts from 1957 to 1961.

voting block from the team he has assembled to govern the nation. How can one reconcile the fact that not even one Italian American has been mentioned as possible candidate for high office, with the other fact that Italian American voters have contributed so much to Kennedy's election…" etcetera. In *Sons of Italy Times*,[15] another similar publication, on January 16 [1961] I found an ironic letter to the editor from an Italian American reader: "I noticed with great interest that, once again…. Italians came out looking like the usual dumb Bertoldo,[16] the nickname they were given—deservedly—years ago. I looked far and wide in the newspapers for news that a Salvatore or a Pasquale has been nominated to this or that position. It goes without saying that the administration has demonstrated the willingness to take into account other minorities, like Blacks and Jews. Well, in the end we can still console ourselves with spaghetti, pizza, Joe Bellino and Frank Sinatra."[17]

These examples document the state of mind of people of Italian descent who believe that official positions are not to be assigned based on merit, but rather as shares of the loot stolen from the enemy. I am not condemning Italians.[18] Even in the Italian democracy, before Fascism, several regions complained that they were neglected if none of their representatives was part of the government. In America instead of regions there are races. Better yet: in addition to regions there are races and religions. In the end, because of all these complaints, a college professor from New York, Edward Re,[19] was appointed under secretary

---

15   *Sons of Italy Times*. Published in Philadelphia, it currently has a circulation of approximately 15,000 copies.

16   Bertoldo is the main character of the novel *Bertoldo, Bertoldino e Cacasenno* by Giulio Cesare Croce (1550-1609). He represents the witty peasant, with no scholarly education but full of common sense. The term is sometimes used, quite inappropriately, to indicate an easily-fooled simpleton.

17   Joseph Bellino (1938-). Former football player for the New England Patriots. Winner of the Heisman Trophy in 1960.

• Frank Sinatra (1915-1998). Arguably the most famous Italian American singers, actor, entertainer of his era and one of the greatest stars of twentieth century America.

18   Should be: Italian Americans.

19   Edward D. Re (1925-2006). Born in the Aeolian Islands, off the Sicilian

of Health and Human Services. Also, an accountant with an Italian name was appointed by the central administration. Still noteworthy is the exclusion of the most prominent Italian American politicians.

New York, February 12, 1961

P.S. In July 1962, President Kennedy appointed a notable individual of Italian origin to the important position of secretary of Health and Human Services: Anthony Celebrezze, famous for his nine scandal-free years as mayor of Cleveland. He is an honest politician, raised in a shack in a poor neighborhood, the ninth of thirteen children of an Italian family from Anzi (in the province of Potenza,[20] in Calabria [sic]). He was born in Italy where his parents had returned for a temporary stay. His appointment is due primarily to his active participation in the Democratic Party where he supported the Kennedy candidature against Stevenson.

---

coast, he was a law professor at Saint John's University before being appointed under secretary in the department of Health and Human Services by the Kennedy administration in 1961. In 1968 he was appointed to the Customs Court and in 1977 became chief judge. He served on the federal bench until 1991.

20 Potenza is the capital and main city of the Basilicata region.

THE NEW YORK MAYORAL ELECTION

Carmine De Sapio, with his black eyeglasses, tall stature, light step, suave and velvety voice; but most of all with his little secret conversations not even a whisper of which reaches the public, in this moment dominates the electoral scenario of the largest American city. In a few days registered Democrats will be asked to choose the party's candidate [for mayor]. The primary elections are one of the remedies that the American democracy is trying to adopt to prevent *organizations* (a fact) from dominating the *free choice* (a myth) of the electorate. *Partitocracy* has been denounced in the United States as the nullification of democracy much earlier than in Italy, for the simple fact that the American democratic system is older. Currently, the Democratic party of New York, which dominates the political scene, is split into several factions due to the lack of a strong unifying personality. This is the result of a series of scandals, revelations and reciprocal accusations among the various contenders, the most prominent being De Sapio—who is not a candidate for office. De Sapio stays away from direct political responsibilities and is satisfied with his role as leader of the Democratic Party of Greenwich Village (a neighborhood that aspires to compete with Montmartre and via Margutta[1]). As secretary of Tammany Hall he is accused of reserving for himself the power of dispensing big and small political appointments, no-show jobs, sinecures, concessions, contracts, commissions, recommendations, favors and awards. The money is hidden in the creases and wrapped in the shadows of New York City's budget, which is larger than that of the Italian state.

What have we learned from the ongoing controversy? De Sapio has been the target of accusations that he wants to be a *boss*. In politics this word comes from the history and political sociology of the United States and has a precise metaphorical meaning. It refers to local political dictatorships that were common in the middle of the nineteen century and that continue to this day, albeit with less frequency. An example

---

1 Montmartre; via Margutta. Bohemian neighborhoods respectively in Paris and Rome. In the 1960s they were hangouts for artists and intellectuals; and locations of avant-garde art galleries and music clubs.

of a classical boss is James Curley[2] in Boston. This phenomenon is one of the many betrayals of the democratic system that flourished in particular in large cities overflowing with masses of people who did not speak English, were disenfranchised from the institutions and were willing to exchange their votes for a minimum of protection in order to survive. *Bossism* [sic] was the remedy that social reality imposed on the democratic theory according to which citizens are independent and their votes are based on conscience and knowledge. Contrary to these principles, even today these citizens vote only in order to gain favors since they do not possess the kind of conscience and knowledge that democracy presupposes. Naturally, the boss dispenses unjust protections as well as just ones. At times he is forced to use immoral or even outright illegal means. At times he has to make compromises even with the criminal element. However, over time the entire enterprise reaches some kind of natural equilibrium, so natural in fact that it is reproduced in city after city. And it tends to return even in those cases where it is temporarily uprooted by reformers, as was in the case of Fiorello La Guardia. In New York the system is at least a hundred years old (the Tweed Ring[3] dates back to 1870). In a city like New York, with so many races, this physical and historic element has great importance. It is noticeable, in fact, how an Irish boss was followed by an Italian one: De Sapio.

Harlem has a Black boss, Adam Clayton Powell, Jr.[4] In thirty years, when, according to projections, the majority of the city's citizens will be Black, he may be able to see one of his successors become mayor, as happened to Fiorello La Guardia who represented Italians and Jews. In the Democratic Party, in the recent past, a coalition against De Sapio has emerged. At the helm of this Jewish-Irish opposition are

---

2 James Curley (1874-1958). Mayor of Boston for four terms, he also served as U.S. House representative and governor of Massachusetts. During his last term as mayor he was convicted and served time in prison.

3 The reference is to William Tweed (1823-1878). He was at the head of the Tammany Hall political club and wielded enormous power and influence in New York City's politics.

4 Adam Clayton Powell (1908-1972). He was the first African American from New York to be elected to Congress. He served in the House of Representatives from 1945 to 1971.

Ms. Roosevelt and Senator Lehman. On February 3, 1961, the current mayor of the city, Robert Wagner, joined the opposition. This is an important development since Wagner owes his election to De Sapio; and, even more damning, Wagner's mayoralty was literally one of De Sapio's creations. Ingratitude being a common feat in life and even more so in politics, this thing did not scandalize anyone. The origin of the divisions among the Democratic party's bosses is to be found in the past presidential election: some supported Kennedy, others Adlai Stevenson and others Stuart Symington.[5] This had nothing to do with ideals: what mattered was feudal loyalty to the candidates. When his adversaries accused him of being the boss of New York, De Sapio had plenty of arguments to defend himself. With his velvety voice he reminded Senator Lehman that he heeded his requests to find a couple of positions for his nephews or cousins and the senator could not deny it. He also reminded Mayor Wagner whom he should thank for his election and the mayor did not dispute this point either. It is the typical justification used by the thief: "Yes, I stole but you held the bag." Mayor Wagner is generally considered an honest person because he didn't enrich himself through politics. However, the common complaint about him is that he has been a weak mayor. During the eight years of his administration he turned a blind eye to the festering scandals that have just now blown up (obviously, the person who lit the fuse is another candidate for mayor) while the conditions of the city have become deplorable. Criminality is up, women and children do not feel safe walking in the streets and even the police are targets of assaults and attacks by hordes of hooligans. Disturbances with the use of firearms are growing; gangs of teen-age thugs are ever more aggressive; school buildings are decrepit, while a large number of cases of corruption among building inspectors has been discovered and tried in court. Investigations targeting the police (which are controlled by the city) have led to the dismissal of entire groups of

---

5   Stuart Symington (1901-1988). U.S. senator from Missouri and a strong ally of President Truman. He was one of the leading candidates for the vice presidency when John F. Kennedy was elected. Kennedy in the end opted for Senator Lyndon Johnson (Texas), who at the time was Democratic majority leader in the Senate, to secure support from the electorate in the south.

corrupt agents and officers. Lately, the mayor forced the resignation of the commissioner of the city's power and gas agency when it was found that he kept in his home, in his piggy bank, more than $60,000 whose origin he could not explain. After he resigned, he accused the mayor of charging the city for his clothes and for Florida vacations with his family. This is incredible stuff; yet, the mayor has not sued him. For eight years none of these scandals became public. And now the firings of dishonest city employees look like a ruse for election's sake or scenes from an electoral drama. At the same time, we saw the mayor and his opponents visit the poorest and most depressed areas of the city to take stock personally of the situation. The mayor showed up in a special car, a convertible limousine that allows people to see him and approach him with complaints and pleas similarly to what used to happen with the kings of yore. His opponents do the same thing and also make promises: public housing, safety, tax reform. The press plays along with these pantomimes worthy of Aristophanes.[6] But does it matter? The public pretends to believe; or, maybe, like people who buy lottery tickets, they think "you never know," while they crowd around the mayor or his opponents with their pleas. To be noted: in this country, where the constitution, the judiciary, teachers, preachers and even politicians are all in agreement (so they claim) in their condemnation of racism, there is visible reliance on the race factor for electoral purposes. Competing slates of candidates always contain at least an Irish, a Jew and an Italian. And the person who, more than anyone else should be against racism, Mr. Powell, the Harlem representative, has used most of his time complaining that there are too few Black candidates, in a percentage that is much lower than that of the Black population. The theoretical premise of democracy is merit not race or religion: we can thus conclude from this that political education has not penetrated very deeply.

When the scandal of the horrible conditions of school buildings came to light, many members of the board of education were forced to resign by the governor. That is when we found out their names: complete mediocrities. In a great city that is a major hub of the film

---

6   Aristophanes (446-386 BCE). Playwright in ancient Athens also known as "the father of comedy" His works ridiculed the rich and powerful.

and television industry; where the most important publishing houses are located; where some of the greatest newspapers are published; with the headquarters of the best and most popular magazines and with some of the best schools of education in the country, the board did not have one single eminent personality. One more interesting detail: membership in the board is a non-paid position. Yet, the members make decisions about millions and millions of dollars on education-related contracts, from construction projects to the purchase of books, pencils and notebooks. What is one supposed to think?

American metropolises have attracted heterogeneous masses of foreigners, unfocused and disorganized; distant both in spatial, cultural and religious terms from their origins; uprooted from their traditions and not yet fully integrated in the new venues. The democratic system is simply inadequate to the task of selecting the best and the brightest. The job of politician is at the same despised and feared and people think that a jack-of-all-trades who decides to pursue a political career is up to no good. However, people are glad someone is doing the job and takes care of deciding, bossing, opposing and pushing. Since the official salary of politicians is very low, people tolerate it when they make money on the side, provided that they do not cause a scandal. Based on what we heard in this period of electoral revelations, the practice of kickbacks, cash donations and shady deals is rather common among vendors and suppliers on one side and public employees on the other, even between criminals and law enforcement agents. It's understandable why many try to fatten their paycheck: taxes are so high that nobody could survive only on a salary. So, everyone pads expense accounts and overcharges private or public employers. Each abuse encourages the next abuse, and soon it's all downhill, careening toward the very serious ones. The entire system encourages lies and the all-pervading lies ensure that corruption does not bother any conscience.

There are other competitors in the battle between Arthur Levitt—the De Sapio-Tammany Hall candidate—and the incumbent Mayor Wagner. Judge Louis Lefkowitz[7] is the Republican Party's sacrificial

7   Arthur Levitt (1900-1980). New York state comptroller from 1955 to 1978. In 1961 he challenged unsuccessfully incumbent Mayor Robert Wagner.
• Louis Lefkowitz (1904-1996). Member of New York state assembly and

lamb, with zero possibilities of winning. There is also an Italian, an honest person, Lawrence Gerosa,[8] who was and still is city comptroller and who, in the last couple of years, has been opposing the anything-goes fiscal policy of the mayor and has scored a significant success in a referendum concerning the issuing of city bonds. The mayor wanted to float a bond for school buildings (from which, as we can guess, many would have profited handsomely). Despite the fact that Gerosa is personally very popular, it is rather improbable that he will be able to get the Democratic nomination for the simple fact that the Democratic Party's machine is not in his hands.

In the smallest Swiss cantons and in small communities in America, like Vermont, where everybody knows everybody else, where the citizens come from a homogeneous background and the problems are not particularly complicated, direct sovereignty by the people is simple, natural and beneficial. But in American cities, those huge caldrons that are similar to imperial Rome, the system is less and less able to work without big unbalances. One of the true counterbalances is a free press, and often this works well. But how many people in this city, so frazzled and high-strung; so rude and badly put-together; so scarred by primitive passions and fertile with bright minds (too bright and therefore sterile); how many will be moved to action or even empathy by an article in a newspaper? Or more precisely: how many actually read the newspapers' opinion pages or the editorials? But then, maybe this is why living in New York is so exciting. It is enjoyable because the city is not made of model citizens. If it were dominated by the spirit of the Salvation Army, it would be mortally boring. Fiorello La Guardia was certainly an honest person and he was the only administrator who did not allow the city's treasury to be looted—with the help of another honest Italian administrator, Portfolio[9] [sic]. Mayor James Walker[10] was

---

municipal judge. He served as New York state attorney general (1957 - 1969).

8   Lawrence Gerosa (1894-1972). Businessman, city comptroller under Mayor Robert Wagner. Dropped by Wagner in 1961, Gerosa ran as an independent as the candidate of "God and the Good People."

9   This name is most likely the result of an oversight by the author or the proofreader.

10   James Walker (1881-1946). In 1926 he became mayor of New York City after

a merry and funny Irishman who accepted $50,000 from friends as if it were a necktie, and in turn gave away cars to actresses and other beautiful women as if they also were neckties. All things considered, the people of New York loved Walker more than La Guardia.

New York, September 3, 1961

P.S. Carmine De Sapio was beaten not only in Tammany Hall but even in his own Greenwich Village district. He has since disappeared from the scene.

---

defeating incumbent John Hylan in the Democratic primary. In 1929 he was re-elected after defeating Fiorello La Guardia.

HIS NAME IS FOX BUT HE WILL BE A WOLF
The Italian Governor of Massachusetts

The governor[1] was punctual for the interview and he stayed longer than he had originally scheduled for the interview, a sign that he was interested in my questions and was enjoying answering them. He only refused to answer one of them. Later, I will explain why.

In a large, white square room the governor was sitting with a portrait of President Dwight Eisenhower[2] behind him. He is a Republican. His secretary's last name is Ghibelline [sic]. When I asked if she knew what that meant, she blushed and said yes, but since I am a professor and I am entitled to show off, I went on to provide a lengthier explanation. The waiting room is open to the public and accessible through an unmanned elevator. A police officer in a white shirt standing in front of the building gave me directions to the floor and the room number. No one stood on ceremonies. In the waiting room there were two couches, a couple of chairs, the secretary's table, three gentlemen who were talking in hushed tones and two women sitting quietly on a couch. From the wall the portraits of former governors were looking down on us: Tobin, Allen, Bradford.[3] In a few years John Volpe will join them. The electorate chose him because he is a *wolf* (not a *fox*[4]) who promised to scare off the corrupt who have dominated after the solemn and boring but honest Yankees had disappeared from the political scene replaced by the cheerful and dishonest Irish. (Not all of them are, of course, but so many that Boston has become the standard background for novels and academic studies on corruption in major American cities.)

---

1   John Volpe (1908-1994). Governor of Massachusetts from 1961 to 1963 and from 1965 to 1969. He was U.S. secretary of transportation from 1969 to 1973 when he was nominated ambassador to Italy, a position he held until 1977.

2   Dwight Eisenhower (1880-1969). President of the United States for two terms from 1953 to 1961. A five-star general, during World War II, he was supreme commander of the Allied Force in Europe

3   Maurice Tobin (1901-1953).
  • Frank Allen (1874-1950).
  • William Bradford (1590- 1657) or Robert Bradford (1902-1983).

4   *Volpe* in Italian means fox.

My first question was: "In your opinion, what is the major contribution made by Italians to the United States?" I came up with this question because in the course of *colonial banquets*,[5] the cliché of Italians' *contribution* is always present. My impression is that the issue is always handled with great exaggerations, maybe due to the banquets' communicative warmth, and also as a result of the combination of two national rhetorical standards of excess: the Italian and the American. In certain occasions I reacted to the rhetoric saying: "If I may, why don't you talk about the contribution that the United States has made to Italian immigrants, helping them up the economic ladder and giving their children a free education, the kind of education that their parents and grandparents never received?" The governor answered: "In the initial phase of Italian immigration the contribution was primarily in the form of sweat and hard labor. Most of them were poor and uneducated and their main concern was to provide sustenance to their families and give their children the basic education they lacked. Their devotion to family life was exemplary, dominated by the attachment to their faith and with of so many examples of honesty and decency. In those years the contribution was smaller than what the size of the population could have given. But in recent years things have changed. Italians have come of age; they participate in the political and cultural life and have achieved prominence in the arts and music. Many second-generation Italian Americans have positions in the sciences, many are engineers and a large number—women as well as men—are in the medical profession. Others in the legal field have given America outstanding lawyers and judges, worthy of those from the ancient University of Bologna..."[6]

---

5   The term refers to the Italian *colony* in America. The term colony derives from ancient Greek and it originally indicated a new settlement of people coming from a different land and still maintaining strong ties with the country of origin. The term took on a new meaning with the rise of European colonial empires in the world. *Colony* then came to indicate a land and a people subjugagted by a foreing power and deprived of political self-determination in its own land. Most likely here the term sarcastically points to people stranded far wawy from the home country, relics of a past and distant culture.

6   The University of Bologna was founded in 1008 and is the world's oldest insitution of higher learning with continuous operation without interruptions.

This answer was both sober and realistic with a distinction between the first extraordinary efforts of the poor immigrants, primarily focused on giving a leg up to their children, and the following efforts of the new generations with their diplomas. I liked it. The governor, however, skipped my second question. "Which is stronger among immigrants: the bond with the Catholic Church or that with their country of origin?" It was a provocative question and of course I knew it was. But I didn't want to limit myself to questions that would only provide the opportunity to open the faucets of clichés. A press secretary had already warned me that the governor probably would not answer because "it wasn't sufficiently clear." I remarked that I do have a lot of faults, but lack of clarity is not one of them. If anything, I have a reputation for being even too clear, so clear in fact that sometimes people get offended. The secretary was a bit of a hypocrite for she knew very well what I wanted to know. In any case, I have already come to my own personal conclusions on this: I have always maintained that Italian immigrants in American were helped much more by the Church than by the [Italian] state, more by priests than by consuls. I am referring here to the first period of immigration, the oceanic current that ripped away from the Italian nation the living and the dead, the healthy and the rotten, the honest and the criminal. Although the immigrants did not have an education, their religious culture was superior to their civic culture. The governor realized he had to provide an explanation for his reluctance. He told me what I already knew: that in America religious issues are not to be discussed and everybody must accept the premise that all individuals are equal, regardless of their faith... This was not a real answer, but it revealed his abeyance to this American taboo, necessary to ensure that so many peoples from all corners of the globe, with different ideas and faiths, can live together.

My third question was: "You have been elected with a *personal vote* and as a protest against the general corruption of the public administration. Now, what will you be able to accomplish, and what do you intend to do?" Here the governor was on friendly ground. It was the kind of question he would get from one of his voters. He acknowledged that there was little he could do, but that he would try hard nevertheless, with diligence and conviction. How would he do

THE TRANSPLANTS • 43

it? The readers should know that John Volpe's victory was personal and not a victory of the Republican Party. Boston has a majority of registered Democrats and is the incubator where President Kennedy grew up. Volpe won because of his charisma and because he is a new face in politics, despite his long activity in Republican circles. "Vote for the Man" was his campaign slogan. In American politics there is always a substantial group of independent voters who end up deciding the outcome of elections, often switching from one party to the other. Moreover, in every party there are voters who, regardless of their registration, often ignore affiliation and follow other principles. It is likely that in the case of Volpe a few hundred thousand voters of Italian origin officially registered as Democrats chose to vote for the Republican candidate. After all, he is Italian and he has charisma. While I usually do not have much feeling for politicos, this time I felt an attraction for this *abruzzese*,[7] not particularly tall but solid and similar to the Roman soldiers carved on Trajan's Column.[8] Apparently he blames his stature on the fact that as a child he used to carry a *còfano*[9] on his head, as in the past both men and women in Abruzzi used to. The women acquired from this practice a solemn and statuary posture and sometimes I still see examples of it in older women in the streets of Little Italy. Men became stocky with powerful backs and shoulders.

"What can I do?" he continued. "Not much. First of all, I promised to myself that I will give an example as a person who does not use political power for his own personal interest, but governs in the interest of the people. I hope this example will inspire others to do the same. I would also like to inspire a sense of responsibility among public employees who are paid by the people to serve the people. I will try to eliminate waste and spend public money with caution. I requested that all the administrators abide by a code of ethics. I pushed for tough rules: I didn't get everything I wanted, but at least we made some

---

7   *Abruzzese*: adjective; from the Abruzzi region of Italy.

8   The Trajan's Column, located in the Trajan's Forum in Rome was erected in honor of Emperor Trajan in 113 to celebrate his conquest of Dacia (now Romania).

9   *Còfano*, is the term used locally to indicate either wicker baskets or water jugs (copper or terracotta) that people –mostly women– used to carry balancing them on their heads.

progress. Just look at what kind of position I find myself in. I am the only politician from my party to get elected [to a state-wide position]. Everybody else, literally every single one of them, is from the other party, the party that I consider responsible for the corruption I want to fight. How can I get them to go along with condemning the state of affairs they are responsible for?"

With these words I took leave of the governor and I am also going to take leave of the readers. The issue is important and it deserves to be discussed. Boston, which once upon a time was the center of Puritan morality, has become one of the worst venues of state and municipal corruption. How did this happen? And how is it possible that the voters' protest elected to the helm of state an honest man like Volpe while at the same time surrounding him with a lieutenant governor, a senate, a house and elected magistrates who belong to and were put in power by the very political groups responsible for the corruption?

Boston, July 5, 1961

P.S. Unfortunately, Volpe was defeated for a few votes in the 1962 election.[10]

---

10   John Volpe was reelected governor for antother term from 1965 to 1969.

THE CIRCULATION DROPS
WITH EVERY OBITUARY THEY PUBLISH

Foreign-language newspapers have always represented a problem for the United States, but it's a problem that soon will be no more. America has always had a wealth of publications and each linguistic community has had its own distinct press with its distinct history: however, all languages went through a similar journey that matches more or less the history of the immigrant groups they represented. The rise and fall of foreign-language news media follows the various groups' economic, cultural and political evolution; and, finally, their progressive integration into the nation's mainstream. With each decade and each new school that is built; with each struggle that picks winners and losers after imposing on them the same trials, the number of readers of foreign-language publications decreases. The human material that descends from different races, traditions, cultures, religions and languages is bent, reshaped, restyled and ground up by societal forces and mandatory public education until it is assimilated and begins to circulate in the country's vascular system. There are still some small benign cysts but they are dying of starvation.

With the exception of new arrivals from Puerto Rico and Canada, the foreign-language press today can acquire only a few thousand new readers every year.

The original purpose of old-style Italian-language dailies was to respond to the needs of a public of immigrants who did not know English well (or not at all) and sought information about the country they had just left. That audience is almost gone: each obituary printed in one of those newspapers means one fewer subscriber because their heirs in the new generation don't read Italian and don't really seek news from and about Italy anymore. Today's immigrants, Italians included, have no reason to buy locally published newspapers since they can get original dailies by air mail from Europe in twenty four hours.

The only reason for the existence of an ethnic press in the United States is to serve minorities that have not yet been fully absorbed into society. For them, the purpose is not to get news from the Old Country, which is getting fainter by the day both in interest and memories, but to get news about their own new society, which speaks English and consists of community life based on social and sports events, on the parish or the temple and, in some cases, on the political club that sponsors the elections of descendants from the same roots who promise to defend the rights of the newer immigrants of the same origin.

Here are some data. In 1884, in the United States there were 525 periodicals in German including sixty-seven daily newspapers. In the same year, the Italian diaspora supported seven periodicals, two of which were dailies. In 1930 the German language periodicals were down to 171, in 1950 to seventy, in 1959 to sixty-four. It has been a constant decline, also accelerated by the wars against Germany. In comparison, Italian-language periodicals in 1900 reached thirty-five, including three dailies. In 1939 there were eighty-six periodicals with six dailies (twenty-one periodicals were already in a mix of Italian and English.) The true history of Italian-language press in the United States—without resorting to clichés—would be very hard to reconstruct. One would have to delve deeply into an unpleasant, smelly reality, often sticky and hot like blacktop in the summer (a comparison that is both adequate and literal). I am not very familiar with the kind of press that is called *colonial journalism*: I have only heard about it and I will not venture an opinion.

The decline of the Italian press started after World War II: in 1959 the periodicals dropped to fifty-two with five dailies. A few statistics will give an idea of the current situation. In 1930 in New York there were three Italian language dailies: the *Bollettino della Sera* with a circulation of 30,433 copies; the *Progresso Italo-Americano* with 99,391; and the *Corriere d'America*[1] with 55,515. In the entire country the circulation of Italian dailies was around 220,000 copies. Today only one newspaper is left, Fortune Pope's[2] *Progresso*. It is impossible to know

---

1 *Il Bollettino della Sera* was published in New York starting in 1898.

• *Il Corriere d'America* was published in New York from 1923 to 1931. Its managing editor (*direttore*) was Luigi Barzini, Sr.

• All three newspapers were owned by Generoso Pope.

2 Fortune Pope (1918-1996). Publisher of *Il Progresso Italo-Americano* and of *The National Enquirer*. He was the son of Generoso Pope who is commonly but erroneously credited with founding *Il Progresso*. The founder and first editor of *Il Progresso* was Carlo Barsotti (1850-1927), who was also the founder of the *Italian*

its circulation for the newspaper no longer publishes data, contrary to the practice of all serious periodicals in the United States. A generous estimate would guess about 50,000 copies. Between 1930 and 1960, despite the new post-WW II immigration and the population growth in New York, there was a net loss of 170,000 readers, more than three quarters from the peak years. Much could be said about the inadequate format and content of Italian-language periodicals; however, it is clear that the decreased circulation is due primarily to the larger picture of social and educational policies that apply pressure on all the organs of linguistic minorities in the United States.

For my Italian readers I just want to report an interesting fact: while Italian-language press is on the way out in the United States, waning in terms of relevance and circulation, a new kind of periodicals is emerging, produced by the new English-speaking generations of Italian Americans who communicate only in English and therefore need English language media. Normally these periodicals are weeklies rather than dailies, thus they function as complementary organs. It is also worth noting that several of these new publications in English are born in smaller urban centers, such as Philadelphia, Boston and Hartford, Connecticut, which in the past were very important hubs of Italian immigration. Thus far their circulation is limited to the local areas, however, some even ship a few copies to Italy where several thousands Italian Americans now live after having moved back to enjoy their savings and Social Security checks or pensions. These *reverse immigrants* want to maintain ties with the places where they worked, saved, raised a family; and where their children, grand children, relatives and friends still live. A nation-wide periodical of this kind, capable of penetrating the Italian communities from Seattle to San Francisco to New Orleans to Boston, does not exist yet. This might happen in the future but so far no visionary mind has conceived it, nor are there entrepreneurs willing to take a chance. Most of all, what is missing is a coalition of local minorities with the *intellighenzia* [sic] and an educated Italian American community.

New York, May 21, 1961

American Bank in 1882.

ITALIAN NEWSPAPERS IN AMERICA

Foreign-language newspapers in America, from Ukrainian to Japanese—not to mention the most obvious ones like Italian and German—were born to meet the immigrants' need for information about relevant events in their countries of origin. It was the only source of information available, since they couldn't read English and—even if they could—the American press would barely mention those faraway places. Moreover, the mainline press completely ignored what was taking place in the immigrants' neighborhoods. Naturally, as these immigrants were absorbed and their feelings for and memories of the old country vanished, the foreign-language press became progressively smaller and focused mostly on the local issues that affected people where they lived. But, there is another factor that must be considered in order to understand the decline of foreign-language press: the journalists. Initially they had all been educated in the coutry of origin, whose language they could write fluently. Speaking specifically about the Italian community, today it is practically impossible to find an Italian American, educated in America, who can write correct and proper Italian. Others, educated in Italian schools, have lost the ability to express themselves with precision and fluidity. Historically, this was similar to what happened to German immigration which was arguably the most educated to come to America. With reference to this community, in a general atmosphere of decline, two different phenomena took place, representative of distinct traditions. After the fall of Nazism, the German population of New York split into two groups: one followed publications that represented, with moderation, the German tradition; the other, mostly Jews of German origin, gravitated around periodicals that reflected a world-wide agenda. In addition there were several periodicals published in Yiddish, the language (or dialect) of the German and Eastern-European Jewry, with a long tradition of renown literary works. Italians, who never had to confront this kind of divisions, were never forced—psychologically or otherwise—to learn English. There are still elderly people in New York who speak only the dialect of Campobasso or Terlizzi,[1] interspersed with a few rough English words; but in general America has been able to absorb the immigrants with the assimilating prowess of big snakes that don't bite their preys but smother them then swallow them whole. This is what mandatory education did to children who, once they had learned English (or American), would become a model, but also a threat, for their parents who never managed to learn the language. Children were also instrumental in keeping and anchoring their parents to this country, preventing them from returning as they had originally dreamt of doing: *fare l'America* [to do America] (that is, to get rich) and then return to Sorrento[2] (or the native village) with a nice nest egg to show off to those who stayed behind.

The new Italian American press, as I mentioned before, is written and read primarily by the new generations, children or grand children of the first poor immigrants. The distinction between these cohorts is very important, not only in terms of language but also economic status. They are better off than their parents and belong to a different social class: they own a house and often a small business; and are members of professional associations. An ever increasing number has gone even farther, especially in business but also in the legal profession and in politics, including the court system (in America judges are elected officials.) In the medical field they are more commonly general practitioners rather than specialists. They are present in considerable numbers in education, especially at the secondary level. Some have achieved great stature in the arts, in particular in painting, sculpting and music (less so in architecture). Many are active labor organizers. Rarely do they excel in theoretical mathematics and scientific research. Many of these choices are due to the natural predisposition of Italians, such as an inclination for the arts, but many are also due to the socio-economic circumstances of their families of origin, most of which urgently needed children to start earning money when still young. Additional reasons are the resistance and diffidence on the part of the

---

1   Campobasso: regional capital of Molise. Terlizzi: small town in the province of Bari in Apulia.

2   Ironic reference to the famous song *Torna a Sorrento* [*Come Back to Sorrento*]. Sorrento is a world-famous resort town on the Gulf of Naples.

rich native Anglo-Saxons toward all immigrants but in particular toward those who did not speak English and did not belong to Protestant churches.[3] It is impossible to conduct an accurate survey since there has never been a serious and credible census of the success stories of Italians in the United States. Millions of dollars have been spent for banquets, monuments and festivals of all kinds, but not even a modest amount was ever spent for a publication that could be the equivalent of the *Golden Book of Italian Americans*.

Returning to the topic of the Italian American press, there are some middle-brow publications written both in Italian and in English, a notable example of which is the *Gazzetta del Massachusetts*,[4] published in Boston by Dr. Giacomo Grillo, a valiant defender of the Italian language and a true journalist who knows how to write about a range of topics, from politics to popular culture. He is also a veritable gold mine of memories and anecdots about the heroic, and at times sordid, colonial press that prospered and whitered in a matter of a few years or even months in the neighborhoods of the Little Italies. Grillo is an expert on the history and literature of the United States and is a lively and competent speaker. Another example is the *Italamerican*,[5] a monthly bilingual magazine published in New York that carries the syndicated column of a notable American writer with strong ties to Italy, Igor Cassini (a Georgian name), better known with the nickname Cholly Knickerbocker.[6] Before I start describing these periodicals, I want to alert my readers that we cannot judge them using Italian criteria. At first glance, the *Italian eye* would equate them to small-town newpapers and, at second glance, to gossip magazines. The right perspective must take into account the great difficulties inherent in publishing in a foreign language with a limited target audience that is

---

3 In Italian the term *Protestante* applies both to Lutheran and Calvinist denominations.

4 *Gazzetta del Massachussets*. Founded in 1896. After several changes, its current name is *Post-Gazette*.

5 *Italamerican* was a monthly magazine published from July-August, 1952, to August-September, 1968.

6 Igor Cassini (1915-2002). Columnist for the Hearst newspaper chain. He wrote the *Cholly Knickerbocker* column.

inevitably not part of the country's cultural avant-garde. A reasonable comparison would be an American citizen who arrived in Rome and, with an American eye, judged the local American tabloid,[7] which looks like a provincial American newpaper, despite the fact that Rome can count on a potential readership of at least ten thousand Americans, both permanent residents and visitors; mostly well off or even wealthy; with well paid jobs in the film industry and similar fields. To the contrary, Italian dailies and periodicals in America could never count on a similarly educated and prosperous audience.

The *Gazzetta del Massachusetts* (current name: *Post-Gazette*) was founded by a courageous, energetic and adventurous southern Italian, James Donnarumma, born on December 26, 1874, in San Valentino Torio in the province of Salerno, who had arrived in America at the age of fifteen. It is profoundly different from comparable Italian publications. Boston by now has become a provincial town, which means it no longer has the power and size of other major urban centers. However, it still has a strong cultural tradition and retains financial power. Little of this, however, is present in the *Gazzetta*.

The first sheets in Italian language published in Boston were born in the North End, near the port, where the Irish had first settled. The Irish were pushed out by the Italian immigrants who presently are still dominant in the area. Boston's North End is a typical neighborhood where monuments of the American Revolution, such as Paul Revere's house and graceful Protestant churches—like the Old North Church— are totally surrounded by Italian stores, cafés, restaurants and small businesses. On the sidewalks, local urchins run around like in Naples, yelling at each other in a Bostonian slang. In the earlier days this neighborhood was full of mutual aid societies, notaries public and fraternities devoted to the organization of parades for the patron saints of Irpinia,[8] Sicily, Liguria and, later, Calabria. Those publications reported the names of people who attended banquets, played the pipe for the rich folks in the community who had a paid subscription and, at times, shamed and intimidated the prominents who were not

---

7   *Rome Daily American*. It started publication in 1946 to serve the U.S. Armed Forces still present in Italy after WWII. It closed in 1984 due to financial difficulties.

8   Region of Campania with capital Avellino.

subscribers into buying space for an ad or at least make a donation. Whether the leaflets were named *Giuseppe Garibaldi* or *The Horsefly* or *The Caudine Forks*[9] the content didn't change much.

To this day the Italian American press consists primarily of reports of weddings, baptisms, deaths and trips to Italy. New entries are college degrees and elections to various offices, from judge to city councilman to governor, all signals of the changing fortunes and the position of Italian Americans on the socio-economic ladder. Aside from gossips, the local newspapers are forgettable and carry very little news with the exception of press clips taken from Italian publications that arrive by ship. Yet, in the past, these little newpapers were watering the plant of nationalism. The editors often were dropouts of Italy's preparatory high schools [liceo classico] and they were responsible for transmitting incomplete notions of Ancient Rome and the *Risorgimento*[10] to the children of the southern peasants who had arrived in America lacking even a primary level education. They taught the immigrants the basics of national pride and how to pronounce the names of Dante, Petrarca, Leonardo and Michelangiolo[11] [sic]; names they had never heard

---

9   Giuseppe Garibaldi (1807-1882). Italy's national hero. Political and military leader, he was one of the major figures of Italy's unification with his band of volunteers, the *Camicie Rosse* [Red Shirts]. He also fought in in Brazil and Uruguay on the side of rebels seeking independence from European powers. He gained the appellative *Hero of Two Worlds*.

• *Caudine Forks*. Site of a famous battle (321 B.C.E.) in which the Romans suffered a humiliating defeat at the hand of the Samnites. The closest cities to the location today are Caserta and Benevento, in the Campania region. In Italian the expression "to pass through the Forche Caudine" is still frequently used metaphorically to indicate an arduous journey of hard trials and setbacks, similarly to "running the guntlet."

10   *Risorgimento*. Nineteenth-century political, social and cultural movement that led to the unification of Italy. It broadly corresponds to the period of the three Wars of Independence of 1848, 1859 and 1871. Historians also include the take-over of Rome in 1870 and the consequent dismanteling of the Papal State.

11   Dante Alighieri (1265-1321). Full name, Durante di Alighiero degli Alighieri. Dante is one of the most celebrated poets in the world's history of literature. Also known in Italy as *Il Divino Poeta* [Divine Poet], or, simply, *Il Poeta*, he is still very much part of Italian schools's curriculum, starting in middle school. His most famous work is *La Divina Commedia* [*Divine Comedy*].

• Francesco Petrarca (1304-1374). Poet, inventor of the sonet. With Dante

before in Italy and that now they would use to defend themselves from the scorn and derision of native Anglo-Saxons. This defensive role, played by even the least respectable of the Italian American press, still continues to this day as demonstrated by the reactions of all the Italian publications in the United States—in English and in Italian—to the recent television broadcast of a drama series on the criminal world of Chicago, which is depicted exclusively as an Italian enterprise.[12] The show was sponsored by some of the most important American companies.

New York, September 10, 1961

---

and Giovanni Boccaccio he is one of the three great writers of the thirteenth and fourteenth centuries, who, working separately but with a similar agenda, created the basis for a common Italian literary language.

• Leonardo da Vinci (1452-1519). Full name, Leonardo di ser Piero da Vinci. He is unanimously considered one of the world's greatest geniuses of all times. He excelled in an almost infinite number of fields of knowledge and practical endevours as an artist, scientist, inventor, engineer, architect, musician and philosopher.

• Michelangelo Buonarroti (1475-1564). *Michelagiolo* is the original Tuscan spelling of the name. Michelangelo is one of the most famous and most celebrated artists and architects of the Renaissance.

12   Most likely it refers to *The Untouchables*. CBS, New York, 1959-1963.

THE ANARCHISTS' PICNIC

I have written often about the Italian American press. It is a product that cannot be understood without direct experience; something that, once tried, can even be enjoyed with a little effort. But for someone who has just arrived from Italy the first approach always produces a rather strange impression. Italians, even the more educated ones, have strange ideas about the population that emigrated from Italy or its descendents. But first we must clarify a fact that is often ignored: the descendents—who are much more numerous than the original migrants—grew up and were schooled in this country, not in Italy, therefore their native language is English and their education is American. Their memories of Italy are filtered through other people's experiences, opinions and contaminations; derived from the image of Italy the way it was fifty or more years ago and very often the way it was in a little southern village.

The Italian American press was born with this framework of reference to serve this population and, therefore, it reflects in every way all the same qualities, shortcomings, limitations and aspirations. The fundamental aspect of its development is the fact that it is becoming more and more Anglophone, while what is left of the Italian-language press is read mostly by people at least fifty years old. It is therefore necessary to view it from this perspective of time and physiology, not from that of the Eternal Italy. One of the most promising signs of the interest by Italian Americans in suitable periodicals in English is the success of Philadelphia's *Italian American Herald*,[1] a very promising weekly. The founder is Dr. Alexander Gregorian, a Romanian[2] who had previously spent many years in Italy as correspondent of British newspapers. The most apparent aspect of this type of press in English, in Italian, or mixed languages is its focus on reporting and celebrating

---

1   *Italian American Herald.* First published in 1961, it has been renamed *Delaware Valley Italian American News Herald.* It has a Facebook page at https://www.facebook.com/pages/The-Delaware-Valley-Italian-American-News-Herald/320067254782854 .

2   This is possibly an oversight, in that Gregorian is a common Armenian last name.

the individual achievements of the descendants of a very humble people that has collectively made great progress and has attained a very high economical, political and social status. It is a remarkable result, particularly when one considers that, despite the foundations of a democratic system, in America the native dominant class—made of rich Anglo-Saxons—has kept foreign-origin populations away from the recognitions that in a democracy are a tangible proof of success. In the Italian American press we see column after column filled with stories of personal success, from college degrees to elections of judges to college professorships. We can also find, for instance, a baptism celebrated in a cathedral or a wedding reception in a top-notch restaurant. We read the announcement of a trip to Italy by an elderly couple that arrived here penniless thirty years earlier and can now afford to travel first class; and their return to the United States to a crowd of children, grandchildren, nephews and nieces. We should not smile condescendingly as if these were cases of infantile and provincial vanity. Behind the ostentation, there is the revenge against silent social ostracism; along with pride for having overcome hardship, competition and pain. Italians, even cultivated ones, when they look at these people see only their economic success. However, one should bear in mind that immigration was an enormous tragedy with years of hunger, hard work, insecurity, death and—always—humiliations. The recent demonstrations of success could probably be more refined, less flashy and less focused on financial success. But if we look at the term of comparison, namely the country that took in the immigrants, we see that it was itself coarse, crude and purely interested in money; a place where everybody was judged by the size of their bank account. A good summary is, for instance, the impressions of count Carlo Vidua[3] in the first years of the century that were recently revealed in the journal *Italica*.[4]

3   Carlo Vidua, Count of Conzano (1785-1830). In 1825 he visited the United States and met with Thomas Jefferson, James Madison, James Monroe and President Quincy Adams.

4   *Italica* is presently the official journal of the American Association of Teachers of Italian (AATI). Joseph Rossi: "The American Myth in the Italian Risorgimento: The *Letters from America* of Carlo Vidua." *Italica*: 38.3 (1961 Sept.) pp. 227-35.

Another aspect that surprises Italians who read these periodicals for the first time is the deep nationalistic tone of the publications. By nationalistic I mean that, without distinctions, the press always supports Italy, whoever may be at the helm of the country at any given moment. In the last century they were first for the Italy of Porta Pia;[5] the next day for the Italy of *Rerum Novarum*;[6] and yesterday they were cheering for Fascism. This is a phenomenon that Italians, no matter how well educated, cannot understand. Among the intellectuals puzzled by this mindset were Gaetano Salvemini and Don Luigi Sturzo[7] who were stunned when they found that in a free and democratic country so many of their fellow countrymen, even without the bombardment of Fascist propaganda or the oppression of a dictatorship, were openly supportive of Mussolini. Those intellectuals did not understand this phenomenon from the very beginning of their American experience; they did not understand that for Italian Americans the exaltation of Italy in that period was a revenge against the dominant Anglo-Saxon class that had humiliated them for decades. For the first time they felt

---

5   The reference is to the war of 1870 when the troops of the king of Italy attacked and took over Rome through a breech in the defensive walls at Porta Pia. This resulted in the annexation of Rome to the kingdom of Italy and the self-exile of the pope inside the Vatican compound.

6   *Rerum Novarum*, 1891 [*About New Things*]. It is one of the most influential papal encyclicals of all times. Issued by Pope Leo XIII, it defined for the first time the Catholic social doctrine within the context of the *modernist* ideology, its institutions and structures: representative democracy, market capitalism, meritocracy and labor unions. The contrast between the Italy of Porta Pia and that of *Rerum Novarum* could not be more striking.

7   Gaetano Salvemini (1873-1957). Political scientist, historian, writer and leading anti-Fascist intellectual. He taught history at Harvard from 1930 to 1948. The correspondence between Salvemini and Prezzolini reveals sharp disagreements and fiery arguments between the two.
    • Don Luigi Sturzo (1871-1959). Catholic priest and founder in 1919 of the Partito Popolare, precursor of the Christian Democratic Party founded after WWII. He was exiled by Mussolini in 1924 and lived in London and New York. A collection of his essays is contained in *Miscellanea Londinese*, a series of several volumes with his writings from 1925 to 1940 published after his death. These and other essays are published in the *Opera Omnia of Luigi Sturzo*, an on-going project lasting several decades by the Istituto Luigi Sturzo. (*Opera Omnia di Luigi Sturzo*. Soveria Mannelli, Rubbettino Editore.)

they belonged to a *nation* that was asserting itself on the international scene. They were not disciples of Georges Sorel or Alfredo Oriani.[8] Even today they do not follow any political theory, which they would not understand anyway. But even when a low-level representative of Italy comes to the United States, they revere him and project onto him their yearning to be part of a great country and a great nation, respected and honored even by those who maintain toward its sons an attitude of condescendence and superiority.

In previous articles I failed to discuss the daily *L'Italia*, founded in 1886 in San Francisco and still alive and well. It represents well the Italian-language press on the West Coast of America. The editor in chief is Renato Marazzini; president of the publishing house is Frank de Bellis,[9] a true apostle of Italian culture and, in particular, music. I am looking at a special issue celebrating its seventy-fifth anniversary. The periodical is written in good Italian with reasonable articles and good-quality print. It reflects, it must be said, the origins of the Italian immigration to California, composed mostly of people from Tuscany, Piedmont, and Liguria. From their ranks came the first big contribution to America, the banker Amadeo Giannini,[10] a Genoese

---

8 Georges Sorel (1847-1922). French philosopher. His theories on the power of myth and revolutionary unionism influenced both Marxism and Fascism.
• Alfredo Oriani (1852-1909). Writer. In the book *La rivolta ideale* (1908) he advocated the creation of a strong state in charge of regulating social life. Mussolini drew from his ideas in shaping the ideology of the Fascist movement.

9 Renato Marazzini (1897-1984). Journalist.
• Frank de Bellis (1898-1968). Born in Italy and migrated with his parents to the United States, de Bellis returned to Italy at age 16 to serve as a volunteer in WWI. After the war, he returned to the United States and settled in San Francisco. He retired in 1941 to devote his whole attention to the study of Italian culture and his true callings: music and ancient-book collecting. In 1948 he launched a weekly radio program, *Records from Italy*, and, later, *Music of Italian Masters*. At the time of his death in 1968 over 100 radio stations nationwide carried the program. In 1963 he donated a collection of 200 incunabula to the Bridwell Library at Southern Methodist University, in University Park, Texas. The following year he donated his collection of 15,000 rare books and manuscripts and 22,000 recordings to San Francisco State College, now stored in the Frank V. de Bellis Collection in the J. Paul Leonard Library. http://www.library.sfsu.edu/about/depts/debellis.php .

10 Amadeo Giannini (1870-1949). The son of Italian immigrants from Genoa, Giannini founded the Bank of Italy in San Francisco in 1904. After the earthquake

who taught the art of fundraising to his competitors, both Anglo-Saxons and New York Jews.

There are other semi-dailies: for example, Boston's *La Notizia*,[11] which is still entirely in Italian. It was quite an impression to find out that the editor, an expert in economics, was also the publisher of *The Boston Free Press*,[12] a non-partisan paper which supports conservative causes (and that is getting more and more popular). Although the target audience is Americans of Italian origin, its content is decidedly national and even more interesting than what appears in *La Notizia*. In Boston there is also a periodical that I believe was the first to adopt English to speak to the new generations of Italians, *The Italian News*, founded in 1921, and "essential for every Italian family that reads." When I visited the newsroom, the interpreter was a skilled and polite Jewish gentleman. These newspapers have peculiar relationships with Italian periodicals. They claim to have correspondents in Italy but, frankly, I never heard about any of them. For instance, I saw the name of a certain C., a lawyer, who was touted to be a national personality in Italy. In another newspaper I read the announcement of an exchange of editors between two periodicals, one in Michigan and the other in Foggia.[13] The first would cover Michigan affairs for the Foggia publication and the other the Foggia affairs for the Michigan paper. The world, apparently, is getting smaller and smaller if Foggia is interested in Michigan, and—even more surprising—if Michigan is interested in Foggia.

Some of these periodicals are printed with offset technology, the cottage-industry standard of publication. And in fact it is a family in Dearborn, Michigan, that publishes a monthly periodical of this kind: *Mondo libero*. Owner and editor-in-chief is Oberdan Rizzo, administrator is Anna Rizzo. It is a literary magazine that publishes poems both in Italian and in English (a typical bad habit of many

---

of 1906, Giannini was the only banker willing to risk lending cash to individuals and businesses. In 1928 Giannini acquired the Los Angeles-based Bank of America which he ran until he retired in 1945.

11 *La Notizia*, 1916-?

12 *The Boston Free Press*, 1960-?

13 Foggia. City in northern Apulia.

Italian American periodicals). Strangely, it also contains copy in Spanish and it claims to be the "only Italian American periodical of this kind in America." I believe it. Among the advertisement I noticed one for the magazine *Controvento* published in Alanno, in the province of Pescara. This is the kind of news that makes me feel the burden of my ignorance, caused by my notoriously long absence from Italy. The *Parola del popolo*[14] (published in Chicago) is a bi-monthly socialist periodical that embraces humanitarian ideals typical of the period of Camillo Prampolini and Filippo Turati.[15] My preference would be for more openly revolutionary ideals. Here I found an example of the cultural exchanges between America and southern Italy: a poetry contest "sponsored by the Columbian Academy of St. Louis, Missouri, and *Pungolo verde* [*The Green Prod*] of Campobasso." I am not saying there is anything wrong with it, but maybe the problem is exactly that there is nothing wrong and that this production resembles too closely that of the bourgeois *Farfalle*[16] [*Butterflies*].

I have good feelings for the New York weekly magazine *Adunata dei refrattari* [*Rally of the Reluctant*], an openly anarchist publication. Nothing to be afraid of, here. I read the announcements of their rallies and I discovered that they consist of open-air picnics or dinners in a *trattoria*. The travel directions to those gatherings clearly imply that today's anarchists own a car (yours truly, a bourgeois, doesn't have one)

---

14   *La parola del popolo* (1959-1963). Published by the *Centro storico uomini rappresentativi del socialismo*, Chicago, Il.

15   Camillo Prampolini (1859-1930). Socialist politician of the reformist, anti-Bolshevik wing. In 1886 he founded the periodical *La Giustizia*, later suppressed by the Fascist regime in 1925. With Filippo Turati and Giacomo Matteotti he founded the *Partito Socialista Unificato* in 1922.
   • Filippo Turati (1857-1932). Sociologist, poet and politician, was one of the founders of the *Partito Socialista Unificato* in 1922 and remained the true intellectual leader of the reformist movement that renounced revolution as a means of political struggle. After Mussolini took power in 1922 he fled to France where he remained in exile until his death in 1932.

16   *La farfalla*. Firenze: Nerbini, 1921-1929. Periodical of provincial and popular poetry. In addition to *La farfalla* published in Florence, there were numerous weekly or monthly local editions in the major Italian cities, among which: *La farfalla italiana*; *La farfalla romana*; *La farfalla sarda*; *La farfalla bolognese*; *La farfalla genovese*; *La farfalla napoletana*; *La farfalla siciliana*; *La farfalla piemontese*; *La farfalla toscana*.

and they have disposable income that allows them to eat out just like I do. I have no idea how the anarchists would be able to get a car in an anarchist society, since factories tend to be rather tyrannical. But this is their problem. They also have drama clubs that produce dewy plays on the fate of the proletarians. Since I was a kid I have always loved picnics and hated melodramatic theater; however, I support the opposition to tyranny in any nation, Russia included. I have always respected and I have dear memories of Camillo Berneri,[17] whom I met in Paris and whose writings are still being published by *L'Adunata*. The ever-present losses on the balance sheet prove that the publishers are not making any money. It is written in solid though a little antiquated Italian, still better than *Il Progresso Italo-Americano*. If I were not afraid of offending them, I would say they remind me of my old professors.

In Boston there exists to this day a little magazine called *Controcorrente* [*Upstream*]. It survived the death of Salvemini, who, in the last years of his stay in America, enriched it with the fervor of his passion against injustice. It was the only publication Salvemini did not abandon. Here he had found a small group of narrow-minded, uncultured individuals always willing to tell him how right he was. They also allowed him to publish the fruit of his sourly spirit, progressively more and more embittered against the Italians who had refused to give him the same power they gave Mussolini.[18]

The *Tribuna italiana* of Phoenix, Arizona, is probably the latest addition to the roster of Italian periodicals. The *Italo-American News* of Orleans [sic] instead must be one of the oldest ones (it claims forty-five years of life.) Despite the fact that both are little more than leaflets, I always try to read them. The social announcements, the little news stories, the photos of the faces in those colonial banquets (unfortunately always too similar) tell a long story. If somebody wanted

---

17   Camillo Berneri (1897-1937). Professor of philosophy, political theorist and anarchist activist.

18   Benito Mussolini (1883-1945). Journalist and politician, founder and leader of the *Fasci di Combattimento*, later renamed *Partito Nazionale Fascista*. He became prime minister in 1922 and in 1925 proceeded to dissolve the parliament, thus transforming the Italian political system from a democracy into a personal dictatorship. He ruled until 1943 when he was removed form office and arrested by the king.

to write the history of Italian immigration to the United States, it would be impossible to find primary sources or original documents. The immigrants got rid of everything that reminded them of their past and the survivors don't even want to talk about it. But for anyone with a bit of imagination, so much can be read on those faces, in those gestures, in the way they dress up for social events. Something that has survived since the era of Enrico Caruso,[19] who represented the ideal of Italian in America, is the monthly *Follìa*[20] [*Madness*]: it really looks like a barber-shop magazine from the era of the Italian king Umberto I.[21]

In Hartford, Connecticut, there is a group of publications that reflects the vitality of a flourishing population of Italian origin. The *Italian Review* is printed on glossy paper with so many illustrations that it looks like a fashion magazine. The editor-in-chief, Venerando Sequenzia[22] has chosen a range of Italian topics that goes from fashion to literature and from cuisine to theater. It contains short capsules, lots of addresses, a culinary dictionary, a list of new books and records and other curiosities. It is a mix of intriguing small items that must be very attractive to the readers. This reminds me of another journal of Italian studies that has been around for a long time, *Italica*, founded in 1924 by Professor Rudolph Altrocchi[23] and currently edited by Professor Joseph Fucilla of Evanston, Illinois, near Chicago. It is the official publication of the Association of Teachers of Italian.[24] The content is

---

19 Enrico Caruso (1873-1921). One of the greatest tenors of all times, Caruso became the most famous Italian in America. According to Wikipedia, his 1904 recording of the aria "Vesti la giubba," from Ruggero Leoncavallo's *I pagliacci*, was the first record in history to sell one million copies.

20 *La Follìa di New York* (1893-present).

21 Umberto I (1844-1900). King of Italy from 1878. He was assassinated during a parade by a gunshot fired by the Italian American anarchist (and possibly police informer) Gaetano Bresci, of Paterson, NJ.

22 Venerando Sequenzia (1918-1986). Publisher of *The Italian Review* and, later, of *The Italian Bulletin*.

23 Rudolph Altrocchi (1882-1953). Professor and chair of the Italian department at the University of California-Berkeley from 1928 to 1947.

24 American Association Teachers of Italian. Founded in 1923. It is currently the largest association of primary, secondary and higher education teachers of Italian in the United States and Canada. Its mission is to "Preserve, Advance, and Promote

generally of the old stuffy kind, mostly historical and documentary. Recently it started publishing more modern critical contributions and functions as a forum for young teachers who want to show off their intellectual ability and get credit for their publications. In my opinion it should be required reading for teachers. The University of California Los Angeles, thanks to an initiative by Professor Charles Golino, publishes the new journal *Italian Quarterly*,[25] which devotes each issue to one specific theme. It shows greater critical liveliness and more openness on the new horizons of Italian literature and social life. Both journals are to be admired for their efforts in the midst of a very strong competition from academic journals devoted to foreign languages, and at the same time in the midst of the general indifference of the Italian American public for anything that goes beyond the immediate and local social life.

New York, 8 dicembre 1961

P.S. I could only mention and describe the periodicals that I have received over the years. There are many others, but I have never seen them and I could not find them at the library.

Italian Language and Culture."

25   Carlo Golino (1913-1991). Professor of Italian at UCLA Riverside campus. He became vice chancellor in 1965. In 1973 he was appointed Chancellor of the University of Massachusetts, Boston.
    • *Italian Quaterly* (1957-present) is a literary journal presently published by Rutgers University of New Jersey.

ALWAYS THE SAME OLD FACES
AT MR. POPE'S SOLEMN BANQUETS

I have already mentioned Fortune Pope, the so-called spokesperson of the New York Italian American community and publisher of the least decrepit among the Italian-language newspapers in the United States. By virtue of this role he has had audiences with the president of Italy and the real pope. Now he has been indicted for fraud against his company's stockholders and the city of New York. Let me begin by saying that there are several people who rejoice at these developments. First of all, the fall of a person in such a visible position (made even more visible by his lust for self promotion) makes the envious happy; the same people who, had they been in his place, would have behaved even worse than he. Then there are those who have been disgusted or hurt by his arrogance. Other happy people, probably, are those who fought battles with him and lost, suffering damages to their interests and ambitions. But it is not his personal case that interests us; rather we are more concerned with the consequences that this disgraceful story might have for the community and for the reputation of Italian Americans.

The aspect that impressed me the most in this unexpected and unwelcome story is the silence of the editor-in-chief and the readers of his newspaper. The news of the accusations has occupied several columns of the *New York Times*, yet nobody in the pages of his own newspaper has risen to defend the accused, despite the fact that here he could have all the space he would ever need to make a counter argument. That hasn't happened. The only thing the readers saw [in the *Progresso*] was a tiny, little news item buried inside the paper, in stark contrasts to the occasions when Mr. Pope is celebrated with honors and praise. In those circumstances the news always appears on the front page accompanied by mandatory photos. It doesn't seem that the readers have expressed any indignation either. Or, at least, I have not seen any letters indicating that the readers were emotionally involved in the story and outraged at this so-called injustice. As far as I am concerned, I have no desire to see the accusation proven. I have no warm feelings for Fortune Pope but I will content myself with the opinion, which I am sure he will be forced to share, that he is nowhere as good as his father, Generoso Pope, if not for anything else, at least for the fact that the son was born with a golden [sic] spoon in his mouth while his father forged the golden spoon with his own hands with tenacity and ingeniousness, in a world much less positively disposed toward Italians than what the son later found. I would be very happy if Fortune Pope could show that he is innocent of all charges with clear and direct evidence rather than by means of crafty lawyers (he can afford to hire the best.) I would be happy, not for him, for I don't care about him, but for the Italian Americans who grew up here and for the Italians who have arrived recently from Italy and haven't yet been beaten down. And finally, I would be happy for all of us, because we always end up having to bear the burden of a public opinion that judges us on the basis on the most sensational scandals and crimes connected to Italian names. For, despite the fact that his father changed his name from Papa to Pope, everybody knows he is Italian.

I am not implying here that all Italian Americans and the recently arrived immigrants from Italy actually want or accept to be represented by Pope and his circle of cronies. To the contrary, we must remark that the group of people that American and Italian official authorities identify as the representatives of Italians and Italian Americans in New York is extremely small. For several years now, if one read the *Progresso* or attended the banquet sponsored by the newspaper, one would find more or less the same old faces gathered around lavishly catered banquet tables, with the same names in the list of participants and honorees. For ten years while I was director of *Casa Italiana*[1] [at Columbia University] I collected the obituaries of important people with Italian last names that appeared in the *New York Times*. These were Italian Americans who had distinguished themselves but whose names, in most cases, never appeared in the reunions of the people who had appointed themselves representative of millions of Italian

---

1   *Casa Italiana*. Established in 1927, it housed the Italian department of Columbia University and functioned as an institute of advanced studies on Italian culture in America. Its first director was Giuseppe Prezzolini, appointed in 1930. Due to its connection with the Fascist regime, it was regarded as a center of enemy political propaganda and was closed down in 1940. It reopened in 1991 thanks to a major donation by the Italian government. It currenlty houses the Italian Academy for Advanced Studies in America.

descendants. None of the Italian consuls had bothered reaching out to these eminent Italians, none of whom had sought to be associated with the *Progresso* or with Pope. They did not contribute to fund-raising events and did not show up at colonial banquets and parades. Everyone knows that the claim by the Pope-led group that they are the de-facto representatives of Italian Americans is a complete fantasy. One could see it very clearly on the occasion of the 1950 mayoral election in New York. The candidate endorsed[2] by the *Progresso* was not elected (rumors circulated that he was also supported by Frank Costello[3]). The winner, Vincent Impellitteri, received the silent treatment from the *Progresso* until he was elected. The same thing happened to the other candidate, the Republican Edward Corsi.[4] In that moment it became clear that the so-called Italian vote does not exist. The first evidence had already surfaced years earlier with the candidature of La Guardia, whom the *Progresso* did not support. He, nevertheless, was elected, not necessarily only with the votes of all Italian Americans, but certainly with the votes of many of them. Yet, [Italian] authorities, as their lackeys call them, never realized this simple fact: the entire prestige of the *Progresso* and Pope's rests only on the attention, the honors and the favors that those authorities themselves bestow on him.

Who is responsible for the myth that Pope and the *Progresso* represent and control the Italian American public opinion in New York and can maneuver its votes? The culprits are primarily the various Italian governments, from the first to the last: the Liberal, the Fascist and the Christian Democrat.[5] I should also add to this list the Catholic

---

2   The Democratic Party candidate, chosen by the Tammany Hall political machine, was Ferdinand Pecora (1882-1971). Most likely he was the candidate endorsed by the *Progresso*.

3   Frank Costello (1891-1973). One of the most notorious Mafia bosses, co-founder of the commission—the self-styled supreme council of Cosa Nostra. He was a close ally of Lucky Luciano and eventually became boss of the Luciano family. He was said to have had very extensive contacts inside the Tammany Hall organization that controlled the Democratic Party's electoral machine in New York City.

4   Edward Corsi (1896-1965). Republican candidate in the 1950 New York City mayoral election.

5   Liberal: from 1892 to 1921. Fascist: from 1922 to 1943. Christian Democrat: from 1946 to 1992.

Church hierarchy, which is much more influential over the souls of Italian believers than any of the consular authorities. Among those who understood the danger of this arrangement was a sharp but unassuming writer (and maybe too shy), Beniamino de Ritis.[6] When the Italian ambassador of that time asked him for his assessment, he expressed— not very forcefully—the opinion that Pope should not be allowed to buy the *Corriere d'America*, founded and directed for a while by Luigi Barzini Sr.,[7] the only Italian newspaper that was competing with the *Progresso*. His recommendation was ignored. Another opportunity to get rid of Pope's influence arrived on the occasion of President Giovanni Gronchi's[8] official state visit to the United States. It would have been the most opportune moment to change the system. The president did not come here to visit only Italian Americans but all Americans. On that occasion, the authoritative voice of Luigi Barzini Jr.,[9] son of the above mentioned Sr., insisted that the traditional banquet offered to honor Italian officials visiting New York should mirror America, not Little Italy, and should not feature Pope as the host. This was not meant as a slight, but Little Italy certainly does not represent America as a whole.

It would take a long time to tell the story of what happened and why the event ended up being the usual colonial banquet with the same faces and the same rhetoric. Other voices have already made the same point, sincere voices, maybe too sincere to carry any weight. And so, many Americans of Italian origin and many Americans who

---

6   Beniamino de Ritis (1889-1956). Journalist and writer, he was the *Corriere della Sera* correspondent from the United States during Luigi Barzini Sr.'s tenure. He also collaborated with *The Evening Post* and other American publications.

7   Luigi Barzini, Sr. (1874-1947). Legendary journalist and war correspondent, he received the highest honors from both the United Kingdom and France (recipient, respectively of the Order of the British Empire and the *Légion d'honneur*). He was correspondent of the *Corriere della Sera* from the United States from 1921 to 1931. In 1923 he bought the *Corriere d'America* which he directed until his return to Italy.

8   Giovanni Gronchi (1887-1978). Third president of Italy from 1955 to 1962 and first Italian head of state to visit the United States in 1956.

9   Luigi Barzini Jr. (1908-1984). Journalist, writer and politician. His most famous book, *The Italians* was published expressly for the American market (New York : Simon & Schuster, 1964).

had honored Italy with their deeds were excluded from the events in honor of the president. Everybody is caught in a vicious circle. Favors from Italian governments created a power structure inside the Italian American community that later Italian governments were forced to tolerate, pacify and buy back, despite the fact that none of its members deserved preeminent positions. Who initiated this state of affairs and when? Was it the local Italian officials or was it the ministry of foreign affairs in Rome? It's hard to tell, but over the years I have heard of quite a few episodes that are just shocking. Unfortunately, I don't have sufficient evidence to prove they are true and therefore I won't report them. However, I feel the moral duty to put forth my observation. The current pathetic situation derives in great part from the tendency of the [Italian] bureaucratic apparatus to seek the easy way out (the banquet with 1800 attendees, paid by banks or labor unions) with frivolous events (dinners, parades, receptions). In the meantime, Italian language programs in American middle schools are the last ones, with a 0.3% attendance among students taking foreign language courses. The leader is Spanish with 18% but even Russian, the latest entry, is higher, with 0.5%. Our bureaucracies do not like long-term plans and they turn to the local organizations only when these agree and go along. The Italian-language publications are read only by the generation of fifty-five years old or older who were never able to learn English and, as a consequence, young Italian Americans do not feel represented by these antiquated relics of the past. What is needed is a long-term perspective and concrete targets. For instance, it is probable that an English-language magazine targeting the new generations of Italian Americans would be successful. We should offer to them the same thing that independent American magazines provide, instead of sycophantic rags that exalt the *prominenti*. The new generations of Italian Americans should no longer be fed stale bread.

So many things should be done..... The list could go on for ever. Let's hope that where experience failed, where advice was rejected or ignored, at least disaster will serve the cause.

New York, October 16, 1960

P.S. The decline of Italian language in elementary, middle and secondary schools, which I had predicted, was confirmed by Professor Henry [sic] Golden in the December 1962 issue of the journal *Italica*.[10]

---

10   Herbert Golden. "The Teaching of Italian: The 1962 Balance Sheet." *Italica*. Vol. 39, No. 4, Dec. 1962 (276-288).

POPE KEEPS THE MARSHAL'S BATON

The Pope affair is unpleasant for everybody. It is unpleasant for American citizens of Italian origin who don't want to be represented by an individual who was found guilty of fraud against his business partners and was labeled an imbecile by the judge. It is unpleasant for the Italian government, which, for the sake of decency, has been forced to stay away from Italian American official events where he plays host. It is unpleasant for those American citizens who have a sense of what is proper and see this individual welcomed and honored by the city's political and Catholic authorities. I hope it is also unpleasant for Pope himself who has been chastised three times by the *New York Times* for committing security fraud and for cheating on a city contract for the supply of road salt.

And, finally, it is unpleasant for those who have to report these events and provide an interpretation that, *par force*, must cast reproach on everyone involved. It would be much more pleasant to write in full conscience that American democracy selects its representatives among the most virtuous individuals; that the editor-in-chief of the most important (or, at least, the least insignificant) newspaper in Italian language in the United States is a shiny example of culture, refinement and financial probity; that none of the highest apostles of the Catholic Church kneeled in front of local politicians; and that the so-called Italian community has such a keen sense of its own individuality among all the other foreign-origin communities of Greater America that it can deny support to people who misbehave. It would be ideal, but it is not the reality.

The scandal erupted on October 9, 1961, when the *New York Times* reported that neither the consul general of Italy in New York nor any other official representative of the Italian government would participate in the October 12 Columbus Day parade and the following official banquet. The official host of both events was Fortune Pope, publisher and editor-in-chief of the *Progresso Italo-Americano*. The reason for breaking with a very long tradition was the sentence Pope and his brother were still serving while on probation. Two days after that report, on October 11, an editorial (an article that expresses the opinion of a newspaper's editorial board) appeared praising Italian authorities (ambassador and consul) for showing a better sense of integrity and dignity than New York's politicos such as Governor Nelson Rockefeller[1] and New York Mayor Wagner, who were explicitly mentioned. The article also mentioned the verdict against the Pope brothers and remarked the inappropriateness for elected officials to associate with parolees.

The origin of Fortune Pope's power lies primarily in a series of errors committed over the years by the various Italian governments in the Liberal, Fascist and Christian Democrat eras. Italian authorities have convinced Italian Americans that the Popes, first the father and now the son, represent Italy abroad and that being mentioned in the *Progresso* is the best route to obtain favors and honors from the Italian government. It so happens, in fact, that Italian government representatives after arriving in New York look for quick personal triumphs. When they realize how hard it is to penetrate the higher American circles, they content themselves with lesser honors, usually brokered by the *Progresso Italo-Americano*. In the Italian community vanity abounds and in recent times there is also an abundance of rich people. Moreover, in America it is common for the rich to spend money to look good in public. From this mentality came the banquets at the Waldorf Astoria that would pump up Italian ministers and undersecretaries in visit to New York, ignorant of the difference between decent people (there are many among the Italian Americans) and enriched lice. Pope sells back to the Italian governments the power that derives to him from being accepted as the go-between with Italian Americans and government officials. From a pure perspective of realpolitik, it has been a terrible investment for the Italian government but a great one for Pope. This series of errors could have ended when President Giovanni Gronchi was on a state visit to America in 1956, the first Italian head of state ever to do so. His should have been a visit to the American people. Instead, it turned out to be a visit to the Italian American friends of Pope.

This year the dinner offered by the Columbus Committee, and the

---

1   Nelson Rockefeller (1908-1978). Businessman and politician. He was governor of New York from 1959 to 1973. He also served as vice president of the United States under President Gerald Ford from 1974 to 1977.

Columbus Day parade the following day, were a great success for Pope. Even though we don't believe the numbers printed in his newspaper (one hundred thousand marchers and one million spectators) it is a fact that the public's participation was enormous—and that the *New York Times* didn't hold anyone back. Is it indeed possible that the *Times* may not be the most popular newspaper among Italian Americans?

In the major American cities the mixing of organized crime and politics is a tradition that started well before Italians arrived here. Italian gangsters eventually absorbed and perfected the lesson learned from the local criminal elements. There is, though, a peculiar aspect that is unique to the Italian American community, namely the tolerance for organized crime. Italians stood by when it was being imported, while it was growing and until it adapted itself to America and began to prosper. None of the Italian-community leaders ever spoke against it and there is no record of a single judge, politician, journalist or even a priest of Italian origin who mounted a campaign against Italian criminality. Anglo-Saxon journalists, pastors, politicians and cartoonists in New York, to the contrary, did wage anti-crime wars against their own kind before Italians arrived.

The marshal leading the October 12 Columbus Day parade was Fortune Pope. In front of Saint Patrick's Cathedral, on Fifth Avenue, he bowed in front of Cardinal Francis Spellman[2] who was waiting at the top of the steps that lead up to the portal. The cardinal responded with a gesture and a smile. If we consider the fact that—as a high Catholic authority explained to me—Fortune Pope is officially excommunicated because he is divorced, one may ask what the meaning of that salute is. The English report says: "He waved," which means the cardinal moved his hand in the air to salute him. Was it a blessing? A scolding? ("Ah, bad boy. That was a big one that you did. But this time I'm going to let you get away with it.") Or was it electoral complicity? Who knows? Maybe a clarification from such a high authority would be welcomed by the many who, in Italy, suffer because they don't have the Catholic Church's permission to divorce. Or, is divorce now a preferential title, necessary to merit the friendship and protection of a cardinal? A little

---

2   Francis Spellman (1889- 1967). Archbishop of New York from 1939 to 1967. He became cardinal in 1946.

later, further down the avenue, Fortune Pope left the parade and climbed onto the viewing platform where the authorities, including Governor Rockefeller, were standing. Here he was warmly welcomed. When Rockefeller left the platform, Pope managed to get his picture taken with Mayor Wagner.

To this day, October 16, nobody has complained.

Obviously, this does not mean that all Italian Americans or all New Yorkers approve of Pope. It simply means that the great majority is not concerned with it, probably doesn't know and certainly doesn't care. I bet that maybe only one out of every ten thousand people understood the objections raised by the *New York Times*. In America parades are public events for the happy sheep that participate: they are eager to march because this is part of society's norms and also a source of fun in these collectivistic times. In the last few years the Columbus Day parade has become an event for all newcomers from every corner of the world who have contributed to America's fortune. The participants are high school students, city employees, union members and political-club members. Some show up only because they can't avoid it. This year there were also political adversaries of the mayor, such as Lawrence Gerosa.

The official banquet was also a great personal triumph for Fortune Pope. When the American anthem played everybody stood up. When the Italian anthem[3] played, everybody continued their conversations sitting down, Pope included. Was this pre-ordained? Was it just a mistake? Was it maybe a warning and a reminder to the Italian government as to who is really in charge? Many expected that after his guilty sentence Pope would retire from public life, at least for some time. After all, he is immensely rich and has no public office. Many recommended a low profile as the best strategy for a time, after which he could reemerge in the circuit of banquets, photo-ops and ceremonies that so please him. That's not the way it went, and to tell

3   In the original: *l'inno di Mameli*. Italians refer to their national anthem with the name of the poet who authored the lyrics, Goffredo Mameli (1827-1849). The music was composed by Michele Novaro (1818-1885). Originally titled *Il canto degli Italiani*, it became the official anthem of the newly born Italian Republic in 1946, following the referendum that suppressed the monarchy. It is also frequently referred to as *Fratelli d'Italia* [*Brothers of Italy*]—the first words of the initial verse.

the truth, he was right. Pope knows the life of the largest American city better than I do. He knew he had the governor, the mayor and the hand-waving cardinal in his vest's pocket. He probably thinks he also has in his pocket the various Italian ministers of foreign affairs, and he probably bets they will soon fire the consul who defied the laws of American cities. The rumors from his circle are that the consul's absence was just a personal pique. I can testify, however, that it is not true and that the ambassador agrees fully with the consul. In Pope's newspaper there was no mention of the New York Times reports. Its readers only read, in a few lines, that he was found guilty on a technicality. What they know is that at the banquet he received a warm applause; that he got to sit next to the governor; that the mayor shook his hand and that the cardinal waved at him. As I said before, Fortune Pope is right and we are wrong because we are ignorant of the unwritten laws that rule American democracy in the biggest cities.

Are these the same laws that also govern older and more venerable institutions? Who knows?

* * *

A spokesperson for Cardinal Spellman informed the press that the gesture toward Mr. Pope was not "a blessing." What was it then? And what did his smile mean?

New York, October 22, 1961

ADDENDUM TO THE POPE SCANDAL

The Editors-in-Chief of *Il Resto del Carlino* and *La Nazione*[1] on October 27, 1961, received the following telegram from New York:

> The article by Giuseppe Prezzolini published in your respected newspaper on October 22, contains several mistakes. One of them is particularly egregious in that it insults and offends the dignity of more than 2,200 dinner guests, including Cardinal Spellman, Governor Rockefeller, Mayor Wagner and hundreds of other respected members of our community, and it accuses them of being disrespectful toward Italy. Mr. Prezzolini states that while the Italian anthem was being played, everyone, including Mr. Pope, continued in their conversation and nobody stood up. This statement is totally false in that the Italian anthem was never played, this time or any other time. The Columbian dinner is an American celebration. The Columbian Committee respectfully requests the retraction of this statement.
>
> Signed: Fortune Pope, President Columbus Citizens Committee.

The telegram by Fortune Pope, editor of the *Progresso Italo-Americano* deserves the following condemnation: it is reckless. And here are the reasons. In my article of October 22 I listed a series of events that prompted the consul general of Italy in New York to refuse to participate in the ceremonies of the Italian American community chaired by Pope. Pope had been found guilty of defrauding his business partners but has been free on parole for a year after returning the money. He and his brother had been labeled "stupid" by the judge.

1) In addition, he had sold road salt to the city defrauding it for about half a million dollars, a sum he was forced to return.

2) None of these facts were ever reported by the *Progresso Italo-Americano*, whose readers were told only that that its editor was found guilty based on a "technicality."

---

1   *Il Resto del Carlino* is Bologna's largest-circulation newspaper, founded in 1885.
   • *La Nazione* is Florence's largest-circulation newspaper, founded in 1859.

3) Despite the requests of civil and religious authorities that he step down, Pope insisted on being again the marshal of the Columbus Day parade and wanted to chair the gala dinner for the same occasion.

4) Despite all this, the parade attracted a large public, on orders from the political bosses, union bosses and the heads of the city's public departments.

5) Despite all this, the parade was attended by the governor of the state, the mayor and Cardinal Spellman, who, from the steps of the cathedral, waved at Pope with a friendly gesture and a smile. The first two personages spent time in friendly chats with him.

6) The entire situation was rather extraordinary and I tried to explain that the reason lies in the corrupt atmosphere of American cities. I also emphasized the moral indifference of many Italian Americans.

7) In the course of my analysis I mentioned that when the Italian anthem was played at the Columbus dinner, the participants did not stand up. I asked a number of questions as to the possible interpretations of this behavior, including the possibility that the report was inaccurate.

I maintain that Mr. Pope's telegram is reckless because he only refutes one point. It is therefore obvious he cannot refute any other facts reported in my article (similarly, he has not refuted any other article I have written about him and his newspaper.) He is also reckless because he does not realize he is implicitly admitting I told the truth about everything else. Even if it turned out, as he claims, that my report on the events at the dinner were false, the fact remains that everything else must be true. The story about the anthem, by the way, was not the premise, nor the central point, nor the conclusion of my article: it was a marginal episode that, whether true or false, does not detract from the value of the larger point I was trying to make. Mr. Pope's protestations remind me the logic of the thief who defended himself in court by saying: "I am accused of stealing a watch at 12:57. In reality I stole it at 12:30, therefore the accusation is false and I must be acquitted."

But, is this circumstance, this detail, this fine point truly false, as Mr. Pope maintains? Let's see. Let me begin with the fact that, unlike several other journalists, I was not invited to the gala and everybody can easily guess why (and it is not an issue). I wasn't there in person, therefore I do not know directly if the Italian national anthem did play, nor whether the guests heard it or not. A journalist is a bit like a historian of the present and historians would never be able to write anything if they could only write about things they witnessed in person. Even newspapers would be half of what they are if journalists could only report what they saw with their own eyes. Thus, since I could not attend the Columbian dinner, I asked Gianfranco Piazzesi, a colleague from my same newspaper, if he knew anything about it. He had not attended the dinner either, however, he had heard that the Italian national anthem had been played and that the guests had not stood up. He gave me the name of the person who had passed the information to him and I talked to this person on the telephone. The person in question is extremely authoritative, with a very important position and is very well equipped to report about this kind of affairs. In no uncertain terms his answer was: he attended the dinner; the anthem was played and some Italians stood up while everybody else remained seated. He also observed that, in that precise moment, at the honor table Pope kept at his conversation without standing up. This detail was not particularly important but it added a bit of color and I used it as a brushstroke to make the painting more vivid. As to the reason for Pope's behavior, whether it was planned that way or if it was an oversight, I mentioned the two possibilities in the form of question since I had no direct knowledge of the real answer. The only thing that matters to me now is whether my report was correct. In retrospect I don't think I would change a thing.

When I found out about Pope's complaint, I asked the same person if he could reconfirm what he had told me. He did; and he also talked to Pope's personal secretary telling him that he and other people had heard the Italian anthem; that they had stood up and noticed that everybody else had remained seated. Pope's secretary responded with a statement by the keyboard player who declared he had not played the Italian anthem. Contrary to this version, I found two more people who confirmed that the anthem had played: they know what it sounds like and it is impossible they could be mistaken. Confronted with these conflicting statements, one could think that the people who confirmed that the anthem had played are victims of a case of collective hallucinations. By the same token, one could also believe that the keyboard player who claims he never played it is the victim of a case of selective amnesia. Either hypothesis is believable. To me it matters that everything I wrote on October 22 about Mr. Pope has been confirmed and accepted without refutation by Pope himself. As to the little story about the anthem, my conscience is clear: I did everything within reason in order to ascertain the truth within the constraints of my sources. For this reason I am addressing my response not to Mr. Pope but to the public that has the right to know if what I wrote is true or false.

New York, November 7, 1961.

GREAT ITALIANS AND HUMBLE IMMIGRANTS

From time to time I stumble upon a list of associations started by Italian immigrants in this country. As I read them, I find them moving and at the same time I smile at their innocent naïveté.

It's a repeat of the same impression I felt when I first arrived here, when, during the colonial banquets, someone would recite a list of names of Great Old Italians mixed together in a random fantasia as if they had been pulled from a hat by the hand of a child, like bingo numbers; and mixed together with no apparent logic. My impression was that those names were like a shield and a consolation; the same way for a thousand years the name of Rome (the imperial Rome of Caesar and Scipio[1]) was a shield and a consolation for Italians after so many lost wars and so many tragedies of foreign invasions and subjugation. As happens to impoverished aristocratic families that still keep alive the memories of powerful and rich ancestors when money gets tight and the daughter must marry a vulgar *nouveau riche*, the names of forefathers serve a special purpose. However, after attending many colonial banquets I realized that the immigrant clubs were not named only after Dante Alighieri, Cristoforo Colombo, Leonardo da Vinci, Giuseppe Verdi and Arturo Toscanini[2] (kneading in the same

---

1 Gaius Julius Caesar (100-44 BCE). Known simply as Caesar, he is Ancient Rome's best known military and political leader. He was also a historian of his own military victories. He was assassinated before he could name himself supreme dictator of the empire.

• Publius Cornelius Scipio Africanus (236-184 BCE). Roman general regarded as one of the greatest strategists of ancient times. He defeated Hannibal in the final battle of Zama, in Tunisia in 202 BCE.

2 Cristoforo Colombo (1451-1506). Probably of Genoese origin, he is known in Spanish as Cristobal Colòn and in English as Christopher Columbus. He was a navigator, explorer and colonizer. His first successful voyage to the American continent in 1492 opened the way for the European colonization of what became known as "The New World."

• Giuseppe Verdi (1813-1901). One of the greatest music composers of all times, he is best known for his lyrical operas. Among them are masterpieces such as *Aida*, *Il trovatore*, *La traviata*, *Otello*, *Falstaff* and *Rigoletto*.

• Arturo Toscanini (1867-1957). One of the highest acclaimed orchestra conductors of all times. In 1949 he was offered the ultimate honor by the Italian Republic: the appointment to the senate as *Senatore a vita* [Lifetime Senator]. He

batch creators and performers). Many of these associations' names are also defensive, but in a different sense. They document the culture and ideals of the immigrants of the old days, and as such, they are a text worthy of study.

I wrote to the Supreme Recording Secretary (equivalent to chief archivist) of the largest national organization, the Sons of Italy (in English: Order of the Sons of Italy. This name gives a better sense of the concept of brotherhood than the Italian word *associazione*). Mr. Joseph Errigo, a lawyer from Wilmington, Delaware, was very courteous and helpful. In a few days my office desk was buried under lists of names of lodges. (One should not worry that those lodges may be similar to what in Italy are the Masonic lodges.)[3] In addition to those lists, I made sure I also researched the minutes of meetings of various associations in the Tri-state Area (New York, New Jersey and Connecticut) published over the course of an entire year in one of the Italian-language newspapers. This is not a comprehensive inventory covering the whole country, obviously. I have no idea what associations exist in the Midwest, in Oregon, in the Northwest, in California or in the Southwest. Nor do I know their names. However, I think this is a fairly representative sample. One could presume that, since Italian immigrants came from the same regions of Italy and encountered similar situations, they must have manifested resistance to the new environment more or less in the same way.

The overall impression one derives from this picture is that all the organizations of Italians in the United States were conceived with the purpose of preservation.

An orange wedge taken from the fruit and left in the open almost instantly develops a rind to preserve the internal moisture. Similarly, the wedges of Italian immigration's waves, after they had been separated from the mother country—about which they knew nothing or close

---

declined. He was the first of only two Italians to do so (the other was journalist Indro Montanelli.)

3   In Italian the term *loggia*—with the meaning of club or association chapter— indicates almost exclusively a chapter of the Free Masons, an association and lobbying power that for centuries has been condemned by the Catholic Church and secular governments. In the last half a century some *logge* have been at the center of sordid political and financial scandals.

to nothing—formed a defensive shield. The associations were all created for preservation, each one of them in a distinct form, for each one had something different to preserve in its own environment. Some associations were named after the location in which they were founded. Here, nostalgia for Italy was kept at bay. Springfield, Roslindale, Medford, Roxbury… Was it indifference or fear that made them ignore Italy? Was the need not to appear foreigner so strong in those immigrants? In the associations that chose an Italian name the preservation motive is quite apparent. Naturally, many were named after Columbus. It's understandable. When Americans badmouth Italy, Italians respond: "Without Christopher Columbus you wouldn't even exist…" After Columbus, Dante Alighieri is rather popular, although, for sure most of the members know the name and nothing else. And then, Francesco Petrarca, Torquato Tasso and, curiously, even Beatrice Portinari, maybe for a women's lodge that wanted to be connected with the *Divino Poeta*. I did not find Laura,[4] and I am quite happy about that.

The *Risorgimento* sector is rather well represented with *Risorgimento Italico* (a term that gives it an 1880 flavor, or maybe a D'Annunzio[5] flavor.) I found a club dedicated to the Four Heroes[6] (of course we know who they are, but if I asked the members, wouldn't it be a bit mischievous?) Then I found the Bandiera brothers, many Garibaldi, a few Mazzini (and this proportion is natural for Italians). Among the other names there is Anita Garibaldi (it is easy to understand Italians' attraction for the personage of a woman who dies for her man); and

---

4   Torquato Tasso (1544-1595). Author of *Gerusalemme liberata* (1581) [*Gerusalem Delivered*], the last of the great epic poems of Italian literature.
 • Beatrice Portinari (1266-1290). She was Dante's muse and the famous Beatrice of the *Divine Comedy* who guides the writer through Purgatory and Paradise.
 • In Italy Dante is known as *il Divino Poeta* or *il Sommo Poeta*.
 • Laura was Petrarch's muse, the woman for whom he wrote his love poems.

5   Gabriele D'Annunzio (1863-1938). Famous poet, writer and rebel rouser. He dominated the Italian literary scene and the gossip columns for half a century. His style was usually overabundant, particularly in his narrative works; and attracted a huge following of admirers as well as very large number of detractors, Prezzolini among them.

6   King Vittorio Emanuele II; Prime Minister Camillo Benso, Count of Cavour; General Giuseppe Garibaldi; Giuseppe Mazzini.

even Adelaide Cairoli (and this is very, very anti-conformist); but also Massimo D'Azeglio[7] (I really cannot understand how his name ended up here. Maybe it was some Piedmontese immigrant who chose it. It sorts of bothers me that a hypocrite like him should be honored and remembered here.) [In the footnote: "This comment caused quite a surprise in some readers, even educated ones, who had never considered the contradictions between D'Azeglio's moralistic principles about marriage in his book *I miei ricordi*[8] and his libertine conduct in two marriages."]

In addition to the early *Risorgimento* period, the final phase of the movement is also remembered with several lodges founded after 1918 and named after Guglielmo Oberdan, Nazario Sauro and Cesare Battisti.[9]

---

7   Attilio Bandiera (1810-1844) and Emilio Bandiera (1819-1844). Born in Venice, the two brothers were officers in the Austrian navy when their city and the Veneto region were part of the Austro-Hungarian empire. They became involved in the independence movement. Betrayed by informers, they were captured and executed by a firing squad.

• Giuseppe Mazzini (1805-1872). Philosoper and political thinker, he was one of the most authoritative proponents of the unification of Italy as a republic, against the existing monarchy. He organized plots and rebellions with very little success. He died in exile in London.

• Anita Ribeiro Garibaldi (1821-1849). Brazilian, wife of Giuseppe Garibaldi. They married in Paraguay while Garibadi was in exile from Italy. She died of malaria while on the run with her husband in Italy.

• Adelaide Cairoli (1806–1871). Four of her children died in combat in the wars that led to unification of Italy: Ernesto, 1859; Luigi, 1860; Enrico, 1867; Giovanni, 1869

• Massimo D'Azeglio (1798–1866). Politician, patriot, writer. He theorized the unification of Italy as a federation of states rather than as a national state united under the Savoy dynasty.

8   *I miei ricordi*. Firenze, Andrea Croci Editore, 1881.

9   Guglielmo Oberdan (1858-1882). Deserter from the Austro-Hungarian army, he joined an irredentist group advocating the liberation of Italian regions under Austrian control. He plotted to assassinate Emperor Franz Joseph during a visit to Trieste. The attempt failed and he was arrested and executed.

• Nazario Sauro (1880-1916). Italian born in Austria-controlled territory, he was a sailor in the Austro-Hungarian imperial navy. He defected to Italy at the beginning of WWI. He was captured and hanged for treason.

• Cesare Battisti (1875-1916). Born in Trento, in the Austo-Hungarian empire, he was elected to the local regional parliament. He espoused the cause of independence

One of these associations is named after Francesco De Sanctis.[10] I happen to know some of the members of this club: they are very good people. They chose that name because the famous literary critic was the most illustrious son of the town where they also were born. They chose him because he was a *paesano*, but they could not care less about helping a student of mine who was working on a dissertation on his work. Wreaths, gala, dinners and speeches? Yes. Books and dissertations? Never.

Just imagine now what these names mean in America. What does an American think when he hears those names? To him they are sounds and nothing else. Yet, to the immigrants they have a meaning, though not the same meaning they have in Italy. They are myths, like the names of saints, symbols of a vague greatness needed to compete with the greatness of America.

New York, May 4, 1961

---

from Austia and joined the Italian army at the beginning of WWI. After being captured, he was charged with high treason and executed by hanging in the Castello del Buon Consiglio in Trent. It is said that most of the people in the area named *Battisti*, ashamed of the name, switched to the German equivalent *Reiner*.

10   Francesco De Sanctis (1817-1883). To this day, he is still considered the most influential critic of Italian literature. He single-handedly shaped the curriculum and the ideological scaffolding for the teaching of Italian literature in all Italian schools. His method and critical/ideological approach dominated throughout the twentyth century, and to this day, more or less all Italian literature texts are still oriented in the same direction. His method, called *storicismo*, consisted in a critical evaluation of authors and works of literature based primarily on the agenda of Italian unification. Texts and authors that served the goal of a historical trajectory toward unification were considered more relevant than those that did not directly approach related themes.

Part Two

Italy's Representatives in America

LETTER TO FELLOW ITALIANS
BY ITALY'S AMBASSADOR TO THE UNITED STATES

Between 1922 and 1925, the Italian ambassador to Washington was Prince Gelasio Caetani di Sermoneta.[1] He is the author of the letter—published below—to a group of Italian engineers sent to America by the Italian government on a work-study program. Caetani was the descendant of one Rome's most prominent aristocratic families whose origins go back to the tenth century; and whose deeds were reported in history books of famous scholars such as Ferdinand Gregorovius.[2] Among his ancestors are generals, diplomats, admirals, cardinals and popes. He was named in honor of one of them, Pope Gelasius II.[3] Onorato Caetani,[4] his father, was a politician, initially elected to the *Camera dei deputati* (the lower house of parliament). He was later appointed senator by the king and went on to become minister of foreign affairs under Prime Minister Antonio Starabba di Rudinì[5] in 1896. In the course of his distinguished public career he also served as mayor of Rome from 1890 to 1892. A talented amateur archeologist, he was president of the Italian Geographic Society, one of Italy's most prestigious scientific institution. Gelasio's aunt, who became Countess Ersilia Locatelli[6] [sic] by marriage, was the hostess of one of Rome's most

---

1   Gelasio Caetani duca di Sermoneta (1877-1934). Minerary engineer and diplomat, he was Italy's ambassador to the United States from 1922 to 1925.

2   Ferdinand Gregorovius (1821-1891). German historian. He spent many years in Rome where he produced the authoritative *Geschichte der Stadt Rom im Mittelalter* (8 vol., 1859-1872); translated into English as *History of the City of Rome in the Middle Ages* (1894-1900); reissued by Cambridge University Press (2010).

3   Pope Gelasius II (1060 ca – 1119). Born Giovanni Caetani, he was elected pope in 1118. He was the first pope to be elected *cum clave*, that is in a secret place where the cardinals could not communicate with the outside. The practice still exists to this day.

4   Onorato Caetani di Sermoneta (1842-1917). Politician. He was mayor of Rome from 1890 to 1892.

5   Antonio Starabba di Rudinì (1839–1908). Politician and minister in serveral cabinets. He was prime minister in 1881-1882 and again from 1892 to 1896.

6   Ersilia Caetani Lovatelli (1840-1925). A self -taught archeology scholar, she became instrumental in starting the first comprehensive archeological studies of ancient Rome.

prestigious literary salons open to the international set; and the first
and only woman to be appointed to the Accademia dei Lincei.[7] Since
he was a boy, Gelasio had an inclination for mathematics and physics.
He attended the Lyceum Gymnasium E. Q. Visconti, graduating in
1896. At the University of Rome he completed the course of studies
in the faculty of engineering in 1901 when he received a *laurea summa
cum laude*. After college, he first went to Liège, Belgium, where he
attended the *École des mines* for one year. In 1902 he moved to New
York to study in the School of Mines at Columbia University.[8] In the
summer of the same year he attended Columbia University's practicum
in mining in the silver mines of Daly West and Ontario, approximately
sixty miles from Utah's Great Salt Lake. He was one of twenty-two
students. At first his classmates only knew him as Mr. Gelasio Caetani.
When they found out about his lineage, a bit intimidated, they started
calling him the Count of Bunker Hill, from one of the locations where
they were working. It was a typical American educational experience.
The students lived in shacks made of wooden boards and slept in bunk
beds like in steerage class, equipped with straw mattresses, a blanket
and a pillow. A cook would prepare lunch which everyone would carry
to the workplace in a tin canteen (that was before the invention of
the thermos, today's standard equipment for all American laborers.)
The job required climbing steep hills to survey and measure the land,
the basic responsibility of any entry-level mining engineer position
in America. Caetani was one of the best in his class. I want to skip
the rhetoric about the democratic spirit of this aristocrat. I never met
him in person; however, I believe I sense in him that simple and very
human thing that goes under the rubric of vocation. Caetani must
have felt good in that environment and must have liked that trade.
He understood that the experience would be beneficial to him and,
in fact, later in life he became involved with a mining company.
(Eventually he left it when he had to return to Italy to tend to more
pressing business. The company resigned itself to the loss only with

---

7   Accademia Nazionale dei Lincèi. One of Italy's oldest academies, it was founded
in 1603 with the aim of contributing to the study of sciences. It later expanded its
horizon to include various fields in the humanities.

8   Now named School of Engineering and Applied Science.

great regret.) In June 1903, when he started working for the business concern Bunker Hill and Sullivan Mining and Concentrating Co., headquartered in Kellogg, Idaho, his salary was three dollars for a nine-hour workday. He tried to absorb as much as he could from this experience and he came to the attention of the management for his interest in extraction methods. His first job consisted in driving a train of cargo wagons into the mine. Later, he was put in charge of perforation and subsequently was promoted inspector. After that experience, he moved to a laboratory for metallurgy research. In the new environment the theoretical foundations he had received in Italian schools and his personal ingenuity served him well. The reports on the experiments he conducted captured the attention of management. In June 1904 he was sent to Alaska; then, in 1905, to the gold mines of California. At the end of the year he was promoted superintendent of Bunker Hill and, with the new title, was dispatched to Mexico to conduct more studies and research. At that time his work was cutting-edge and his studies were published in prestigious scientific journals. In the five years he spent in the profession he made lots of friends everywhere. In 1912 in San Francisco, with two other partners, he founded the mining company Bursch, Caetani and Hershey. Caetani was in charge of metallurgy research and invented a fusion method with arsenic that later became an industry standard. Between 1912 and 1914, he was working on a book on this subject when his efforts were interrupted by the beginning of World War I. He intuited that Italy would eventually end up entering the war.[9] He put aside the plan to open a new office in New York and decided to return home. The company kept his name until 1918 when it became clear that he would not return to his old profession. Back in Italy he distinguished himself in all of his endeavors. In the war, the mining experience served him well. Decorated three times for military valor, his most impressive deed was the explosion that destroyed the mountain top of the Col di Lana,[10] allowing the Italian army to take it after an endless

9   World War I started in 1914. Italy decided to enter on the side of the Triple Entente (Russia, France, Great Britan) on May 24, 1915.

10   Col di Lana: A mountain peak in the Venetian Dolomites, and the site of one of the bloodiest battles of WWI.

futile siege that had cost, up to that point, more than 10,000 lives. In a round-about way, we can say that this really was an American contribution to Italian history.

When the Fascist movement appeared on the political scene, Caetani was a member of the Nationalist Party and, with his comrades, embraced the new political entity with the contained enthusiasm the well-bred harbors for the less intelligent but more able. (I personally believe that, without the alliance with the Fascist Party, the Nationalist movement would have never attained power.) When he was appointed ambassador to the United States everything and everybody was in his favor: the Italians, with whom he had fought valiantly; the historical moment that saw Italy and the United States allied; the Americans, who were proud to salute the Italian product of American schools; his bilingual fluency and his ability to relate to people also in dialect and slang. He seemed the ideal person for the post. The only ones who objected were the Fascists of New York who started attacking him in the publication *Il Carroccio*[11] in the period between January and June 1924. They didn't think he was Fascist enough, or maybe he wasn't coarse enough or not condescending enough. Were they able to have his head handed over to them? Officially nothing is known. However, in 1925 he was called back to Italy. He died on October 20, 1934. I did some research on his life and I noticed that only the *Corriere della Sera* published his obituary (paid for by the family). Even the *Nuova Antologia* is silent about him. Apparently the *Piccolo Giornale d'Italia* [sic] published an account that I wasn't able to find. The *Enciclopedia Italiana*[12] gives no details as well. For this reason I am devoting so

11   *Il Carroccio*. Italian review journal, was published between 1914 and 1927.

12   *Corriere della Sera*. The major daily newspaper of Milan and one of the most influential nationwide. It was founded in 1876.

• *Nuova Antologia*. Quarterly jounal of "letters, sciences and arts," founded in 1866 by Francesco Protonotari. Published in Florence, it is one of Italy's most prestigious publications.

• Most likely *Il Piccolo*, the major newspaper of Trieste, founded in 1881. It was owned by the publishing company Il Giornale d'Italia, which owned the homonymous newspaper and the daily *La Voce d'Italia*.

• Founded by Giovanni Treccani in 1925, the Istituto dell'Enciclopedia Italiana publishes the most comprehensive general encyclopedia in Italian language.

much space to talking about him here.

The letter I am publishing below was addressed to a group of Italian engineers sent by the Italian government to the United States on a scholarship. It is remarkable in that it lacks the usual international rhetoric (so prevalent these days as soon as a student pokes his head out of his home country) on the inevitable and immediate effect that just a little trip abroad will have on the friendly relations among the peoples of the earth; and on the future prospect of the entire humanity embracing peace and prosperity. It is also noteworthy for its realism: not the realism of an ambassador addressing citizens abroad but the realism of a man who was tested by other men who were also being tested. And finally, it is memorable for the deep sense of national identity, not at all rhetorical, that allows one who lives abroad to accept without idolatry, but with respect, the mores of a different people. I have always been deeply impressed by this letter. Obviously, I can't claim to have seen all the letters that ambassadors (not only Italian) must have written in similar occasions but I doubt that, if more existed, they would be of this caliber. In any case, this is a great document of style that, in my opinion, would make for a great reading in school anthologies. (Even mining engineers know how to write when they have something to say.) Another remarkable detail: the dignified building that houses the Italian embassy in Washington is the result of his work. I also want to add something that is not known about Caetani: while the edifice was being built he was extremely irritated with the Italian bureaucracy.

Royal Italian Embassy
Washington

Dear Engineer:

Enclosed with this letter please find your paperwork. I am taking this opportunity to extend my cordial and paternal welcome to this hospitable land, together with my best wishes for the difficult task you have endeavored to undertake of starting your career in humility, from the lowest rung of the ladder. You will be following the same path I walked on when I was your age. You will respond with the same curiosity, illusions, hopes, disappointments that I experienced in the first years of my career and that are now the pleasant memories of an adventurous past. You too will find out that reality is almost always different (and most of the times less attractive) than what is at first envisioned. But, behind this facade you will discover horizons and opportunities that you now ignore and that could lead to a reality even more attractive than what you had imagined. It will be difficult for you, with an academic degree in engineering, to start working as a simple laborer. Moreover, you will be a foreigner, a person whose trustworthiness people will instinctively question; and you will be the representative of a race whose history, traits and achievements are ignored by ninety percent of Americans.

More than once I felt the impulse to give up, but what kept me here was the wish to demonstrate personally the qualities of our people, and I think I succeeded. This was one of my greatest gratifications. My first advice is to work tirelessly to perfect your knowledge of English. Most of your success will depend on this. You should also try to penetrate the mentality and adapt to the American lifestyle without prejudging, without being critical and without inhibitions. Your success is inseparable from this kind of attitude. You will never be able to advance if the Americans you will meet do not feel you are attuned to the spirit and the social dynamics of the United States. You should not be afraid to become Americanized on the outside. Your Italian soul won't change. Do not express generalized and gratuitous criticism and forget about persuading Americans with the usual clichés of all Italians being geniuses. If you do not criticize them, you will see that Americans will criticize themselves. Let them speak and do not comment. If you want to prove our [Italian] superiority, do it with your deeds. Do not lose heart if you have to work for months with pick and shovel; or if you are asked to monitor the monotonous work of a machine; or spend the whole day working on boring drawings. I personally endured, physically and emotionally, more than anyone can imagine. I don't believe we only learn what our mind believes it is learning. I don't believe that three months spent on a monotonous, repetitive and boring task is time wasted. We always learn something even when we don't realize it: we learn by breathing the atmosphere and absorbing impressions almost unconsciously. Once assimilated, the sum of these small bits of knowledge will turn out to be extremely useful in the future. You won't be able to reach a high position unless you immerse completely in the psychology and the mores of the American people, and unless you learn to distinguish, in all its details, the state of the art of the particular sector where you work. A career depends obviously on an individual's intelligence, willpower and character. But it also depends on time, and time—Einstein's theories notwithstanding—remains immutable and unperturbed by our impatience. Be aware that in America nepotistic connections and impressive academic titles count for naught. The only things that matter are personal performance and the ability to deal with human beings. The best *connection* you can count on is what you can prove about yourself. Do not rely, as they do in Italy, on the friendly push of an ambassador or some other big wig. Americans will discard it mercilessly. What really matters is *character*.[13] fairness, loyalty, frankness, moral courage and honesty. Your bosses will observe with attention how you treat your associates and subordinates. Those who don't know how to treat people cannot lead them. Your chances of a successful career are all there. You will have to soften your personality and eliminate impulsive reactions, angry moments and big blow outs. One must be calm, dignified yet ready, when necessary, to engage in a good fist fight to demand respect. Keep your eyes open to catch new opportunities. Nobody will blame you if you leave a company and move to another job. But you should do so openly and earnestly.

Your future is in your own hands. Do not count on the ambassador if you tire of a job and want something else. The ambassador is very interested in helping you getting started but he is not a job referral service. In the United States there are many opportunities for those who have the right stuff. If a person does not succeed, he should not blame the circumstances or other people. One should look into himself to understand what is lacking. I am certain that ninety percent of our newly graduated engineers will go very far, but it will happen only after working hard… for years. Those who will decide to return to Italy will

---

13   In English in the original.

bring back something more important than money: the treasure of the American experience. Thus far, the only people who have come from Italy have been peasants and laborers but, unfortunately, not Italy's best minds. This has had a negative effect on our reputation. You, my young colleague, have the very arduous and noble task of demonstrating that Italy is not inferior to any other nation. Please, keep me informed about your progress. I have no interest in helping the inept but I will give all my support to those who will demonstrate their worthiness. I wish you the greatest success. The future of my younger colleagues and the prestige of Italy are very dear to my heart. Be well.

CAETANI
January 7, 1955

ITALY'S REPRESENTATIVES IN NEW YORK

Italian affairs are not my concern and I am not interested in talking about this topic, especially in this forum. However, when Italy sends its representatives to America, they fall in my crosshair. A while ago Italy sent to New York a great and beautiful ocean liner together with an undersecretary who was neither great nor beautiful. The ship spoke very good American, namely it showed every aspect of the ingenuity, the craftsmanship and the flexibility of a people that can learn new languages from other peoples. The representative of the Italian government, to the contrary, was endowed with none of these qualities. He arrived here with a great desire to speak in public, but, since he didn't know the local language, he was limited to speaking to an Italian audience, any Italian audience, indiscriminately, no matter where and when, as long as he could speak. Out of curiosity I went to his speech at the consulate with a crowd of about a hundred people that the functionaries had managed to herd for the occasion. In front of this public the orator spoke for one hour about the rebirth of Italy after World War II. He didn't say anything new for we have heard the same things in reports of the Italian Chamber of Commerce, in press releases by ANSA,[1] in Italian newspapers and even by American correspondents in Italy. And yet, apparently, these facts must have been new to the undersecretary because he had to read them from a cheat sheet. And poorly did he read them, in fits and starts, stumbling on words, with long and extremely boring lists of statistics. As an excuse he claimed that in America speeches are full of data—something that is manifestly not true. If anything, speeches by Americans are full of funny anecdotes. Every so often the undersecretary would get stuck trying to decipher whether the figure he was reading was millions or billions. The difference is not irrelevant, and he should have been better prepared. Despite the fact that he was a long-term member of parliament, his Italian pronunciation was awful; with words like

---

1   ANSA: Agenzia Nazionale Stampa Associata, the leading Italian wire service, founded in 1945, after the fall of the Fascist regime, replacing the state official press agency Angezia Stefani. Agenzia Stefani was founded in 1853 and shut down on April 29, 1945.

burocrassia and *democrassia*[2] [sic] that reminded me of vernacular theater. Obviously, he had never bothered to correct it. For an entire hour I did not hear a single meaningful word, an intriguing thought, a new idea or a sharp observation that would catch my attention. He paraded in front of us all the trite clichés of propaganda, including the myth that the electoral success of the communist ideology in Italy is the result of poverty; even though even children know that it is the richest areas of Italy that vote for the Communist Party. The other shopworn cliché was that the common sense of the Italian people would eventually reject communism. This would have given us a shiver if we had not already become frozen solid by the time he raised that point. The parade of banalities, of cookie-cutter slogans, saccharine and bromides reached the peak when he begged the public to press the *generossa democrassia americana*[3] to help Italy. This shocked me more than any other mediocrity that had come out of his mouth because the tone was humiliating and the hope was phony. Nothing of what he said would ever go farther than that room because nobody in New York would ever pay attention to a speech on provincial topics in front of a public of a hundred people. If one wants to be heard in New York, one must reach a different public, in English, via radio or television.

In his speech the undersecretary kept going back to the fact that he had been "close to De Gasperi";[4] that he "had spoken to De Gasperi"; that he "had seen De Gasperi"; that he "had heard De Gasperi" and he "had worked very close to De Gasperi". Finally, the entire credit for the reconstruction of Italy was De Gasperi's, with the help, of course, of the pathetic orator who was gratifying us with his presence. I am not an expert of Italian affairs, but from what I read it seems to

---

2   *Burocrassia; democrassia.* The phonetic spelling is meant to reproduce the speaker's regional pronunciation (most likely from northern Italy, possibly Emilia-Romagna) of *burocrazia* and *democrazia*.

3   Ditto.

4   Alcide De Gasperi (1881-1954). One of the founders of the political party Democrazia Cristiana that dominated Italian politics until 1992. He was prime minister from 1945 to 1953 in the post-WWII period known as *Ricostruzione* [reconstruction]. His major accomplishment was the electoral defeat of the leftist coalition *Fronte Popolare* [Popular Front] in 1948, and the alignment of Italy with the Western alliance of liberal democracies lead by the United States.

me that De Gasperi's major achievement was doing good and some bad, allowing all the political factions, communists included, to take advantage of his government's passivity.

Earlier this year, another government representative had arrived on a visit. This one was a lady and the result was even worse. She stayed two months (presumably at tax payers' expense) with the excuse of a sprained ankle that she could have easily taken care of on a ship heading home. She enjoyed herself by delivering speeches, in Italian of course, to those same identical audiences that understand Italian. In terms of ideas her speeches were at the level of a domestic servant's; and, in terms of rhetorical flourish, of a bigoted church lady's. Long and tedious as a rosary, they gave me the impression of a long skirt that is dragging on the floor and is about to fall off but is still hanging by a thread while everybody is waiting for the moment when it will slip down revealing long underwear.

I have seen several representatives of the official Italy in the United States. Before the Fascist period the representatives of the liberal governments were often good people, lazy and uninterested. They were happy with a good meal and a good cigar sitting in a comfortable armchair: at least they didn't bother anyone. The Fascists were arrogant know-it-alls who annoyed everyone; commanded the best cabins on a ship; hit on girls and demanded to stay at the Waldorf Astoria. The latest ones, the Christian Democrats, poor saps, grew up in the most remote parishes of provincial Italy; have never stuck their noses outside their native hamlets; have never traveled first class and are just childishly happy for having the kind of power they had never dreamed of. And of course they have no idea what to do with it. The functionaries who know America well but who must comply with the wishes and orders of these ignoramuses look at them with a diplomatic smirk while they fulfill their desire to speak in front of a hundred Italian Americans, reassuring them that they are really addressing the *generossa democrassia americana*. In the past it seemed to me that some of the Italians in power wanted to make Italy bigger than it really was, but now I wonder if the remedy isn't worse than the problem, since they are making it much smaller than it is.

New York, September 17, 1954

PRESIDENT GRONCHI SHOULD REPRESENT
ALL ITALIANS, NOT JUST THE IMMIGRANTS

The visit to America by the president of the Italian republic has been the object of discussions and negotiations in Washington, not only at the state department but also in the Italian diplomatic and consular circles. This event could provide a new opening and raise the profile of Italy to a new level of responsibility and respectability. Will this happen or will the visit run the usual course? In a few words, the Italian president's agenda could finally signal the visit of a representative of all Italians, not just of Italian Americans. By now, practically all Italian Americans are American citizens and they constitute a small percentage of the population. Therefore, in order to emphasize the difference between the two groups, it would be necessary for Mr. Gronchi to visit American institutions and associations. This, at least, is what leaders of other countries do on a regular basis. And this approach is desirable and possible and even necessary for Italy as well: Gronchi's visit to the United States is the first ever by an Italian head of state. In the past, until now, the highest Italian authorities to visit have been prime ministers, not presidents. The unique role of the president's office and its functions, which are more symbolic than political, offers an ideal opportunity to introduce the entire Italy as a whole to the American people, marking a distinction with the country that sent here millions of workers who—by now—have been absorbed into society.

Without getting into too many unpleasant details, we can say that the previous visits by Italian statesmen contained more folkloric elements than political goals. For the American public, Italy is a country that has given a significant demographic contribution of enterprising and hard-working citizens to the development of their country but that now—in the historical context of post-war developments—represents something different in terms of institutions and goals. In other words, Americans incorrectly believe that Italian American immigrants, and nothing else, constitute the fundamental ties between Italy and the United States; a belief that is confirmed by the choices made by politicians and diplomats in charge of Italian foreign affairs. But this notion is wrong and outdated, first and foremost because we live in different times. As the years go by, the old immigrants are replaced by new generations of Italian Americans who are completely Americanized and whose feelings for Italy are—at most—a residual form of affection and reverence, due more to social habits than culture. It is also wrong because the two countries, the old and the new, are different places. Italian exports to the United States are targeting all Americans, not just Italian Americans. In other words, we are moving from chestnuts and olive oil to machinery and fashion. The new relationship with America is based on the taste of a rich and sophisticated international middle class, not a civilization of common foods.

Many think President Gronchi's visit could be the best opportunity to mark a change in the official relations between the United States and Italy, moving away from the limited platform of Italian American issues to a much wider one that encompasses shared political and cultural interests. The same people also suggest that President Gronchi spend time visiting and learning about organizations such as the *New York Times* or the *Daily News*[1] (each with a circulation of 3,500,000) rather than local little Italian-language newspapers. They also think it would be worthy for the president to study the workings (since he is an academic it should not be difficult for him) of one of the many large foundations that donate huge amounts of money for the advancement of science, such as the Rockefeller or Ford foundations. This seems a better way to allocate resources instead of wasting time and prestige in order to raise funds for small enterprises with limited vision. These people also believe that, in the interest of all Italians in America, the president should emphasize that the recent immigration from Italy, unlike that of the past, is characterized by individuals with technical skills and a higher level of education, with needs that are different from those of the immigrants of yore. It should not be difficult for the organizers of the president's visit to find in American society people suitable for a welcoming committee. From Wall Street bankers to Broadway playwrights; from film producers to museum directors in Washington and New York; from novelists enamored of Italy to the CEOs of multinational corporations with a presence in

---

1 Official name of the newspaper, also commonly known as *New York Daily News*. It was founded in 1919.

Italy; there is an endless list of names that in America have a much deeper meaning than the usual, worn-out ones. There are also serious organizations that could take care of the logistics and the meeting agenda of the president. The America-Italy Society,[2] whose president is former ambassador Ellsworth Bunker,[3] was originally created with this goal but has been excluded in favor of committees with a much narrower focus. What matters is that President Gronchi is received by America as a whole and not only by a small sect, even if his Italian heart is closer to them. The issue is political relations, not emotions.

This may be hard to swallow for those who consider themselves the irreplaceable operatives of every official visit because they have been taking care of the various ignorant and dialect-speaking ministers who routinely visit here. Isn't it about time Italy's representatives learn—metaphorically—to speak Italian instead of their regional dialect?

Italy today enjoys a new reputation in America. Educated Americans and their newspapers and magazines are captured by the charming image of modern Italians, elegant, refined but at the same time grounded in the ancient traditions of high quality craftsmanship. You can't open an American periodical today without seeing Italy being mentioned in its pages. To understand this enormous change in status, one should remember what used to be published in the past. Examples are the caricatures that appeared in *Harper's Weekly*[4] between 1880 and 1900. The visitors of the exhibition *Four Centuries of Italian Influence in New York*[5] at the Museum of the City of New York in 1955, surely noticed that Italy was represented by a stocky man with handlebar moustache, grinding the organ with a monkey on his shoulder. Today, advertisements in major newspapers and magazines show the slim figures of classy ladies or the puzzling and fantastic paintings of famous artists. In the past, to the American public, Italy meant pick-and-

---

2   The America-Italy Society was founded in 1925 and dissolved in 1959. Its records are kept at the University of Minnesota's Archives and Special Collections.

3   Ellsworth Bunker (1894-1984). U.S. Ambassador to Italy in 1953-1954.

4   *Harper's Weekly* (1857-1916). Subtitled *A Journal of Civilization*, it was a general interest magazine dealing with politics, culture and other contemporary topics.

5   *Four Centuries of Italian Influence in New York*. Special exhibit, Museum of the City of New York, Sept 15, 1955.

shovel workers. Now the name is invoked in discussions about shoes made in Florence so fine they seem chiseled by Benvenuto Cellini[6] himself. We should make it clear that we do not want to disparage millions of Italians who came here in the past and confronted the most difficult challenge a person can face, namely being transplanted from one civilization to another, without any support from the Italian government and no welcome from the American ruling class. Those who have *survived* deserve our respect, and, most of all among them, those who have not put up airs and become pretentious. Their names only appear in newspapers when they die and only at that point do we find out about their achievements in American life and the modest wealth they have accumulated without hurting anyone.

Some say that the monopoly on Italy's image should not be delegated to small minorities dominated by arrogant, self-important and self-promoting individuals. The problem is two-faced. Italian Americans should not be the only ones to represent the ties between Italy and the United States. Moreover, among Italian Americans there are many valiant individuals who disdain showing off and, therefore, never appear in official ceremonies, pushed aside by the bombast of others more able at making noise with drums and trumpets. The visit by President Gronchi could mark the beginning of new relations and in this sense it takes a historic meaning. Only this president, who has already shown his independence of judgment in many other circumstances, could take this step. Will this be the time, or will he take the path of least resistance allowing the old forces and the traditional power to prevail? This is the question many are asking.

New York, January 23, 1958.

---

6   Benvenuto Cellini (1500-1571). Most renown for his work as a goldsmith and cast-bronze sculptor. His most famous work is the *Perseus* statue (1554) located in the Loggia dei Lanzi outside Palazzo Vecchio in Florence.

NEW YORK'S POLITICOS PUT THEIR STAKES IN GRONCHI TO CAPTURE THE ITALIAN AMERICAN VOTE

When I stuck my head out of the taxi this morning, wrapped in my cashmere scarf to fight the cold, I saw the ocean liner Cristoforo Colombo.[1] She was gorgeous with her streamlined bow pointing upwards into the sky; white in a day whitened by frost and sunlight; so peaceful, moored at the friendly pier, unaware of the more than thousand people it was carrying; all happy to have arrived and yet sad to leave behind the warmth, the fine foods and the new friends they had just made onboard.

As inhabitants of this port city, we know the port gives us life. We know the outlines of the many ships that approach, blowing their sirens, helped by little hustling tugboats covered in icicles. All we need to identify them is a glimpse at the smokestacks. Their colors are like flags and we feel we almost hold them in our hands when they dock at the piers. They are our guests of honor and, whenever a newcomer arrives, the whole city of New York seems to take on a festive tone. Sirens wail; airplanes fly overhead; balloons float in the sky; newspapers have huge headlines and TV and radio stations fill the air with their broadcasts. Even priests sometimes mention the event in their sermons. There is happiness in the air and often the mayor himself comes to welcome the new arrival.

Welcome, ocean liner Colombo, for carrying new people to this land made of many people. Welcome for ferrying across the globe these hurried Americans, voluble, restless and eager to embrace new ideas and challenges. Welcome for representing Italian ingenuity, Italian cuisine, Italian hospitality and Italian unpredictability. You are our champion. Forget about politicians and ministers. A ship like you is the symbol of a nation that was able to design, build, equip, make comfortable and hospitable an industrial marvel and point it in the right direction at the right time. This is a real ambassador because it knows how to communicate, and its reputation becomes the reputation of the country of origin. Those who travel to Italy will form here a

---

1   Cristoforo Colombo. At the time of launching in 1953 she was Italy's largest ocean liner. The maiden voyage took place in 1954. She was scrapped in 1982.

first impression they will never forget and when they return they will be left with a last and lasting one. Ninety percent of the impressions Americans have about Italy are now shaped by the ocean liners that carry them. In this context we heard great news about Italian passenger ships on the Italy-America route: they are the second in the world by traffic volume and they are acquiring new routes around the world. This will enhance their visibility and status in the United States.

Meanwhile, the city's politicians are waiting for president Gronchi with anticipation and some anxiety. This is an election year in the United States and maybe the Italian president is not fully aware that this is the most exciting game and the most important lottery in America. The fortunes of the two parties are rejuvenated at the prospect of distributing a handful of plum jobs worth a hundred thousand dollars a year as well as thousands and thousands of lesser jobs worth much less, sometimes so little that they are barely enough to live by. But everybody is out to get something for himself/herself in this game and all is grist for the electoral mill.

As soon as the visit of the president of Italy was announced, the city's politicos hurried to picture him as the president of Italian Americans, or, at least, of those among them who bother to vote. Meetings have been held in private offices in the skyscrapers overlooking Central Park and lunches in clubs overlooking the harbor. Everybody is asking the same questions: who will win the race to be the first in line to greet Italy's president; and who will appear with him in the right photos with the usual say-cheese faces and the one-more-time handshakes? Those photos; the printed programs with the list of names; the mention of the seat of honor at the inevitable banquets; or the chairmanship of an honorary committee aren't just ink stains on useless pieces of paper. They are true electoral IOUs. They convince the little voter who still can't read English newspapers that the old country is represented in America by such and such party and such and such politician. Past Italian governments have given legitimacy to local authorities in this manner, and they, in turn, spent it on the local political market. Everyone knows that in politics selling illusions on the market for power is an essential function.

All these things would be tolerable if they were limited to awarding cheap, meaningless medals. Instead, they also touch and affect American interests. In the off years, when no elections are held, nobody pays attention to these ceremonies, and the gratifications they dispense are purely personal. But this year the competition is fierce, and the bets even involve the health of the American president's heart.[2] Thus, any little preference for one candidate instead of another could be wrongly interpreted. It so happens that the [Republican] party, currently in power in Washington, is the party less favored by Italian Americans; at least by those who live on the eastern seaboard. It is a problem that complicates things for the Italian president. Italy, as a nation, could pay the price for unknowingly favoring one party and offending the other. But it is a problem that could be solved by relying on other forces, outside the sphere or partisan politics.

New York, February 12, 1958

---

2 President Dwight Eisenhower suffered from heart disease and his health condition was an issue of particular concern in the last years of his presidency.

THE POLITICS OF AN ITALIAN CONSUL IN NEW YORK

The post of consul general of Italy in New York is difficult. Indeed, I would venture to say that, for the Italian diplomatic corps, it is the most difficult of all similar positions in the world..

First of all, the location: all sorts of important personalities pass through here, including those who outrank the consul and who blame him if the city doesn't notice them or the mayor doesn't run to welcome them with the key to the city on a golden tray. Then there are true tragedies, like the sinking of the Andrea Doria,[1] when the telephone rings incessantly for days and days. One more problem is the close relationship with the embassy. When the ambassador is a gentleman like Manlio Brosio,[2] the consul doesn't have to worry about pettiness and backstabs: but with other ambassadors? The consul, moreover, has to constantly worry about his actions and words on a big stage like New York, where everything is under scrutiny and analyzed with a magnifying glass. Things that would go undetected in Seattle quickly become reasons for scandal in New York. The biggest current problem concerns criminals of Italian origin that America wants to get rid of by expelling and dumping them in Italy like garbage bags. The consul must oppose these moves despite the fact that international law allows it. Another test of patience for the consul must be the distorted, confused and mistaken image harbored by all Italians about America, Americans and Italian Americans. From top ministers to humble shoeshines, from the Marquis of Forlimpopoli to Guccio Imbratta,[3]

---

1   Andrea Doria. Italy's largest ocean liner at the time, was launched in 1951 and had her maiden voyage in 1953. She sunk in 1956 near Nantucket island, off the Massachusetts coast, after a collision with the ocean liner *Stockholm*. Fifty-one people died while 1,600 were rescued by the crew using lifeboats.

2   Manlio Brosio (1897-1980). Minister of foreign affairs in 1945, he became the first Italian ambassador to the Soviet Union in 1947. He was also ambassador to the United Kingdom, the United States and France. In 1964 he was appointed secretary general of NATO where he remained until 1971. He was awarded the Presidential Medal of Freedom by President Richard Nixon in 1971.

3   Marchese di Forlimpopoli. A character in Carlo Goldoni's comedy *La locandiera* (1782). He represents arrogant and impoverished aristocracy, contrasted with the

they all have irrational expectations that America will shower them with support and warm feelings of friendship.

As if this were not enough the biggest headaches, like icing on the cake, come from the Italian American community. This mass of people is divided along lines of personal loyalties; of thousands of narrow-minded, parochial associations; full of insatiable vanity, grandiose ambitions and incurable thin-skinnedness; full of *nouveau-riche* delusions and contempt for the poor. In theory they should not be in the purview of the Italian consul, in that almost all are American citizens. However, in reality, based on my observations, this has always been the main preoccupation of consuls, whether they were from the liberal, Fascist or republican regimes. This happens by virtue of sophistry and the complicity of the money that Italian Americans send to Italy to support various organizations and the little hopes that the dream of money from America triggers in the majority of Italians, from university professors to shoes exporters.

Thus, it's not hard to understand why some consuls only lasted for a short time: some left unhappy and others left behind much unhappiness. For those who understand the situation—and I think I am one of them—the function of the Italian consul in New York generates much admiration together with a sense of pity for the man who occupies that post. High doses of admiration and pity saluted Baron Carlo De Ferrariis[4] who managed to stay here for five and a half years in addition to a year and a half in Chicago. When he left, he was honored by so many cocktail parties, private dinners, lunches and banquets that he probably had to skip regular meals to avoid dying of overeating. Even if we discount some obligatory homage required by etiquette and the general hypocrisy of social functions, such a unanimous choir of approval was rather impressive. It should also be said that the departure of Consul De Ferrariis was even mentioned

---

Conte d'Albafiorita, a rich merchant who bought his aristocratic title.

• Guccio Imbratta. Translated into English as Sloppy Hugh, is a character in one of Boccaccio's short stories in the *Decameron*. He is the lazy, glutton, unreliable, messy, hair-brained servant of the shrewd Frate Cipolla (Day VI, n. 10).

4   Carlo De Ferrariis Salzano (1905-1985). Career diplomat, consul general of Italy in New York from 1953 to 1958.

in a short editorial by the *New York Times*. (I seemed to recognize the style of Herbert Matthews, a former correspondent from Italy who has maintained a great interest in the country and its cultural and political developments.) The consuls of other countries also gave him a good-bye dinner party. Last but not least was the so-called Italian community, namely those Italian Americans who are constantly trying to show off and appear on the pages of newspapers that are still printed in a language that approximates Italian; or composed of clips from newspapers from Italy to which the only local contribution are typos, grammatical errors, layout mistakes and headlines that have nothing to do with the story they cap.

If nothing else, De Ferrariis was able to navigate around rocks and shallow waters. A year ago, in recognition of his high-quality diplomatic work, he was promoted to the rank of minister and was appointed director of the office in charge of relations with the United Nations, which is a very sensitive job. It was a very well deserved promotion. Later, he became general secretary of the ministry, and, after some major changes under Prime Minister Amintore Fanfani,[5] he was promoted ambassador to Canada.

All this notwithstanding, I will repeat here what I told him privately: my opinion is that his political approach in New York (his strategy was approved by Rome) was profoundly wrong. Personally I had a very good relationship with Baron De Ferrariis. We would meet once in a while, alone or with other worthwhile guests (otherwise I would have declined). His conversation was refined, elegant and erudite. He was the scion of one of the few Neapolitan aristocratic families that—after the military conquest of the south by the Piedmontese in 1860—understood immediately that the Bourbon regime was over and that the Savoy[6] dynasty was going to stay. They recognized the new situation and decided to cooperate with the new liberal Italian state

5   Amintore Fanfani (1908-1999). Politician. He served as prime minister in five governments: 1954; 1958-1959; 1960-1963; 1982-1983; 1987.

6   Royal House of Bourbon. This royal dynasty lorded over southern Italy for 150 years until it was defeated by the house of Savoy in 1860 in the long battle for the unification of Italy.

• Royal House of Savoy. Piedmontese dynasty that lead the process of unification of Italy.

out of a sense of duty. This is something that still remains as a vestigial trait, at least in part, in the aristocracy that lost its power. I have met very few *servitori dello stato*[7] who had the same sense of commitment toward the government as De Ferrariis. I was deeply impressed by the long days he put in at work; by his patience in dealing with situations that were often both unpleasant and ridiculous; by his self control and skills in time management. Except for the long hours, I have none of those qualities. Without ostentation, he would keep me informed about books that I should know about. His criteria in judging Italy, from the *Risorgimento* to recent events, often found me in agreement and, to my great surprise, I wasn't able to get into a fight with him about these topics. I also knew, from other sources, about his efforts to prevent the American government from dumping back in Italy the garbage of gangsters who are properly a by-product of American culture.

One evening I ran into him near my house. He had come to pick up his daughter who was studying architecture and was staying at her studio until very late at night. He told me she worked past midnight five days a week and he had to pick her up after a long day of work, with more meetings in one day that I would have in a month. But what about his strategy and politics? It was based on Italian Americans. I want to make it clear that I don't want to diminish their merits and importance. Indeed, I have always maintained that the great majority of Italian immigrants ought to be admired for the economic success they have attained. Moreover, they owe these achievements only to their vitality as they owe nothing to the various Italian governments that abandoned them in America without an education, without leaders and without support. They also owe nothing to the American government that, in those days, did nothing to protect immigrants. However, Italian consuls ignore the healthy, successful majority of our fellow Italians. The only part of this population they pay attention to is also the worst: vain, loud, ignorant, often connected with criminal elements or at least in silent complicity with the criminals whom they never dare oppose or denounce. The complicity of all Italian consuls with this minority has always stunned me, not because of its immorality, but because

---

7   *Servitori dello stato.* Public servants. The Italian expression implies that the state, not the public, is the ultimate holder of legimate sovereignty.

it's the wrong political strategy. These individuals, a minority, sell to the Italian government the influence they claims to have, but they would have no influence in the community if the Italian governments just refused to treat them with favors, protections, honors and with coveted invitations to banquets and social events. Moreover, the new generations of Italian Americans couldn't care less about this minority that is losing strength with every passing year.

This minority survives by exploiting the myth of the Italian American vote despite the fact that this vote doesn't exist. Those who claim to control it are just like Dulcamara,[8] as the victories of Fiorello La Guardia (who fought against political machines) and Vincent Impellitteri clearly demonstrated. Both these candidates defeated their Italian American adversaries supported by their respective parties' electoral machines. Meanwhile, new generations of Italian Americans have emerged who speak American and don't read the community newspapers printed in what passes for Italian language. If Italy cares about its long-term relationship with Italian Americans, it must learn to invest in these new generations instead of aiming at quick-and-dirty immediate results with the old ones. Italy can still be very appealing to young Italian Americans on the condition that a new tone and new policies are put in place. Obviously, the consul general of Italy in New York can't be like Don Quixote and can't be a moralist either. He still finds in many Italians a mentality that is stuck in the past, as if we were still in 1880 when America was only concerned with getting workers from Italy to replace Blacks who were no longer slaves, or more labor to employ in the emerging industries. A consul is a consul, not a miracle worker, but he should not be nearsighted.

Italy's major political problem in these times is how to establish new relations with the American people, not with Italian Americans. The visit to the United States by President Gronchi should have been a splendid opportunity to engage in a dialogue with the real leadership of America. The president should have taken the opportunity to step up to a higher level and explain that Italy and Italians are not longer like those who arrived here in 1880. Italy should also be more careful

8   Dulcamara. The charlatan doctor in Gaetano Donizetti's opera *Elisir d'amore* (1832).

about the kind of Americans it invites to Italy. Many Professor Sausage (a caricature of teachers of Italian I created), people with very little understanding of Italy, have been introduced to Italian universities as ambassadors of American culture. These people harbor notions about Italy that are based on old clichés while their academic work is worthy that of a typist. Many fake and so-called valuable individuals have passed through the consulate's filter and have been welcome by ministers, universities and even by the Vatican. Venality and vanity dominate these relations. This is why I thought Consul De Ferrariis' politics were wrong; despite the fact that I spent some delightful hours in conversation with him and that I greatly respect him as a functionary. But maybe it wasn't his fault. Maybe he just followed orders. I don't know which one is true. In five years he never asked me what I thought about anything. I never felt more useless as an Italian than when I was with him.

New York, December 19, 1958

Part Three

Criminality

HOW AMERICANS IN 1891
BECAME ACQUAINTED WITH MAFIA

The Oxford English Dictionary mentions 1875 as the year when the word Mafia appeared for first time in a London newspaper. The term started spreading worldwide with the mass emigration of Sicilians from their island, following the military *Spedizione dei Mille*[1] headed by Giuseppe Garibaldi that resulted in the annexation of Sicily to the kingdom of Italy. The word Mafia surfaced with great sensation in America in 1891, related to the New Orleans lynchings;[2] a historical event that has been forgotten on both sides of the Atlantic, but that at the time created huge sensation in the press both in Italy and in the United States and caused a break in diplomatic relations between the two countries. In 1958 I happened to be in New Orleans and so I started looking into the collection of old local newspapers preserved in the city's library. I noticed that the newspapers' pages with the reports of those events were rather worn, often held together by tissue paper; a sign that several people must have studied them. I also learned that a local, impartial scholar had published his findings in a journal devoted to the history of Louisiana. Outside New Orleans, when it took place, this episode of violence became the object of congressional investigations; sociological essays; fictionalized history and a lot of diplomatic correspondence between the federal government of the United States and the state of Louisiana. I will give here as faithful

---

1   *Spedizione dei Mille* [Expedition of the Thousand]. This military venture took place in 1860 and became the single most important and almost mythical episode of the *Risorgimento*. Sponsored by the Savoy King Vittorio Emanuale II, a corps of volunteers—the famed *Camicie Rosse* [Red Shirts] under the command of General Garibaldi—left Genoa by ship and landed in Sicily. Here they fought the poorly organized and demoralized army of the kingdom of the Two Sicilies ruled by the Bourbon dinasty. With support in part from the local population, they made their way to the capital, Naples, deposing King Francis II. The kingdom was annexed to the kingdom of Sardinia which, at the time, was the official name of the Savoy state before it was renamed kingdom of Italy in 1861.

2   See Patrizia Salvetti's *Corda e sapone* (Roma, Sellerio, 2003); *Rope and Soap* (Bloomington, Bordighera Press, 2016) for the history of lynchings of Italians in the United States.

a report as possible of the events that left a very deep impression on America. It can be said that it was in that moment that the word Mafia became associated with Italians and with time the association has become even stronger and more widespread.

The evening of October 15, 1891 was humid and rainy. The New Orleans Chief of Police David Hennessey[3] was walking home with a friend, a detective from a private agency. While they were walking, they did not pay attention to a boy ahead of them who kept turning to check which direction they were going. From time to time the boy would whistle two high notes followed by three low notes. Some said it was the *Marcia Reale*, Italy's national anthem. Not far from Hennessy's house the two split up and went separate ways.

Hennessey lived in a poor section of town. His biography states that his father was a mercenary soldier who had named his son after himself. Allegedly, Hennessy senior was a veteran of the Civil War on the Confederate side under General Godfrey Witzel.[4] After the war, during a period of intense struggle between whites and Blacks for the control of the city, he had joined the police. Wounded several times in war, he died in 1867 in a tavern brawl, killed by a certain Guerin who, in turn, was later killed on the steps of a court house. In 1878, the future chief of police killed some unidentified person during a fight in a bar. He was arrested and tried with his cousin Mike, but both were acquitted by the jury. Cousin Mike was a policeman, but the scandal forced him to resign from the force and eventually ended up getting killed in Houston, where he had become a private investigator.

In 1888 Dave Hennessey was appointed chief of police by a mayor named Shakspeare.[5] Prior to that, he had been working for a private security agency owned by a certain Ferrel. When Ferrel died, Hennessey bought the agency. Both names, Hennessey and Ferrel, are clearly Irish. In that period the biggest American cities were dominated

3 David Hennessy (1858-1890). New Orleans's chief of police from 1888 to 1890.

4 Godfrey Witzel (1835-1884). German American major general in the Union Army and interim mayor of New Orleans.

5 Joseph Shakspeare (1837-1896). Mayor of New Orleans in 1880-1882 and 1888-1892.

by bands of tough, fearless, violent troublemakers of Irish descent. Many elected politicians were Irish as well; as were the majority of the police, a true force in the city. The law-and-order situation was such that the official police were like a little private army that could not be bothered to catch criminals. Private citizens or businesses that could not count on the protection of the police had to turn for security and protection to one of the innumerable private detective agencies, as did the Sicilians who had emigrated to New Orleans and who quickly learned the local customs.

These details illustrate the environment and the local conditions on the ground. People who hung out in taverns, where one could kill or get killed, could be gangsters one day and become policemen the next without any screening. This made me think back to the time of the Papal States when the authorities recruited into the police bandits that were roaming the countryside if they agreed to drop the old profession.

Hennessey is described as tall, massive and attractive (if you like a face like that of a bulldog), with hazel eyes, black mustache and jet-black hair kept together by shiny grease with bangs on the forehead. His description reminded me of the *bravi*[6] and their hairstyle in the *Promessi sposi*.[7] He was considered a typical policeman for those days: courageous, merciless and with no morals. In the words of an historian who wrote about him: "Today we would call him a gangster who happened to be on the side of the law." He was the first official American victim of Mafia, thus it is important to describe him with precision. Sicilian immigrants had been suspected of several murders, but the real killers had never been found. Local newspapers talked

---

6   *Bravi*. The term indicates thuggish private guards hired by local lords as security force in the sixteenth and seventeenth centuries. They were usually outlaws. Manzoni in *I promessi sposi* described them as sporting a characteristic look, with long hair and flashy clothes.

7   *I promessi sposi*. Written by Alessandro Manzoni, the most famous Italian novel (for Italians) was published in several dispersed editions with major changes between 1825 and 1842. The first edition was printed in 1825-6 by printer Vincenzo Ferrario in Milan. The final and definitive edition was published by printer Guglielmini e Radaelli in Milan in 1840. The events narrated take place in the Milan and Lake Como areas around 1630 during the Spanish domination.

about them and the vow of *omertà*,[8] the wall of silence that the police could not penetrate. Some of the murders probably were motivated by honor; or by the desire to avenge the death of a friend or relative; or by business disputes. The police, as often is the case in America in these kinds of situations, didn't really put many resources into investigating crimes that involved those damn foreigners. However, it looks like Hennessey made a mistake. He got in the middle of a fight between two Sicilian gangs that were fighting for the control of the fresh-produce business. In those days New Orleans had become the capital of Sicilian immigration. Typical of all immigration waves, one Sicilian would call another and so forth. The southern climate; its looks and character; along with the presence of a large contingent of French and Spanish people gave the city a distinct Mediterranean flavor with lots of Catholic churches. This was at the time when no passports, police controls or consular visas were required to immigrate.

The citizens of New Orleans were descendents of pirates, smugglers and other scum of the Caribbean seas. As in many other port cities, morality was rather wobbly; but here it was more so than in other places; mostly as a consequence of the Civil War and the defeat of the South, which had brought turmoil and a period of oppression by the winners on the losers.

Brothels had sprouted on every corner so brazenly and loudly that they caused consternation in other parts of a more hypocritical America. It is no surprise that Sicilian criminality saw New Orleans as an attractive new turf for its activities and also as a safe harbor, far from the *anti-banditismo*[9] campaign launched by the new Italian state after the unification. Certainly, among them were honest citizens but these tended to settle mostly in the countryside where they created

---

8 *Omertà* is the implicit vow of non-cooperation with the authorities by an entire community. The term derives from *uomo* [man] and refers to the fundamental property of manliness. *Omertoso* would be the opposite of a *snitch*.

9 *Banditismo*. In the years after the annexation of the south to the kingdom of Italy, bands of oulaws were controlling the territory and the population in large swaths of the countryside, especially in Calabria and Sicily. In addition to criminal intent, these gangs also had—albeit vague—political goals of resistance and self-determination in opposition to the oppressive regime imposed by the new northern regime.

important agricultural centers. (Edmondo Mayor de Planches,[10] one of the first high level Italian diplomats to write about Italian immigrants, visited them a few years later and left a historical description.) However, it is also a fact that the Italian consulate had a list of criminals, at least a hundred-names long, that were sought for extradition back to Italy. The ambassador wanted to share it with the local authorities, but these didn't know what to do with it or how to handle the entire situation. At the time of the Hennessy murder trial, which turned out to be the real fulcrum of the tragedy, the list had grown to 1,100. The consul was successful only in the case of a notorious bandit from Calabria, Giovanni Esposito, who, according to the accusations, had committed eighteen murders in Italy. In Louisiana he kidnapped for ransom a protestant minister, Rev. Rose. To prove that the pastor was in his hands, and also show his determination, he cut his ears off and sent them to the family.

Esposito was discovered thanks to a tip from an informant while he was living in New Orleans under a new name. He had a nice life and a second wife who swore he was a great husband and father. After Hennessey arrested him and the consul obtained the extradition, his friends collected several thousand of dollars to pay for his lawyer and tried everything possible to keep him in the country. Rumors among the population had that Esposito had been betrayed by a certain Abbruzzo who was later found murdered. The police could not find his killer. Esposito was deported to Italy, tried, sentenced to life and imprisoned at Santo Stefano.[11] The history of his trial and his portrait were reported in the periodical *Illustrazione Italiana*[12] of 1890. After that, I don't know what happened to him. His reputation on this side of the world is that he was the person responsible for importing Mafia to New Orleans and the United States.

This was Hennessey's first battle with the Sicilian Mafia. The

---

10   Edmondo Mayor de Planches (1851-1920). He was ambassador to the Unites States between 1901 and 1903.

11   The little island of Santo Stefano, where a penitentiary was located, is a few miles from the port of Naples.

12   *L'Illustrazione italiana* (1873 - 1962). Published in Milan, it was one of Italy's best selling illustrated weeklies.

second battle led to his death. The war for the control of the fresh-produce business was waged by two families, Provenzano and Matranga. Apparently, Hennessey backed the former. One episode accelerated the events: the Matrangas were ambushed by the Provenzanos while they were leaving the port in a horse-drawn carriage. Many shots were fired and one of the Matrangas lost a leg. At the trial, the Matrangas realized that Hennessey was backing the Provenzanos. Among other clues, the lavish treatment and excellent food enjoyed by the Provenzanos in jail were attributed to Hennessy's influence. Hennessey was a member of the Red Lantern Club (one can easily guess what kind of place this club was.) Ostensibly it had a social mission but one cannot avoid noticing that red lanterns were the common signal for brothels. Red Lantern is the generic name given to a district where brothels line the streets and prostitution is practiced openly—despite the laws—under the protection of corrupt police. (In those days their locations were reported in a tourist guide called *Blue Book*,[13] which is now a rarity sought after by collectors.) Among the club's members was a certain Joseph Macheca, most likely from Malta, a man with power and influence, who, in association with other Sicilians, owned ships for the transport of fruit in the Gulf of Mexico. He warned Hennessey not to get involved in the business of other people and particularly that of the Sicilians or he "would end up in a box." Hennessey dismissed the threat. On the evening of October 15, 1891, as he was about to step into his house, Hennessey was targeted by a volley of shots from rifles and pistols. He managed to return fire with his pistol as two of the assailants approached him and shot him at close range. He then stumbled for a few steps toward the friend that, upon hearing the shots, had run back to help him. When asked who the killers were Hennessey replied: "It was them." "Them who?" "Dagoes."[14] This was the derogatory term used to indicate Spanish, Italian, Portuguese and in general all southern Europeans with darker skin and a foreign accent. In this case the accusation pointed clearly to the Italians. Hennessey

---

13   Author Unknown. *Blue Book*. New Orleans: Thomas C. Anderson, circa 1911.

14   The footnote in the original text explains the origin of the term: "*Dago* (pronounced *deigo*) is probably the metathesis of Diego, a very common name among Iberians and in countries they dominated, Sicily included."

did not personally recognize any of the killers, since it is (still) standard practice for these operations to be carried out by hired gunmen that cannot be identified. Moreover, the killers wore the typical kerchief that conceals the bottom half of the face, leaving only a small slit open for the eyes, under a hat's wide brim.

As long as Sicilian immigrants in New Orleans kept to themselves and took care of their rivalries of honor and business among themselves, the New Orleans police (a misnomer) weren't particularly concerned. But when it became known that Mafia was involved in Chief Hennessey's assassination, popular resentment started growing and became so intense that it eventually led to one of the worst cases of lynching in history. Carlo Matranga was probably the most notorious of the suspects and was in fact the first to be arrested. He had a bomb-proof alibi: that evening he was playing cards with some *paesani*. In a way his alibi was a bit too strong and it seemed planned. The suspicion against him was based on the fact that the abandoned house from which some of shots were fired had been rented with his money. To get rid of the indictment, Matranga hired one of the many private detectives that, due to lax rules, were working in a gray area between private and public law enforcement agencies. When Matranga was acquitted, the initiatives of detective Dominic O'Malley—the man he had hired— became the basis for the accusations of jury corruption. O'Malley, by the way, was Irish.[15] Twenty other Italians were arrested together with Matranga. Some were friends of his: Antonio Scaffidi, already known to the police for attempted extortion of a merchant named Messina; Emanuele Polizzi, otherwise identified with the name Polissi; Pietro Monastero, a landlord; Bastian Incardona, whose brother was working for Matranga; Charles Traina, James Caruso and Antonio Marchese. Antonio Bagnetto, a guard at the fruit market who for his superior intellectual abilities—he knew both languages and translated for the other men—was called *il professore*, was found in possession of three revolvers. All the names were of Sicilian origin. Others involved were Loretto Comitez [sic][16] and Frank Romero, presumably Hispanic,

---

15   Italian readers would not recognize the name as Irish, thus the author added the detail for clarity.

16   Loretto Comitz.

although in those days it was common for people to change name upon receiving U.S. citizenship, a practice that is often mentioned in the correspondence of many Italian consuls to the central government. Alternatively, one should always be aware of the chance of simple spelling errors. Marchese was the father of the boy accused of giving signals for the ambush by whistling in code. Another one of the crew was Rocco Geraci, who had already been accused of killing an Italian shoemaker. With the exception of Matranga and the Maltese Macheca, the rest were petty criminals who, at one point or another, had had problems with the police. An incident that took place while they were behind bars gives an idea of the kind of atmosphere at the time. In the discovery phase, a certain Duffy, an Irishman and a friend of Hennessey, picked one of the accused to carry out his personal vendetta. He applied for a permit to visit in jail Antonio Scoffietti, whom he blamed more than anyone else for the death of his friend; and shot him with a gun, wounding him only superficially. Duffy himself was arrested and tried but got away with only a few months behind bars.

The chief of the Pinkerton Agency[17] reported a story, widely circulated in Italy as well, that I personally find questionable and that was never proved to be true. He claimed to be a friend of Hennessey and said he had planted a spy in the jail where the Sicilians were being held. The spy's name was Di Dio. His cover was as a counterfeit expert who had been jailed after being mistreated by the police. Ostensibly, he struck up a friendship with the Sicilians persuading them he was a member of organized crime and managed to get the story of the assassination conspiracy from Polizzi (or Polissi). The newspapers of the time did not report anything about it. Polizzi, in all likelihood, was frazzled and on the verge of mental collapse. During the debate in court he suffered from seizures. He first confessed but later withdrew his confession, which was then thrown out by the judge. This entire episode feels like a cheap mystery novel or some dramatization thereof; something that would fit a whodunit play, but that leaves serious

---

17 Pinkerton National Detective Agency. Founded in 1850, it was for decades the most notorious private security agency in the country, often working in concert with government law-enforcement agencies to maintain public order; disrupt labor strikes; and conduct clandestine operations of dubious legality.

historians very skeptical. The truth is that there was no need for spies. Everyone believed the Sicilians were guilty and everybody expected the jury would find them guilty.

At that time the city had a vigilance committee appointed by the mayor composed of fifty members, charged with looking into public safety issue. Its chairperson initially was E.H. Farrar (an Irish surname) and, later, a certain Flower. The committee was the peculiar re-incarnation of similar volunteer groups that, in other occasions, had taken over the reins of armed control in the city in periods when the police seemed paralyzed and City Hall was similarly indecisive. The history of New Orleans before 1900 shows several periods when these kinds of arrangements had taken place, with the corollary of erudite debates by American jurists about the right of the people to take direct control of public order when elected officials are patently derelict in their duties. In Italy we have had similar situations even in the twentieth century. History doesn't care about justifications or reprimands: it is what it is. However, we should remember that the apparition of a similar explosion of popular furor by irregular forces in New Orleans had already taken place only a few years earlier with the White League,[18] a movement that fought against the alleged excesses of the Union administration after the victory in the Civil War. These forces, one way or another, always appeal to the supremacy of white Anglo Americans. In this case they targeted Italians. Professor Giovanni Cecchetti,[19] a personal friend who works at Tulane University in New Orleans, hypothesized that this popular uprising was connected to the election of President Grover Cleveland[20] who had campaigned with an anti-foreigner agenda.

In these circumstances the official function of the committee was

---

18   The White League was active in the years 1874 and 1875 in Louisiana. It was one of many paramilitary organizations whose goal was the defeat of Republican politicians in local elections.

19   Giovanni Cecchetti (1922-1998). Professor of Italian at Tulane University, Stanford University and finally at the University of California, Los Angeles, where he was chair of the Italian department from 1969 to 1977.

20   Stephen Grover Cleveland (1837--1908). He served as president of the United States for two separate, noncontiguous terms in 1885–1889 and 1893–1897.

to secure law and order. In reality it fostered a climate of tension and danger in Italian neighborhoods where, in those days, the windows and the doors of houses and businesses were kept shut. The trial lasted from November 20, 1890, until March 13 of the following year. It took two juries to reach a verdict. The first one was dissolved after nine days due to irregularities. Apparently the Italian community, or at least the best organized group, the one called Mafia, was able to collect enough money to hire top lawyers and private investigators. The court heard 319 witnesses. The judge in person exonerated Matranga. For three of the accused the outcome was a hung jury, and, according the local laws, they were either to be retried or let go. The others were all found not guilty.

When the verdict was announced, the city erupted with outrage and cries for justice. The revenge plan was organized in the open with the vigilance committee taking responsibility for all that would ensue. We know the names of the organizers who signed a manifesto published by the newspapers. (A few years later, the main organizer was elected governor.) We also know who incited the populace; who distributed the arms; and who led the armed volunteers. The way the plan unfolded shows it was put together carefully to make sure it would appear it fell within the boundaries of legality, or at least that its execution would avoid implicating directly the organizers. For this reason, for instance, some of the Italians were taken from the prison and formally handed to the crowd, so as to avoid the possible accusation that they were killed by identifiable individuals inside the jail.

George C. Parke died at age 87 in Tampa, Florida, a few years ago. In a sealed envelope, to be opened after his death, he revealed that he had lived in New Orleans where he had been part of a squad of twelve people armed with rifles and to whom the lynching's organizers assigned the goal of killing the Italians. He also said that he had been living in hiding his whole life in fear of retribution by the Italians. Could it be true? None of the organizers was alive at that time and even if someone had been, nobody would have ever confirmed his version.

In an exclusive club in New Orleans, a couple of days ago, I met the son of attorney A., the lawyer who defended the Italians. He looked quite nervous and, in too many nervous words, told me that his father had taken that case as a pique. After the assassination of Hennessey, he had volunteered to be one of the prosecutors but was rebuffed. Thus, to show his professional skills, he took the opposite role and succeeded in getting the not-guilty verdict. I reminded him that, based on what I had read in the local newspapers, his father, during the closing argument boasted that he was a personal friend of the victims and that he would have never accepted to defend the accused if he doubted their innocence. I am not sure whether for the son historical truth trumped his antipathy for Sicilians: what was evident was that he didn't hold much respect for his father.

The reason for the massacre was the indignation of the whole city at the verdict. Mobs do not normally follow the light of reason or the law. The jury, instead, in this case, used reason and the result was a careful, cautious and free decision. The jurors were all native New Orleans citizens, of French, Anglo-Saxon or German ancestry and, probably, a Jew, Seligman. There were no members of the Italian community. Regardless of this, the jury was accused of being corrupt. Italians or, better, Mafia was believed to have paid large sums of money to ensure the acquittals or at least a hung jury. In old documents, yellowed by time and typed in the tiniest of fonts, I read the interviews with the jurors. At first they all refused to talk, as was their right. They were unanimous in saying that they were not convinced by the evidence presented by the prosecutor and that they made their decision without pressure. Some complained about the low cultural level of fellow jurors, who were basically illiterate and, conceptually and intellectually, inadequate to the task at hand. They all denied they had received money from the Mafia. Nevertheless, the press published figures that even today look ridiculous. One of the jurors allegedly received $150, another one $500. I am not claiming here that a conscience is necessarily more expensive, but I would like to note that to risk one's life is worth more than $150, even if it's only for the conscience. The risk of being the target of violence for the jurors was indeed real to the point that some of them had to leave the city to protect themselves, at least temporarily. The jury's foreman, Mr. Seligman, a professional jeweler, took a coach to a train station near New Orleans. Due to a mishap, he found himself walking in public. He was recognized and

was surrounded by a menacing crowd. Luckily, a police officer was nearby and intervened after calling for reinforcements. Other jurors hired armed guards to protect them even in their own homes. It took a while for things to settle down. The son of the lawyer who defended the Italians assured me that his father's business was not affected negatively; indeed, it boomed, as he gained a reputation as the kind of lawyer who could handle hopeless cases. Anyway, if corruption had taken place, it is nevertheless sure that the Sicilians of New Orleans had learned a very important lesson very quickly: American justice in those days was worth its weight in gold, and in order to get justice they had to fork out all the gold they could. I am not claiming they were moral individuals; I claim, though, that they were quite smart.

A crowded calculated to be around 6,000 people, a big number for a small city, gathered in front of the statue of the patriot Henry Clay[21] on Canal Street, to this day the most elegant street in New Orleans. It was March 15, 1891. The population was angry at the verdict that acquitted all the Italians accused of murdering Hennessey. Probably everything would have ended with shouts and maybe some fist fights if it hadn't been for an organization, the so-called Fifty, which prepared, planned, directed and quite openly took charge of the operation. "When law enforcement is lacking, the people have the right to take control of public interest and see that justice is done." This is a theory that has surfaced often and in many different times and places around the world, and it was applied that very day. Was it justice? Or wasn't it rather a barbaric act? History is what it is and it allows for no corrections. No argument will give back life and honor, if indeed they had honor, to the Sicilians who were massacred. Later, and after long and protracted fights, the American government paid the sum of 125,000 Lira (in 1891 the currency was the gold-lira) to the families of three victims who at that time were still Italian citizens. All the protagonists are dead and probably their descendents meet in some political club and shake hands at a costume ball during Mardi Gras. But in New Orleans people still talk about it, albeit in hushed tones.

If we could foresee the final outcome of our passions, or what

21 Henry Clay (1777-1852). Congressman and senator from Kentucky for several terms, and speaker of the House. He served as secretary of state from 1825 to 1829.

our sacrifices will produce, including the compromises with our own conscience, it is probable we would never get much done, or, at least, nothing great and nothing big. In and by itself a crowd is nothing. A crowd does not think or decide or act. But there is always someone who directs and leads it. At times, a crazy rider grabs the reins and in those cases we know how things end up. In Renaissance Florence we have the written accounts of events when (as Florentine historians told us) leaders called the people to gatherings. This usually was the beginning of arson, vandalism, looting and killing. The long speech given that day by in New Orleans by a self-appointed leader inflamed the souls. The crowd had only a marginal role, limited to shouts and threats, but with its presence it supported the tragic operation of the real operatives organized in an armed team. At the right time they picked up the arms that had been kept in storage nearby and used them as badges to get through the mob. Only twenty-five people entered the jail where the Italians were kept. Nobody in a position of authority bothered to protect the prisoners: not the governor, the mayor, or even the new chief of police who, predictably, had a personal animus against them. The prison warden, when he saw the crowd and the armed squad, opened the cells of the Italian prisoners and told them to hide in the women's section. From the reports of the journalists of the time and from the autopsies of the victims, it is possible to reconstruct what happened to each of the prisoners. Only one of the Sicilians was lucky enough to be able to mingle with the common prisoners who stayed behind on the ground floor. He wasn't recognized and thus was saved. Everyone else was in a state of sheer terror. Who wouldn't be? Some incredible things happened. Sunseri[22] and Polizzi were found inside a dog shed so small that people wondered how two human bodies could possibly fit in it. Another one, Incardona, crouched in a fetal position, hid in a garbage bin and survived.

Macheca, Scaffidi and Marchese Sr. ran back to the third floor where their cells were but found them locked. The corridor leading to the cells was exposed to the lynch squad that, as soon as they saw them, started shooting. Macheca brandishing a club tried to break the lock of a cell where he thought he could protect himself. He

---

22   It is possible the author may be referring to Salvatore Sinceri.

was found dead clutching the club, his hand smashed by a bullet. Marchese Jr., the child who was the alleged lookout for the ambush, was recognized but was spared due to his young age. Matranga and Charles Patorno were able to hide only to re-emerge later, dirty and slimy, from another room where they had hidden under a pile of garbage. They also survived.

In New Orleans a descendant of one of the victims of this tragedy told me that Matranga later managed to become a big shot in the local longshoremen union. He was murdered by a professional killer from Chicago, hired by an enemy faction inside the same organization. Before dying he shouted to his son: "Get that son of a bitch." The son gave chase and shot the killer. According to the witnesses, the wound his son inflicted onto the killer was identical to the wound suffered by Matranga: two bullets to the heart, the only two that were fired. The implication may be that both belonged to the same school.

The group that entered the jail placed sentries at the door and didn't allow access to anybody. The vigilantes immediately killed three Italians but, in order to avoid being singled out and to assert the democratic principle of popular justice, they brought two of them outside and gave them to the crowd. One of them was Polizzi, one of the strangest characters in the trial, during which he kept moving and shaking uncontrollably, screaming and shouting for the entire time. Today he would certainly be committed to a mental institution for epilepsy. He was the only one who, approached by a fake Italian criminal—a Pinkerton spy—allegedly confessed he committed the crime, a confession he later recanted. He was brought out of jail held up by the shirt collar by a gigantic individual, someone the press described only as "a well known cotton grower." It could be that the name was not mentioned to protect him and other members of his family; or because he was part of the agrarian aristocracy that shared control of the city (but that was slowly surrendering power to the industrial neo-capitalists from the north). Polizzi was taken to the Old Quarter to a street corner that borders Canal Street and hanged from one of the gas lamps that, to this day, make the area so charming and picturesque for the delight of tourists.

Often, as I was wandering in that part of town, I asked myself if the lamp in front of me may be the one where the poor epileptic was hanged. One particular was reported by the press, and it is so crude and realistic that it helps explain the madness of the whole thing. As soon as the body of Polizzi was hanged from the street lamp, the crowd, of its own initiative and in an act worthy of them, started grabbing him to take a souvenir of the event. So, they ripped off shoes and clothes until he was left naked. But apparently that wasn't enough because eventually his body was cut up in parts. Maybe in an old New Orleans house, preserved under a glass dome or between the pages of a book, there still are strips of skin or scalp, with the date of the fateful day neatly written on them.

The second public victim was Bagnetto. Back in the prison, when people approached, he pretended to be dead but he could not fake it long enough. He was dragged out of the jail with a rope around his neck. The mob decided to hang him from a tree. A child climbed up to tie the knot, but the branch snapped so the operation had to be repeated a second time until it finally succeeded.

After Bagnetto, six other Sicilians were taken from the prison and killed one by one: Geraci, Monastero, Traina, Caruso, Comitez and Romero. At 9:15 AM the massacre was over. There were no more people to kill. The day ended with a triumphal parade culminating with a speech, given from the platform of a statue, to inform everyone, at 11:00 am, that the execution was complete. When it was all over, eleven people had been lynched. After the tragedy, none of the relatives dared go looking for the bodies. Only a woman, Polizzi's companion, went to the prison while thousands of people were still crowding the area with bellicose and hostile disposition. The woman must have been half crazy herself. The reporters noted that she was wearing a worn-out print cotton dress with a wool blue shawl on her head and a yellow ribbon around her neck. She was in her mid thirties, with a Mediterranean complexion. With the exceptions of two dead that ended up in a common grave, the bodies were returned to the families who gave them funerals, some quite elaborate and some in the city cathedral. Apparently, in attendance were not only relatives, friends and other Italians, but also Anglo-Saxons. According to a reporter who visited the Italian quarter near Poydras Market[23] by the port, the survivors "showed neither anger nor fear, although they said those few hours felt like years. Everyone thanked God for having been saved from such a horrible destiny." I imagine that quite a few candles were lit in the New Orleans cathedral. In the pockets of the dead, a rosary, images of saints and even a small statue of Saint Joseph were found. In the pockets of Comitez, instead, a German calendar was found.

After the verdict, suspicion and animosity were high against the jurors. Some were openly accused by the press of having been corrupted by Mafia. It appears that the price of a conscience in those days was rather low but, conscience notwithstanding, a vote to acquit the Italians certainly meant troubles for the rest of one's life.

The jury's foreman, as I mentioned earlier, was almost killed by the mob that recognized him while he was trying to get out of town by train. All the jurors who were interviewed denied there had been attempts to corrupt them and maintained that the decision to acquit depended only on the fact that the prosecutor had failed to present convincing evidence. One of the jurors gave the most eloquent answer to a journalist: "There were two Black folks who claimed they recognized the killers. But, how can I believe the word of two Blacks against that of a white man?" The detective hired by Matranga to find evidence to support his alibi was also forced to leave town for a while.

The Italian quarter is centered around Orsoline Street,[24] that is, ironically, the place where the first proper girls from France found a home and an education in America. As soon as the news of the verdict reached the quarter, Italian flags were flying in front of all windows. But when, later, after the massacre, the reporters stormed the area, they found that all the flags had disappeared while the women were busy taking care of the green grocery stores and the men had all gone into hiding.

---

23 Also known as the Poydras Street Market, it was an early market area in New Orleans.

24 Congregazione delle Orsoline is a Catholic organization founded by nuns in 1535 with the mission to educate young girls. In the course of the centuries the oder prospered and created a world-wide network of schools for girls and young women that is now present in every continent.

The city-appointed commission charged with investigating the facts didn't find anything wrong. The chairperson of the commission, who was believed by most to be corrupt, was expelled from the chamber of commerce. The American government was forced to explain to the Italian government that the autonomous sovereignty of the state of Louisiana precluded federal intervention; therefore Washington couldn't even provide that the killers would be tried in court. Diplomatic relations between Italy and the United States were broken for a time; then, the American government paid the puny sum I mentioned at the beginning. In the state of Louisiana, the organizer of the lynching was elected governor. Historians emphasize the fact that, after the massacre, Mafia continued to commit crimes but never attacked the police directly. That is to say: what happened was not right, but at least it was efficient.

The readers are probably asking: what is the point of talking about those sad pages? And who do I think was right: organized crime (that actually did have a fair trial) or those who took the law into their own hands? These are good and heavy questions, and, of course, I have given them a lot of thought. It is a fact that the episode always made a deep impression on me from the moment I found out about it. When I was in New Orleans I searched those places and tried to envision what happened. Nowadays, all is quiet for Italians in New Orleans, although American writers are still talking about it. The impeccable newspaper collection at the public library (with extremely polite service) counts innumerable documents with articles on Mafia updated to today. As far as who was right and who was wrong, I side with Alessandro Manzoni[25] who said that no one has yet invented the knife that can separate exactly right from wrong. For me it is enough to say that this historical episode is to be considered as evidence of the fact that the immigration was a tragedy; that the difficulties of communication among different peoples and races are immense; and that, for sure, humans are not kind to one another; particularly when they gather in

25 Alessandro Manzoni (1785-18730). Novelist, poet and playwright. He is considered by Italians one of the country's greatest writers. He is best known for his novel *I promessi sposi* (1840) which was instrumental and enormously influential in reforming the Italian language. To this day he is regarded as a master of prose.

groups and don't think for themselves but give in to group thinking. I am saying all these things a bit crudely, and, provisionally.

New Orleans, January-February 1958

A BIOGRAPHY OF SALVATORE LUCANIA
ALSO KNOWN AS LUCKY LUCIANO

A new biography of Lucky Luciano, *The Luciano Story*,[1] recently landed on my table. The famous gangster, whom Italy is now honored (and burdened) to host, and the crime syndicate are also the subject of a Broadway show I saw not long ago; and of the movie *New York Confidential*,[2] based on a book with the same title written by journalists Lee [sic] and Mortimer that came out a couple of years ago. All these coincidences made me revisit this particular aspect of American life and the questions that surround it: how much of what is told about gangster life is true? How important is it in the life of the United States? And what does all this mean? First of all, I wonder where the information comes from. As we know, the number one rule of criminals is to not attract any attention. Gangsters surround themselves with silence; they use the phone cautiously in fear that their conversations may be monitored and; as far as I know, there are no collections of gangsters' letters. The only physical documentation available is lists of their clothes and hotel bills. Their operations presumably must be recorded by some form of bookkeeping, although nothing has ever been brought to light during trials. At the same time, every single witness that has testified in court against them was a criminal himself, involved in the same activities, and therefore with very little credibility. In order to find out what gangsters do, one must spend time with them and participate in the same activities, and in fact the little we know comes from spies, traitors, prostitutes and informants. The first

---

1 Salvatore Lucania, also known as Lucky Luciano (1897-1962). He is considered the founder of modern Mafia in America. He was instrumental in dividing the control of illegal operations in New York among five families; and in setting up the *Commission*, the ruling board composed of the heads of families that acted in the best common interest.

    • *The Luciano Story*. Sid Feder and Joachim Joensten. David McKay, New York, 1955.

2 *New York Confidential*. Directed by Roussel Rouse. Edward Small Productions, 1955. Based on the homonymous novel by Jack Lait and Lee Mortimer. Crown Publishers, New York, 1951.

operations of the little Mafia of Giuseppe Masseria[3] concerned the illegal smuggling of fellow Sicilians to the United States. Once they had settled down, their main occupation was extortion of small retail businesses and protection from possible troubles, troubles that the Mafia itself would cause. It is the old concept of the medieval tribute in a society dominated by the powerful, still present in a modern society that was still in part medieval.

Many gangsters of the new generation, like Luciano, were born in Italy but went to crime school in the slums of the Lower East Side, starting in first grade. They would graduate from the juvenile penal system and, finally, complete their academic training in penitentiaries where they were taught by elderly, experienced criminals. Here they would learn how the system works and how to adapt the criminal networks to take advantage of the new developments in society. The kind of *gangsterism* [sic] invented by Lucky Luciano had a broader vision and bigger ambitions. To begin, one must bear in mind that organized crime, or, as I call it here, *gangsterism*, flourished in response to the law that for several years prohibited the sale of alcohol, the period known as *Prohibition*.[4] The law was very unpopular even among the citizens who had voted for a senator or house representative who, for political opportunism, supported the law. Paradoxically, in those circumstances organized crime provided a social service. Luciano and others jumped to the opportunity to supply liquors, wine and beer to a whole nation thirsty for alcohol and deeply unhappy with the new restrictions. This was the turning point for all gangsters. They were no longer the small bore Mafiosi of yore, illiterate and narrow minded. The new generation was thinking bigger and had sharper organizational skills, indispensible to manage a web of intricate and complex commercial

---

3   Giuseppe Masseria (1886-1931). Also known as *Joe the Boss* was an Italian criminal who escaped to America in 1903. He became associated with the Mafia and eventually became the head of one of the New York families and the first *boss of bosses*.

4   The 18th Amendment to the American Constitution was passed in 1920. It prohibited the manufacture, sale, transport, import or export of alcoholic beverages. It is not generally well known that the amendment did not prohibit the purchase or consumption of alcohol. It was repealed in 1932 by the adoption of the 21th Amendment.

networks. To make things even more difficult was the fact that their business was entirely illegal and, therefore, required secrecy; with safe houses and hide-outs; far from the eye of law enforcement. A national enterprise of this kind required executives with great talent; able to adapt instantly to new circumstances and maintain control over clandestine distilleries and transportation networks, active mostly at night; that reached all the way into the heart of the cities and from there to individual outlets. It was also necessary to bribe the police in order to ensure a certain degree of safety and, of course, to use violence to punish traitors; induce fear in possible spies and get rid of the competition. Countless murders have been attributed to the big bosses of this enterprise, although the large majority of the victims were also mobsters, often from competing gangs. Very few of these crimes were committed against innocent citizens, and the death toll for these was certainly lower than that for car accidents due to drunk driving or the distraction of drivers who fool around with a girl friend instead of paying attention to the road.

In the absence of reliable sources of information, with a bit of imagination, American journalists have tried to reconstruct the lives of the new generation of gangsters. It's a little bit like the *Storia della rivoluzione americana* [sic] by Carlo Botta,[5] who filled his pages with passages from speeches by Washington and Jefferson who, if they could read the book, would be quite surprised to find in it things they never said. Lucky Luciano's biography, for instance, is full of dialogues that, had they been recorded with a tape recorder, would sound very plausible. In reality all they show is the virtuosity and creativity of the writers and their knowledge of street slang.

There are two kinds of wrongs in analyzing this phenomenon. Some, with an anti-American agenda, tend to simplify things greatly and see the entire life of this continent as dominated by gangsters. Some minimize it, as if it were irrelevant and meaningless. The entire gangster world is not particularly large but what is really important is the fact that it's not going away despite the efforts of law enforcement. It is a phenomenon

5   Carlo Botta (1766-1837). Historian. *Storia della guerra dell'indipendenza degli Stati Uniti d'America.* D. Colas, Paris, 1809. First Italian edition: Milano, Vincenzo Ferrario, 1819.

on the margin of American life; it is being fought vigorously; it has been squeezed into a corner; forced into a clandestine life, in hiding and invisible; except for the times when it explodes in extreme forms of violence. The mob only dominates certain environments and more precisely the least American of them: the areas of cities with recent immigrants that have not yet been assimilated. But despite this fact, the phenomenon is connected to American life and it is a product of American life itself. The criminal element is present in all societies; however, the form that crime takes in American life is America's own and it will never change until America remains America. Take for instance the chapter in Lucky Luciano's biography about the blossoming of a new modern mentality in Sicilian Mafia. When Luciano was a boy, Mafia was a culture and a habit limited to Italian immigrants. The boss, Giuseppe Masseria, enjoyed playing traditional card games with friends; didn't own a car and wouldn't dream of sitting in a box at the Metropolitan Opera House; nor of going to the track to bet on horses in the company of a flashy and dumb starlet wrapped in a mink fur coat. He would never think of expanding his operations, based in New York, to Chicago or Los Angeles or Miami. Forget then about keeping on top of the developments that took place after World War II, when the networks expanded all the way to Italy, France, Turkey and China. Giuseppe Masseria was eliminated in a non-descript Italian restaurant while Luciano, who had ordered the hit, was washing his hands in the men's room. From that day he has come a long way, engaged in a journey that is perfectly compatible with that of America and mirrors her expansionist policies, her vitality, her risk-taking mentality and finally the vagaries of political life.

The question everybody asks is why Luciano was set free after World War II, after being sentenced to thirty-five years in prison following a world-famous trial whose prosecutor was New York's Attorney General Thomas Dewey.[6] It is definitely a mysterious *affaire* that not even the recent biography can explain. The widespread rumor, never disputed—by the way—was that during World War II Luciano helped

---

6   Thomas E. Dewey (1902-1971). Attorney general of New York state from 1937 to 1942; governor from 1943 to 1954. He ran twice unsuccessfully in presidential elections.

the U.S. Army intelligence before and after the invasion of Sicily. With his help, American intelligence established solid relationships with the local Mafia bosses. Another possible explanation attributes the judicial pardon to the presidential election in which Dewey was a candidate. The gangsters' real strength is not in their viciousness or their courage. It resides in the fact that American society, or at least a significant portion thereof, needs certain services that are prohibited by law. In order to provide those services it is necessary to find men willing to take the risk. *Gangsterism* was and is still today the expression of a form of social dissent, not simply a case of thugs and bullies who impose themselves onto society (although this aspect does exist in some particular cases). The gangsters' principal activity consists in supplying the paying public with forbidden forms of entertainment. At this time in America, one of the biggest forms of entertainment is gambling, from lotteries to horse races and other sports events. Gambling is a pleasure that attracts an enormous public: maybe it is a metaphor for our own lives. Don't we gamble when we get married; when we choose one career rather than another; and even when we accept an invitation to dinner? And let's not even talk about decisions like investing in real estate; or buying merchandise on sale that we don't immediately need but that, we hope, we will already own when the prices rise. Morally there is the additional fact that nobody forces a gambler to gamble. Just providing the opportunity is not like hurting someone intentionally. No one has ever heard of gangsters that would threaten people who don't gamble. Organized crime also engages in another, rather unsavory, activity: providing mercenary love, where suppliers are generally not the cream of society. This is a topic that would require a long disquisition, but suffice it to say that American gangsters are doing in this country what many ancient and modern states consider useful for the public good. From the documentation presented at the trial, it would be hard to conclude that Luciano—who was tried and convicted by Dewey for this crime—was any worse than people in other countries that practice the same trade openly with a license and with no need for secrecy.

My conviction that gangsters perform a social function has been reinforced by an additional issue: narcotics. Recently, I read several proposals supported by medical doctors who maintain that the government should supply narcotics at a fair price to addicts, under strict surveillance. The most dangerous aspect of drug addiction is the need to procure money, at any cost, to buy the substance. The addicts pay exorbitant prices to the dealers and, in order to get the money, they end up as prostitutes, thieves and murderers. These are awful consequences. It is nevertheless true that it's impossible to correct these consequences by prohibition alone. When laws and society reveal themselves to be inadequate, full of errors and unrealistic absurdities, there come the gangsters, ready to fill a desperate need. Obviously, they do so with moral indifference, brutal callousness and vampirism; which are made even worse by the risk and the secrecy of illegal activities. With gambling, thus, it is not surprising that many newspapers in New York support the public take-over of this business; with the goal of absorbing into its coffers the millions of dollars that end up in the gangsters' pockets.

There have been and there still are other gangster activities that would be difficult to list under the rubric of social usefulness. Organized crime is involved in counterfeit currency distribution; extortion of labor unions; and protection of unscrupulous business people, among others. But even in these sectors, gangsters would not be able to operate unless the general climate of society didn't give them the opportunity. One last thing must be said: in America the tradition of fighting outlaws is an old and established duty that is often left to a free press. It is not a coincidence that one of the few activities immune from the effects of organized crime is precisely journalism.

New York, March 16, 1955

MAFIA OR THE MORAL SEPARATISM OF SICILIANS

The American public is convinced that all over the United States there exists a very well organized association of criminals called Mafia, composed of Italians. Instead, according to the experts, this association is composed mostly of people of Sicilian origin and not Italians in general. Complaints and protestations about this generalization by Italian American newspapers and organizations of descendants of Italians have had no effect whatsoever; first of all, because Italian Americans are not as well organized and powerful as, for instance, the Jews; second, because the Italian-language press has limited circulation and practically no influence in society at large; and finally, because Italian American associations lack in members and resources. But, to top it all, these protestations have little or no credibility because Italian Americans have never denounced, or manifested their opposition to, or distanced themselves from the various local versions of Mafias in their backyards. There has never been a campaign in the Italian language press; there has never been a public meeting; there has never been an Italian American judge or a political leader at the head of a movement who fought and denounced those among them who victimized—first of all—the Italian communities, even before they victimized American society. The proof is in a book by Frederic Sondern,[1] also available in Italian. This book can be called the first public indictment against Sicilians by a branch of the Federal Department of Narcotics [sic].[2] This special federal unit has always maintained that the American criminal underworld is organized along racial lines and that the entire organization is headed by a group of Sicilians. This transpires quite clearly from the deposition of Carlo Siragusa, a special agent in the narcotic squad, in front of the Kefauver Investigation Committee [sic].[3]

---

1 Frederic Sondern. *Brotherhood of Evil: The Mafia.* New York: Farrar, Straus, and Cudahy, 1959. *La mafia oggi.* Milano: Bompiani, 1960.

2 Federal Bureau of Narcotics. Agency of the Department of Treasury established in 1930. In 1968 it merged with other agencies to form the Bureau of Narcotics and Dangerous Drugs, the predecessor of the present Drug Enforcement Administration.

3 Estes Kefauver (1903-1963). Politician from Tennessee. He served as senator from 1949 to 1963.

Siragusa is of Sicilian descent and has sworn war against his country fellowmen who dishonor the island and who, in his opinion, are the minds of history's largest criminal enterprise ever. This organization concentrates its dominance in the United States but extends its tentacles on the international stage, from Turkey and Syria to Italy and France. From the Al Capone[4] era, when criminals were at most operating on a national scale, we have moved to the [Lucky] Luciano era, with an international dimension. The world has shrunk in size not only for good but also for evil. Airplanes that carry medicines that save people in far away lands are also used for the drug trade that poisons the young. Progress is progress also for crime.

The stories narrated in this very interesting book come from the archives of the FBI, from the Narcotic Department, the IRS, the Secret Service and the Postal Police. All these organizations operate with secret agents that are independent of local state governments and are therefore considered immune from political pressure, particularly from elected state attorney generals. They are the most respected and most feared law enforcement agencies, with great resources, and shielded even from pressures from Congress. This book isn't particularly sensationalistic, but exactly for this reason it has caused enormous sensation. The raw material is pretty well known already but the fact that it is confirmed through the depositions of federal authorities makes it that more striking. Even the Kefauver investigation almost disappears when compared with the details of these stories. The most important aspect of this documentation is that it refutes the Kefauver investigation's thesis about Mafia as the center of organized crime in the United States. This theory was based on the hypothesis that Mafia, at least from a law enforcement perspective, was structured like a regular corporation, with a chairman and regular meetings. The report, to the contrary, concedes that nothing of that sort exists. What really

• *Special Committee to Investigate Organized Crime in Interstate Commerce.* Created in 1950 at the urging of Tennessee Senator Estes Kefauver. The hearings were broadcast live on television and even shown in movie theaters, in front of an estimated audience of 30 million viewers. They had a huge influence in shaping the attitude of American public opinion toward Italian Americans.

4 Alphonse "Al" Capone (1899-1947). Arguably the most notorious American Mafia boss.

exists, according to the writer, is an association of Sicilian families that exploits the environment by means of the systematic violation of the law. Their common characteristics are cohesion, discipline, intelligence and a basic philosophy. (I am using the word *philosophy* in the American sense, meaning a certain concept of life.) These families utilize all the guarantees that American law has put in place to protect the innocent, and use them skillfully to avoid the punishment they deserve. The problem, thus, is not in the actions of certain individuals: it is in the habits, mentality and identity of a group of Sicilians who live in a state of semi-isolation in the United States.

What are the fundamental characteristics of these Mafiosi? The book emphasizes, in particular, the tight cohesion within each family. These are strong, proud and hard-working people. The women are taught to understand, forgive and ignore the lifestyle of their men, be they fathers, brothers or husbands. Even when their dignity and feelings are offended by marital infidelity, they would never turn to the police. They are excellent cooks and devoted mothers.

If the family becomes rich—and it happens quite often—they don't seek social recognition. Their tendency is to stay in a separate world. They only visit with family members and trusted friends. They don't commingle with neighbors, and social relations with the outside world are limited to the minimum necessary. When they are arrested they are always courteous: they smile, bow and immediately ask to see a lawyer. Their fundamental rule of life is a very strong sense of self-control. In general they are not ostentatious with their wealth: they are happy dressing modestly, living in two-storey detached single-family homes furnished in the style of the European middle class of fifty years ago. Only when it comes to cars they choose luxury brands, like every other solid American businessman. They are usually good family men, they don't get drunk and they attend mass at the local parish church to which they give generously. They are always willing to do favors for people in power and then they return inside their protective shell.

The bosses command respect even when they end up behind bars. This phenomenon has been observed also in Italian prisons: lower-rank Mafiosi take care of their bosses as if they were domestic servants. Predominance is not acquired by means of a popularity

contest. It is earned. The implicit hierarchy among Mafia members is
not communicated by secret handshakes or special signals. Rather, it's
a matter of intuition and instinct and it reflects control over a network
of common acquaintances. The most appreciated quality is secrecy,
particularly with law enforcement. The infraction to the rule of silence
is punished with the harshest retaliation. There is also a very strong
sense of brotherhood among members so that when a member is put
away in prison his family is adequately provided for in all its needs.
Though they were once migrants now they don't like to travel much.
They don't stray far from a thin strip on the Mediterranean Sea in Sicily
or their new residences in the United States. Their business model
is based on extracting a profit from transactions centered on illegal
goods and services. The golden age of Mafia was the era of Prohibition
when a large portion of the population was implicitly supporting its
activities. With alcohol trafficking also came gambling and prostitution.
Law enforcement forces have also investigated Mafia's infiltration into
legitimate activities, such as the trade unions; distribution networks
of alcoholic beverages [after Prohibition]; import of Italian products,
in particular cheese, oil and canned tomatoes; control of wholesale
fish and fresh produce markets; bakeries; distribution and servicing
of jukeboxes; management of restaurants, pizzerias, coffee shops and
night clubs. In many cases these activities operate legally and are headed
by professional managers; in other cases they serve as covers for much
more lucrative illegal trafficking. The most important decisions, such as
eliminating traitors or dividing up the territory among competitors, are
administered by a council in the course of secret meetings. Only one of
these meetings has ever been discovered, in the town of Apalachin in
the mountains of northern New York state. The discovery was in part
the result of the determination and curiosity of a local police officer
who wanted to find out the source of wealth of an Italian resident,
Joseph "Joe the Barber" Barbara,[5] who was living in a villa with a lavish
lifestyle and no visible means of support. About seventy Mafiosi were
interrogated by federal authorities who, in the end, could not find a

5   Joseph "Joe the Barber" Barbara (1905-1959). Head of the Bufalino Mafia
family of Scranton, Wilkes-Barre, PA. He hosted a meeting of bosses in his residence
of Apalachin, in Upstate New York in 1957.

single compromising piece of evidence. All the suspects declined to answer questions, pleading the protection of the fifth amendment which guarantees the right against self-incrimination. Many of them came forth with the same identical excuse: they stopped by Mr. Barbara's villa on a courtesy call and spent time with him enjoying the landscape and playing cards.

According to the book, the favorite setup for the quick and unexpected execution of traitors is often during a banquet with other members of the brotherhood: surrounded by Italian wine and large portions of pasta, the victim is *taken care of* discretely, and the body later dumped in a remote location. In reality, though, the modes of execution have been quite varied depending on the circumstances. Albert Anastasia[6] was gunned down while sitting in a barber chair in a fancy hotel. Al Capone lined up his enemies against a wall in a car garage.[7] The victims thought they were being frisked and robbed by police agents; instead they ended up shot in the back by a machine gun fusillade. Some of these scenes appear in the movie *Some Like it Hot*, with Marilyn Monroe[8] (with the exception of the Italian gangsters' scenes, it is one of the most idiotic products ever to come out of Hollywood.) The initial scene of the film refers to the Chicago massacre I just mentioned. Another movie I am familiar with is based on a banquet of Italian mobsters in Florida. In the course of the meeting of a fictional Italian opera house society five traitors are executed. The first scene is extremely realistic while the second is definitely humorous with the chairman giving a speech in pidgin English. Meanwhile, at this time, a new film is being shot on the life of Al Capone, who already was the subject of previous films such as *Little Caesar* (1931) with Edward G.

---

6   Albert Anastasia, born Umberto Anastasio (1902-1957). In the 1950s he was the head of the Gambino family and one of the most powerful Mafia bosses of his time.

7   The reference is to the Saint Valentine's Day massacre in 1929, ordered by Al Capone against members of the Irish Mafia.

8   *Some Like it Hot*. Dir. Billy Wilder. United Artists, 1959.
   • Marilyn Monroe (1926-1962). Born Norma Jeane Mortenson. World-famous actor, singer and performer.

Robinson[9] and *Scarface* (1932), starring Paul Muni.[10] I am mentioning these movies to illustrate how vivid the Mafia phenomenon still appears to be in the American collective imagination.

Sicilians in general are very upset with the Sondern book despite the fact that the writer acknowledges with great clarity that the overwhelming majority of Sicilians are honest people who have contributed mightily to building this country. But he also confronts the nagging problem I mentioned at the beginning: "How come these good and brave people did not show any kind of initiative against the black sheep in their midst, unlike the Anglo-Saxon communities? Why didn't they protest and resist, even resorting to violence, against a few bandits that were exploiting them?" The writer quotes the answer of a prestigious—albeit unnamed—member of the community who explains that silence is caused by fear. To me, it is an excuse even worse than the sin itself.

Should some of my readers be offended, I shall also report that the Sondern books talks at length in an admiring tone about the intelligence and the abilities of the top Italian crime figures in the United States. Al Capone invented the concept of criminal operations on a national base. "This short, ugly man, with a powerful body and enormous energy, had incredible managerial creativity. If he was operating in a normal environment he would have become the leader of a large American corporation (...) His organization was a model of efficiency." Al Capone, incidentally, was not Sicilian,[11] unlike Lucky Luciano who is from Lercara Friddi in the province of Palermo. Also Sicilian was Luciano's mentor *don* Giuseppe Masseria,[12] "a first-class businessman,

---

9   *Little Caesar*. Dir. Mervyn LeRoy. Warner Brothers, 1931.
   • Edward G. Robinson (1893-1973). Born Emanuel Goldenberg, film and stage actor.

10   *Scarface*. Dir. Howard Hawks. Universal, 1932.
   • Paul Muni (1895-1967). Born Frederich Meshilem Meier Weisenfreund, film and stage actor.

11   Al Capone's parents emigrated from the province of Salerno to New York City, where he was born.

12   Giuseppe "Joe the Boss" Masseria (1886-1931). He was one of the first Mafia bosses and head of the Genovese family. The honorific title *don* is used primarily in southern Italy. It derives from the Latin *dominus* (lord, house master). It is also used

with leadership skills." Sicily was also the land of origin of Giuseppe Lanza,[13] "an organizer with immense energy who dominated the fish market." The psychological portraits of Sicilian crime figures in the United States correspond to a large degree to what we also observe in Italy. However, the thesis presented in the book, according to which the roots of the criminal mind are in the family history, doesn't hold water. There is no proof that these criminals came from dynasties of felons. One should always bear in mind that the United States has been host to several organized crime syndicates that have no connections with Sicilians. For instance Meyer Lansky, Wady David, Louis Buchalter, Abner Zwillman and Abe Reles[14] were all members of gangs that either cooperated or were in direct competition with the Sicilian Mafia. And finally, how can anyone talk about Mafia as if it were a single entity while the author himself, in every page of this book, shows that among the Sicilians there were constant fights, turf battles and personal rivalries? Masseria was killed to clear the way for a younger competitor. Frank Costello was the target of an assassination attempt caused probably by disagreements on splitting booty. Albert Anastasia was killed after trying to take over a territory controlled by Cubans. Any honest historian will recognize that there have been several Mafias, some of which composed largely of Sicilians. However, there has never been *one* Mafia that controls and dominates all others.

In the end the writer unfortunately reveals poor knowledge of things Italian. Italian words are often misspelled; glaring errors of geography and history keep appearing, as, for instance, the peculiar assertion that "in 1925 Mussolini decided that Sicily would become the political and intellectual center of the Fascist empire in the Mediterranean." So many absurdities in so few words! All in all, though, one should

---

for Catholic priests as the equivalent of the English *Father*.

13   Giuseppe Lanza (1904-1968). Union organizer at the Fulton Street Fish market and prominent member of the Genovese crime family.

14   Meyer Lansky (1902-1983). Mobster and close ally of Lucky Luciano.
  • Wady David (1914-1965). Gangster from Boston's South End.
  • Louis Buchalter (1897-1944).
  • Abner Zwillman (1904-1959).
  • Abe Reles (1906-1941).

not judge the book based on these or other blunders. The relevant aspect is the research based on documents from the archives of various federal agencies. For instance, the book reports an anecdote about the gangster Eugenio Giannini[15] (not a Sicilian name, by the way). Siragusa met with him in Milan in a hotel near Piazza del Duomo[16] while he was in the company of an alleged countess. Giannini had arranged the meeting to sell information to the American agent during a visit to Italy whose purpose was to organize the purchase and shipment of cocaine to the United States. Very interesting indeed.

April 5, 1959

---

15   Eugenio Giannini (1906-1952). Soldier in the Lucchese crime family turned FBI informant.

16   Piazza del Duomo is Milan's main square.

HOW THE MAFIA MET THE NEEDS
OF THE AMERICAN PEOPLE

Setting aside moral considerations, my definition of the criminal association that the American press calls Mafia would be the following: the convergence of Italian vitality (audacity and creativity) with the needs and the means of a rich country such as America.

A few days ago at dinner with a small group of acquaintances we started discussing this very hot topic: in addition to yours truly, the others were a journalist from Italy, an Italian diplomat, an importer of Italian foods and two ladies whose contribution to the conversation was exclusively their grace and beauty. It is rather interesting how the arrest of Italian gangsters during a business meeting in the town of Apalachin, in Upstate New York, generated an unprecedented flurry of comments and reactions in the Italian community. Some Italian Americans have even gone as far as writing letters to newspapers complaining about alleged insinuations made against their community by some of the commentaries. Until now it seemed to me that Italian Americans barely noticed and barely worried about what was being said and written about them. The books that have been published on the topic of organized crime did not become best sellers in the Italian American communities; and even books that celebrate Italian American success stories, some of which contain historical exaggerations, have been barely noticed. Occasionally, from time to time there are complaints when a movie comes out portraying gangsters with Italian names. However, I have never read an analysis or a refutation of the criminal activities that have been regularly reported in newspapers and books, including those that are mentioned in the Kefauver congressional inquiry. And no denunciations either. My observation is that Italian Americans have been defensive; always sensitive to the offense of an Italian name used in a movie, but never eager to understand and fight this internal problem. The outcome is that the American public opinion by now is convinced that there is a connection between some specific forms of criminality and the Italian origin of many citizens. No one, so far as I know, has given a convincing rebuttal to this opinion.

In the course of the evening I noticed that we were served the inevitable dish of pasta and a few bottles of wine from an august Italian winery—long defunct—whose name is still being used in the United States. This is not uncommon: many relics of the European past are still present here, like specimens in the glass cases of a museum. During the course of our animated conversation (not so *Italian* though that we would keep interrupting each other) I was able to form an opinion on several points that I am going to expose to the Italian public.

First of all, Mafia, be it in New York or in the United States, does not exist in the form of a true association. The Kefauver investigation uses the name in generic terms to indicate groups of criminals from the same hometowns and on the margin of American society. No proof has been presented that it is an all-encompassing federation of gangsters. In contrast to this, we all agreed that there is such a thing as a *Mafioso mentality* that is observable in the protagonists of several recent famous criminal cases. The same mentality is also widely present in a large part of the Italian communities in the United States. With this I don't mean that the Italian communities are composed of gangsters. Rather, I claim that they have tolerated the existence of these gangsters whose activities are well known to the Italian-language press published in this country and to Italian American politicians who have never done anything to denounce the bosses and their methods while they were expanding their reach into the communities with banquets, formal dances and parades. Someone also mentioned that organized crime supports politicians and their electoral campaigns, rallies and charities. One of us made a useful distinction between two kinds of gangsters: those imported from Italy and those who grow up locally. In the Apalachin dragnet, the Mafiosi were all between forty and sixty-five years old. Their specialties were the protection racket of small grocery stores; ballot stuffing in elections; and, more recently, trade-union activities of extortion against entrepreneurs. One of the emblematic representatives of this cohort was a certain Giuseppe Profaci,[1] a distributor of counterfeit olive oil. The natives, meanwhile, have a different mind set and, so to speak, a different education and vision. Their model is Frank Costello, who has a wide

---

1   Giuseppe Profaci (1897-1962). Founder of the Colombo crime family.

range of interests that reach into California and New Orleans. He still uses the old provincial gangsters as soldiers, but he has a very sharp financial mind and good political connections on a national scale. This kind of Mafioso has greater familiarity with the American culture and lifestyle, knows how to push the right buttons and is de-facto perfectly assimilated into the forces of American capitalism.

It is also important to mention another set of facts that the defenders of Italian Americans often point to, namely the responsibility that capitalist, protestant, Anglo-Saxon America has had in the development of this particular kind of Italian entrepreneurial spirit. It is not enough to say that before the arrival of the large mass of Italian immigrants America already had several criminal organizations composed of Anglo-Saxons, Irish and Jews; and that these were very active with extortions, murders, robberies and other crimes. In fact, the responsibility of America is even deeper. We should not forget that when Italian immigrants were brought here to replace the recently-emancipated slaves, they were kept on the outside of mainstream American society, with no educational opportunities, no support and not even charity. They were left to fend for themselves without protection in the hands of a very corrupt Italian leadership made of bankers that stole their money; demagogues; extortionists and exploiters. This class of people dominated the communities for decade and controlled an unreliable, corrupt Italian-language press. All these aspects are mentioned in the reports made by visitors from Italy between 1880 and 1900. The self-appointed community leaders took advantage of the immigrants' ignorance and prepared the terrain for the low-level criminals who later evolved into today's high-flying Mafiosi. An additional observation concerns the split between American legislation and its prohibitions against alcohol, gambling and prostitution on one side; and, on the other side, an enormous market willing to pay for these very vices. Without these prohibitions Italian criminal activities would not have been possible. Leaving aside for a moment the hypocritical posturing of laws that are systematically violated, we must recognize that entrepreneurial and often ingenious Italian criminals had a very important function in American society. There was a vacuum to be filled and they filled it. Thus, I wasn't surprised when one of us said that he was prouder to be from the same town of Frank Costello than from that of a cobbler who made a pair of ornate slippers and sent them to President Eisenhower as a gift.

One of our dinner companions recalled that when Italians first arrived the only education they received was the violence they suffered at the hand of the Irish under the indifferent glance of policemen who also were Irish. How can one blame the poor Italian who pulled a knife to defend himself? These people actually saw the Mafia as a badly needed protector. Today the treatment of the new immigrants who are coming to America is very different, as can be seen in the case of Puerto Ricans who, when they arrive, find schools, social workers and religious institutions eager to help them settle in the new environment and get an education. The press is full of stories that focus on the positive aspects of their presence, contrary of what happened in the decades after 1880 when newspapers were full of insults against Italians. Yet, even with social support, these communities lack a leadership class that can provide role models and guidance and they are beginning to show the initial signs of the formation of criminal organizations commonly found among immigrants uprooted from their native countries for economical reasons. Today it is Puerto Ricans who pull out their knives. The ascent of Puerto Ricans in trades and professions, preceded by thirty years of American presence in the island, is being helped in many ways. They have two newspapers where they can debate their issues and at least fifty movie theaters. On Broadway one of the greatest hits in recent history was *West Side Story*,[2] the moving tale of a young Puerto Rican woman who in the end marries an American man. Seventy years ago Broadway would have never produced similar stories about poor Italians.

Today's America is different. The America of the past had the immigrants she deserved. As I said before, the large majority of Italian Americans is composed of honest, tenacious, patient people. Some of them are ingenious businessmen and entrepreneurs. Their only fault is that they never joined the American press in denouncing and fighting the gangsters in their midst, the very people who exploited the Italian community for decades and that still today, even in their old age, still manage to give it a generally negative reputation.

---

2 *West Side Story.* Music by Leonard Bernstein; lyrics by Stephen Sondheim, 1957.

ITALIAN AMERICAN GANGSTERS
ARE AGING AND GRAYING

For a long time the federal government, the police, magistrates, prosecutors and journalists tried to remove Albert Anastasia from the streets of New York, as he was considered by many a murderer and one of the big bosses of the local Mafia. What they failed to do—legally—for years, someone from his same line of business managed to accomplish in a couple of minutes—someone who presumably wanted to take his position or sought vengeance for something Anastasia had done in his position.

The morning of October 25, 1957, at 10:30 a.m., Umberto (also known as Alberto) Anastasia was relaxing in the reclining chair of his favorite barber shop in the Park Sheraton Hotel. It was the same hotel where Arnold Rohestein,[1] also a mafia boss, had been killed twenty years earlier. Before lying back, Anastasia chatted and joked with the owner, Arturo Grosso. Suddenly, two men entered the establishment wearing black gloves and with faces partially covered by bandanas. They pulled revolvers from their pockets; pistol-whipped the owner and started firing at Anastasia who, from his position, had not seen them entering. For some strange coincidence, Antonio Coppola, a fishmonger considered to be Anastasia's bodyguard, was not with him. Each killer shot five bullets two of which lethal: one to the back and one to the head. Two more bullets went through the right hand that the victim had raised to protect himself. Wrapped in a bathrobe with tissue paper around his neck, Anastasia spun around and fell between two barber chairs. Death was instantaneous. The lights overhead shone on a large diamond ring on his left hand. In the shop, besides the owner, were two other clients, a manicure lady, two barbers and a shoeshine. Screaming in horror and fear, they ran out of the shop bumping into the killers as they were fleeing, thus making it impossible for witnesses to discern who was who and identify the shooters. The descriptions given to the police turned out to be so vague that an

---

1 Arnold Rohestein (1882-1928). Notorious gambler and racketeer, he was reputed to have conspired to fix the 1919 baseball World Series lost by the White Sox.

officer on the scene commented that he had never seen such a large assembly of blind people in his lifetime. Thusly ended the life of an individual who had carved a niche and found a role for himself in New York's society; owner of a hundred thousand dollar Spanish-style villa where he lived with his brother Tony (nicknamed "Tough Tony"), surrounded by a 10-feet high metal fence topped with barbed wire and with a great view of the Hudson River. The grounds were guarded by three great Danes and, at night, illuminated by search lights. His was an exemplary family—so to speak—at least so far as the history of Italian crime families in America goes. One of the seven Anastasia brothers actually turned out right and became a priest and revered pastor in the Bronx.

At some point in the past I did some research and reconstructed part of their life history. The seven brothers were born in Calabria to a railroad worker that operated a railroad crossing in the countryside. One can imagine what kind of life they lived: the noise of the sea on one side; the monotonous passing of trains; school and church far away in town. One can also understand why those seven brothers who decided they would make it to America at all cost were exceptional people. For sure they did not bring with them from Italy a criminal organization or criminal experience. Some of them could not obtain passports, so they entered the country illegally. In New York they started working in the worst and most corrupt environment, the same piers that the movie *On the Waterfront*[2] has popularized all over the globe, exposing the tragic violence that dominates that world. Step by step they climbed the ladder and became the toughest, most tyrannical, most violent and thuggish mobsters in the whole place. Their leadership style was legendary: in the world of trade unions, the brothers Antonio, Alberto and Geraldo were respected but, most of all, feared. Their lives were a sequence of arrests, trials, and acquittals (thank to the deaths of potential witnesses) that can only be explained with the liberal procedures of American justice that gives the accused the presumption of innocence and easily releases them on bail. Antonio, who, on one occasion, was facing charges that could lead to a death sentence, was able to get away unscathed because four witnesses that

---

2 *On the Waterfront*. Dir. Elia Kazan. Columbia Pictures, 1954.

were scheduled to testify against him disappeared before the trial began. In one occasion, Antonio was accused of beating a longshoreman who refused to obey his orders. His version was that the poor man had fallen down and that he had simply dusted off his coat. The judge accepted his explanation.

As a way to explain the conditions in which they operated, we must consider that this empire-building and leadership style were similar in brutality to the regime of slavery in the American south. The only mitigating factor appears to be the fact that, ostensibly, the longshoremen themselves, or at least a majority of them, accepted it. After long political fights; investigations and, most of all, the work of a Jesuit father[3] who fought long and hard for the rehabilitation of longshoremen; finally the union agreed to regular elections supervised by observers from other independent labor organizations. It was quite a surprise for all, Jesuit father included, when the results showed that the majority of the workers opted to continue with the same leadership and the slavery-like system.

In the neighborhood where they lived, Anastasia and his family enjoyed a good reputation and even the police officers who kept an eye on their house declared to the press that they were model citizens and were even involved in public charities. In fact, I remember that in one occasion the longshoremen's marching band, led by Tony Anastasia [sic],[4] opened the procession of the *Madonna del Carmelo*[5] with great satisfaction of the local priest and his flock.

As Albert Anastasia was having his last shave, miles away his wife was leaving the villa to run some errands. A reporter who went to the villa managed to approach a groundkeeper who was working in the garden. The dialogue he reported is worthy of the best Hemingway.

"Is Mrs. Anastasia in?"

---

3   Most likely the reference is to John M. Corridan (1911-1984), a Jesuit known as the "Waterfront Priest." He was the inspiration for the character of Father Barry in the film *On the Waterfront*.

4   Anthony Anastasio (1906-1963). He kept the original spelling of the last name *Anastasio*, unlike his brother Albert who changed his to *Anastasia*.

5   Most likely the reference is to the annual procession of Our Lady of Mount Carmel and San Paolino di Nola in the Williamsburg section of Brooklyn.

"Why?"

"*Cumpà*,[6] Anastasia was gunned down."

"Which one?"

"Albert."

"Father or son?"

"I believe it must be the father."

The reporter tells that the gardener remained impassible and said he could not let him in because the lady of the house was out shopping. Then he turned around and kept to his work without a word.

The police believe that this is the sequel to the attempted murder of Frank Costello, the mob's minister of finance. Nobody will ever find out who gave the killers their orders or who pulled the trigger. For sure these killers were more brazen and better shots than the one who tried to get rid of Costello. The murder took place in a central location in New York and the assassins, following a protocol that could have come directly from Edgar Allan Poe,[7] disappeared in the crowd that, in that location, is always massive as it enters and exits the dark tunnels of the subway. The weapons were later found in a garbage can: foreign made, imported to the United States several years earlier and sold in other cities. Out of sheer curiosity, here are the names of the first people interrogated by the police: Mike Miranti, sixty years old, an old friend of Anastasia; Antonio Coppola, forty-nine years old, one of Anastasia's body guards; Ercole Anniello, a big shot of organized crime from Brooklyn, plus some other minor characters. All of them were Italian. Despite intense detective work, the police could not find the murderers, nor did they discover a motive for the killing. It certainly wasn't the first time that the efforts of the police could not break through the power of the mob. This organization is based on fear: witnesses and people with information do not want to talk. Anastasia in particular was known to go after witnesses to get rid of them. Despite all the secrecy, however, a couple of days ago an

6   *Cumpà* is the dialect version of compare [companion, comrade], derived from Late Latin *compatrem*. In southern Italy it is used with selected friends and acquaintances to indicate a status of social equality and confidentiality but also respect [buddy, pal].

7   Edgar Allan Poe (1809-1849). Writer, editor and literary critic.

extraordinary fact happened. The police learned that a special meeting of big mafia bosses was going to take place in a plush villa out of the way and far from busy roads.[8] The villa is owned by Joseph Barbara, fifty-one years old, owner of a local tavern and believed to be one of the crime bosses of Upstate New York. The police operation worked to perfection. Fifty-seven notorious crime figures were stopped and questioned. None of them was carrying guns; none of them was out on parole and everybody told the same story: they were visiting their dear friend, Barbara, who had fallen ill. All the last names of the fifty-seven were Italian, with the exception of a couple of Hispanic. It was interesting to see that the age of these individuals was between forty and sixty-five, with an average of over fifty. There were no young people. All of them are people who have made it and, like all the other senior people involved in organized crime, in the last few years have adopted the strategy of having a legitimate business as a cover; anything from liquor stores to car garages to moving companies. The purpose is to hide the real activity that is responsible for their comfortable lifestyle: luxury cars, expensive night clubs, top notch restaurants, villas and second and third homes at the beach and in the mountains. At their age they feel the need for a peaceful existence. After all, they all are good family fathers, they send their children to private schools and colleges, and they help them set up legitimate businesses or pursue respectable careers. The nephew of one of them is a criminal lawyer in New York.

The police could not find out what the purpose of the meeting was. Some believe that the attempted murder of Frank Costello and the assassination of Albert Anastasia indicate some kind of revolt by the young gangsters against the old guard. Others believe the meeting was called to agree on a strategic plan and avoid the consequences of an investigation into the garbage hauling industry in New York. Practically every company in this business is owned by Italians and their connections to organized crime are well known. Let's just say there is something that doesn't smell right, here. [The original footnote reads: "The Court of Appeal with a verdict on Nov. 28, 1960, stated

8   The reference is to the meeting that took place in the town of Apalachin, N.Y. in 1957, and discussed in previous chapters.

that the charges of conspiracy were not proven and all the people indicted were acquitted. They all maintained that the only reason for the gathering was to visit their ailing friend."]

Among the people who were interrogated we find the peculiar figure of Caspar [sic] Donald Modica,[9] who bragged about "having been in contact with some of the most illustrious figures in the country." He looks much more dignified than the rest of the garbage collectors; with white hair contrasting with the dark southern complexion of his skin; big turtle-framed glasses; a thin mustache; a cigarette hanging from his lips and fluent and smooth English. He looks like what he is, a professor at New York University (a private institution), where he teaches philosophy of education and safety regulation in manufacturing. He is proud of his expertise in industrial psychology and in the relations between management and labor. He is thus qualified to practice public relations, a novelty management discipline invented in America that recently has become all the rage in Italy. Unfortunately, in addition to a résumé as a professor, he also has a rap sheet with two convictions, one for practicing medicine without a license and one for attempted robbery. The crime world holds him in high esteem, as signaled by the fact that his wife is the goddaughter of Albert Anastasia's wife. Modica was also the private tutor of the children of Albert Anastasia, Joe Adonis and Willie Moretti,[10] three high ranking figures in organized crime. His lawyer claims that Modica has been rehabilitated. In 1952 he became director of the educational programs sponsored by a social club founded by Anastasia whose members are primarily longshoremen.

Meanwhile, all fifty-seven participants caught at Barbara's house

---

9   Casper Modica (1904-?). He was an instructor at New York University where he taught an extension course on philosophy of education from 1939 to 1943. In 1957 he was interrogated by a senate committee investigating the garbage hauling industry in New York. In the issue of November 15, 1957, the *New York Times* published the profile "Mob Psychologist: Casper Donald Modica," with no by-line, in which he was reported stating: "I taught the children of some of the most illustrious men in the United States" (meaning the children of mobsters). "One of them is practising [sic] law, criminal law," he added.

10   Joe Adonis (1902-1971). Born Giuseppe Antonio Doto. High profile mobster.
   • Willie Moretti (1894-1951). He was an underboss in the Genovese family and a cousin of Frank Costello.

are now out free because the authorities could find nothing against them. Whatever they were discussing in that meeting remains a mystery. Moreover, if a few days from now the police should find the dead body of some Mafia veteran, killed with no witnesses, even if the assassination took place in broad daylight in a crowded place, it will still be a mystery.

It is important, however, to observe that Italian American youngsters give minimal contribution to organized crime. All the elderly are settled down, they live off their assets and are accepted in their communities under the guise of real estate agents, salesmen, soft drink distributors and other similar activities. Organized crime is already all grey-haired.

New York, December 8, 1957.

CRIMINALS WITH ITALIAN NAMES
AND AMERICAN UPBRINGING

Correspondents of Italian newspapers in the United States have been reporting that several Italian American organizations are protesting a television show about organized crime that mixes together famous known criminals—beginning with Al Capone—and many fictional characters, all with Italian last names. The show, *The Untouchables*,[1] will not return next year and the Italian organizations took it as a sign that their complaints were successful in forcing its cancellation. The producers, on the other hand, insist that the reasons are purely business related. But it is still significant that a promise had previously been made that the characters would no longer have Italian names.

In the past, Italian immigrants in the United States were represented in cartoons as little men with olive complexion, short and squatty, with a mustache, grinding an organ while a monkey extracted fortune-telling colored cards from a hat and handed them out to passer-bys in exchange for a few pennies in the beggar's tin cup. When I first arrived in New York I still remember seeing maybe four or five of them, with the kind of pathetic *frinfrin* that showed up in the poetry of the young Aldo Palazzeschi and Sergio Corazzini.[2] By now they are all gone. After being elected mayor, Fiorello La Guardia stopped issuing new licenses; and, despite the fact that their presence was a picturesque and even moving feature of this city, I must agree that it was the right decision. In any case, it is improbable that any young second-generation Italian American would have continued the tradition and the nomadic existence of a beggar—their peculiar charm notwithstanding. By the time new licenses stopped being issued factories, businesses and other job opportunities in the private and public sectors were offering far

---

1   *The Untouchables*. Prod. Quinn Martin. ABC, New York, 1959-1963. Based on the memoirs of Eliot Ness about a team of law enforcement agents who led the charge against Al Capone in Chicago in the 1930s.

2   Aldo Palazzeschi (1885-1974). Pen name of Aldo Giurlani; avant-garde novelist, poet and essayist.

  • Sergio Corazzini (1886-1907). Poet. The reference to these poets is an inside joke and a jab at two of the most important avant-garde Italian poets of their time. Needless to say, Prezzolini did not appreciate their style.

superior and more respectable living wages and social status.

My personal opinion about the effects of the complaints by Italian American associations against that television show is that they will have no influence whatsoever on the attitude of American public opinion. In the United States today nobody harbors prejudices against citizens of Italian descent based on the reason that there have been numerous crime figures of Italian origin. I never felt around me the suspicion that I was carrying a knife in my pocket; or that at night I was hanging out with people who were planning a break-in into a store; or a hit to get rid of a traitor. Other Italians feel the same way. I asked people who moved from humble origins to relevant social positions: in school well-behaved Italian American boys and girls aren't singled out for harassment nor are they targeted or taunted for alleged connections to the mob. On the other hand, the American public believes that the major criminal organizations are in the hands of people of Italian descent and, more specifically, of Sicilians. This opinion derives from the fact that Italian names often appear in news stories on organized crime and also because of fiction-like episodes such as the meeting of crime figures in the small town of Apalachin, where all the participants had Italian last names.

All symbolic representations of a people and the general opinions expressed about them from the outside are always inadequate, often negative and sometimes even openly libelous. Simplification and generalization neglect many positive aspects. The little organ grinder could not possibly symbolize an entire population that had proved time and again to be composed by a large majority of very hard-working people. However, these stereotypical representations also contain elements of truth. Both the organ grinders and the Mafiosi did exist. Indeed, Mafiosi still exist today. But I believe the habit of connecting an Italian name to organized-crime activities will probably disappear from city streets the same way Italian organ grinders did.

The legends surrounding Mafia aren't born in a vacuum. I confess and maintain that I am much happier to associate myself with the *race* of Al Capone than with that of the organ grinders. I also prefer the characters in the *Inferno* to those in the *Limbo*.[3] It is nevertheless

3   *Inferno* is the first cantica of Dante's *Divine Comedy.*

perfectly understandable why the Italian population, which has so successfully become integrated into American life, is disturbed to find itself described in such negative terms in a popular show. There is also no doubt that the official doctrine (but not the outright practice) of the media and the American government is that discrimination against citizens based on race or religion should not exist. Lastly, Italians have witnessed other racial minorities rebel against offensive representations and obtain reparation (although they seem to me to be rather inconsequential victories). Therefore, if Italian Americans have protested in the typical American way, using the media and with demonstrations in front of the television stations that broadcast *The Untouchables*; and, finally, if they have boycotted products from American companies that sponsored the show with advertisements; well, more power to them. They did the right thing. Moreover, if the cancellation was truly caused by their protest, that would mean that they have political muscle too. In every country in the world this counts a lot, but in America it counts even more.

In the end, however, I don't agree with the protest strategy of Italian Americans. I believe they should have let sleeping dogs lie. If the names of our fellow-countrymen disappeared from television, they would pop up on radio. And if they were removed from radio, they would show up in newspapers and in depositions during trials. Finally, it seems to me that Italian Americans, who are so worried about the good name of Italians, behave like those who hide the thermometer that shows a fever: the fever doesn't go away. I also fear the counter-reactions caused by these demonstrations: the protest movement should not be headed by certain individuals whose reputation raises even larger doubts.[4] I was comforted that my opinion is indeed correct

---

• In Dante's *Divine Comedy*, the circle called *Limbo* comes before the *Inferno* proper. It is populated by illustrious men and noble spirits who died before Christianity and, therefore, did not receive a baptism. They live in a state of angst, yearning for the vision of god. In contemporary language, it means a dimension of upsetting uncertainty, lack of clarity and psychological anxiety.

4   This thinly veiled reference alludes to one of the leaders of the demonstrations, reported to be Anthony Anastasio, brother of Albert Anastasia, the recognized boss of the union that dominated New York's docks.

when I read a column by John Crosby in the *Herald Tribune*.[5] Crosby is a very accomplished journalist, with a great reputation for integrity, independence and straightforwardness. Here is what he wrote:

> This campaign is hard to take for a writer. A writer, crazy as he may be, uses his ears and eyes to observe society and to report how society is faring and how life is. He writes what he sees and hears. For instance, a writer who read about the dragnet of dubious characters in Apalachin certainly would have noticed that every single last name was Italian and could have concluded that there is a quite a number of Italians in criminal organizations. And in fact it would be rather difficult for any writer to write the history of criminal organizations in this country without going back to Al Capone—and even farther in the past—without filling the story almost exclusively with Italian names. At the risk of drawing the ire of the Italian American Anti-Defamation League I must point to the fact that Italians and particularly Sicilians have a genius for thuggery and criminal organizations in a percentage larger than other national groups. True, Arturo Toscanini is also one of them! Italians are a pleasant people, with a warm heart and they know how to sing. But they have also produced a bunch of criminals.

The article is much longer. It is strong and funny. I can't reproduce more here, lest I get accused by Crosby of being an Italian literary criminal who plagiarizes from an American colleague to look good. Now, Crosby's pieces are read by people more numerous and more important than those who read the flighty and irrelevant Italian American press. It seems to me that demonstrations in front of movie theaters and television studios have only had the effect of reinforcing the general opinion still existing in America on organized crime; on Italian Mafia and, in particular, Sicilian Mafia. There is a second order of considerations: these demonstrations in defense of the good name of Italians were organized by a newspaper[6] whose owners and editors pleaded guilty of what they called a "technical violation," but that the

5   John Crosby (1912-1991). Media critic for the *New York Herald Tribune*.
   • *New York Herald Tribune*. Founded in 1924. It was *New York Times*'s closest competitor. It closed in 1966.

6   A not-so-cryptic reference to the *Progresso Italo-Americano*.

law actually calls *fraud*. The frauds (plural), perpetrated against the company's stockholders and the municipality of New York, totaled one million dollars. Nobody in the Italian American community wants to mention these facts. Of course the less this is discussed the better, but, in exchange, that newspaper should stay out of endorsing this campaign for the "good name of Italians." There are many of us of Italian origin who live happily in America without the need for a newspaper to defend our good name.

The Italian-language newspaper that instigated the demonstrations found itself on the same side of the boss[7] of a union organization active in the infamous New York harbor. His name is very well known because his brother was killed in a barber shop downtown New York; and everybody presumes the reason of the killing was related to internal affairs of organized crime. Now, isn't it a bit preposterous to ask for support from the American public opinion with champions like this?

If the organizers of the protest had been model citizens, one could respond to Crosby that, although what he said is accurate, he did not mention many of the circumstances and responsibilities at the root of Italian and Sicilian criminality. First of all, these criminals with Italian names were not educated in Italy but in the United States; second, the nature of their organization is typically American and not Italian; and, finally, this is not a provincial enterprise: it is industrial. Before Al Capone and other Italian Americans like him, there were dozens of criminal gangs in America whose bosses had Anglo-Saxon names or names of other ethnic groups. Moreover, the American public could have chosen not to support criminals by avoiding buying alcohol during Prohibition; or by not using prostitutes after the bordellos were closed by law; or by not gambling illegally. Without the support of Americans, Italian criminals would not have survived. American society needed them: that's all. These people risked their lives or years in prison and operated with great skill in order to give the public the services and goods society had hypocritically prohibited.

One last thing remains to be said. When these Italians, or their parents, came to the United States, they were not treated with white gloves, as now happens to Puerto Ricans, for example. They were

---

7 Anthony Anastasio.

welcomed in America with the hugs of bosses that wanted to suffocate them. They got help by bankers who robbed them. They received no protection from laws they didn't know existed and didn't understand. The strongest ones among them understood that they had to take matters into their own hands. It's remarkable that only such a small number became criminals.

This is what one should reply to Crosby, if only the dialogue had not been spoiled by those who do not have the stature to engage in it.

New York, April 9, 1961

ORGANIZED CRIME
IN THE SMALL FRONTIER TOWN OF TUCSON

The very day I arrived in this growing town I had the impression that the only things worth reporting were the warm sun of winter days and the blackbirds that fly around cypresses. Then, in the hotel lobby I picked up a newspaper with the story of a mysterious crime that had taken place a weak earlier and that seemed just perfect to tickle the interest of my readers, probably bored with my observations and commentaries. The newspaper reported the grand jury deposition of the nineteen-year-old Dorothy Janssen, the victim's widow. In her testimony she revealed some curious facts about the crime that was enthralling the city. She said that the night her husband was killed he had taken about three thousand dollars out of a safe full of cash and had armed himself with three handguns. He put one in his belt, one under his armpit and strapped the third to the lower leg. He left without a word and a little later he was found dead. A trail of blood led from his car, where the body was found, to a nearby apartment complex where a certain Victor Colletti lived. Colletti told the grand jury that he didn't know Janssen, that he had never seen him before and that at the time of the crime he was in a different location engaged in a conversation with a University of Arizona professor in one of the modern, safe and respectable residential areas of this growing city. The widow also said she ignored what her husband did for a living. She added that she had never questioned her husband about the source of his money. She would see him open the magic box to take out money when she needed cash for their expenses, and that was it. Maybe another wife would have been a bit concerned knowing that her husband kept so much cash at home, but she was unfazed: "He came home every night," she said. Her parents said the same thing. To them it was enough that "he came back at night." He must have been a really nice boy. But, on that night he went out and did not returned. Apparently, he had mentioned a few times that he was receiving money from his family in Belgium. The police discovered that *he* was the one who was sending money abroad to a person with his same last name. From Belgium, so far, nothing has been learned. The police also discovered that Victor Colletti was the son of one of the Italian Americans who attended the famous meeting in Apalachin, NY, which, according to the police, was a Mafia summit. But Colletti's alibi was confirmed by the college professor who, by the way, does not have an Italian name. The widow never heard her husband mention Colletti but she remembered the name of another person: Rudy. The name corresponded to that of Rudy Perfecto, or Perfetto, the vice president of a company that owns a chain of Italian restaurants in the city. I visited one of them: it's like a glass box with a horse-shoe counter where, according to the local custom, one sits to eat spaghetti or pizza. When the police started looking for Rudy they found out that he had left town for an unknown destination four hours after the crime had been committed. Also vanished was a certain Morris Brady who had been previously arrested and sentenced twice for illegal gambling. Gone with them, apparently, are the three thousand dollars that nobody has been able to find anywhere. The grand jury in the meantime received the following information: Rudy Perfetto had been scheduled to appear in front of a different judge to face charges of domestic violence against his pregnant wife. After he had been arrested for that crime, Perfetto had been released on a bail set at three thousand dollars. When he didn't show up for his hearing, he forfeited the money and an arrest warrant was issued for him as a "fugitive from justice." Colletti's landlord, a certain Mr. Grande, declared he had never met Janssen and that the day of the crime he too was out of town. Colletti apparently ran away with the help of Frank Fiore, who was never deposed as witness. Unable to solve the mystery with their own resources, the police asked for help from the FBI—which has jurisdiction across state lines—but so far nothing has emerged. To this day nobody knows how Janssen earned a living. Nobody knows why he was killed or who killed him (with a single shot to the stomach after a struggle). It is also not known whether this episode may be related to other crimes in the city or elsewhere in the United States. The silence of the witnesses is as disturbing as the crime itself. There is a smell of *omertà* and the general impression is that some of the witnesses have been threatened.

This probably would be a small story if it happened in a large city;

if the motive didn't appear so mysterious; if it didn't suggest analogies with similar small episodes in other American cities and, finally, if the circumstances weren't so strange. To add to the oddity of the whole situation, we have the unusual marriage of a nineteen-year-old woman with two children who lives comfortably with an abundance of cash whose origin she does not question. This hardly feels like the typical image of the American family to me, although it is *an* image. But the aspect that really attracted my attention was that all the individuals involved have Italian names.

The more the police investigate, the more intricate things look, more than they had appeared at first. Tucson is a very pleasant town with no local organized-crime community. Whatever crime element exists, it has been imported from Mexico following a rapid expansion in recent years. A century ago it was a frontier town where poor Mexicans and European miners (some from Italy's Piedmont) settled. Cotton farming, copper mining and smuggling were the main industries and the city's lifeblood. Today the first industry is tourism followed by agriculture and manufacturing. What used to be a little oasis in the middle of the desert has been transformed into a source of wealth by human ingenuity. Tucson sells its desert view the same way Posillipo[1] sells the view of the gulf [of Naples] and its climate.

The origin of Tucson's fortune is in its climate. Doctors first discovered that the weather was ideal for tuberculosis patients and for people with arthritis: dry and warm in winter, cool during summer nights, with clean air and no wind. Slowly it has become a very desirable location and today at least a third of the tourists that come to visit end up moving here. Although the city has expanded and continues to grow, there is no shortage of space, with wide roads and very little traffic. Each house is surrounded by a garden planted with palms and other local trees that give a picturesque look to the area. It almost feels a bit like an American Egypt. The cost of living so far has not gone up, contrary to what has happened in Florida, for instance; and, based on the information I could gather, it is certainly lower than in other American metropolitan areas. The population is

---

1   One of the most picturesque Naples neighborhoods, located on the gulf, north of downtown.

mixed but in general they all share the same desire for peace and quiet. Around a nucleus of tuberculosis patients, retirees and elderly people with savings, a whole community of service providers has sprung up. Real estate investors, developers, builders, business owners, lawyers and manufacturing companies all want to take advantage of the low cost of setting up business here without spoiling the environment. Nearby there are also several military bases, primarily belonging to the Air Force. There are lots of swimming pools, good hotels, a large number of motels and, finally, ranches for people in search of a rustic and simpler life. One drawback is the scarcity of water. Huge pumps work day and night to suck water from the underground to allow plants, animals and people to survive. Everybody is worried that the water is getting harder and harder to reach and it is necessary to drill deeper and deeper into the ground.

The goal of the citizens is to live in peace and quiet and, maybe for the same reason, the criminal underworld has also begun to move here. But the newly arrived gangsters don't indulge in their preferred activities, such as extortion, prostitution, gambling, and loan sharking. They want a quiet life and enjoy the wealth they accumulated in Chicago or Los Angeles, like dignified retirees with a rap sheet long on arrests but short on convictions. Some bought a ranch, some speculate in real estate and everyone flaunts money. The native population is a bit nervous and even the mayor doesn't like this trend. The undesirables, unfortunately, are largely Italian, or at least this is what their names suggest.

Although this region is far from the port cities where Italian immigrants settled in mass, there are still a few tens of thousands Italians living in this area. Recently, a new periodical started publication, the *Tribuna Italiana*, mercifully written almost entirely in English (the few articles in Italian are a graveyard of crimes committed against grammar, syntax and history.) The problem of the arrival of individuals with a checkered past and a history of criminal activities was even discussed on local television by the mayor and the chief of police. Since these people cannot be rejected or sent elsewhere, the local community believes that the best strategy is to follow the recommendations of the Kefauver commission, according to which criminals, like parasites, fear sunlight. Therefore, the worst for members of organized crime is to be exposed, denounced and to have the spotlight pointed directly at them since, in order to operate effectively, they need the cloak of darkness.

In the meantime, so far nothing has come to light about Janssen and the people who disappeared. We know nothing and, chances are, we will never find out about the murder motive and the missing money.

A couple of years ago there was another case of a man who was found dead. His name ended in a vowel and his features suggested he could be from southern Europe. He was in the trunk of a car, nicely folded like a blanket. Nobody knows who put him there. From what we can surmise, it seems evident that this was a conflict among small fish in the crime underworld: maybe it was a dispute on splitting the loot, or maybe someone shortchanged the big bosses of the money they were owed. The big bosses, meanwhile, remain unknown in their comfortable villas; they attend mass with their families; their children enroll in the best private schools and, when the die, they will have grandiose funerals. When the police interrogate them they never know anything and they always have a perfect alibi, confirmed by the people they were with. If, at a previous point in life, they were convicted of felonies, they have already paid the price to society and now they can be free—often on parole. Once upon a time, when Tucson was just an agglomeration of huts surrounded by the desert and the people didn't have air conditioners, swimming pools and radiators for cold nights, it could happen that a horse thief, captured in the middle of the night, would end up hanging from a tree. If an Indian killed a white, chances are he would end up crucified. Those were tough times, uncivilized times, they say. And it's true. Progress brings swimming pools, radiators, bank accounts, real estate speculation, people released on parole and also a tiny bit of organized crime.

Tucson, Arizona, January 15, 1961

Part Four

Mafia Returns to Italy

THE ONLY THING ITALIAN
IN ITALIAN AMERICAN GANGSTERS IS THE NAMES

Under President Harry Truman the United States Attorney General James McGrannery [sic],[1] started the implementation of a policy whereby foreign citizens or naturalized American citizens who had distinguished themselves in criminal activities would be expelled and returned to their respective countries of origin. Political and subversive activities were also included in this category. In the past the deportation process had been used rarely and mostly for political reasons rather than for law-and-order purposes. After Eisenhower's election in 1952, the attorney general started applying much stricter enforcement and compiled a list of hundreds of people targeted for expulsion. The list contained the names of people from all sorts of countries: Stromberg is Russian; Voiler, Romanian; Chaplin[2] (not exactly a criminal, but nevertheless undesirable because of his unpleasant political views), British. Not surprisingly, several of the undesirable guests on the list were born in Italy and have Italian names. However, I question whether they can be properly classified as *Italiani*. As I have often reported in the past, these individuals were brought here as little children and have never even learned a word of decent Italian. They grew up in the mean streets of American cities where they received a basic criminal education, then moved up to middle school in juvenile detention centers, and, finally, graduated from the penitentiaries of higher learning such as Sing Sing and other infamous places. Legally, some of these people are still Italian citizens because they never bothered or forgot to request American citizenship. Others, before they could be deported, had to be stripped of American citizenship first. In some cases this process took years: with the help of smart defense lawyers, they were able to

---

1 Harry Truman (1874-1972). President of the United States from 1945 to 1953.
• James McGranery (1895-1962). U.S. attorney general in the Truman administration 1952-1953.

2 Charlie Chaplin (1889-1997). British actor, co-founder of United Artists. Accused of being a communist sympathizer after an FBI investigation, he left the U.S. in 1952 to attend the opening of a new film in London. The next day his re-entry visa was revoked.

drag on the legal procedure for eons. In the meantime they would get arrested for other crimes, released on bail, re-arrested and re-released many times. Expelling the big fish takes longer than dispatching the small fish, obviously. The rich and powerful can afford to spend huge amounts of money on lawyers, thus forcing the government to also invest large sums into the process to prove that the citizenship is invalid because of lies on the naturalization applications. For the suspects of politically subversive activities, usually the lie involves denied having been part, either abroad or in the United States, of any organization whose goal is the overthrow of the government itself.[3] For criminal elements, the pretext is lies about previous convictions in the country of origin or a fake date or place of birth. Everybody knows that in the United States it is extremely easy to forge or fabricate identification documents. On the other hand, the punishment for such an act is extremely harsh. If someone wants to get a second wife, all he needs to do is swear that he is not married, but in case the law finds out the consequences are rather severe.

We should also add that in many circumstances Italian criminals had questionable papers not due to forgery or outright cheating but simply because their parents were either ignorant or sloppy. In many cases when they arrived to America they didn't even think about bringing documents for their children. Once they had settled, rather than starting the long process of requesting birth certificates from the hometown, they quickly learned that all they had to do was find a couple of witnesses willing to give sworn statements about the children's date and place of birth. Frank Costello's parents most likely never imagined he would have such a brilliant career in the Neapolitan *camorra*,[4] at least not at the time when they procured a birth certificate that declared he was born in the United States, which, unfortunately, contradicted another much more reliable birth certificate issued in Italy that showed that he was Italian by birth. For this reason he is now a

---

3   The most common charge was membership in communist or communist-leaning organizations in the home country, labor unions included.

4   *Camorra*. Criminal organization with origins in Naples. It is often compared to the Sicilian Mafia. The word *camorra* is also used generically in vernacular to indicate a state of diffuse illegality, corruption of institutions and racketeering.

target for deportation and he is in prison in the U.S., where he would prefer to stay rather than being forced back to Italy. Since the order of deportation is a police act, not a judicial one, it means that the deportation is an administrative decision and is not determined by a trial by jury. Many deportees appeal the measure and the fight can drag on for years. However, some of those who are facing long sentences in the United States accept immediate deportation in exchange for a pardon that allows them to get out of prison. This is the case of Lucky Luciano whose sentence was commuted by the governor of New York[5] in mysterious circumstances and went straight from a prison cell to the ship that took him to Italy.

The United States was unable to get rid of a certain Iccardi [sic],[6] accused in Italy of murdering for political reasons and then robbing a U.S. Army major who, during World War II, worked as intelligence agent and liaison with the Italian Resistance movement. Iccardi is an American citizen and legally cannot be tried in Italy because he was[7] under American jurisdiction when the crime was committed. He also cannot be prosecuted in America because the crime was committed in Italy. In this case the Italian government requested his extradition but the request was denied. Many of these complications stem from the fact that there is no bilateral treaty between the United States and Italy about circumstances of this kind.

In addition to Lucky Luciano, other criminals of Italian descent were deported back to Italy: Frank "the Cripple" Coppola,[8] Joe "Peachy"

---

5 Governor Thomas Dewey. As attorney general he prosecuted Luciano and succeeded in having him convicted.

6 Aldo Icardi (1921-2011). Second Lieutenant in the U.S. Army, he served in the Office of Strategic Services (OSS). He was parachuted behind enemy lines in northern Italy in 1944 to help partisan fighters. He was accused of the murder of Major William Holohan.

7 In the original text: "[P]erché Iccardi è suddito americano legalmente non può essere giudicato in Italia, perché *non* era sotto la giurisdizione americana." (Emphasis mine.) I edited this passage deleting the negative *non*. Most likely the original text contains an error and should read: "perché ~~non~~ era sotto giurisdizione americana." It would be otherwise impossible to comprehend the legal argument and the causal relations. Iccardi was an American citizen and a soldier in the U.S. Army when he committed the murder; therefore he was under American jurisdiction.

8 Frank Coppola (1899-1982). Nicknamed "Frank Three Fingers," he was

Pici, Carmine Tufarelli and a few personal friends of Luciano, such as Gaetano Chiofalo, Nicola Gentile and Raffaele Liguori. Common wisdom in the media and the opinion of the Kefauver commission is that Luciano and the rest of his gang continue to maintain close working relations with the New York Mafia. It has been even hypothesized that they are actually still running the New York operations where suspicions and allegations of their involvement in the traffic of narcotics are rampant. To this regard, the murder of Eugenio Giannini[9] is at least mysterious. A common criminal, while he was held in Rome's prison he gave information to American authorities about the international drug traffic. It is rather obscure how he managed to come back to New York despite the fact that he was supposed to be still in prison in Italy and, on top of it, at a time when there were active investigations about him in New York. None of the newspapers I read had an explanation. All we know is that he was found dead, killed in typical execution style, with a bullet to the back of his head.

All the deportees tried to fight deportation orders and now are not particularly happy living in Italy where they feel like—and they are—foreigners. They had never been there, they don't speak the language and they don't know the customs. In America they appear to be Italian imports but in reality they are the products of America's tolerance toward immigrants. There is a funny story that illustrates the true feelings of deportees forced to return to Italy. In August 1953 a deportee, Michele Spinella, expelled at age 59, wrote a letter on the stationery of the Igea Grand Hotel in Palermo to the state attorney general who prosecuted him. He mentioned he was thrilled that the officer's daughter had fallen and broken a leg. "Too bad it happened to her and not to you" he said, and continued warning the father that "those who did me wrong will be punished. Wait and see."

After conducting many interviews with the deportees, a correspondent of the *Herald Tribune* observed that the deportations didn't make anybody happy. The Italian authorities are extremely irritated; public opinion is also irritated and in some cases has even

---

deported to Italy in 1948.

9 Eugenio Giannini (1906-1952). Soldier in the Lucchese crime family, he became a Narcotic Bureau's informer.

shown sympathy for the deportees; and the deportees are depressed and dream of returning to the United States—even at the cost of ending up in prison to finish their sentences. One of the reasons Giannini cooperated with the American authorities, supposedly, was the filth and the rats he encountered in Rome's prison. He liked American prisons better.

Giuseppe Lo Curto, who, according to American police was a close friend of Luciano and was deported with him in 1946, returned to America in 1952 and was caught in May of the following year while he was watching television with his friend Muriel McCormack. Found guilty of killing two police officers, his sentence was commuted and he was deported to Italy again in 1964. After his last arrest he admitted he had already come back to the United States three times.

And here comes the question: how did he manage to get back and forth three times? Any honest Italian gentleman gets the chills just thinking about the procedure to get permission to travel to America. First, one must obtain a passport from Italian authorities, then comes the application for a visa that entails an investigation by the American consulate, medical records, vaccinations and financial and criminal records. The last step is the interrogation by immigration officials on the ship and more interrogations at the port of arrival. To top it all, there are all sorts of physical barriers, uniformed inspectors, precautions, security measures, documents and translated certificates. Yet, a convicted felon sentenced to life in prison came and went three times. As if this were not enough, he was only caught because someone passed information to the police about his whereabouts in New York. It must be true what they say: laws are made to bother honest people and to sharpen the intelligence of scoundrels.

New York, September 23, 1953

ITALY AND THE RENDITION OF CRIMINALS

In the last few months, almost all Italian newspapers of all political inclinations, from left to right, have published strongly-worded editorials against the United States, accusing it of dumping a bunch of common criminals and other undesirables onto the peninsula's shores as if throwing trash overboard. The issue is causing a lot of worries to people interested in preserving good relations between the two countries, and, naturally, it raises concerns inside the respective governments. To this end, I thought it would be useful to investigate the facts by digging into official documents. I am not at liberty to disclose the sources of my information for I am bound by the promise that I would protect the privacy of the people who helped me. I also promised I would not reveal their positions. However, I want to assure my readers that the information in my possession comes from credible functionaries of both countries at all levels, from high to low. The only people I did not consult with are the deportees themselves—for obvious reasons. I spoke, however, with their defense attorneys.

For this article I followed an uncommon approach: first I formulated the kind of questions and doubts that any Italian citizen would like to ask, and then I tried to give answers from the point of view of an American citizen. It's a straightforward method that takes away biases and has the advantage of clarity. Here is the imaginary dialogue between an Italian (I) and an American (A).

I: *Is it true that American citizens are deported from America just because they are criminals?*

A: Untrue. It would be impossible to deport an American citizen from the United States. The Constitution doesn't allow it. Exile as a form of punishment does not exist in American jurisprudence.

I: *How come, then, even Prezzolini calls them "exiled"?*

A: It's just a metaphor, not a legal term. The term refers to a moral condition, not a legal one. Many of these deportees haven't lived in Italy since they were children and when they are brought back there they are totally lost: they feel like foreigners.

I: *Why does the American government send them to Italy?*

A: Because, based on a strictly legal argument, they are Italian citizens. Some never acquired American citizenship. Others, who were naturalized, have been accused of using fraudulent means to obtain U.S. citizenship and, therefore, were not entitled to it. The decision is made by a judge after a regular court hearing. The American government claims that the moment they lost their American citizenship they reverted back to the status of Italian citizens and they must return to their homeland. The Italian government often does not agree with these legal arguments. Thus far, all the people who have returned have done so either voluntarily or with the approval of the Italian government.

I: *Is it unusual for a modern state to expel or deport foreigners, or people that are considered foreigners?*

A: Not at all. Indeed, it is a very common practice. Every country has the right to expel from its soil foreigners that are considered *undesirable*. In some countries, for instance in France, all is needed is a police order. France has used it against journalists who, according to the French government, did not "tell the truth" and did not contribute to good relations between the two states [sic].[1]

I: *What are the conditions of these deportations? Are they brutal and rough?*

A: Deportation is always brutal and taxing for anyone. In legal terms, deportation is a punishment. In many cases it really is one of the most severe punishments that can be imposed. People who live in a country for a long time create human relationships and often have a family. They speak the language of the country, know the customs and are comfortable with their lives. And then, suddenly, they are thrown out. The punishment is so brutal that people often choose to serve a prison sentence rather than being deported so that, after they are released from prison, at least they can go back to their families and their lives. The circumstances vary greatly by country. Some countries implement much more cruel measures than the United States. Argentina, for instance, gives a deportee three days to get out. New Zealand—which is a very democratic and progressive country—gives them twenty eight days. In France the waiting period is very short. In the United States the term is six months. Moreover, in America the law is tilted in favor of the accused and a good lawyer can drag

1 France and, presumably, the home country of the offending journalist.

on the process for years.

I: *While they await the final disposition of the case, are the deportees kept in prison?*

A: Very few of them are. Legally they are under arrest. However, they can be free on bail and go about their business until the deportation order is finalized. For instance, as of January 31, 1951, the total number of people awaiting deportation was 39,743: only 1,545 were in prison; 5,742 were out on bail; 28,919 were out on their own reconnaissance and 3,537 were in hiding and considered fugitive from the law. These figures demonstrate a rather lax attitude, reinforced by the number of people at large. Of course, if the people who decided to go into hiding were caught, they would end up back in prison with no chance of bail. In France, to the contrary, there was a case of a deportee who was kept in prison for nine years eight months and twenty one days (from a report published by the United Nations).

I: *What are the reasons that can trigger expulsion from the United States?*

A: More or less the same reasons apply all over the world. The main, generic but fundamental reason is the interest of the "public good." This term can cover a lot of legal areas: it may refer to security, public safety, the economy etc. In some cases the laws are more specific. In some countries panhandling and vagrancy are enough to warrant an expulsion. Other common reasons are illegal possession of firearms, traffic of narcotics, abuse of minors, homosexuality, prostitution and smuggling. In Argentina all is needed is "offenses" to foreign heads of states, or offenses against a foreign flag, or even the dissemination of information that could damage good relations with other countries. The last one is the kind of clause that makes it almost impossible to be a foreign correspondent in Argentina. The United States doesn't have that long a list. Only recently, with the passage of the McCarran law,[2] the enforcement has become more active. For instance, the United

---

2 *Immigration and Nationality Act.* Also known as McCarran-Walter Act (1952), the law was meant to prevent certain individuals from immigrating to the United States. One of the innovations was a strict policy against individuals who were in any way connected to communist organizations.

States honors the recent international Brussels Convention[3] and does not expel foreigners just for being indigent, as long as the person is not a criminal. This has never happened, not even during the Great Depression.

I: *Is the number of Italians that have been deported really significant? Is it one of the biggest groups ever deported from the United States?*

A: In 1953-1954 the total number of deportees from the United States was 26,951. Of these, 351 were rendered back to Italy. The number is not very high and it certainly is not the largest group by nationality. Moreover, it is rather small compared to the overall population of Italian descent living in the United States.

I: *What about the other deportees? For the sake of information and also for comparison purposes, what were their countries of origin?*

A: Illegal entries into the United States are much easier by land than by air of sea, obviously. Of the total number of deportees, 22,628 were Mexican and 1,296 were Canadian.

I: *Many in Italy contend that Americans are much more lenient with political allies and so-called blood relatives, particularly the British. Is it so?*

A: It doesn't look that way. The number of British subjects expelled was 299 against 351 Italians. One should remember that the overall size of the British population in the United States is much, much smaller than the Italian. When we compare the treatment of Italians to that of citizens of other countries, the gap is even wider: 200 people from Greece were deported although the Greek population in the United States is one tenth of the Italian. At the same ratio, the Italian deportees should have been over two thousand.

I: *Why does America worries so much about such a tiny amount of undesirable foreigners? Yours is a big country: why do you get caught up in such small things?*

A: Italians cannot fully appreciate the enormity of problems that are caused by the influx of foreigners, useful and useless, honest and dishonest, suitable for integration and indigestible. Just think what it would mean if Italy had to educate fifteen million people of foreign origin in the national language for at least two generations before they

---

3   *International Convention for the unification of certain rules relating to Arrest of Sea-going Ships.* Brussels, 1952.

could become fully functional citizens. Starting from 1892, skipping the first hundred years of the Republic, the total number of people expelled from the United States to this day is 5,416,313—or five and half million. Of these, 443,210—almost half a million—had to be forcibly expelled, or deported. In addition to six thousand miles of border with Mexico and Canada, there are thousands and thousands of miles of coast where it's easy to get ashore. Only in 1953 the border police inspected 45,000 ships and 85,000 airplanes. Over two million sailors were processed with temporary permits lasting from a few hours to a few days. Inspections were conducted on more than 2,000 diplomats and 10,000 consular or other officials from overseas.

I: *Why is surveillance necessary at all?*

A: First of all, these are common measures. In Italy, by the way, if the police were to follow to the letter the exact provisions of the law the screening process would be even more intrusive and unforgiving. Immigration is a real headache for the United States. In the past the doors were open to all. However, that policy created problems, social unrest and political fights. The first legislative initiative to defend America from foreign invasions dates back to 1789 [sic],[4] a few years after the foundation of the Republic. Americans are rather liberal and tolerant by nature, tradition and law. But these virtues are not common to all the humans who were dumped onto these shores. As a consequence, some illiberal and intolerant corrections had to be introduced. America is founded on principles, some of which so absurd that once in a while they need to be modified with common-sense corrections and a few hypocritical patches, all the while without ever denying the principles themselves. As Americans have become richer and more powerful, the immigration pressure from all over the world has increased and applications to migrate now arrive from all corners of the globe. It's hard to believe that George Washington would have imagined that Chinese would migrate to the United States by the tens of thousands and that it would be necessary to make a special

---

4   *Naturalization Act (An act to establish an uniform rule of naturalization). Sess. II, Chap. 3; 1 stat 103. First Congress; March 26, 1790.* The original title reported by the Library of Congress uses the indefinite article *an* in front of *uniform* (Philadelphia: Printed by Francis Childs, 1795).

law to keep them out.[5] It was a law that contradicted basic principles and values. Nevertheless, it was an essential law that saved America from the deluge of people who, otherwise, would have flooded the country, wiping out all the efforts to create a rich, independent and modern nation. Moreover, despite the racial laws and the provision to sift through the immigrants, the United States has taken in forty million people. Consider that every year thousands of individuals try to enter the country illegally. A Senate inquiry has determined that there are already millions of illegal residents. New York alone has about 200,000. Immigration experts estimate that in some Brooklyn neighborhoods the percentage of illegal residents is as high as ten percent of the population.

The number of career criminals among Italians deportees is rather low. In 1953-1954 there were forty-four criminals: four were accused of crimes against morality; six were drug traffickers; one was mentally ill and four were subversives. The large majority, 218 cases, were people without legal papers. A curiosity is the number of sailors who ended up being deported because they overstayed the terms of their visas. In 1953-1954 the total was 295, 130 of which Italian. Probably they were staying with relatives or a girlfriend... Inevitably, in this huge mass of cases, some injustices and unnecessary harshness have been committed.

I: *How is it that the data for deportees are so small, while those for the expulsions are so large?*

A: There is a rather simple explanation. The primary reason for being expelled from this country is lack of official papers. These people normally don't fight the system and reluctantly return to their home countries. Deportees are those who refused to leave voluntarily and decided to fight the expulsion decrees in court. Often in this category are individuals who defend personal as well as group interests. A Senate investigation revealed that their legal expenses are often paid for by criminal organizations that want to keep their members in the

---

5 It probably refers to the 1882 so-called *Chinese Exclusion Act (An act to inaugurate certain treaty stipulations relating to Chinese)*. Previously, Congress had passed another law targeting Chinese nationals, the 1862 *Anti-coolie law (An act to prohibit the "coolie trade" by American citizens in American vessels)*.

country, such as in the [Francesco] Brancato case.[6] At times the trials drag on for years at very high cost.

I: *But there are cases when the law is truly inhumane.*

A: True. Although even the McCarran law asks for some leniency when the deportation results in the separation of family members, cases of inhumanity do occur. Maybe this has to do with the insensitivity of individual police officers and immigration agents who get progressively de-sensitized after dealing with so many cases of deceptive practices, trickery, lawlessness and outright criminal behavior.

I: *Is it possible to appeal to a higher court?*

A: The only possibility is to have a member of congress introduce legislation dealing with that specific case granting citizenship to an individual. It is a very unusual case but it does happen: every year about a thousand such laws are proposed, but only two hundred are approved.

I: *What happens to those foreigners who, if they were sent back, would face political persecution, like in Russia or Poland, for instance? How would they be treated if one tried to flee illegally to the United States?*

A: These cases follow a different process. In 1953 the Commissioner received 110 requests.[7] Eighty-four were rejected, eight were accepted and thirty-four are still under consideration. It is not a very reassuring outcome. However, it is not hard to see how a Romanian or a Polish would be willing to make up lots of stories in order to stay in the United States. One should not forget the cases of communists who feigned being victims of communism in order to penetrate the United States and work as spies. Now another phenomenon is under way: representatives of communist countries are trying to persuade some of the fugitives to return home promising them a normal life, even better than in America. But this would take another long conversation, and I think this is already long enough as it is.

New York, July 5, 1956

---

6   Documents from the legal case about Francesco Brancato are published online at the following URL: https://www.courtlistener.com/opinion/241028/united-states-of-america-ex-rel-francesco-brancato-v-john-m-lehmann/.

7   Presumably these are petitions for political asylum.

ITALY SHOULD REJECT CRIMINALS
FROM FOREIGN COUNTRIES

The United States wants to deport to Italy a certain Carlos Marcello[1] whose name also appears in criminal records with the aliases Calogero Minacari or Minacore. He was born in Tunis, Tunisia,[2] on the sixth or tenth of February 1910 and never set foot on Italian soil. He considers himself a French citizen and asked to be deported to France. The French government, however, rejected his claim stating that his French citizenship has never been proven in the United States. Thus, the United States proposed to deport him to Italy. Will Italy be able to resist the pressure? Carlos's father, Giuseppe Minacore, was born in Ravanusa, in the province of Agrigento, Sicily, in 1892. When he was eight years old his family moved to Tunis. In 1910, at age eighteen, he immigrated to the United States but the same year he returned to Tunis to marry Luigia Feruggia (or Ferruggia), born in Roccamena, Sicily, in 1893. Luigia's father had moved the family to Tunis when she was nine months old. In October 1910 she gave birth to Carlos and later joined her husband in America, more precisely in New Orleans. She has been living there ever since while her entire family still lives in Tunis and some of her brothers served in the French army.

Carlos Marcello is therefore the son of parents born in Italy who emigrated to Tunisia with their respective families when they were still children. He never even visited Italy and has always lived in Louisiana. Starting in the 1930s, Marcello was found guilty of a series of crimes, from armed robbery to trafficking in narcotics. He has also been under investigation for a long list of other crimes for which he could not be tried for lack of witnesses. American federal authorities maintain that he is one of the most powerful and dangerous Mafia bosses in the United States and, therefore, nobody dares testify against him.

Marcello does not have American citizenship. He is legally a foreign resident and, as such, the United States does have the right to expel

1   Carlos Marcello (1910-1993). Head of the New Orleans Mafia. He was suspected by some of having played a major role in the assassination of President Kennedy.

2   Tunisia in that period was officially a French protectorate, but a de-facto colony.

him. However, there is no proof that it has the right to deport him to Italy. First of all, there is no proof that he has maintained Italian citizenship even in the case that, by mistake, some consular authority might have issued an Italian passport. Moreover, the reason for his expulsion is drug trafficking, an offense that has been added to the statutes by the new McCarran law but was not in existence at the time he committed the crime. Technically, however, the McCarran law is applicable retroactively and can be used to punish people for acts that were not previously considered unlawful.

Researches conducted in Tunisia on Marcello's nationality have not yielded any results. There is no definitive proof that he is a French citizen, just as there is no proof that he is Italian. Moreover, Italy cannot demonstrate that this less-than-desirable individual lost Italian citizenship any more than can the United States demonstrate that he acquired French citizenship. The McCarran law is an American law, but it is not part of international law nor is it accepted by Italy. The law gives the American government the power to expel from its territory criminals convicted of certain crimes; however, in order to ship these individuals to another country, it goes without saying that U.S. authorities need the approval of the receiving country (in this case, Italy). The same law also contemplates the possibility that the country of citizenship may reject the deportation order. The law, then, has provisions that list alternative countries where criminals may be deported, such as the country from which the persons last embarked for the United States. For Marcello, the country was Tunisia, at that time a French protectorate. It is also possible to deport a person to other countries that are willing to accept the deportees—with the exception of bordering neighbors Mexico and Canada. Obviously, no country will volunteer to take in a character of the likes of Marcello. Finally, if all this weren't enough, Marcello does not want to go to Italy! He doesn't feel Italian. He was educated in French-language schools in Tunisia and graduated from Crime College in America. Why should he go back to elementary school in Italy?

From this point of view, the Marcello case exemplifies one of the aspects that have most affected both Italian and American public opinions from a moral perspective. As I mentioned in the previous chapter, Italy has only received a small number of deportees. However, many of them had a very large resonance in that they were top racketeers, born in Italy or of Italian descent.

After Lucky Luciano, the United States would now like to deport to Italy Joe Adonis;[3] Frank Costello, who is considered the ringleader of Murder, Inc.; Albert Anastasia, the boss of the New York piers; Sam Accardi,[4] who, according to American authorities, is one of the bosses of the international drugs trade; Nicolò Impostato [sic],[5] one of the Kansas City's bosses; and Nicola Amaruzza, boss of illegal gambling in New Jersey. In addition to these big names there is a whole another list of individuals involved in organized crime. Many have already been sent back to Italy with the consent of the Italian government and with rather dismal results. The deportees have found themselves without means of support in a society they didn't know, much poorer than America, less favorable in terms of their usual trade and also more resistant to crime, at least in individual terms. They ended up confined to villages or small towns where there is nothing to steal except chickens and where gambling is limited to church *tómbola*[6] and state-run lotteries. These masters of major operations are starving, like surgeons exiled among the Eskimos. I read somewhere that they wanted to organize a march on the American embassy in Rome to demand financial aid, maybe because the only language they can speak is American. In fact, even though legally they are Italian citizens, in reality they are and remain American. Marcello clearly belongs to this category. Here is, therefore, the perfect opportunity for the Italian government to take an official stand and present the question to the public opinion.

Some argue that these criminals are the product of the American environment, therefore, deportation for crimes they committed in America after they grew up in the American society is equivalent to

3   He accepted deportation to Italy in 1956. In Italy he was subjected to internal exile (*confino di polizia*) for his suspected connection with the Mafia.

4   Settimo Accardi (1902-1977). He fled to Italy in 1955. Extradited to the U.S. in 1964, he was sentenced to 15 years in prison.

5   Nicola Impastato (1906-1979). He left Italy during the Mussolini anti-Mafia repression campaign and became a major crime figure in Kansas City, Mo.

6   *Tómbola*. A game similar to bingo.

declaring that they harbor some kind of race-based criminal disposition. I beg to differ. I never shared the horror and scorn cast on Italian criminals in America. In my opinion in many cases these are very remarkable individuals in terms of intelligence, cleverness, political savvy and courage. After being abandoned by their country of origin and being taken in with disdain by a new country, they were able to adapt to the new environment, thrive and achieve excellence. Some even took care of social needs and performed historically useful functions, as during Prohibition. Presently they are doing the same with regard to gambling. Without the support—either willing or unaware—of a large part of American society, they could have never created the kind of powerful organizations that show how useless and pernicious those laws were and are. Of course, these individuals are violating the laws of the land, therefore they must be prosecuted. But why should we deny that their activities reveal the natural talents of many Italians who, neglected, exploited and oppressed by tyrannical governments for centuries, developed and brought to the new country the great talent of creating a state inside the state?

My point is that here they found the most propitious conditions for their natural genius to blossom and prosper. The fact that these developments are considered criminal by American laws is not the fault of their country of origin: the fault resides with the country that did not know how to take advantage of their intelligence in order to turn them into functionaries, captains of industry or courageous soldiers. These were exceptional individuals who had to find an outlet for their dynamism and found it in crime and criminal organizations. In this sense, yes, they were made by America and America should not send them back to the country of their *biological* origin, which is not the country of their *moral* origin.

Italy is under no obligation to accept criminals who are clearly not Italian citizens. Unfortunately, the absence of a treaty between the two countries on this issue has created misunderstandings and confusion for over a hundred years. Italy also has contributed to this confusion with its military draft laws: American-born children of Italian citizens born in Italy who visited Italy with an American passport often discovered they were wanted by Italian *carabinieri*[7] as military draft dodgers. There remains the fact, however, that the Italian government has no obligation, either domestic or international, to take back Marcello or any other individual of Italian origin whose nationality is uncertain. The Italian constitution,[8] by the way, contains an article that refers to the heirs of the former Italian royal house of Savoy. This article spells out that Italy is under no obligation to readmit all of her citizens, even when their citizenship is not in question. The members of the house of Savoy, in fact, are Italian citizens; however, the constitution bans them from Italian territory.[9]

Some functionaries of the Italian government are clearly worried that the McCarran law may provide an excuse for potential reprisals. If Italy refuses to take back its citizens after they are expelled, the United States may deny entry visas to all Italian citizens. The functionaries that have reluctantly already accepted some undesirable criminal champions are right to argue that they had no choice if they wanted to avoid reprisals. However, they should have also evaluated that the United States would be very careful in applying this kind of sanctions (I am not aware that there have been any such threats.) Moreover, in the Marcello case, Italian authorities should have cited a precedent with France that did not result in the suspension of entry visas for French citizens. According to the 1947 Peace Treaty,[10] Italy enjoys the status of most preferred country concerning immigration. It is

---

7   *Carabinieri* are one of Italy's national police forces. *Carabinieri* are part of the ministry of defense. The major duties are law enforcement and public order, with a capillary network of stations that covers the entire Italian territory. Their mandate includes a role as military police.

8   The constitution of the Italian Republic, promulgated on December 27, 1947, came into force January 1, 1948.

9   In 2002 the Italian parliament approved a law that rescinded the prohibition for members of the direct descendants of the last king to enter Italian territory. They were allowed to enter Italy effective November 10 of the same year. The law encountered fierce opposition from several segments of Italian society of all political orientations.

10   The Peace Treaty with Italy was one of the Paris Peace Treaties signed in February 1947 by the participants in World War II. It was ratified by the U.S. Senate in June 1947.

therefore clear that the rules that were not applied to France cannot be applied to Italy.

The tone of the relationship between the Italy and the United States is such that problems of this kind should be easily solved without reprisals. The Italian government should find an agreement with the United States and establish some principles concerning the treatment of Italian citizens who were accepted by the United States and grew up there. It is the responsibility of the United States to deal with them. First of all, these people were accepted after going through an extensive screening process that included questionnaires, interviews, documentation etc. Second, they became criminals and a danger to society, instead of model citizens, because of the way they were treated by society, the schools, the streets and the press; and because of the examples they grew up with.

In the past the attitude of the Italian government was too lax for opposite reasons. During Fascism emigrants were encouraged to return to Italy and during the military occupation after Word War II, after the peace treaty was signed, Italy was rather accommodating toward America, which was providing crucial financial aid in the years of reconstruction. This submissive attitude depended on the circumstances of the moment but is no longer sustainable. Many diplomats, members of parliament, ministers and even Italian presidents have visited the United States. Why didn't anyone bring up the issue and get concrete results? I don't recall reading anything about this problem in the memoirs of former Ambassador Alberto Tarchiani.[11] Let's hope we will find something in the future memoirs of Manlio Brosio.

New York, July 8, 1956

---

11   Alberto Tarchiani (1885-1964). Journalist and diplomat. He was ambassador to the United States from 1945 to 1955.

Part Five

The Language and Culture of the Immigrants

THE IMMIGRANTS' CHILDREN

While I was in a hospital for a minor operation I received a letter from one of my Canadian readers. I don't get much mail and usually I tend to answer right away. This time I had to put my reader on hold with the promise that I would get back to her later. In the meantime, I had a chance to discuss the issue she raised with a friend who is an expert in the field.

But I haven't told you yet what it was about. The letter came from a woman, yet (apologies to my female readers) I was struck by its quasi-masculine tone, that is, its lack of sentimentalities. Moreover, while it was presenting a personal experience, it showed a remarkable grasp of a general problem of great relevance. To use a big word in vogue among scholars, the problem is bilingualism among immigrants. Sooner or later immigrants must learn a second language and they are thus using two communication instruments. I wonder what consequences this has on their minds and especially on the minds of children. I am sure the letter from this lady and my answer will interest my readers. And here it is.

Chatham, September 13

Dear Sir:

I trust that your reply to my letter will help me solve a delicate problem of great importance to me. In order to provide you with a context, I will first introduce myself in hopes that it will make my situation a bit clearer. My husband and I are from Bologna. We are 34 years old and we immigrated to Canada in 1955. We are from an upper middle-class background, politically liberal and economically secure. After the Liberation[1] we became disillusioned… So, we decided

---

1   The term *Liberation* is generally understood to be the period between 1943 and 1948. It includes the fall of the Fascist regime (July 25, 1943); the armistice with the Allies (September 8, 1943); the civil war that ended with the liberation proper from the German occupation and the surrender of the Repubblica Sociale Italiana, the Mussolini puppet government of northern Italy (April 25, 1945); the plebiscite that ended Italy's monarchic rule and established the new republic (June 2, 1946); and the election of the first post-war democratically elected parliament (April 18, 1948).

to move to a new country and we chose Canada. To make our break even more drastic, we bought a farm (130 acres) a few miles from the town of Chatham,[2] and we started farming.

Back in Italy my husband owned his own business, a metal shop. I was a middle-school teacher. The jump was both huge and exhilarating. I discovered that manual work, which in Italy is needlessly disdained, actually leaves the mind free to explore and get to know oneself in depth. The parcel of land we own, the huge maple tree outside my window, the tall corn that ripens in the sun, all this makes us feel we are part of this country and no longer foreigners. We have been married for nine years and last June I gave birth to a baby. He is an authentic natural born Canadian. And here is my problem: what language should we teach our child? We always speak Italian at home and my mother, who lives with us, barely speaks any English at all. The most natural thing would be to teach him first Italian and, later, English. But I am afraid that this may make it difficult for my child to make friends in the first years, or that he may be self-conscious and unable to communicate with other children. I am also afraid that if we taught him both languages at the same time he might become confused. I would like him to possess his own words deep inside. I know how much you like clarity and, since you belong to two worlds, I feel nobody else could help me as much as you. I apologize if I imposed on you, but I trust you will understand. With many thanks for your attention.

With great admiration,
Maria Vera Corsini[3]

And here is my answer:

Dear Ms. Corsini:
My answer is very simple and concise: teach your child the language

---

2   Presently, Chatam-Kent, Ontario.

3   Maria Vera Corsini (1923-) is a published poet. *The Immigrant's Two Souls: Le Due Anime Dell'Immigrante*. Edited and with an introduction by Guido Pugliese. Welland, Ont., Éditions Soleil, 2006. Attempts to reach Maria Vera Corsini through her publisher were unsuccessful. We were told she now lives in Florida but no further information was available.

of the country where you live. From the little I know, Chatham is a small town of about 30,000 people in Ontario where English is spoken. Make sure your child learns English from the beginning without mixing it with Italian, at least until he is eight years old. Later he will be able to learn other languages, but first he must absorb the language of his country. The roots of his expression must penetrate deeply into the national soil.

You touched a very important point when you expressed your fear that two languages may cause confusion in your child's mind. This kind of mental confusion in life at times can lead to hesitations and uncertainties in making decisions. This is the central point of this issue and I will return to it later. I will also provide you with the opinion of a specialist, but, before I do that, please allow me to present another reason why you should teach English to your child from the beginning. One day in the future he will inherit your land with the big maple tree and the corn fields. You should not turn this child into a Canadian who speaks some kind of Italian Canadian dialect. As an adult he will have to buy, sell, negotiate; maybe argue and, let's hope, make love to girls from his hometown—in English. If you start speaking Italian with him while he is a child, chances are his English will be a bit deficient, crooked and unnatural. If you speak English to him, his English will have a bit of a foreign accent but he will correct it in school. His words will have a natural flavor, the same way Italian feels to me, and French to a French and so forth. This sense of ownership, the kinship with one's own language, is essential to form the spirit of a person. Undoubtedly there are a few exceptional individuals who can withstand the hardship of learning foreign languages in childhood at the same time as they absorb the national language. One of the most unusual cases is described by Michel de Montaigne[4] in his *Les Essais*. While he was a child his overbearing father gave him a German tutor who only spoke Latin to him. At age six, he could only speak Latin and not a word of French. He grew up lively and alert despite the fact that he was nourished with a dead language. Yet, not everyone can have the resilience to withstand a similar treatment. We are all familiar

---

4   Michel de Montaigne (1533-1592). Philosopher and de-facto inventor of the essay as a new literary genre. *Les Essais* [*The Essays*] was published in 1595.

with people from the upper classes raised by foreign nannies. They can speak with ease two or more languages but the concepts they express are a bit gauzy, as if the words had been smoothened and polished. Even when they have brilliant minds and shiny personalities, their speech lacks the color, the flavor and, I dare say, the smell that are present in the words of a peasant.

Obviously you and your husband will have practical problems to solve. First of all, you will have to make an effort to speak English to your child. However, the other approach would present a different order of problems: what would happen when your child goes to nursery school, kindergarten and finally elementary school? This is the problem facing parents who speak Italian at home. The social environment is more powerful than the family and, after a few months spent with peers, children start speaking English to their parents even when they are spoken to in a different language. At times, in less educated families, children develop contempt for their parents when they cannot speak the educated language of their schooling. And finally there is an ethical issue that concerns your duty toward the country that you chose and that adopted you. The official language and the language of your community is English. Language is an integral part of the sense of unity that is necessary for the health of a country. I remember reading that child-development specialists advise against using two languages with children. I talked to a friend, a renowned scholar who studies these issues and I asked him for his opinion. Here is his answer:

> The majority of scholars who study this issue believes that bilingualism is harmful. The leading Italian scholar in this field is Giovanni Calò. Here is the argument in brief: Jean-Jacques Rousseau stated that children should first learn the mother tongue and begin to *reason*. Later they can learn a second language. In favor of bilingualism are Louis Necker, Ferdinand de Saussure and Antonio Rosmini. The first experimental findings prove that this optimistic theory is wrong. I remember the work of John Smith, Frank Saer and James Hughes, who conducted field work in some areas of Wales where children spoke Welsh at home and English in school. They found that these children were one to two years behind their peers in intellectual development. Izhac Epstein and Gonzague de Reynold reached the same conclusions. Giulio [sic] Ronjat studied the phenomenon of

bilingualism using his son for his observations. The child was raised in French and German, respectively the father's and the mother's languages. Their house servants were French or German speakers. The result was that the child showed signs of what is now called bipolarization of linguistic activity in bilingual individuals. This consists in a phenomenon whereby each language has a different role in the consciousness. Ronjat's son finds it more natural to discuss scientific matters in French and literary matters in German. At the 1932 Nice, France, convention on new education, in the section dedicated to bilingualism one of the speakers stated: "As children in primary and secondary school we were taught to understand and use two languages simultaneously. As a result, our tendency was to focus more on words than on ideas. When we spoke, we created utterances in one language while we were thinking in another. Our consciousness became accustomed to this lie since infanthood and would not longer rebel. We became full of nuances and different shades of meaning. We could shine but we could not concentrate and burn: our soul is made of changing colors, not stainless steel." (This passage is taken from a text by Luigi Volpicelli,[5] a renowned scholar of pedagogy and social criticism.)

To be fair I want to clarify that there are scholars who favor bilingualism. Some of them think that having two languages means having two souls. I personally believe that we have only one soul and

5   Giovanni Calò (1882-1970). Professor of pedagogy at the University of Florence from 1911 to 1952.
 • Jean-Jacques Rousseau (1718-1778). Swiss philosopher and social scientist. His most influential book is *The Social Contract* (1762).
 • Louis Albert Necker (1786-1861). Swiss scientist.
 • Ferdinand de Saussure (1857-1913). Swiss linguist. He is recognized as the founder of modern linguistics, and in particular structural linguistics.
 • Antonio Rosmini (1797-1855). Catholic priest and philosopher.
 • John David Saer, Frank Smith, James Hughes. *The Bilingual Problem*. A Study Based Upon Experiments and Observations in Wales. Aberystwyth, Hughes and Son for University College of Wales, 1924.
 • Izhac Epstein (1862-1943). *La pensée et la polyglossie; essai psychologique et didactique*. Lausanne, Payot et Cie, 1910.
 • Gonzague de Reynold (1880-1970). Swiss political philosopher and nationalist activist.
 • Jules Ronjat (1864-1925). French philologist. His studies focused primarily on Provençal and Occitan.
 • Luigi Volpicelli (1900-1983). Professor of pedagogy at the University of Rome.

that the other languages we know are just instruments. I observed often that Italian immigrants do not have two souls but two half-souls. They are able to speak neither the language of their fathers nor that of their children. I assume you and your husband are proud of your Italian culture. You can transmit it to your child with photos and books translated into English. Then, when he is 17 or 18 years old, you should send him to Italy to learn Italian in a course for foreigners. One of my principles is never to give advice, but this is a special circumstance and I believe there are no doubts about this. If you don't want to take it as advice, you can consider it a consultation. Free of charge, of course.

Sincerely,

New York, November 21, 1957

Dear Mr. Pagani:

While reading the *Giornale della Libreria* n. 18, 1957, page 128, I found a passage that concerns me directly:

> In a recent article [August 15,] by Giuseppe Prezzolini published in the Florence newspaper *La Nazione*, the famous writer—whose illustrious reputation is due to other pursuits—advised Italians living abroad against "teaching children Italian in addition to the language of the host country" because children and "young people" are not able to learn well two different languages at the same time. His conclusion is that it is better to teach only the language of the new country where the youngsters will grow up and build their careers.

Mr. Pagani, please calm down. I never wrote those words. I also have the impression you did not read my article directly, first of all because you do not mention the publication date. You probably read some interpretation of my words that were circulated by representatives of Italian immigrants not in a generic place called *abroad* but specifically in Argentina. According to those *smart* Argentine readers, I basically stated that "children and youngsters" should not learn a foreign language

---

6   *Il Giornale della Libreria*. It is the official organ of the Associazione tipografico-libraria italiana. It began publication in 1888.

and that only "old people" should. Mr. Pagani: I never wrote crap like that. Here is a brief summary of my article: "The majority of pedagogy experts, starting with Rousseau, believe that teaching two languages simultaneously to *children* under eight years old is harmful and creates confusion in their minds. *Foreign languages* should be studied only after the *national* language is well rooted in the mind. This opinion is supported by several studies (not all of them) conducted in bilingual areas such as Switzerland, Belgium and even China and Korea. The findings show that children before eight years of age who grow up in a bilingual environment have a lower IQ than their peers raised in a monolingual setting."

This concept apparently was too complicated for those Argentines who took it upon themselves to scold me with an interpretation that you, in turn, took at face value without bothering to check the original. The Argentines were happy with their misunderstanding and reported things incorrectly. I have a long experience with immigrants, not only in the United States and not only Italian. I am convinced that the experts are right. Of course, there are exceptions and I reported a very famous one, that of Montaigne. My article advised against the use of two languages during *childhood*. Parenthetically, I wonder how many Italian immigrants speak the *Italian language* that you so ardently defend as opposed to some crude dialect. The study of foreign languages is fine in middle school, not during nursery school or even elementary school. In most countries foreign languages are not taught in elementary school. The exceptions are those countries where bilingualism is a *political* issue. It seems to me you believe that our immigrants are still *Italian*. In this you are incorrect: in reality the large majority is composed of *citizens* of their host countries. Moreover, immigrants want their children to be respected and considered true citizens of the countries where they are growing up. They want them to be equal in everything, be it dating, doing business, working etc. My realism tells me that their natural language is not Italian; it is American English, Spanish, Portuguese, whatever.

I won't bother to discuss other statements in your letter because they are not directly related to my article. All I want to say is that, in my opinion, your arguments are pulled out of thin air and fit with the rhetorical strategy used to solving problems that one doesn't know how to solve. Your opinions on Italian immigration, on Italian schools abroad, on textbooks and so forth belong to that category. They are not based on reality. Believe me: if Italians abroad had been minimally united; if they had real knowledge of Italian language; and if they really had the will; they would have been able to open lots of Italian language schools even without the support of the Italian government. They would have done so with their own means and the support of the countries where they once were guests and where they now are in charge. Isn't it time that Italians abroad stop expecting the Italian government to do what they cannot do by themselves because they lack the will, knowledge and unity?

Yours "realistically," not "illustriously," because I am not illustrious among rhetoricians.

October 2, 1957

P.S. As I expected the *Giornale della Libreria* did not publish my reply. The editor of this periodical cannot read and when he makes mistakes he doesn't want anyone to correct him. But he wants to teach.

ITALIAN IMMIGRANTS IN AMERICA
ARE AGAINST EDUCATION FOR THEIR CHILDREN

I was researching the history of Italian immigration to the United States in Italian sources when I ran into a very interesting book, *Gli americani nella vita moderna osservati da un italiano* by Alberto Pecorini.[1] I remember that I first read it in 1911 when it was published by Fratelli Treves,[2] the leading Italian publishing house of that era. Back then I wrote a very favorable review and I probably corresponded directly with the author. The book is about fifty years old and I am afraid it won't last much longer as it was printed on wood-pulp paper and the pages crumble as one leafs through them. In these kinds of books the decay begins at the edge of the pages then spreads to the printed part and soon only dust is left. Pecorini's work is not a literary masterpiece and it is not a great loss that nobody will be able to read it fifty years hence. However, it is a very interesting eyewitness account, probably the most relevant text after the volume by journalist Dario Papa[3] which, in my opinion, was the first remarkable travel reportage from America by an educated and cultivated Italian not from consular ranks.

In those days Pecorini was well known in the Italian press community in America. It would take a picaresque writer to depict with appropriately colorful adjectives the condition of the other pigmy-like descendants of Pietro Sbarbato's [sic] *Le Forche Caudine*.[4]

---

1   Alberto Pecorini. *Gli americani nella vita moderna osservati da un italiano*. Milano, Treves, 1909.

2   *Fratelli Treves* was a prestigious publishing house, founded in 1861. In 1939, due to financial difficulties, the company was sold to industrialist Aldo Garzanti who gave it his own name in order to avoid controversies with the Fascist authorities with regard to the recently promulgated anti-Jewish laws (Treves is a Jewish name.)

3   Dario Papa (1846–1897). *New York*. Milano, Giuseppe Galli Editore, 1884.

4   Pietro Sbarbaro (1838–1893). Journalist and editor of *Le Forche Caudine* (1884-1885), a satirical magazine that regularly denounced corruption in the Italian parliament. He was found guilty of libel and served several years in prison. Prezzolini is making a rather obscure and sarcastic comparison between journalists working for Italian-language publications and Sbarbaro, who, in addition to great skills as a writer and satirist, was a man of great moral integrity. Prezzolini mockingly calls Italian journalists "descendants" of *Le Forche*'s tradition.

Pecorini deserves credit for being, or, better said, for trying to be a reformer in the community of Italian journalists in America, which was composed of a motley crew of mostly kooks, adventurers, crazy geniuses, blackmailers, weird-and-excitable exploited artists, some subversives, some nationalists, some anarchists, some half-doctors and some total failures. Regardless, they all were always eager to get into fights both with the pen and often with their fists to defend their ideals and attack those of others; always over the top and beyond the pale; with a tone of superiority that vastly exceeded the influence and the importance of the newspapers they were working for.

There are no archives of the close-minded press that mushroomed for decades until quality writers and editors arrived from Italy, such as Luigi Barzini Sr. and Italo Carlo Falbo.[5] More serious publications emerged when, finally, true professionals brought with them the highest standards Italy could offer.

With regard to Pecorini, I heard two different versions of his life. I wanted to check which one was true. I thus wrote to a relative of his and to one of his friends in Argentina where he died. Unfortunately, neither one answered my letters. It seems that Pecorini's mother was from Austria and his father was an Italian Jew. He came to America with a recommendation by Luigi Luzzatti,[6] studied theology at the Divinity School of Springfield, Massachusetts, and, according to one account, converted to Protestantism. Some sources claim that he sold the periodical *Il Cittadino* to the businessman Alberto Tarchiani,[7] but I could not verify the correctness of this information. (Incidentally, I remember that when I was editor of *La Voce*[8] I corresponded with Tarchiani.)

---

5   Italo Carlo Falbo (1876-1946). Journalist and politician. With Luigi Pirandello he founded the journal *Ariel* (1893-1933).

6   Luigi Luzzatti (1841–1927). Economist and politician. He was Italy's prime minister from 1910 to 1911. He is also considered the founder of the Italian credit union system (*Banche popolari*).

7   *Il Cittadino*. Italian language periodical published in New York (1907-1919).
   • Alberto Tarchiani (1885–1964). Journalist and publisher, he founded the weekly *Il cittadino* in New York. He later served as ambassador of Italy to the United States from 1945 to 1955.

8   *La Voce* (1908-1916). Weekly magazine of culture and social criticism founded in 1908 by Giuseppe Prezzolini and Giovanni Papini. Despite its short life, it is still

Pecorini's book is one of about two dozen serious accounts and reportages on America written by Italian visitors and travelers. In this case we are presented with observations and analyses based on real research. It is not clear how deeply Pecorini dug, but for sure at least he tried. My impression is that he combined research with direct knowledge of people and places, complemented by personal interpretations based on his biases and a general conceptual framework. That's a lot if one considers the times. In hindsight, we now know that there are methodological approximations in the interpretative framework of the statistics he reports (he gives no sources for them.) The book was written after the economic crisis of 1907[9] which was as serious as that of 1930.[10] His conclusions surprisingly contain very sound theories. The ideas may not be original, but, for sure, Pecorini was smart enough to choose the right ones. Here are some passages worthy of quoting:

> There is no other country in the world with a potential for continuous and abundant prosperity as great as that of the United States, for it is endowed with unparalleled natural resources, advantageous geographical position and vastness of territory. But it is necessary for the economic life to be regulated: it must stop being so tumultuous and without control. So far the United States has been similar to a person who, instead of eating regular meals three times a day, prefers to binge all at once and spend the rest of the day taking care of indigestion.

How many times have I heard this very same concept in the years after the 1930s depression? A hundred times? A thousand times?

One chapter is devoted to the conditions of Italian immigrants. It is a very sober and truthful summary that can shed light on some peculiar phenomena still present today even in communities of Italian descent that have been fully integrated into American life.

---

regarded as one of the most influential publications of twentieth century's Italy.

9   The financial crisis is also known as "The Panic of 1907." In the course of three weeks, in mid-October, the New York Stock Exchange fell fifty percent.

10   The reference is to the Great Depression whose beginning is usually dated in the year 1929, although it exploded in all its fury only a year later.

Ninety percent of the typical Italian colony in a large city is composed of laborers and their families. Fifty percent are illiterate and a third is comprised of newly arrived individuals who depend on contractors or middlemen to survive. One way or another, these people are systematically exploited by those they depend on. The remaining ten percent is made of individuals whose only interest is making money as fast as possible: small business people whose commercial activity is primarily the import of foodstuff for the *paesani* from their regions of origin in Italy; some bankers; travel and shipping agents and notaries public, most of whom so irresponsible and unscrupulous they would sign anything for money. The so-called community leaders could not be bothered with the social and moral improvement of the masses. They want to make money any way they can and spend the remaining time partying and dining. If the thirst for gold in Americans is a sad spectacle, among Italians it is totally revolting.

Today the situation is different for the better. However, the consequences of those beginnings are still felt. For instance, one of the least known aspects of Italian immigration was the opposition, or at least the indifference, of Italian parents to education for their children. The individuals who went to school and now constitute the middle class of professionals, doctors, lawyers, judges, senators and representatives don't owe their education to involved parents. Indeed, they owe it to American laws that made it mandatory for children to attend school (recently the age has been raised to sixteen) while making it illegal for them to work. Dario Papa was the first to notice it, and Pecorini confirms it:

An Italian boy who arrives in the United States at twelve or thirteen years of age goes to work with his parents instead of going to school, violating the provisions of the law. Very often parents lie about the real age of their children so that they can start working immediately, often in industrial plants, in dirty and unhealthy environments. The only things a child learns about Italy is the horrendous dialect spoken at home; the obscene words he picks up in the neighborhood streets; and the primitive reasoning and thoughts of his illiterate parents. He never sees an Italian book because nobody in his home can read. And then, when he grows up smart and educated he develops a sense of repulsion for everything Italian.

Pecorini didn't realize that the hostility by peasants from southern Italy toward education also existed in Italy. This was one of the causes (though not the main one) of illiteracy. Southern peasants had been afflicted by such poverty; by such need to get out of the brutal conditions of life; that their immediate instinct was to focus only and exclusively on making money. In America they ran into the American thirst for money that results from collective excitement and dynamism—the kind of excitement that extends to spending all the money earned or to invest it in risky adventures. This mentality merged with the hunger for money (which was hunger for bread) of Italian peasants with the significant difference that the first priority of Italian immigrants was to build a house for their families. Education was never considered a way out of poverty. The antipathy toward education can be seen in the fact that, especially in the older generations, the Italians who did go to school chose professional careers, such as medical and legal, that would lead to the exploitation of their clients. Very few of them chose careers in the sciences, which in those days promised only moral and idealistic rewards. Jewish immigrants, in comparison, made different choices. These observations came to mind while I was reflecting on a recent play, written by an Italian American policeman, titled *The Opening of a Window*. The author, Gene Radanò,[11] took as subject the story of a smart boy, from an immigrant Italian family, whose father did not want him to get an education. I found the root of this mentality in old books about immigration. Sometimes, it pays to look back to find the origins of things that are coming to the surface in our time.

New York, October 29, 1961

---

11   Gene Radanò (1917–2007). Police officer in New York City from 1946 to 1966. He was also a playwright, novelist and screenwriter for television shows. His play *The Opening of a Window* opened on September 20, 1961.

YES TO PARTIES, NO TO CULTURE

When I was appointed director of Columbia University's *Casa Italiana* in 1930, I tried to develop several initiatives for the Italian American community of New York City. It was a complete fiasco. A cursory review of my columns may give an idea of the cultural level and close-mindedness of Italians in the new homeland.

One of my first proposals was to pool together the financial resources of the many Italian American associations. I had noticed that every year these associations would compete with banquets, socials, balls and other events to attract donations from people of Italian descent whose collective wealth has increased significantly over the years. My idea was not a novelty in New York: the Jewish community was doing something similar, reflecting both its wealthier status and a much more modern mindset. They have long understood that it is pointless to waste energy in too many initiatives; thus, they created a committee to select a few but very relevant events worthy of support. The Italian consul agreed with my concept but nothing came of it. From the very beginning I noticed that my proposal of working together never drew any open opposition. However, it was received coolly and with a silent deliberation not to cooperate. In another case, I reached out to the local Italian language press proposing the creation of a collection of archival materials on immigration. There was no answer. Nobody was keeping mementos of personal immigration stories or those of their relatives. If anything, they were trying to forget.

Left to my own devices, I concentrated my efforts on an initiative that I cared about personally, namely the creation of scholarships for students of Italian in advanced college courses.[1] My logic was that it made sense to invest in them because any effort to improve the cultural and linguistic level of potential future teachers would be more effective than the encouragement given to high school students. A good teacher who had the opportunity to live in Italy for a few months, in the future would be able to affect hundreds of students. I was not interested in helping children of Italian American parents

---

1   Presumably, the scholarship was for education students.

pass a generic language test. I wanted to help the diffusion of Italian among non-Italian students. Indeed, to tell the truth, I thought it was more important to recruit students from other ethnic backgrounds. My ideas about this issue were not welcome: the local newspapers didn't even consider my proposals and continued to publicize the usual banquets and fundraisers to endow scholarships reserved for Italian American students. The only time I succeeded in gaining the support of Italian Americans was when I proposed the creation of a scholarship fund to send Columbia University students to Italy to improve their language skills. I organized a ball on one of the transatlantic ships of an Italian cruise line, generously made available free of charge by the owners. I charged much less than the customary ticket in order to make it possible for all members of the Italian American associations to participate; shoemakers and barbers included, not just the well-offs. It seemed that this time I hit the right note: more than four hundred associations joined and we collected 6,000 dollars.[2] The money was deposited in a special account where it is accruing interest until it reaches the 100,000 dollar mark. To honor the participants I called the account *Italian American Associations Fund.* I also suggested that these associations continue their contribution with a five percent surcharge on the tickets they sell for the lavish and endless colonial banquets they keep organizing. But nobody listened. Not only: the following year, when I proposed repeating the initiative, nobody joined me. I thus concluded that the so-called Italian American community lacks a sense of commitment and continuity. Most likely, the first time they were attracted by the novel concept of a low-cost ball organized on a ship, not by the goal of the initiative.

For several years I also dedicated my energies to the publication of a *giornalino*[3] destined for the schools where Italian is taught. At that time there were similar publications in French, German and even Latin; in addition to several ones in Spanish. The number of students of Italian in high school and college was high enough to support that

---

2   Most likely this is a typo. From the context, the correct figure is probably $60,000.

3   Literally, little newspaper.

kind of initiative. With the help of publisher Vanni,[4] I started working on this project but I soon realized that the teachers of Italian origin were very cold. The only ones who showed some enthusiasm were usually non-Italian. The two associations of teachers I contacted, one of teachers of Italian, the other of teachers of Italian origin, didn't want to have anything to do with it. One of my best students, who had in turn become a teacher, finally explained with great honesty: "Your Italian is too good for us." A few years later, the publisher and I decided to give up.

I also tried to experiment with music, to see if I could awake some interest in my fellow countrymen who, as legend has it, are musically inclined and have great musical taste. Together with Mrs. Perera, a well known and highly respected organizer of fundraising events, I tried to organize a *concertino* of Italian classical music. As long as the events were free, people showed up; but the moment we mentioned charging a small fee, nobody was interested anymore. Better luck had a choir, organized by Maestro Benelli, the brother of poet Sem Benelli.[5] The choir, dressed in traditional costumes, specialized in old Italian folk songs. In that occasion I noticed how far Italians have fallen from their traditions. Despite my efforts, I could not find even a single elderly Italian woman who had preserved a dress from the Old Country. We had to resort to photos in folklore books in order to have them recreated by a tailor. The only times the auditorium of *Casa Italiana* filled up (only 300 seats) was when we had performances by opera singers. Opera is the only artistic passion of the Italian American population.

Immediately after the end of World War II, when I was no longer director of *Casa Italiana*, in agreement with the new director and with publisher Vanni, I tried a bigger initiative, namely the publication of a special series of classical Italian texts with front translation. I was under the illusion that I would find support from a large Italian American association with many chapters all over the United States that every year organizes major gala events and very nutritious banquets. One of the top leaders, a banker that I thought was a very serious person,

---

4   S.F. Vanni is a publishing house located in New York City with a catalog of books in Italian.

5   Sem Benelli (1877–1949). Playwright and librettist.

made lots of promises. In order to develop the series, all the publisher needed were commitments for five hundred copies. The person who made the promises disappeared: his interests remained alive only the time to satisfy his vanity and be introduced to Eisenhower, who at that time was president of Columbia University. In the end we could not find one single Italian American family willing to purchase a series of twenty volumes of Italian classics with English translation. When I developed the project, I submitted it for revision and suggestions to five of the most important professors of Italian in the United States. Two of them, both Anglo-Saxon, approved it and promised they would help. The remaining three, Italian American, didn't even bother to answer. The publisher decided to try anyway.[6] He thought that once the volumes had been printed, the public would buy them. He published a new translation of the *Divina Commedia* in three volumes; the *Ricordi* by Francesco Guicciardini; the *Odi Barbare* by Giosuè Carducci and even the first complete translation of Ludovico Ariosto's *Orlando Furioso.*[7] The majority of those volumes is still languishing in a storage room in some dark basement.

My most recent experience with Italian Americans goes back a couple of years. By now Americans of Italian origin are almost completely absorbed into the mixture of races in the United States. Some families have been here for four generations. Starting with the

---

6   Library of Italian Classics. Disambiguation: a series with the same title is also published by Oxford University Press.

7   *La Divinia Commedia.* Translated by Harry Morgan Ayres. New York, S.F. Vanni, 1949.

• Francesco Guicciardini (1483– 1540). Renaissance historian and political writer. None of his books were published during his lifetime. His most famous work is *Storia d'Italia*, first published in 1561. *Ricordi.* Translated by Ninian Hill Thomson. New York, S.F. Vanni, 1949. Written over the course of several decades, the book was first edited and published in its present form in 10 volumes by Giuseppe Canestrini in *Opere Inedite di Francesco Guicciardini.* Firenze, 1857-1867.

• Giosuè Carducci (1835–1907). Poet. He was the first Italian to win the Nobel Prize for literature in 1906. *Odi barbare.* Translated by William Fletcher Smith. New York, S.F. Vanni 1950. *Odi barbare* is a sylloge composed between 1873 and 1893. The title refers to the topic of the collection, primarily the world of antiquity.

• Ludovico Ariosto (1474-1533). Poet. *Orlando furioso.* Translated by Allan H. Gilbert. New York, S.F. Vanni, 1954. It is the most famous chivalric poem of Italian literature, first published in 1532.

second generation the dominant language has been English and, with the disappearance of Italian, other surviving remnants of Italian culture are also being wiped out. I thought it was time to examine the outcomes of our immigration and compile a list of names and addresses of prominent people of Italian descent. I drafted the project of a *Who's Who* of Italian Americans, based on an impartial and rational approach. There are already two similar publications but they contain very few names, mostly chosen with sloppy criteria or for reasons of friendship and personal connections. We don't have yet any compilation with brief biographies of the names of, let's say, all the doctors; pharmacists; judges; members of prestigious orchestras; priests and so forth of Italian origin. My idea was to publish a catalog with at least 10,000 names, with regular updates. The concept was received with favor by Ambassador Manlio Brosio who supported it to the extent possible with the Italian American Chamber of Commerce [sic].[8] Several functionaries of the Istituto commercio estero (ICE)[9] and several Italian consuls in America also liked the idea a lot. However, not a single Italian American I presented my project to showed any interest. I mentioned that mine was not some kind of self-promotional effort, and in fact I was willing to do it without any compensation. Nevertheless, the Italy America Chamber of Commerce did not even want to talk to me—literally. This organization, which mostly comprises Italian American business people from New York City, regularly buys expensive advertisements in periodicals that nobody reads; and spends tons of money for social events that have nothing to do with commerce and trade. The leaders of the group didn't even think they should at least listen to my presentation before rejecting it. I remember that, later, one of the authorities who had supported my project asked me if I was disappointed that nothing had come of it. "To the contrary," I answered. "You see, I have the impression I made that proposal in hope they would say no." "What do you mean?" "Well, most of all I wanted final proof that Italian Americans, even the rich ones who are

---

8   Italy America Chamber of Commerce. Founded in 1887.

9   Istituto Nazionale per il Commercio Estero [Foreign Trade Institute]. Founded in 1920, it is the state agency of the ministry of economic development [Ministero dello sviluppo economico] responsible for the promotion of Italian export.

so full of themselves and their success, have not reached the American level. This is already evident in newspapers, books and speeches where they demonstrate an inability to come to terms with a wider and more modern perspective. With a few exceptions, they are close-minded, backward and provincial. They are like a self-enveloped cyst, closed to the most modern country in the world. They have climbed the ladder of wealth but not that of thought. They have risen because America has risen and the rise has brought them up, the same way a ship carries around the world the barnacles attached to her keel. And, by the way, this image is not mine: it comes from banker Giannini, one of the few who could actually say it because he was one of them."

The only initiative that has achieved a measure of success is the poetry festival. Every year New York public schools students of Italian recite Italian poems chosen by them or, unfortunately, by their teachers; and for their efforts they receive small gifts consisting of books, boxes of chocolates and cakes. This initiative costs nothing, doesn't bother anyone and only tickles the ambition and curiosity of those kids and their teachers. Probably this is the reason it's still going on. However, in the next pages you will be able to read my observations about this as well.

POETRY AS AN EMBALMED CADAVER

During my tenure as director of Columbia University's *Casa Italiana*, I had the unfortunate idea to organize an Italian Poetry Day and to invite all the New York schools where Italian was taught. Students and pupils would compete for prizes by reading Italian poems of their choice. Events like poetry readings and staging of contemporary or ancient plays in a foreign language are very common in American schools. The winners were to be selected by a committee composed of teachers whose students did not partake in the competition. The initiative was successful and continued for a number of years. I am not sure, however, how much it has contributed to the popularity and love of Italian poetry. My guess is that the students of Italian I had to listen to every year were not worse than those who acted in Molière's[1] farces in French or in Cechov's [sic][2] tragedies in Russian. It was in this context that I had a revelation. The poems, as is bound to happen, were obviously chosen by the teachers, not the students. And the choices were a window on those teachers' culture and taste. I remember distinctly that three particular poems kept coming up for years and years, recited by more than one student. These were, in order of preference: *La spigolatrice di Sapri* by Luigi Mercantini; *A mia madre* by Edmondo de Amicis; and a poem by the same title by Aleardo Aleardi.[3] How many times did I hear:

---

1   Molière (1622-1673). Stage name of Jean-Baptiste Poquelin. French playwright and actor.

2   Anton Chekhov (1860-1904). Russian playwright and short-story writer.

3   Luigi Mercantini (1821–1872). Poet and member of the Italian parliament famous for patriotic poems.

  • *La spigolatrice di Sapri* [*The Gleaner of Sapri*], his most famous poem was written in 1858 to memorialize a disastrous expedition of volunteers whose goal was to liberate southern Italy from Bourbon rule in 1857.

  • "A mia madre." *Poesie*. Milano, Treves 1881.

  • Aleardo Aleardi (1812–1878). Poet of the late-Romantic period.

They were three hundred, they were young and strong
and now they are dead.[4]

(La spigolatrice di Sapri)

I didn't count, but to me it felt like a thousand times and every time
it felt like nine hundred and ninety nine times too many. After these
poems, best sellers were the works by Giovanni Prati;[5] sometimes
Giosuè Carducci and, the most recent, Gabriele D'Annunzio. Among
the classics, the best known was *A Silvia* by Giacomo Leopardi.[6]
Clearly we were witnessing the literary stratification of the Romantic
period. The teachers who were showing off personal knowledge and
preferences through their students had, in turn, been taught by teachers
who had gone to school in Italy between 1880 and 1900 and were
exposed to poetry anthologies that reflected the sentimental choices
of those days. Nothing had broken the tradition. The poetical baggage
of those new teachers was the same as that of *their* teachers when
they were high school students in Italy. In the meantime in Italy
things had been evolving dramatically. Poetry had undergone great
changes with deep transformations. New sensibilities, new issues, new
sources of inspiration, new and different poetical languages had—and
have—recently emerged. The trauma of World War I hasn't had any
influence on these teachers; nor has the social transformation from
an agricultural to an industrial society; nor a different psychological
landscape and the absorption of realistic language into poetic expression.
In America everything has remained the same, as if fossilized. Not
even the most recent immigrants had brought with them the new
Italy. However, the aspect that struck me the most was the almost
complete impermeability of the teachers to *new* country, where many
were born and schooled; and where most of them completed their
studies in English and were exposed to Anglo-Saxon literature. At the

---

4 This is the most famous refrain from *La spigolatrice di Sapri*, a couplet that
practically every Italian knows by heart.

5 Giovanni Prati (1814-1884). Poet and senator.

6 Giacomo Leopardi (1798–1837). Poet and philosopher. He is universally
known as one of the greatest poets of Italian literature.
  • *A Silvia* (1828).

beginning of the [twentieth] century, Italy started absorbing literary experiences, styles and concepts from other countries. In the meantime, in the immigrant communities the patriotic and provincial taste and the languid and frayed vocabulary of Italian late-Romanticism[7] were still honored and preserved, like in a museum glass case. The poetry festival resembled the exhumation of embalmed cadavers.

In this as in many other cases, the image that came to my mind to describe Italian immigration (although, in all honesty, the image applies to other immigrations as well,) was that of a cyst, an image I used in previous occasions. A cyst is a blister of sorts that shows up in the body and surrounds itself with resistant tissue for protection. Cysts remain isolated and do not respond to the evolution and renewal of the surrounding tissues. Most of the times they are harmless and live on, until the body dies. The literature of the last gasps of bloodless and exhausted sentimental Romanticism will last until the death of Italian immigration; despite the fact that it no longer has any relation with the body of Italy and it is an anomaly even within the body of America, against which Italian immigration still seeks protection.

Other residues of this phenomenon grab the attention of Italians who visit the United States for the first time. These residues are the names of Italian associations that honor the likes of Giordano Bruno, Camillo Sbarbaro or Giovanni Bovio.[8] Or they can be on the shelves of an old bar where a yellow liqueur is sold, the *Galliano*,[9] something that takes me back to Italy's colonial wars in Africa before 1900. The festival of Italian poetry revealed to me the existence of a literary cyst

---

7 Romanticism was an artistic movement that emerged in Europe in the late eighteenth century. It emphasized the expression of individual emotions, passion and a fascination with the grieving soul of the artist. In Italy, literary Romanticism was closely related to the political movement known as *Risorgimento*. Late-Romanticism took the same themes and style and brought them to an extreme, becoming repetitive and bombastic, without genuine inspiration.

8 Giordano Bruno (1548–1600). Dominican friar and hermetic philosopher. He was accused of heresy and burned at the stake in Campo de' Fiori in Rome.

• Camillo Sbarbaro (1888–1967). Poet and translator from French and Greek.

• Giovanni Bovio (1837-1903). Philosopher, politician with republican leanings and member of the Italian parliament.

9 Sweet liqueur created in 1896.

that doesn't hurt anybody and that no doctor with common sense would recommend removing.

The literary cyst, present in Italian teachers, is identical to the literary cyst carried by the old wave of literate immigrants from the same social class. By old immigration I mean the stream that arrived before the great break of World War II. That hiatus constitutes an enormous abyss between the old and the new wave. In the first wave of the great migration, the educated immigrants brought with them the literary taste, level and style of that time; therefore, this is how they expressed themselves as soon as they were in the position to "make the presses squeal"—as we used to say before the linotype machine was invented. Today there are still several Italian poets in the United States who use the language of Aleardi and Prati. Isn't this an interesting phenomenon from a social, anthropological and folkloristic standpoint? There are daily and monthly publications that print these works. Here is, for example, a passage from the self-introduction to a poetry book. This is fascinating to me in that it is a mix of classical and American languages, in a total unselfconscious way, of course. Hear Ye, Hear Ye:[10]

> I am enamored of the old form and I abhor the extravagances that today [1931] pass for poetry, extravagances that deface the melodiousness and levity of Calliope's[11] divine art and tend to condemn the beautiful and harmonious Italian muse to a shameful decadence. I wrote what this soul of mine dictated with no sophistry or hesitations and without worrying about the poisonous arrows flung by jealous people and the eunuchs sitting in the first rows and high price theater boxes... I wrote for those who suffer like me, for those who know the cramps of hunger and the torment of seeing one's child cry for a miserable *penny*, for those whose heart is not petrified.... I abhor pedantic individuals because they have given nothing to the world; they are relentless naggers, repugnant orthodox who feign being scandalized at every chance they get, people who splash themselves in a stagnant pond; they cannot comprehend my verses, the same way they ignore the *speed-up* in the factories of America...

---

10   No bibliographical information is provided in the original text.

11   Calliope. The foremost of the nine muses. In Greek mythology she was the patron of eloquence and epic poetry.

And do you want to hear one of the poems of this enamored of the ancient form? I am selecting a passage that talks about the life of those who, like the poet, took the big step of immigration:

> And there they go! go! away, toward unknown
> shores, pushed by indecent fever
> for gold, always they are the eternal Helot[12] servants
> who only know of trouble and hunger.

Here is someone who probably really endured suffering and paid a heavy price, but that experience has triggered only trite clichés in his poetry. This immigrant carried some literature in his baggage and when he tried to say what he perhaps felt but could not express, he just repeated what he had read. When one examines the poetics, or, better yet, the versification that was born from immigration and was transplanted in America and survived like a cyst, it is incredible how little reality, how little novelty and sincerity it contains. There are dozens and dozens of poetry volumes whose publication is paid for by the authors themselves. They are a literary tragedy even more painful than the social ones they describe. In the passage I quoted above, the only hint of reality comes from the two English words: the child desperate for a *penny* and the technical term—which becomes poetic in this rhetorical context—of the mechanical cruelty of the *speed-up* ("quicker-or-you-are-fired"). The word *penny* that came out of his pen in America is an almost archaic expression, because generally the word used is *cent*; the child that cries for a penny takes on an almost mythical character. The *speed-up* sounds like the tyrannical order given by a supervisor. These two English expressions are more lively than the Italian. Curiously, in order to find expressions that are born from a poetic, non-literary spirit, one needs to search in popular songs.

If the so-called poets of the old immigration that are still alive should happen to read this article, god knows how much they would despise me. The paradox is that I respect and appreciate them for the love they kept for that kind of literature that cost them a lot of disappointments, sorrows and, I presume, money. In addition to the

---

12   Helots. A class of serfs or slaves in ancient Sparta.

unhappiness for being far removed from Italy's new sensibilities and expressive modes that were evolving in a different direction, they also were met by the silence of fellow immigrants who couldn't care less about their poetry; didn't even notice their existence and, naturally, didn't spend a dime to buy those volumes. As a result, these poets were pushed toward becoming lachrymose beggars and they now make for a curious chapter in the history of Italian immigration. They wanted to be poets in a language that is foreign to the country that took them in; they wanted to live off their poetry which, by the way, is no longer considered poetry even in their country of origin.

New York, April 8, 1960

ITALIAN AMERICAN POETS
ARE AN UNHAPPY BUNCH

Among the five million Italians who came to America looking for work, a few had some education—and wrote poetry. The Italian-language newspapers of those days regularly published their poems in every issue—a tradition that continues to this day. How many of these poets have seen their work published? Nobody knows. A detailed analysis would yield funny and even surprising results, but nobody has bothered to investigate because, frankly, not many readers would be interested in finding out how many individuals brought from Italy a baggage full of clichés, worn-out words and banal meters. Their survival, though, is an interesting phenomenon. It is similar to the phenomenon studied by biologists who observed that animals that are transferred to an environment with a different climate continue to give birth to descendants with unchanged characteristics, even if those characteristics do not serve any purpose in terms of sustenance and preservation. The environment apparently has no influence on them. This happens to humans as well. There are families of white people who migrated to Africa centuries ago who keep generating children with blond hair and blue eyes. The sun does not change those traits as the power of the seed is stronger than that of the environment. Residues of immigrations or of invasions from foreign peoples can be found, for instance, in the foothills of the Italian Alps, where small communities of Germanic people still speak dialects by now extinct in Germany. These Italian American writers are the same: they use a poetical dialect that nobody in Italy has used in a long time. The size of their production, published in America, is significant. There are many books, probably published at the authors' expense, that look like they came out of the presses of small, marginal printers. And now, there is a cottage industry of publishers in Italy, mostly unknown, who publish the works of the last survivors of the literary migrations. They take advantage of these authors who are willing to spend their hard-earned money in hope of gaining fame in Italy.

I am not referring here to Italians who ended up in America for a variety of reasons and published their work in American journals, as fiction writers like Nicola [sic] Tucci and Antonio Barolini; or political essayists like Giuseppe Borgese.[1] These authors are integrated in the American system and now enjoy good success and a loyal following. I am not even talking about the phenomenon of writers of Italian origin who are writing in English. This is a phenomenon that deserves attention in a different context and concerns writers who sprung out of Italian roots but whose thoughts and imagination are primarily American.

These others survive perpetually nostalgic, spending their own money to publish their work. In a poem dedicated to his unfortunate comrades, namely the "Italian poets in America," one of the most famous of them sang this song:

> Oh poets who came here
> To end your lives
> After living
> For many years in that desirable
> Land where the sun almost
> Always shines, and where
> Sweet love sparkles
> Deep in everyone's pupils
> I know you are oppressed
> And cannot find peace
> Because although you are messengers
> Of true Beauty
> Nobody listens to you here
> For here there aren't enough people
> Cultured enough to understand a cantor.
> And all those beautiful
> Rhymes that you write
> Pushed by the sublime inspiration that you know
> Are like flowers lost in the wind
> Stars that for one moment
> Shine in the firmament

1 Niccolò Tucci (1908--1999). Writer of short stories and journalist. He interviewed Albert Einstein for *The New Yorker*.

• Antonio Barolini (1910-1971). Poet and novelist. Some of his work appeared in translation in *The New Yorker*.

• Giuseppe Antonio Borgese (1882–1952). Writer, essayist and journalist. He was professor of Italian at University of California-Berkeley; Smith College, Northampton, Ma; and at the University of Chicago.

And then disappear in the darkness.

[O poeti venuti/ venuti a finir qui la vita/ dopo esser vissuti/ molt'anni in quell'ambita /terra ove il sol brilla /quasi sempre, e sfavilla/ in fondo alla pupilla/ /di tutti un dolce amor,/ io so che siete oppressi/ e non trovate pace,/ giacché sebbene messi/ della Beltà verace,/ nessuno qui v'ascolta,/ perché qui non c'è molta/ gente abbastanza colta/ da intender un cantor./ E tutte quelle rime/ belle che voi scrivete,/ spinte da quel sublime/ afflato che sapete,/ son fiori sparsi al vento,/ stelle che un sol momento/ raggian nel firmamento/ e spaion nel buio.]

I cannot fathom how, with all the real tragedies that immigration caused (about which the survivors feign amnesia and the dead keep silent), anybody one could also include the tragedy of poets, a supposed tragedy that consumed only paper and it spread—at least so I hope— more ink than blood and tears. There is something pathetic about a group of decent people who stuck faithfully to their love for what they claim are the pure Italian words. At a time when their language, or better yet, their dialects, were mutating into a barbaric mix contaminated by low-class English learned from the American plebes, they kept writing in grammatically perfect Italian, following the rhymes and the same identical century-old so-called poetical words, untouched by the changes that were taking place in Italy. At their core lies the rhetoric of the late-Romantic period, undisturbed even by the influence of more modern poets such as Carducci or D'Annunzio.

Italian-language poets were a deeply unhappy bunch, at least judging from the wailings of their poems and the introductions of their books. Actually, since many of them are still alive, they are still unhappy. Everywhere one can hear the same lament over and over: "Philosophy, ye poor and naked go"[2] (with the only difference that here it is not philosophy but poetry). I guess it was inevitable. These people grew up locked inside the mass of Italian immigrants who either spoke only dialects and couldn't read and write; or, if they could read, they didn't read books. On the other side they saw the masses of American

---

2 The quote is from a sonnet by Petrarch. *Canzoniere*, VII, *La gola e 'l sonno e l'oziose piume*. 1336- 1374.

natives, indifferent to what they called the "beautiful language of Italy" unless it was sung by opera singers. Their merchandise had no value in this country. Riccardo Cordiferro,[3] one of the best known and most appreciated practitioners of this trade and who, to this day, is held in high esteem by the members of this poetic tribe, in an article inveighed with epithets like "filthy, loutish, cheap" against the solid Italian businessmen who were making a lot of money trading chestnuts, olive oil and wine but would not buy their poetry books. It could be that those businessmen deserved the epithets for other reasons, yet I don't understand how and why importers of cured salami and tomato paste with a bit of the color and scent of Italy should have supported a literature that was alien to them, that nobody understood and that the host country didn't even know existed. It was not a product worth patronizing.

In Italy their poetic language had already disappeared. Books no longer swooned about "swallows that chirp about love" and "weave fair love-carols in the sky." You couldn't find anywhere in print "Hyrcanian tigers,"[4] "the deep maelstrom of sin," "fate that ridicules and threatens me," "hours of pleasure, days of inebriation." Really, were they dreaming of making money—by the hatful—in America—with this kind of imagery? Almost none of these poets had any contact with American schools. Some went through high school in Italy and called themselves *professor*, a title that enjoys very little consideration in Italy, particularly in the south, where even kindergarten teachers are called professor. Whatever the case, they never got regular jobs as teachers. I met many teachers of Italian in American schools and none of them, as far as I can remember, mentioned being a poet. They all used prose to write their idiocies, which is exactly what I do when I write my own idiocies.

---

3   Riccardo Cordiferro, (1875–1940). Pen name of Alessandro Sisca His *nom de plume*, translated as Richard Ironheart, is a clear reference to "Lionheart." He is best known as author of the lyrics of *Core 'ngrato* [*Ungrateful Heart*] (1911), one of the most famous Neapolitan songs.

4   Hyrcania in antiquity was a region along the southern border of the Caspian Sea. Hyrcanian tigers have long been extinct, exterminated by ancient Romans who used them in gladiator games.

* * *

Note: I want to immortalize the colonial bard Riccardo Cordiferro with a few quotations from his work because I don't want my readers to think that I am making things up. Italian provincial poetry, the kind that is published by the *Farfalla illustrata*, came to shore here and here it is preserved with mothballs in a museum glass case. And let's not talk about the cravings for publicity and praise pursued by these poets. Cordiferro, for example, in his own periodical reprinted press reviews of his work taken, respectively, from *Colombo* (Houston, Texas), *La Rassegna letteraria* (Palmi, Reggio Calabria) and *La Sentinella* (Bridgeport, Connecticut).

Here are a few lines from his sonnets. From "*T'ho troppo amata*" [I Too Much Loved You], first quatrain:

> If a Hyrcanian tiger ripped apart my chest
> And if it tore up piece by piece my heart,
> No, I would not sense as much pain
> As I feel, oh ungrateful one, in front of you.

> [Se ircana tigre mi squarciasse il petto/ e mi facesse a brano a brano il cuore,/ no, io non sentirei tanto dolore/ quanto ne provo, o ingrata, al tuo cospetto.]

Here is another example from "*Perché?...*" [Why].

> Why are you asking me for love rhymes,
> Why are you asking me for winged song,
> Now that a gelid tomb is my heart,
> Now that of my lyre broken are
> All the strings and mute it lies..?

> [Perché mi chiedi tu versi d'amore,/ perché mi chiedi tu canzoni alate,/ se una gelida tomba è questo cuore, /se della cetra mia si son spezzate/ tutte le corde e muta se ne sta?...]

Is it possible to imagine a collection of worse worn-out words, of falser feelings, of more banal rhymes; of a sentimental vacuum rendered even worse by the show of the ellipse, those infamous three dots, the ineffably romantic poetry's specks of dust that fell from the skies on those "love rhymes"; on those "songs" that, of course, are "winged"; over the tomb that had to be "gelid" and on the "lyre" (where could he buy it, if not from a junk dealer?) with, it goes without saying, "broken strings?" Why didn't someone grab a mop and do a clean up?

New York, June 26, 1960

NOSTALGIA FOR THE PAST: GIUSEPPE INCALICCHIO

This name jumped to my eyes twice in the last few days. It appeared below of a bunch of poetry lines in a local newspaper that is allegedly written in Italian. Just around that time, the same newspaper reported the arrival in New York of Giuseppe Ungaretti[1] with an interview and a photo. To be noticed: that newspaper had never previously published even a single poem by Ungaretti or any kind of articles about him. As far as I can tell, its readers know about Ungaretti just as much as I knew about Incalicchio[2] until that moment. Such was the situation when I opened my column for the November 15, 1959, issue of the weekly *Il Borghese*[3] with an ironic observation that stated: "I was shown an Italian-language newspaper with the photo of Ungaretti visiting New York. I wonder who told the newspaper that quenches[4] its readers' thirst for poetry with Giuseppe Incalicchio's verses that Ungaretti is a poet."

On January 5, 1960, poet Incalicchio wrote to the *Borghese* and the editor forwarded his letter to me asking if I wanted to reply. I answered that they should publish it without changing a single comma because that would be the best possible reply to himself. And so it goes that it appeared in the section *Small Mail* in the January 28, 1960 issue.

> Dear Editor,
> I am an occasional reader of Your magazine. In the number 48 issue, in the column *New York Diary*, Giuseppe Prezzolini mentioned my name. I shall premise that I don't know the above-mentioned individual, who, from what I can surmise, must be your correspondent in New York. In his column my name is mentioned in a comparison

---

1 Giuseppe Ungaretti (1888–1970). One of the most celebrated Italian poets of the twentieth century, representative of the movement called *ermetismo*.

2 Giuseppe Incalicchio (1889-1971). Poet.

3 *Il Borghese* (1950-1993). Political periodical with center-right leanings, founded by Leo Longanesi.

4 In the original: "*abbevera i lettori.*" In Italian the verb abbeverare [to water] is primarily used in association with animals. For plants, the verb is *innaffiare*. For humans, *dissetare*.

with the poets Giuseppe Ungaretti and Salvatore Quasimodo.[5] It doesn't take a genius to notice the sarcasm contained in the note about me. Most likely your Italian readers wondered: "Who is this guy, anyway?"

The answer is easy. I am one of the millions of immigrants who fifty years ago left Italy because in Italy there were no opportunities for us. And if in these fifty years I have been naïve and idealistic enough to cultivate, as best I could, Italian poetry, could you in all honesty say that this was a crime? (In reality, there is nothing worse and also more stupid than cultivating Italian poetry in this country.) Certainly, I never had the hubris to expect that my name would be glorified in the literary anthologies of my motherland. Frankly, believe me, I can do without such honor (?) Consequently, it is very hard for me to comprehend the obscure reasons that motivated your correspondent to mention my name. In any case, let's just forget about it.

In conclusion, dear Editor, please heed my curiosity. Isn't it true that the so-called hermetic poets represent a literary current that, when it's not conscious mystification of art, is nothing more than a manifestation of mental unbalance?

Sincerely,

Giuseppe Incalicchio

Staten Island, January 5, 1960

P.S. With reference to the Nobel Prize awarded to Salvatore Quasimodo, I have a question: did the Swedish government award the prize to an Italian poet because of the sinking of the ship *Andrea Doria*?[6] If that were the case, it wouldn't be the first time Italians are made fools of.

However, on January 27, 1960, ignoring that his first letter would appear in a later issue of the magazine, Incalicchio wrote again. I am publishing his second letter here for the first time.

---

5 Salvatore Quasimodo (1901-1968). Italian author and poet, winner of the Nobel Prize for literature, 1959.

6 The writer refers to the Italian ocean liner Andrea Doria that sunk on July 25, 1956, off Nantucket Island, after a collision with the Swedish ocean liner Stockholm. Forty-six passengers of the Andrea Doria and five of the Stockholm died in the collision. International investigations attributed the responsibility of the collision to the Swedish ship. The writer insinuates that the Nobel Prize for literature to Italian poet Salvatore Quasimodo was awarded by the Royal Swedish Academy as a sort of compensation for the maritime disaster.

Illustrious Editor:

As you know, Italians in America, in addition to reading almost all the publications that arrive from Italy, also read the magazine you so wisely edit, *Il Borghese*, which is probably more eloquent than others for its strictly literary content that eschews images and flashiness, two things that in these days are overused. I am one of those who read with interest *Il Borghese*, which, since I am not a subscriber, I purchase every week at one of New York's newsstands. Having said so, I want to share with you my surprise when I read in the issue number 48 a column by Professor Giuseppe Prezzolini that mentions my name directly, and more specifically: "I was shown an Italian language newspaper with the photograph of Ungaretti visiting New York. I wonder who told the newspaper that waters its readers with Giuseppe Incalicchio's verses that Ungaretti is a poet." With these words Eminent Professor Prezzolini obviously wanted to offend me because the term "to water" is used for animals when they are taken to the watering tank; and this definition does not bring honor to the pedagogue Prezzolini. The newspaper he alluded to is read not only by educated Italians but also by scholars of other nationalities who love our language; and is read by Prezzolini himself, who, otherwise, couldn't have found out about my poems; which, maybe, are not appreciated by him if he thinks he should compare them with those of his great friend Giuseppe Ungaretti with whom he had lunch, as he wrote in the first part of the same article. As to the newspaper in question, I am not the only one whose poems have been published there. The works of many other Italian Americans have also been published, and Prezzolini knows this very well. Why did he choose only me as his target to water his readers? Isn't this an obvious insult? Let him continue to write his overblown columns but tell him to leave me alone. My poems have nothing to be ashamed of when compared to those of Ungaretti and they would have nothing to be ashamed of compared to those of Prezzolini if he were a poet.

I would be grateful, dear Editor, if you should make public my complaint that objects to the arbitrary and less-than-noble utterances of the illustrious Professor Giuseppe Prezzolini.[7]

---

7 The translation attempts to faithfully reproduce the style and syntax of the original Italian text.

In the period between the first and the second letter, Incalicchio's mood and attitude changed. In the first letter, to him I was an "unknown," presumably "a correspondent for *Il Borghese*." In the second I became "Professor," indeed, "Eminent Professor." In his first letter, Incalicchio is an occasional reader of the magazine; in the second we learn that he buys it regularly at newsstands, although he is not a subscriber. To demonstrate his knowledge of the magazine, Incalicchio qualifies it as outstanding in term of its "strictly literary content"! In his second letter, Incalicchio asks how come I chose him as a target, and "only him" instead of the many Italian Americans whose poems are published in that newspaper.

I am more than happy to answer his questions. The meaning of my first note in the column was: there is a huge gap between Ungaretti's poetry and the poems that appear regularly in said newspaper. Given those standards, it is evident that Ungaretti's poems for the editors are worth zero; exactly as Incalicchio himself stated when he wrote that in his opinion hermetic poetry is the stuff of nuts or crooks. There is nothing offensive against Incalicchio in my words. Incalicchio's poems and the poems of many other people like him that appear in those sheets are regular poems, written in the poetic language we have been accustomed to for centuries. There are no dangerous innovations, there are no images that make one jump up and they require no effort to understand what they mean. Their meaning can only elicit approval on the part of the good and proper people who read them. The verses follow an order, metric rules are applied, all the words can be found in an Italian dictionary and they are always used with their conventional meaning. Incalicchio's verses, as well as those of his friends, march on like soldiers in a platoon at the orders of a corporal. In short, Ungaretti's poetry is the opposite of Incalicchio's. My note was not directed at Incalicchio. Rather, I was pointing out a contradiction in the newspaper that publishes his poems but had never mentioned Ungaretti even once before, and only became aware of him the day when he showed up in New York. Now Incalicchio asks me why I chose his name instead of that of another poet's whose verses appear in the same publication. Here is the reason why: in those days his name appeared twice in the newspaper. And I also liked the musicality of that name. I didn't know who he was and not even now do I have any idea who he may be. I chose him because of the frequency of his apparitions.

Not yet satisfied with the two letters I am publishing here, Incalicchio wrote yet another letter to a different magazine that had mentioned my column. And, to top it off, he wrote a poem about me, a poem that I really want to share with my readers. Here it is:

COMPARISON
(Dedicated to an illustrious pedagogue)
You are a brilliant and wise mentor
And I believe you were a student of Carducci;
You are a good writer and this brings you honor
And you enjoy the autumn sky.
You are famous for a book
About that Florentine secretary.[8]
We all know about your renowned acumen
And your vigorous Latin spirit.
Yet sometimes from so high up
You come down here and cast into a bad light
Those you don't believe are at your height
Of knowledge and you reduce them to nothing.
And if you are proud to be Tuscan
And as such you feel superior
You should know I am from Latium,[9] I am a Roman
And I have of Horace[10] the strength and good humor.
There was a time when your words didn't fail
To advise the love of poetry
The time when you were schoolmaster
And spoke about art and philosophy.
Now, I don't know why it came to you
To put my name in the note
You sent to the Italian people
Who, with reason, notice the beautiful and the ugly.

---

8 The reference is to Prezzolini's *Vita di Nicolò Machiavelli, fiorentino*. Milano: Mondadori, 1927.

9 Latium. Region of Italy with capital Rome.

10 Quintus Horatius Flaccus (65 BCE-8 BCE). He was the most acclaimed poet at the time of Emperor Augustus. His work *Odes* was considered the highest form of lyrical poetry.

That newspaper does not water people
With my flowing and exciting rhymes;
If anything, it delights them. That is the error
That you made: the first mistake
Of a Titan that is slowly dropping
From open hills toward the highplains[11]
And it seems indeed that in you is disappearing
Into vain dreams the genius of your early years.

[*CONFRONTI* -- Tu sei brillante e savio precettore/ e credo del
Carducci fosti alunno:/ tu scrivi bene, e ciò ti rende onore./ E ti
diletta il cielo de l'autunno./ Già sei famoso per quel tuo volume/
intorno al segretario fiorentino:/ tutti sappiam del tuo provato
acume,/ del tuo vigore e spirito latino./ Ma qualche volta pur da
tanta altezza/ scendi un po' giù mettendo in scarsa luce/ chi tu non
credi essere a l'altezza/ del tuo saper e a nulla si riduce./ Pur se tu
vanti d'essere toscano,/ e come tal ti senti superiore,/ sappi ch'io
son del Lazio, son romano/ ed ho d'Orazio forza e buon umore./
Un tempo non mancò la tua parola/ a consigliar d'amar la poesia/
e questo quando a capo della scuola/ d'arte parlasti e di filosofia./
Or, io non so perché ti venne in mente/ d'apporre il mio nome in
quella nota/ mandata a quella nostra itala gente/ che con ragione
il brutto e il bello annota/ quel foglio non abbevera il lettore/ delle
fluenti e fervide mie rime;/ si diletta, se mai. Questo è l'errore/
da te commesso, e son le pecche prime/ d'un titano che lento va
scendendo/ dai colli aprichi giù pei falsi piani;/ e sembra inver che
in te va scomparendo/ l'ingegno giovanil fra sogni vani.]

I probably overdid it with the narration of this colonial episode but
I thought my readers would find it useful to understand certain
phenomena of Italian immigration directly from written documents.
I don't believe it is possible to fake letters and poems like those of
Incalicchio. For this reason alone their value is incalculable.

I want to add that Mr. Incalicchio is wrong when he demands to
be "left alone." Writing verses, good or bad, is private business when
one keeps them in a drawer. Once they are published everybody has

---

11   In the original: *falsi piani*. Play on words: *falsopiano* (singular) means high
plains. The compound word is composed of *falso* [false, fake, phony] and *piano*
[plain.] By separating the two words the writer stresses the allusion to dishonesty.
The correct morphology of the plural word is *falsopiani*.

the right to critique them. By the way, I didn't even characterize them negatively. I only observed that a newspaper that publishes his verses most likely will ignore Ungaretti's. I didn't say that Mr. Incalicchio is a bigamous or a forger. I didn't even say that he writes poems identical to those that fifty years ago used to appear in *La Farfalla illustrata*. I just limited myself to comparing him with another poet. To conclude: I gave him the gratification of publishing his polemical prose and his satirical verses for a public that would have never read him. I did not change even a single comma. The readers will pass their own personal judgments.

New York, April 21, 1960

LETTER TO THE EDITOR OF
IL PROGRESSO ITALO-AMERICANO

To the Editor:

I was shown an article you wrote on October 23, 1958, about Columbia University's *Casa Italiana* where I served as director from 1930 to 1940. I know well its history and I am one of the few who has the courage to talk about it without fears. Your article is like a *corbello* [basket] full of a variety of inaccuracies and outright fabrications, which, according to the Italian dictionary, can be also defined as a bunch of *corbellerie* [howlers]. Allow me please to provide some examples. If you so wish, I could follow up with more, or, as the old saying goes, I could "tackle on to the foodstuff shipment."

You stated, for instance, that the *Società Dante Alighieri*[1] was housed in its quarters during the Fascist period and that the *Casa* degenerated into a propaganda agency. Now, the *Dante Alighieri* was never housed in *Casa Italiana*; it never even had an office on its premises, nor I believe it ever held a meeting of its board in those rooms. At most, it organized lectures, concerts and dances the same way as many other associations did, not only Italian and American, but, for instance, even Irish. In one occasion, during the colonial war in Ethiopia,[2] the *Dante Alighieri* had the gall to organize a lecture supporting the war, with an audience of about forty people. I personally threw them out and they never set foot in the *Casa* again. You should know these things because in those days the *Dante Alighieri* was directed by Dr. Italo Falbo[3] who is currently managing editor of the newspaper you are working for, which is also the same publication you were also working for at that time. Moreover, in those very days the *Dante Alighieri Society*'s headquarters

---

1 *Società Dante Alighieri*. Founded in 1889, it received a royal charter in 1893 with the mission of promoting Italian culture abroad. The Fascist regime turned it into a propaganda outlet. The United States government banned it during the WWII years.

2 Second Italian-Ethiopian War (also known as Abyssinian War), 1935-1936. Italy invaded and occupied Ethiopia deposing its emperor and imposing colonial rule.

3 Italo Falbo (1876-1946). Journalist. He was editor in chief of the Rome newspaper *Il Messaggero*. After moving to the United States he became editor of *Il Progresso Italo-Americano*.

was in Dr. Falbo's office, that it to say, right where your newspaper is. The *Dante Alighieri* had no official status as an association: it had no by-laws and no registered fee-paying members. It was basically Dr. Falbo's private business. What you wrote is even more bizarre since at that time the *Progresso Italo-Americano* openly supported the Ethiopia campaign and was a source of the kind of propaganda for which you blame *Casa Italiana*!

You also stated that at the beginning of World War II Italians were excluded from *Casa Italiana* ("The *Casa* was closed to Italians.") I can assure you that this is not true. I could give you a long list of witnesses to back me up. *Casa Italiana* remained open to everyone, Italians and non-Italians, and even to Black people. And how could *Casa Italiana* sort out Italians from Americans or people of other nationalities? After all, thank god, Italians aren't black or yellow. Were Italians required to hang a bell around their necks, like lepers in the Middle Ages? Or, maybe, should have they worn a yellow ribbon like Jews in Rome? Where did you see the edict that shut Italians out of the *Casa*? In case you were tempted to change the terminology stating that you meant to say "Italian Americans," not "Italians," that would be even worse. All Italian Americans always found open doors at *Casa Italiana*.

You also state that *Casa Italiana* "has finally reopened its doors" just because it has recently hosted the musical company of a friend of yours that performed *La Wally*.[4] Again, I can assure you that those doors were always open, except during the university-scheduled academic vacations. Since it looks like you wrote a couple of articles full of inaccuracies, I beg you to look up an Italian dictionary and choose an adjective that fits your work. You have also neglected to mention the main goal of *Casa Italiana*. First of all, the *Casa* was not "donated to Columbia University to host people looking for an oasis of peace, to nourish the spirit with the most beautiful things and elevate the soul toward the mystery of art, poetry and music," as you wrote. I have no idea where you found those swooning, cutesy words. Its goal is much more serious and, most of all, very clearly defined. *Casa Italiana* was donated to Columbia University by a number of donors in order to

---

4   *La Wally*. Opera by Alfredo Catalani (1854–1893). The opera had its première in 1892.

make available to the university a venue where the language, literature and history of Italy could be taught in a supporting environment. It was not created for singers, dancers and people in search of an oasis of peace. Rather, it was created for students who wanted to study, and, as a matter of fact, hundreds of students have gone through those halls. Some of them now teach Italian in American universities and colleges. Hundreds of dissertations on literature and philosophy have been drafted in those rooms. Here the *Repertorio bibliografico della storia e della critica della letteratura italiana*[5] was born, a work that is owned by the most important libraries in the world, and that you, I bet, so busy contemplating the "mystery of art," never looked up even once.

In the Italian magazine *Il Borghese*, Vol. 7, n. 47, I showed how *Il Progresso Italo-Americano* is written in an Italian language that is often ridiculous and false. I also exposed its poor quality: it's full of typos, layout mistakes, history and geography blunders. It's a slapdash job. Not long ago, I read the announcement of a banquet sponsored by an Italian American society in honor of an Italian general who "having enlisted as a private in 1915"[6] later became "commander of the Third and Fourth Army Corps." Apparently none of the editors realized that this was simply impossible. In reality the poor sap was a modest colonel who, as is customary, on the day of his retirement was promoted to the rank of general, but who never had the intention to steal the job from the duke of Aosta.[7]

This is the kind of disinformation you perpetrate against your readers in the belief that they must be much more ignorant than they really are. In the meantime you serve to the public swoony speeches like the one on *Casa Italiana* about whose past and present you know very little. On top of that, the little you know is all wrong. I am not going to lower myself by asking that my letter be published in your

---

5 Giuseppe Prezzolini; Columbia University. Council for Research in the Humanities. Columbia University. Casa italiana. *Repertorio bibliografico della storia e della critica della letteratura italiana dal 1902 al 1932*. Roma: Edizioni Roma, 1937-1939.

6 In 1915 Italy entered the war (WWI) that had started the previous year.

7 Emanuele Filiberto di Savoia-Aosta (1869-1931). Member of the royal house of Savoy, he was commander of the Third Army Corps in WWI.

paper as would be my right. I really don't care about what you write and I can live happily without a correction.

Devotedly yours,

New York, November 12, 1956

THE NEW LANGUAGE INVENTED
BY ITALIAN IMMIGRANTS IN AMERICA

Italians who visit the United States, when they come in contact with the second or third generation immigrants' descendents, are often puzzled, stunned, and sometimes horrified by the language used by people they consider Italian like themselves. It is the same reaction experienced by visitors, journalists and consular employees who arrived here decades ago. The language they heard was not Italian; it was not a dialect of Italian and certainly it was not English; but a hodge-podge that contained a bit of Italian and a bit of dialect (which varied with the geographical origin of the individual), built over a foundation of English pronounced the Italian way, with a rounded vowel at the end of each word. Examples: *contrattore* [contractor], *tracca* [track], *picco* [pick], *grosseria* [grocery], *bordante* [boarder]. Their surprise grew when they found the written version of this lingo[1] (often with many variations) in restaurant menus, classified ads in newspapers and even in official documents drafted by American authorities who wanted to make sure they were understood by Italian immigrants. A couple of examples are *scalloppini* [it should be *scaloppine*] and *tailors of cotti* [coats]. The language of Italian Americans, therefore, is composed of a series of distortions of English rather than the Anglicization of Italian. This was clearly the result of an effort by a mass of poor, ignorant peasants who wanted to communicate with foreign-language workmates and with the bosses their livelihood depended on. It wasn't a spontaneous, poetic language that individuals developed for themselves. It was a form of forced communication, similar—if I may use this comparison—to cooking food in a pressure cooker that readies a meal in a few minutes instead of hours.

An analysis of the words of this lingo easily reveals that it contains

---

1   The author uses the word *gergo* which normally is translated with *jargon*. As linguistics and in particular dialectology have evolved in the last fifty years, the definitions of these technical terms have also changed. In English *lingo* reflects the casual nature of a language used for every-day informal exchanges, while *jargon* is used to describe a highly specialized language dense with technical terms with fixed value used in a particular sector of human activity.

mostly nouns. A small percentage of adjectives are also present but with much lower frequency than in Italian or English. In shaping this language the immigrants satisfied the urgency of their communicative needs. We find: *pezze* [pieces, meaning dollars], *bosso* [boss] and *olivetta* [elevated railroad]. But we don't find words for *good, beautiful, true, false, right, wrong*. At most we see *orrè* [hurray], a cry heard in theaters or stadiums to express emotional admiration; and *naise* [nice], a positive evaluation. The need to find and keep a job and the pressure to earn money explain the structure, dictionary and intonation of this *interlingua*.[2] The lexicon is functional and pragmatic, containing just a list of nouns. There are no adaptations or transformations of words that convey emotions or subjective evaluation. Those who hear it, after a while can pick up a certain tone of disdain, spite, rancor and revolt: the Italian ear doesn't respond favorably to it because the words contain something harsh and broken and, often, forcibly hard-pushed. Even love is presented as a physical function; different from the role it has in Italian dialects where it occupies a preeminent position in popular poetry to express emotions even deeper than those of the literary language. Here it becomes less spiritual and more materialistic, betraying a sense of hostility toward non-Italian women who are described as mocking and taking advantage of immigrant males. The *ghella* is far removed from the concept of *girl* and even more from that of *ragazza*. To be noted is also the linguistic phenomenon called *phonetic adaptation* whereby, when a foreign word enters a language, speakers find in their own language a word with a similar sound. The speakers' native words lose their original meaning and adopt those of the foreign words, thus changing the former original meaning. This is how *shovel* became *sciabola* [in Italian it means saber] and the worker that uses it is a *sciabolatore* [in the sport of fencing *sciabolatore*

---

2   *Interlingua.* The author uses this term to describe the phenomenon of an intermediate language in which elements of the source language and the target language are present simultaneously, as in a sort of linguistic purgatory. A more precise term, depending on the state of refinement of this intermediate language would be *Pidgin* or *Creole*. In strictly technical and linguistic terms, *Interlingua* refers to an artificial language, similar to Esperanto, based on Romance languages, whose development began in the 1920s.

is *sabreur*, a swordsman with a saber.] *Elevated railways* became *olivetta* [little olive], *tunnel* became *tonno* [tuna fish], later replaced by *tubo* [tube]. *Mulberry Street*, the center of New York's Little Italy became *Mòrbeda*, with obvious phonetic assonance with *morbida* [soft]. The town of Hoboken, in New Jersey, morphed into *Obocchino*, resonant of *bocchino* [cigarette holder]. At the top of them all is *Broccolino*, that transforms *Brooklyn* into a vegetable [small broccoli.]

A curious phenomenon, albeit rare, is the imitation of English words such as *officer* that, converted into the immigrants' language, became *ufficiale*. Presently, in Italian the noun *ufficiale* is used only to define the highest range of military ranks. Interestingly, by extending the meaning to cover functionaries and elected office-holders, the word reverted back to the original Italian meaning, with a semantic value similar to that of contemporary English. It thus has the appearance of a thirteen century Tuscan term rather than a nineteenth century foreign borrowing: instead of being lifted from the pages of the *Progresso Italo-Americano*, it looks like it was taken from Dino Compagni's *Cronica*. [3] Not to be mistaken: the members of Italian associations that use this term are unaware of its history and evolution. They saw it in English-language newspapers or in the bylaws of American associations and they copied it as it was.

At times the marriage of Italian and English is steeped in dialect, as in the case of *coppetane* ['ncuop + town]: *'ncuop* literally means on top, above, over; and it designates the section of town that is *up*. Thus, *coppetane* designates New York's *Uptown*. This, at least, is the Neapolitan version. Sicilians say *oppitani*, with a different phonetic rendition of *up*. Regardless of the version, it all feels chopped up, stuttered, maltreated and minced. Another noticeable phenomenon is the disappearance from the lingo of words that are no longer needed. For example, since sanitary conditions have improved over the years and new buildings have indoor plumbing and bathrooms; the word

---

3   Dino Compagni (ca. 1255–1324). Florentine historian and politician. He wrote *Cronica delle cose occorrenti ne' tempi suoi* [*Chronicle of Events Occurring in His Own Times*] between 1310 and 1312. He never published his work in fear it would bring retaliation for his provocative and sharp opinions about contemporary Florentine political figures. The manuscript remained hidden until the late fifteenth century.

baccauso [backhouse, outdoors latrines in the back of the house] has disappeared.

In a few generations this entire terminology will be gone as the few new immigrants who are still arriving face different conditions. In Italy they learned the grammatical foundations of Italian and here, as soon as they go to school and learn English (adults included), they are the first ones to be horrified by the rough linguistic mixture used by the old immigrants. This difference in linguistic sensibility first appeared between two groups of immigrants separated by the historical landmark of World War II: those who arrived before 1940 and those who emigrated after 1945. This also marks the abyss that exists between these generations. The fact that these two don't speak the same language represents one of the most important phenomena in the history of Italian immigration.

It is also important to notice that in the field of journalism two different trends developed after a protracted struggle. At the very beginning, Italian-language dailies and periodicals were written and edited by professionals who came from Italy and who knew Italian quite well. Approximately after 1900 the innovation of classified ads was introduced and it became impossible for editors to hide or translate into proper Italian the lingo created by Italian American workers. Leafing through the newspaper *Bollettino della Sera* of 1917, I found classified ads containing words like *giobbisti* [jobbers], *pressatori* and *sottopressatori* [pressers, pressers' helpers], *operatori* [operators] and *sceperi* [garment shapers]. I also found announcements for a *mezzo-giovane*,[4] *mezzo-sciainatore* and *mezzo-barista*. *Mezzo* [half] stands for part-time; and the jobs respectively refer shop helper, shoeshine and bartender. A farmhouse is always a *farma*; the trolley is the *carro elettrico* [electric wagon] and heat is *stima* [steam], whence the frequent and involuntarily ironic announcements about houses for sale *without stima*, i.e. without appreciable value.[5]

---

4 *Giovane* literally means young. The full context of this word is *giovane di bottega*, shop apprentice, usually the youngest person in an artisan's shop who is still learning the trade.

5 *Stima* in Italian means appraisal, estimate, but also good reputation and admiring respect.

Today the situation is quite different. In the classified ads of the *Progresso Italo-Americano* those expressions are almost gone. The old generation that still uses them has retired with nice pensions and their children—comfortable and secure in society—no longer need to look for jobs in the pages of Italian-language newspapers. The most recent immigrants from Italy looking for jobs speak a decent Italian and don't need to read the announcements translated into the old lingo. Nobody looks anymore to buy or lease a *fruttistenne* [fruit stand]. At the same time words like *bar* and *barista*[6] are now commonly used in Italy. Even the newly-arrived *grignollo* [green horn] knows them.

The ignorance of English words assimilated into Italian created a doubling of the meaning as, for instance, in the case observed by linguists of the word *canabuldog*. This word reproduces the Italian duplication in *cane bulldog* [dog bulldog].[7] By the way, because of phonetic preferences, Florentines call it *cane busdroghe*. The same phenomenon appeared in Sicily during the Arabic domination of the island,[8] with the creation of the toponymies *Mongibello* (in Arabic *Gebel* means mount, therefore *Mongibello*, crasis of *Monte Gebel*, means *Mount Mount*); and *Porto di Marsala* (*Marsala* means *Allah's port*: the literal meaning is *Port of Allah's port*). The most recent repetition/duplication[9] that has spread all over America is *pizza-pie*, which, translated into Italian, means *pizza-pizza*. This term is not having much success in advertisement or in store signs, although it is very common in everyday language. It should also be noted that in the last

---

6 Curiously, the word *barista*, an Italian neologism created on the root of the American word *bar*, has crossed the ocean in the opposite direction and is now used in the U.S. to identify a person working in an Italian-style coffee shop.

7 Translator's note: term *canabuldog* results from the crasis of different lemmas, namely *cane a bulldog*. The preposition *a* in Italian indicates the distinctive property of an otherwise generic entity. For instance, Italian uses "*barca a remi, barca a motore*" to indicate respectively *row boat* and *motor boat*. The same applies to flavored foods or particular styles to indicate "in the manner of." In these cases the preposition *a* is followed by a definite article. We thus have: "gelato *al* limone" [lemon-flavored ice-cream], "pasta *alla* puttanesca" (no need for translation here).

8 The Arabs invaded Sicily in 652 CE. Sicily was an emirate (state) with capital Palermo from 831 to 1072.

9 The technical term in linguistics is "pleonasm."

decade, starting around 1950, Italy's improved economical conditions and the stream of American tourists who visit Italy along with the considerable amount of imported Italian products to the United States, from craft to advanced manufacture, have injected new genuine Italian words into English. For instance, the word *pizza* is winning the battle against *pizza-pie* and stands by itself against the English duplication.

And now it is time to ask: what kind of footprints will be left by this half-a-century-long linguistic torment? I have reported only a fragment of the information that was collected by linguists like Arthur Livingston, Alberto Menarini and Samuel Scalia; or by observers like Dario Papa, Adolfo Rossi, Amy Bernardy[10] and other visitors to the United States who became familiar with Italian immigrants. From the literary standpoint maybe the only traces left by the lingo will be the ironic intonation, the caricature and parody by a few who "stooped down" to listen to that "horrendous speech" and took a look at the "monsters"[11] generated by cross-breeding the English language with Italian dialects. The scions of Italian bourgeoisie educated in Italian lyceums, practiced their satirical vein by making fun of the ignorant *cafoni* and their primitive language, thus following in the wake of a long tradition of writers from the beginning of Italian poetry to this very day, from Ciullo d'Alcamo to Renato Fucini.[12] The Italian America

10   Arthur Livingston (1883-1944). Professor of Romance Languages at Columbia University, translator and curator of several works from Italian. He investigated the language of immigrants.

• Alberto Menarini (1904-1984). Linguist and author, he was awarded the Laurea Honoris Causa from the Università di Bologna in 1984.

• Samuel Eugene Scalia (1900-1986). Professor of Italian at Brooklyn College (and father of the late Supreme Court Justice Antonin Scalia).

• Dario Papa (1846-1897). Journalist, author of *New-York* (Milano, Galli, 1884); *La donna in America* (Milano, Aliprandi, 1889).

• Adolfo Rossi (1857-1921). Journalist, author of *Un italiano in America* (Milano, Treves, 1894).

• Amy Bernardy (1880-1959). Author of several books on Italy and Italians, among which *Italia randagia attraverso gli Stati Uniti* (Torino, Bocca, 1913).

11   "Stooped down," "Horrendous speech," "Monsters": these terms are direct citation of comments by the above-mentioned authors.

12   Cielo d'Alcamo, also known as Ciullo d'Alcamo. Thirteenth century Sicilian poet and satirist. Only one poem remains: *Rosa fresca aulentissima* [*Most Fresh and Scented Rose*].

lingo was not even adopted by Italian American novelists who staged their works in the milieu of family life. At most, the lingo appears in bits and pieces only as a device to add local color to the stories.

P.S. Mr. Angelo Ricaldone from Biella, Italy, wrote to tell me about his experience in Australia. As I suspected, he confirmed that Italian immigrants in Australia did the same thing by creating a new lingo. He supplied the following examples. A mother yells at her daughter who is running on the front yard: "*Non andare lì che spogli la grassa.*" [Meaning: Don't go there or you will spoil the grass. Literal translation of *spogli la grassa*: you will undress the fat woman.] Two friends are talking and one describes his relax activities: "*Siedo in giardino e rido il buco.*" [Meaning: I sit in the backyard and I read a book. Literal translation of *rido il buco*: I laugh at the hole.] The old Italian immigration to America didn't even have *rido il buco* since they were illiterate, unlike the immigration to Australia that took place after World War II.

• Renato Fucini (1843–1921). Poet, essayist and novelist he is best known for short stories set in rural Tuscany.

SPEAKING ITALIAN, DREAMING IN ENGLISH

In the previous chapter I tried to describe the lingo, the language-by-necessity, used for a long time by Italian immigrants in the United States. That language is slowly disappearing. The second and third generation descendants of those immigrants grew up speaking English while the new immigrants who arrive from Italy today have a better knowledge of the Italian language and tend to learn English rather quickly. One of the interesting aspects of this lingo was that it comprised only few words, mostly nouns, with a small amount of verbs and almost no adjectives. Generally the words were formed from English terms with a vowel attached at the end. The English phonemes were approximated to the corresponding inventory of Italian sounds. Sometimes the words were assimilated into existing Italian words, changing the latter's meaning. In a way this language was forced onto the immigrants rather than being the product of their creativity. In 1889 Edmondo de Amicis, in the short essay *Sull'oceano*,[1] noticed this phenomenon among the immigrants who had moved to Argentina:

> What a strange vocabulary! I heard a sample of the strange language spoken by our folks in Argentina after they had mixed with the local population and with other Italians from different parts of the country. Almost all of them had lost a chunk of their dialects, acquired a bit of Italian and mixed Italian and dialect with the local language, adding vernacular suffixes to Spanish words and vice versa, with literal translation of idiomatic expressions from the two languages. As a result, in the new language these words and expressions took on a new meaning, so that these people ended up speaking what feels like four languages in one sentence simultaneously, jumping from language to language as if they were insane.

Similar descriptions also come from North America with an abundance of examples reported by Italian journalists and writers who observed and wrote about the immigrants. From this coarse, incomplete, totally concrete language no important literary works emerged. Those who had received some education in Italy before emigrating continued

---

1 *Sull'oceano*. Milano, Fratelli Treves, 1889.

to write the way they had been taught, as if they had been kept in a glass cabinet in a museum. Their language style was taken directly from the late-Romantic period, steeped in sentimentality and vacuity. The tradition, by the way, alas, is still alive and well and present to these days in the schools where Italian is taught. (At the latest poetry-reading competition at *Casa Italiana* two of the readers chose poems by Aleardo Aleardi!) They were using this dusty, sap-dripping language at the same time as they were looking down on the new choppy dialect, mocking it at every possible occasion and targeting it with ridicule, thus perpetuating the other eternal Italian tradition, that of making fun of peasants. More about this later.

Meanwhile, the new generations—the American children of Italians—began communicating and expressing themselves in English, both in poetry and prose. Some of these writers, in addition to using the Italian American dialect to give local color to childhood memories, became aware of the linguistic contrast that existed between themselves, fluent English speakers, and their parents who, due to a total lack of cultural consciousness about their language, were losing the original dialect and were not able to acquire English; with the sad result that they were uneasy and embarrassed in both languages. There are accounts of this stage that are worthy of examination. Jerre Mangione, a second generation American, born in Rochester, NY, in 1909, is one of them. His major work is *Mount Allegro*,[2] the name of one of the Italian neighborhoods in Rochester thus named by a large community of Sicilians, many of whom still live in the area. It probably is the name of some hill in one of the hometowns[3] on the native island. The volume is autobiographical, a rather common genre among American writers growing up in ethnic communities who turned to the folkloric material that could capture the interest of American readers. The memoirs of the Swedish-origin poet Carl Sandburg[4] are

---

2   Jerre Mangione (1909-1998). Writer of the Italian American experience.
• *Mount Allegro*. Boston, Houghton Mifflin, 1943. The publisher decided to market the book as fiction rather than as an autobiography.

3   *Montallegro* is a small town in the province of Agrigento in Sicily.

4   Carl Sandburg (1878-1967). Poet and historian. The child of poor Swedish immigrants, he won the Pulitzer Prize for poetry in 1951 and again in 1959 for history.

another typical example of this genre. This kind of works should be analyzed from this perspective.

As soon as he entered school, Mangione realized he was living a "double existence": he had to speak English in school and Sicilian at home. Like in many other cases, his mother was the agent of conservation of language and old traditions. Mangione had to hide when he wanted to read books because his parents believed that too much reading could be harmful to the child's brain. More than once have I read about the hostility of Italian parents toward educating their children. They preferred that the children started working as early as possible to earn money. My analysis isn't based on the details of Mangione's experience; however, it is interesting to read that the first time he went to Sicily, the mythical land described with vivid and fascinating images by his parents, he was struck by two visions: the poverty of the people and the nakedness of the landscape (I understand him so well!) Moreover, he was struck by the fact that the Sicilian language he was speaking could not be understood by Sicilians. The words that were coming out of his mouth, taught by his mother, were not Sicilian. They were Italian American. At home Mangione was not allowed to speak English. His younger sister, Maria, in her dreams would speak English but she was excused because dreaming was not a conscious act. His mother had learned unconsciously a basic vocabulary of English words with Italian endings that had become some kind of family lingo. As a boy, Mangione realized that when fellow Sicilians met for the first time, they would start communicating in Italian, but, as soon as they learned their respective origins, would instantly switch to Sicilian. Someone who insisted on speaking Italian would be considered pretentious or "a socialist." From early on, Mangione had a very fine ear. He realized, for instance, that Sicilian language has no unity, in that there are many intonations and dialects depending on the area.

> Relatives whose origins were from Sicilian cities on the coast, like my father, spoke as if they were shooting their words against the wind or through fog, with a sharp singing accent. People from the center of the island spoke as if they had never heard happy music. Their language was heavy with funereal and massive sounds.

This is a very beautiful musical description. His parents did not have serious problems living their lives in America, despite the fact that his father spoke barely-comprehensible English and his mother had learned only a few words from her children. Except for the *bosso* [boss] who was an English speaker, all their co-workers were Italian and Italian was the language spoken in the stores. It so happened that one day the *bosso* figured out what Mangione's father was saying in Italian about him and fired him. An uncle of his who knew even less English used to tell a story from his first days in Rochester when he had to deal with non-Italian storekeepers who could not understand a word he was saying. Nobody wanted to sell to Italians and nobody wanted to rent rooms to them. One day, having lost all patience, his uncle gathered a group of people and, brandishing pickaxes, engaged in a demonstration in front of the shop; explaining with gestures that they were hungry and wanted a place to sleep. The demonstration, supported by the presence of pickaxes, impressed the locals. The storekeepers changed policy and town hall provided Italian workers with some habitations. As I was reading these true stories about immigration—the kind of stories one does not hear during today's colonial banquets—I thought about the philosopher Gianbattista Vico[5] and his theory according to which, before developing an oral language, humans were communicating with a gestural language. The Italian American word that struck Mangione most deeply was *baccauso* [backhouse], one of the words that are rapidly disappearing because backhouses no longer exists, replaced by bathrooms built inside living quarters.

The word that struck Anthony Turano the most was *morgheggio* [mortgage]. Born in 1894 in Calabria, he was a lawyer and writer of social and juridical essays.[6] He ran into this word when a judge asked for his help in translating a letter written by a poor immigrant. Turano took his time and finally figured out that the word meant mortgage, the English word for the Italian *ipoteca.*[7] This brings back

5   Giambattista Vico (1668-1744). Philosopher, historian and jurist.

6   The 1940 U.S. Census lists one Anthony Turano—born in 1894 in Italy—as living in Reno, Nevada.

7   Modern Italian now uses the word *mutuo.*

to my memory the confusion of a court interpreter in New York who, during a murder trial, had to translate the testimony of a witness who was testifying that he had seen the criminal near a *sciocchezza*. The word in standard Italian means foolishness, but the witness meant showcase, as in store window. Turano observed correctly that the large majority of Italian immigrants were peasants who had to face an industrial reality. Ignorant of the Italian terminology, they were forced to use English terms in order to express their needs. But, for the words to fit in the flow of their language, first they had to be converted phonetically into the closest thing that sounded like their language. Turano divided the English words that had been transliterated into three categories. The first refers to things outside the immediate realm of reality, terms such as *sexa* or *sescia* [section], referring in particulars to railroad rails. Other words of this kind would be *rancio* [ranch], *rodomastro* [road master], and so forth. The second category covered words referring to entities unknown before the immigration, things such as the *morgheggio* or *lista* [lease] and *fensa* [picket fence]. The third, finally, listed words the immigrants were hearing constantly around them, despite the fact that Italian words for those entities did exist and they were rather common: *stritto* instead of *strada* [street], *carro* instead of *automobile* [car], *denso* instead of *danza* [dance]. He observed that, once the word had been formed and accepted, it would follow Italian grammatical rules. If it were a verb, it would be conjugated, as in the case of *faitàre* [to fight]. All these observations, interesting as they may be, are rather empirical and approximated, particularly for what pertains to the semantic analysis. Probably it has to do to the fact that Turano was an Italian American who first went through the lingo phase and only later acquired English. Some of the examples are not exactly correct, as is the case of *tomate* [tomatoes]. The adoption probably was facilitated by the presence of immigrants from some regions of northern Italy where tomatoes [in Italian *pomodoro*] are called *tomati*. In 1932, the year of his writing, it wasn't difficult to realize that, as a consequence of the reduced immigration flux, the Italian American lingo was destined to undergo further bastardization and Americanization. Turano, correctly, predicted that it would eventually disappear. No Italian American writer has felt the compelling urge to write an entire book in the language of his youth. Despite the fact that probably they still remember it quite well, they only use it in their narratives as tiles of realism. Interestingly, there is only one poetry book written in a language that wants to reproduce the Italian American lingo without turning its speakers into caricatures, as was instead the case with Neapolitan singers when they came to perform in New York theaters. Even more interesting is the fact that that the book was written by an Irish.

New York, April 29, 1962

CARNEVALI AND OTHER ITALIANS
WHO WROTE IN *AMERICANO*

The group of people who gathered around my journal, *La Voce*, myself included, had a friend in Emanuele Carnevali,[1] despite the fact that we didn't know he existed. I first found out about him in 1950 when I happened to get my hands on a rare publication of his critical writings and poems. The volumes, strangely, were not published in the United States but in Paris, around 1925, by a small house, Contact Editions,[2] located in one of the most beautiful spots in the French capital, the Isle Saint Louis on the Quai d'Anjou. This was the time of the expatriates, a small group of American intellectuals who ran away rather than facing the materialism of their country, and ended up living in Paris. Here they basked in the illusion of the false liberation of American prose; with the promises of the phony *Bohème* of the *Rive Gauche*,[3] where they set camp; protected by the fistful of dollars they, for better or for worse, were getting from the materialistic motherland.

The little volume that collects whatever is left of Carnevali's production is 268 pages long and was edited by Dorothy Dudley.[4] Her meritorious work exempts us from having to rummage through the pages of small journals like *Poetry, The Little Review, Others, The Lyric, Youth, The Modern Review* and so forth. Carnevali, the introduction tells us, was a very smart child who grew up without a mother and an indifferent, absent father. After leaving Italy, he lived in New York and Chicago for eight years, leading a miserable and rudderless existence,

---

1   Emanuel Carnevali (1897–1942). Emigrated to the United States at sixteen, he started writing poetry and became very well known in avant-garde circles. He wrote exclusively in English.

2   Contact Editions (1923-1929). Founded by an American expatriate in Paris, it published volumes by some of the greatest authors of the period, such as Gertrude Stein, Ernest Hemingway and William Carlos Williams.

3   *Rive Gauche* [Left Bank]. The left bank of river Seine was the cradle of avant-garde movements in the first decades of the twentieth century. In the original Prezzolini calls it "*Riva sinistra*" and adds in parenthesis: "sometimes really *sinistra*," playing on the *triple entendre* of the term which in Italian also means both "sinister" and politically "left-leaning."

4   Dorothy Dudley (1884-1962). Poet and literary critic.

working a variety of jobs: dishwasher in restaurants and private clubs; extemporaneous translator; teacher of Italian language; secretary etc. He always maintained the sense of urgency and entitlement of someone who is forced to do things below his stature but is not sufficiently coward, nor courageous enough, to resign to it. He died in Italy where he had returned after falling ill with tuberculosis. He held Arthur Rimbaud[5] as his life model and, like Rimbaud, was enamored of poetic greatness.

Born in Florence in 1898 he died in Italy in 1925 [sic].[6] After his death Carlo Linati[7] wrote an article in the Sept. 1, 1934, issue of *Nuova Antologia*: "A very promising rising star (...) He was admired by the latest American poets, the most demanding and critical, the most *avant-garde* in experimental techniques (...) and received an award from the journal *Poetry*."[8] Any American with an average culture who happened to read this article in 1934 would have asked: "How come I have never heard of this person? Who is he? I want to find out more and read more of his stuff." But his research soon would end up in a blind alley. The American *Who's Who*,[9] with a list of thousands of American personages, does not have an entry for Carnevali. The catalogue of the New York Public Library (four million volumes) does not have his book. And it doesn't appear in the catalogue of the famous Library of Congress either. Our American reader could look up Stanley Kunitz's *Authors Today and Yesterday*: nothing; or Alberta Chamberlain Lawrence's *Who is Who among Living Authors*: same result. He could grab the Cambridge history of American literature: no mention. If he called even the best bookstore in town, the clerks wouldn't know where to look. After a long and patient investigation he would find five lines hidden in the three hundred pages of a recent history book

---

5   Arthur Rimbaud (1854-1891). French poet precursor of modernism. He had with a very precocious literary career and stopped writing at age twenty-one.

6   The correct year of his death is 1942. Carnevali returned to Italy in 1925 and spent the rest of his life battling a mental illness that required frequent hospitalizations.

7   Carlo Linati (1878-1949). Writer and literary critic.

8   *Poetry*. Founded in 1912. The extant website claims: "The oldest monthly devoted to verse in the English-speaking world."

9   *Who's Who in America* is a directory published by Marquis Who's Who Ventures. The directory contains short biographies of individuals deemed worthy of mention.

244 • THE TRANSPLANTS

on American literature by Alfred Kreymborg.[10] In the general index of American periodicals finally he would locate a bibliographical note that would bring him to the obscure journal *Poetry* with a few of his poems. I don't mean with this to diminish his value nor dismiss the rare case (or, as Linati puts it, unique) of a young Italian who lived for a short time in America and was able to take possession of the secrets of its language to the point where he could write both original prose and poetry. His fame and success, however, were limited. His works in prose or in free verse have a thin yet lyrical vein, except when they focus on notations of facts and sensations: in theses case images tend to appear and, with them, the hint of a rhythm. It was easier for Carnevali to find a niche in contemporary lyricism which does not protect itself behind the moats of prosody and the defensive walls of metric. The samples I read clearly demonstrate it. From a social standpoint, both Carnevali and our immigrants in general did not have a vision of America as a sweet friend or a gentle host. Speaking metaphorically about the boarding rooms where he lived, Carnevali wrote:

> I brought you illness and illness you gave back to me; I brought you poverty and poverty you returned. I brought you joy and you returned disgust, a disgust so powerful I would have broken up in thousand pieces had I left myself be led by it.

As a person he must have been rather difficult, both by nature and by purpose. In America he made lots of friends of both sexes, he fought with them and then made up. Some American writers of the period gave him positive reviews, some with reservations. I am afraid

---

10   The New York Public Library currently owns a copy of *A Hurried Man*, Paris: Contact Editions, 1925.

   • The Library of Congress holds four books, three of them essays about him and an "autobiography." The earliest was published in 1967.

   • Stanley Kunitz (1905-2006). Poet Laureate. *Authors Today and Yesterday: A Companion Volume to Living Authors*. Kunitz, Hadden, Haycraft, ed. New York, The H. W. Wilson Company, 1933.

   • Alberta Chamberlain Lawrence (1875-1956). *Who's Who Among Living Authors of Older Nations*. Los Angeles, Golden Syndicate Publishing Company, 1931.

   • Alfred Kreymborg (1883–1966). Poet, novelist, playwright. He is best known as literary editor and anthologist.

he expected to obtain from his genius more than it could actually produce. However, it is a miracle that in such a brief time he was able to immerse himself so deeply into the language. In one of his first poems, dedicated to clichés, he wrote:

> The headwaiter says: "Such nice weather today!"
> And flashes a sentimental smile…
> But I haven't slept and have been waiting for sunrise.
> One day I would like to be born
> With a trumpet as powerful as the wind
> To announces to the world
> That wonderful cliché, "such nice weather today."

There were many other days, however, when he was so desperate he wanted to cry and wanted to announce "It's going to rain today," to every old lady, every young couple, every scoundrel who came to the flophouse where he lived.

After discovering his poetry I wrote about it in a Turin newspaper. Yet, only in 1950 did I become aware of his work as a critic. He had written in a penetrating way about *La Voce* and the writers whose works were published in this journal. His observations were much deeper than those of many academics. This means he had the talent to discover new values and not simply accept and analyze them. Far away from Italy, with a modest education (it seems he briefly attended school in Venice,) he discovered the poets of *La Voce* and *Lacerba*. Here are some of his notes.

Aldo Palazzeschi: "Simple and naive like a modern Saint Francis of Assisi. A rascal with eyes full of wonder, a quick and luminous artist."

Giovanni Papini: "After great suffering we all have lots of remedies we can recommend. Yet, after age twenty, often after a defeat, most of us shrivel up, become humble. But Papini fulfilled his vow when he was twenty and did not shrivel up (…) He could be sixteen, twenty or sixty. He was born with "Genesis' and spoke in the 'Apocalypse.'"

Scipio Slapater: "Hard, strong, clean young man."

Corrado Govoni: "Delicate like a young girl, he sings about the filthiest, most obscene affairs of an old Italian city, always with his delicate voice."

Piero Jahier: "Too many scruples in this man. He must believe that every man perturbed by a punishing conscience is a poet. He works in an office for a living. No dictionary, no grammar book are enough for him. They must expand and stretch in order to contain him. Jahier knows that the poet makes the dictionary and the grammar and many other things."

Ardengo Soffici: "He is the most avant-garde and, through French influences, he has achieved a jagged form of poetry; free words and lyrical simultaneity, which are accidental like life itself."

Clemente Rebora:[11] "Very serious, very rich, he overflows with images with an orgy of cold emotions and he consumes himself in a unanimity that is too emotional and vague."

Now, these critical judgments are not always extraordinary or profound and would benefit from some fine tuning. In my opinion, they also need the support of a cultural background and knowledge that Carnevali did not possess. Yet, if one considers the time when they were written, they are certainly noteworthy. He also talks about me and I wasn't sure whether I should quote it here or not, mostly because I thought my neighbors would think I would do it out of vanity. I hope for myself, however, that at my age there were more important things than other people's opinions. Therefore, here it is:

Prezzolini: "Amiable critic(!),[12] clean and forceful, he put Marinetti and his gang back in their place with the only intelligent articles on Futurism[13] ever to appear in an Italian journal, where dull and

---

11 *Lacerba* (1913-1915). Political intellectual journal founded by Giovanni Papini and Ardengo Soffici.

• Giovanni Papini (1881-1956). Writer and poet, active in the avant-garde movement. He converted to Catholicism and took progressively more conservative positions.

• Scipio Slataper (1888–1915). Writer and supporter of the intervention of Italy in WWI

• Corrado Govoni (1884–1965). Poet in the Futurist movement.

• Piero Jahier (1884–1966). Writer and poet. He edited *La Voce* with Prezzolini.

• Ardengo Soffici (1879–1964). Writer, poet and painter.

• Clemente Rèbora (1885–1957). Poet of the avant-garde. He later took the vows as a Catholic priest.

12 In the original "*amabile.*"

13 Filippo Tommaso Marinetti (1876–1944). Poet and editor, founder of the

hard-headed academicians waged war against it and disgusting, ignorant Young Turks defended it."

Certainly I didn't deserve the adjective *amabile*, and if it came from another source I would consider it sarcastic. I am very committed, though, to "critical cleanliness" and I am happy Carnevali noticed it. Poor Carnevali! I wanted to write this piece because I don't want anyone to say that I am like one of those critics who keep a notebook with the list of reviews received on one page and, on the opposite page, the list of reviews returned. When one of their creditors dies, they cross out the debt with a deep sigh of relief. I was attracted to writing about him because I thought he was a man who, in many ways, could talk to me; but he was already dying the very moment I set foot in America.

Carnevali is not the only Italian who came here as a teenager and learned English to the point of handling it like a native born. I will mention the cases of Pascal d'Angelo and Arturo Giovannitti. Giovannitti too, like Carnevali, learned political and social hate and rebellion, but went beyond the literary realm. His poetry today feels long on eloquence but short on sensibility, based on rhetorical cardboard cut-outs of "Judges and Accused," "Rich and Poor," "Rebels and Wardens," all generic and abstract. His verses, collected in the 1914 volume *Arrows in the Gale*,[14] go back to the traditional models of Walt

---

Futurism movement.

• Futurism: artistic, poetic and social avant-garde movement of the early twentieth century. It emphasized modernity and technology against tradition and academic conformism. It was very influential in figurative arts.

14   Pascal d'Angelo (1894-1932). Author of *Son of Italy* (New York, McMillan, 1924); one of the most compelling autobiographies written by an Italian immigrant. Functionally illiterate when he arrived in the United States at age sixteen, D'Angelo learned the language as an autodidact and published poetry in several important journals. *Son of Italy* is currently in print, published by Guernica Editions, Toronto, Canada.

• Arturo Giovannitti (1884-1959). Socialist political activist and union organizer. He was accused of murder after violent incidents during the Bread and Roses labor strike of 1912 in Lawrence, Massachusetts. He defended himself in court with a memorable closing argument and was acquitted, thus escaping a death sentence.

• *Arrows in the Gale*. Riverside, Connecticut, Hillacre Bookhouse, 1914.

Whitman, Edgar Allan Poe and Oscar Wilde.[15] His language is rich but contrived, like an exercise in oratorical scales that reaches the climax with a sonorous conclusion, like a political speech.[16]

New York, September 13, 1954

---

15   Walter Whitman (1819-1892). American poet and essayist.
  • Edgar Allan Poe (1809-1849). American writer, editor and literary critic.
  • Oscar Wilde (1854-1900). Irish playwright, novelist, essayist and poet.

16   Prezzolini returned to Giovannitti in an article published in the newspaper *Il Tempo*: "Elogio di un 'trapiantato' molisano bardo della libertà negli Stati Uniti." Anno XXI, N. 128 , 10 Maggio 1964, 3. (Translator's note.)

Part Five

The Italian American Contribution to America

THE ITALIAN AMERICAN
CONTRIBUTION TO AMERICA

Foreign words tend to appear in a literary text and even more in poetry primarily to render the local color or the national identity of a given character. It is a touch of realism. It is true, though, that Manzoni does not let Renzo speak dialect and Petrarch does not need French words to add local color to Laura. Many other artists took other routes. Dante, for instance, used Latin and Provençal. Manzoni himself made the Spanish governor of Milan speak in his native tongue in addressing his driver. In the nineteenth century the use of foreign words increased. Sixty years ago Antonio Fogazzaro used Venetian dialect to better define some of his characters, and today, novelists like Pier Paolo Pasolini and Emilio Gadda, think directly in dialect even before they make their characters speak it. At times, artists with a satirical bent enjoy themselves with difficult rhymes, like Luigi Pulci who rhymed *salamelec* with *Melchisedec*.[1] In this case the excitement for this ingenious trick must have surpassed the intention to create local color. A tepid example of this local color is in Giuseppe Parini's *Il giorno*,[2] where

---

1   Renzo Tramaglino is one of the main characters in Alessandro Manzoni's novel *I promessi sposi* [*The Bethrothed*]. The character is from Lecco, at the southern tip of Lake Como's eastern branch.

  • Laura was Petrarch's muse. They met while living in Avignon, France.

  • Antonio Fogazzaro (1842-1911). Poet and novelist. His most famous novel is *Piccolo mondo antico* (Milano: Galli, 1895).

  • Pier Paolo Pasolini (1922–1975). Poet, novelist, essayist and public intellectual. He wrote poetry in his native Friulian language. His novels take place in working class neighborhoods in Rome.

  • Carlo Emilio Gadda (1893–1973). Novelist. He used the dialects of Rome and Milan in his works.

  • Luigi Pulci (1432-1484). Writer of *Morgante*, a satirical parody of chivalric poems, published in 1478. *Salamelec* is the Italian distortion of Arabic *sa·laam alai·kum* ("May peace be upon you.") In Italian the word *salamelecco* means insincere, excessively effusive greetings or salutations (such as deep bows or hand kissing). The rhyme appears in *Morgante*, XVIII, 194.

  • *Melchisedec* is a biblical king mentioned in the Bible's *Book of Genesis*.

2   Giuseppe Parini (1729-1799). Poet and social critic, representative of the Italian Enlightenment.

  • *Il giorno* (1763-1765). A satirical poem, it is Parini's most famous work.

the terms *monsieur* and *toilette* appear. Franco Sacchetti,[3] who usually loved crazy and weird rhymes, never used foreign words, although he was well aware of many borrowings from French used by Florentine merchants who traded with Lyon, France. Machiavelli in his reports from France seemed to forget Italian and threw in several words taken from French, although he never used them in poetry. Verses with a mix of Italian and Spanish are in Ludovico Ariosto's *Satira II*:[4]

> Ajora no se puede; etse mejore
> que vos torneis a la mañana; almeno
> fate ch'io sappia, ch'io son qui di fuore.

> [Right now it can't be done; it's best/ that you return tomorrow morning; at least/ make sure that I know, since I am right outside.]

Each artist took a different approach. In examining Italian American writers who used the lingo of their families, it seems to me there are no conscious traces of the aesthetic value of those words. They used them only for the sake of realism to reproduce local color and, sometimes, for scorn of the uneducated. The same disdain and ridicule toward the ignorant peasant is present in the Italian theatrical tradition from its origin. The comical effect is emphasized by a poor sap's attempt to use difficult words to show off, as does a shepherd from Dalmatia in Poliziano's *Orfeo*.[5] Giovanni Berchet[6] mixed French and Italian for comical effect: *ma chère amie/io crepo qui* [My dear girl friend/I will croak right here.]

---

3   Franco Sacchetti (1332-1400). Poet and writer. His most famous work is the collection of short stories *Il Trecentonovelle*.

4   Ludovico Ariosto (1474-1533). Poet, author of *Orlando Furioso*, Italy's most famous epic poem.
   • *Satira II* (1517).

5   Poliziano, born Agnolo Ambrogini (1454-1494). Poet, humanist and playwright. He was considered the most important poet at the court of Lorenzo de' Medici.
   • *Orfeo*. Short dramatic composition in vernacular by Poliziano, based on the myth of Orpheus and Eurydice. Composed in Mantua around 1480, it was published in 1555 ca.

6   Giovanni Berchet (1783–1851). Poet and patriot. He was the author of the Romanticism manifesto *Lettera semiseria di Grisostomo* (1816).

In all the fiction books in English by Italian Americans there was never sufficient artistic power to really penetrate the mainstream of American taste. I would submit that the authors didn't even try. The most important works of narrative, in terms of artistic merit and success (meaning, accepted by the American public) are *Son of Italy* by Pascal D'Angelo; *The Grand Gennaro*, by Garibaldi Lapolla; *Dago Red*, by John Fante; *Mount Allegro*, by Jerre Mangione and *Maria*, by Michael De Capite.

All of these books are out of print and they can be simply considered as documentation.[7] More or less, they all dealt with poverty and the poor according to the norms of *Verismo*.[8] Except for Lapolla, none of them tried to create grand characters. They give the impression that the authors realized they had in their hands folkloric material that was both physically close and potentially interesting to the American public, although the same public was very distant in spiritual terms. Thus, they rendered this reality with nostalgic affection toward the past but also with rancor toward the present, using a tone that became more and more similar to that of a tour guide. "Here are the Italians" they seem to tell the American public, pointing to them as if they were animals in a zoo. "See..? They are not so bad... or stupid... at least not as much as they look. Really. Actually, you were a bit mean and a bit arrogant when you judged them." In the books of these pseudo-novelists the *story* basically does not exist. The structure is based on a series of scenes that follow sequentially and where autobiographical elements prevail. Often there is one canonic chapter dedicated to the

---

7   Garibaldi Lapolla (1930-1976). Educator and writer. *The Grand Gennaro*. New York, Vanguard Press, 1935.

• *Dago Red*. New York, The Viking press, 1940.

• John Fante (1909-1983). Novelist, short-story writer and screenwriter. His best known work is *Ask the Dust*. New York, Stackpole, 1939.

• Michael De Capite (1915-1958). Novelist. Among his works is *Maria*. New York, The John Day Company, 1943.

• As of today all these works have been re-issued, with the exception of *Maria*.

8   *Verismo*. Literary movement between the end of the nineteenth and the beginning of the twentieth centuries. Its goal was the objective representation of the lower class, with simple and direct language and dialogues. *Verismo* is sometimes rendered in English as *Verism* to distinguish it from *Realism*, name of the French current *Réalisme*.

pranzo,[9] which takes on an almost ideological dimension. The meal is always based on spaghetti and flasks of Chianti wrapped in straw. The abundance of the culinary feasts in these folkloric novels obviously has to do with the poverty endured by the families before the present success. One observation I read that can be applied to all of them is that hunger is always the main character. Hunger, first suffered then conquered, is defeated again and again by eating and drinking more than necessary.

Beside hunger, the most common theme of these novels is the conflict between the immigrants and America. This makes sense since the autobiographical nature of the texts leans toward the sociological essay. Conflicts abound: the first generation that came from Italy clashes with the second that grew up in America; person-to-person loans and unpaid debts; expenditures to bring relatives from the old country; rivalries between northerners and southerners; the dominance of family interest to which everything else must be subordinated; the patriarchal system imported from Italy; the festive spirit of social gatherings for funerals, weddings and baptisms. There are no real Christian feelings but there is a lot of superstition. No priest appears, similarly to Italian novels of the *Verismo* period, although it must be said that Italian American writers learned their lesson more from Theodore Dreiser than Giovanni Verga.[10] The *Verismo* of these writers feels dry, conventional and detached. It's like reading a list of items in an inventory. Conflicts between immigrants and America are not represented by means of characters with a symbolic function. America appears as a sort of test tube, closed and immense; where a little colony of Italian insects is placed, destined to undergo mutations. At times America is embodied in the figures of a policeman, a judge or a teacher. Yet, they are fleeting apparitions that never manage to become symbols. The Italian groups described in these novels fall

---

9   The big Sunday lunch, traditional in Italian American (and Italian) households.

10   Theodore Dreiser (1871-1945). Writer and poet. He is considered the father of modern American novel and a representative of realism.

• Giovanni Verga (1840-1922). Novelist and short-stories writer. He is the major representative of *Verismo*. He depicted in particular the reality of his native Sicily. The famous melodrama *Cavalleria rusticana* by Pietro Mascagni is based on one of his short stories.

apart in a couple of generations without even becoming aware of it. In order to be absorbed they have to renounce what they were. What else is assimilation? It is not the product of a law. It is not an exchange. It is not a federation of forces that remain intact while cooperating (like the French speaking community of Canada.) The notion of the contribution that Italians gave to America can only be heard in the in the speeches of those who made American assimilation a sort of profession, like Leonard Covello,[11] for instance. I am not denying that this contribution exists, but it resembles the sharp joke I heard from an Italian fruit merchant, who, by the way, was much smarter than the above-mentioned professional. The green grocer obtained the permit to position his cart in front of the house of a millionaire banker: "The banker and I signed an agreement. I will not compete with his bank and he promised he won't sell apples in this spot." The individual work of Italians has certainly contributed to America's success. In turn, America's economic progress and its imperial size and structure have elevated and multiplied the individual energies of Italian Americans. The Italian banker Giannini gave America a novel concept of a bank's national function. But this was not an Italian cultural contribution. It was his personal genius, awakened and magnified by American dynamism. Thousands of Italian Americans have become rich simply by buying a parcel of land to cultivate as a vegetable garden at the edge of the city. As cities expanded, the land would be rezoned for development and the value increased. Hundreds of Italian American doctors today have rich patients due to the fact that America got richer and distributed wealth among the middle and working classes. When in the course of the colonial banquets I hear that American railroads were made by Italians, I inevitably think that in reality the railroads were conceived, planned and designed—thus they were *made*—by engineers who were not Italian. Italians at most brought a contribution as beasts of burden, working here and there, without really understanding what

---

11   The reference is to Leonard Covello (1887-1982), one of the most admired figures in the Italian American community at large: educator, community leader, and intellectual with a deep commitment to the advancement of Italian people. Among his other achievements was a Pulitzer scholarship that allowed him to enroll at Columbia University. He was the first Italian American principal of a high school and a founding member of the American Italian Historical Association (1966).

they were working for. Until the latest generations—that is until the time students of Italian descent started coming out of medical schools or architecture schools—Italians had been only patients in hospitals and exploited tenants. They were not scientists, researchers, architects, designers or engineers. And, please, let's not talk about the arts, a field where we would expect Italians to bring a contribution. Suffices to say that about five million people came to America from Italy, more or less the entire population of Lombardy.[12] And what have they produced in terms of art? Let's make a comparison with that region between 1880 and 1940.[13] Unfortunately, the majority of monuments that people with taste would like to destroy in New York and other places were built by able Italian artisans with zero genius who had worked in the quarries of Carrara[14] or graduated from the Fine Arts academies of provincial Italian towns. In the field of music, in particular opera, things are a little different. However, we must remember that it wasn't Italian Americans who gave America the best singers, soloists and orchestra conductors. It was Italy. Toscanini, who in the colonial banquets is often mentioned with other great names in the list of debts America owes to Italians, never learned English well and never applied for American citizenship. He was the purest product of Italy's nineteenth century musical culture and technique. He resided in the United States for a few months a year for financial reasons, inside a cyst of Italian culture. The same thing can be said about the only other important Italian name in the contemporary music world, Gian Carlo Menotti,[15] with the difference that Menotti's English is as good as his Italian.

---

12   The population of Lombardy, the Northern region whose capital is Milan, was 10 million in 2018 (most recent data available).

13   Ambiguous statement: it probably suggests a comparison between the artistic production in Lombardy and in New York (following sentence) in the period 1880-1940, implicitly upholding the output in Italy as far superior.

14   Carrara. City in Tuscany. In this area are quarries with the best quality white marble. It is the source of the marble used by Michelangelo and other major artists for their sculptures.

15   Giancarlo Menotti (1911-2007). Musician, composer and entrepreneur. In 1958 he founded the *Festival dei Due Mondi* and in 1977 organized the American branch of the *Festival di Spoleto* in Charleston (South Carolina).

And now, back to our Italian American writers. First of all there aren't that many, they aren't great, and they haven't become part of the American literary tradition. For example, none of them has achieved the same relevance as the German Dreiser or the Swedish Sandburg. They are decent, average American writers who looked at their families and wrote about those environments with some detachment, sometimes with humor, sometimes treating them as anthropological specimens. The process of assimilation never encountered a resistance grounded in culture and consciousness, only in traditions and habits. Although the immigrants were in the large majority ignorant, they did have a moral and social structure based on centuries-old habits centered on the family; on religious rituals followed with reverence albeit with no profundity; and on a capital of common notions made of folkloric traditions and superstitions. The immigrants had to go from a culture limited in scope but sedimented over centuries of experience to the American culture, more complex and more volatile. It was a difficult transition. The reaction of first-generation immigrants was to insulate themselves inside the family and small groups of fellow *paesani* in the local Little Italies or in the countryside. The second generation created a rip: they felt American and even a bit anti-Italian. The rip took place right in the middle of an even more radical and faster transformation that took America from a predominantly agricultural country to a fully industrial one. This revolution had gigantic consequences at every level, with profoundly alienating effects on the human masses that had to endure it. All social relations that had existed up to that point were scrambled, and at the same time it became extremely difficult to create new ones. It was like jumping on a moving train to find out that all the seats were taken by passengers that barely bother to look up, and being forced to travel the entire distance standing up hanging from a strap. Starting from the crucial aspect of the difference between the languages of the two generations of Italian American immigrants, in her thesis at Columbia University, Fiorella Forti, wrote:

> In the majority of Italian households, children were forced to speak Italian at home[16] and to follow traditions and ideas even

---

16 Prezzolini comments in parentheses: "The correct term should be *dialect*."

when they were openly in conflict with the outside world. Like all other parents, and even more than the majority of parents, Italian immigrants forced their children to adopt the habits and social customs they had inherited. However, the children, due primarily to the education and the social environment in which they were present and active, and to the knowledge of English, wanted to act and be American. They realized that their parents' culture was not American and started sharing the opinion that the outside world had toward them. They also learned that their parents' behavior was considered inferior and, as a consequence, even [the children] were being kept at the margin because of their origin. For a certain period the children of Italian American immigrants went through hard times marked by severe internal conflicts. On the one hand they loved and respected their parents, yet they had no choice but to resist their authority if they wanted to become American, although they didn't really have a clear notion of what being American meant. On the other hand, they longed for acceptance as Americans by those who considered themselves such. Sadly, these attempts were not always successful.

When we look at individual achievements, Italian American immigrants were unquestionably successful. Millions of people from the peasant class improved their economic condition and saw their children become doctors, businesspeople, lawyers, builders, magistrates, politicians and more. Had they not come to the United States their children probably would still be fighting poverty. In contrast, here they now belong to the lower middle class, some to the solid middle class, and some to the upper middle class. [In the footnote: A list of economic and political successes of Italians, particularly those of the second and third generations, would be too long. I recommend two publications: *The Italians in Contemporary America*, by Harold Lord Varney.[17] This pamphlet contains a directory of Italian Americans with important positions in politics and education in the United States. It also contains numerous entries for businesspeople.

The second is *The Italian in America: A Social Study and History*, by

---

17   Harold Lord Varney (1893-1984).
   • *The Italians in Contemporary America*. Unknown binding, Published by the Italian Historical Society of New York, n. 10: 1931. This organization was later dissolved.

Lawrence Frank Pisani[1] (New York: Exposition Press, 1957). Initially this was a dissertation defended at Yale University. A more recent revision contains many names, but it also contains errors, some of which concerns me directly. The author in a letter acknowledged them and accepted the corrections. I should also add the many biographical repertories, such as the *Who's Who* published in several volumes by Giovanni Schiavo or Ario Flamma. Both works are inspired by the wish to please their readership.]

The contribution of Italian Americans to America was exclusively in terms of size and energy, rarely of quality, at least in proportion to the size of the community. When we give the word *contribution* the specific meaning of *influence on American life style*, we come up with very little. Millions of Italian American basically didn't bring anything Italian that has remained significantly so. The majority of immigrants had no distinct Italian taste and no Italian culture: they did not own a national patrimony but only local traditions.

No matter how we cut it, all we can say concretely about the contribution of Italians to their adoptive country is that it was physically important but with very limited intellectual value. It can be reduced to growing vegetables and the fact that they now appear on American tables. This was definitely a contribution and a merit of Italians: they taught Americans the vital force of artichokes, zucchini, salads and string beans even before dieticians discovered the importance of vitamins. These were real Italian novelties and imports. If the American diet changed from the traditional boiled-meat-with-cabbage; pork-and-beans; roast beef and steaks; and fish and oysters to make room for fruits and vegetables, it was because of the influence of Italians. It isn't much but it's a real contribution. All the rest is rhetoric good for the colonial banquets or political speeches.

The crowning achievement of Italian culinary influence in America was the word *spaghetti* that acquired the meaning of *pasta*. More recently we had the introduction of *pizza*. However, the American influence can be seen in dishes like *spaghetti with meat balls*, which is pasta with tomato sauce mixed with small globs of meat, an obvious derivation from German or Swedish cuisines. This hybrid dish surprises all the

---

1 Lawrence Frank Pisani (1921-?).

Italians who sit down in run-of-the-mill Italian restaurants in New York. Not even with wine were Italian immigrants able to impose their taste. Wine drinkers in America generally are descendants of Europeans, not Americans converted to wine. Or, if they converted, it's because they visited Italy or France; not because they tasted California wines.

One thing Italians contributed to was the growth of Catholicism in the United States. But even here their contribution was in terms of numbers, not quality. The Italian clergy had very little to do with it. The high echelons of Church hierarchy are inhabited by the Irish clergy. The literary and theological production in the United States does not have a single Italian name. There is an influence through Catholicism, but not by means of Italian Americans. Rome is filtered by way Dublin and Munich, not Calabria or Sicily; nor by way of Italian seminaries in Naples and Palermo.

THE LANGUAGE OF THE HALF-FOREIGNERS

With a few, rare exceptions, Italians who migrated to North America never learned English all that well. Many, especially women, didn't learn it at all. The majority stopped at five hundred mangled words, with English roots and Italian endings, to be used in a life that was restricted to work, saving and raising children. The best study conducted on the topic is an essay by Alberto Menarini.[2]

The situation was greatly different for their children, with a series of unexpected and dire consequences. The children went to school, played in the streets, went to the movies, practice sports and, in so doing, learned English. The new language put them on the same level as their peers and the rest of the population, but separated them from their parents. Even the old folks who had managed to learn English could only pronounce it with a strong accent that embarrassed their own children and was ridiculed by native speakers. This phenomenon is not discussed in the official statistics, nor is it present in diplomatic reports and it is never mentioned during colonial banquets. Generally, the phenomenon was barely noticed even in the memoires of the few second-generation Italians who wrote those stories after they had gone on to great success and brilliant careers in other fields. A few instances appear in autobiographies and novels written in English by the second generation. I was able to secure one of these autobiographies, full of interesting biographical and family information, from a student of mine, Olga Peragallo.[3]

One of the best American writers of Italian origin was John Fante, whose autobiography, *Dago Red*, was translated into Italian. First of all, we must pay attention to the fact that the title includes one of the most common slurs used by Americans to demean Italians: *Dago*. This is a word that provoked many fist fights and occasionally pushed enraged Italians to draw knives from their pockets.

---

2   Alberto Menarini (1904-1984). Linguist and scholar. The book mentioned is *Ai margini della lingua*. Firenze, Sansoni, 1947.

3   Olga Peragallo (1910-1943). *Italian American Authors and their Contribution to American Literature*. New York, Vanni, 1949. The book was published posthumously with an introduction by Prezzolini.

I am nervous when I bring friends to my house; the place looks so Italian. Here hangs a picture of Victor Emmanuel,[4] and over there is one of the cathedral of Milan, and next to it is one of St. Peter's, and on the buffet stands a wine pitcher of medieval design; it's forever brimming, forever red and brilliant with wine. These things are heirloom belonging to my father, and no matter who may come to our house, he likes to stand under them and brag.

So I begin to shout to him. I tell him to cut out to be a Wop and be an American once in a while. Immediately he gets his razor strop and whales hell out of me, clouting me from room to room and finally out the back door. I go into the woodshed and pull down my pants and stretch my neck to examine the blue slices across my romp. A Wop, that's what my father is! Nowhere is there an American father who beats his son this way. Well, he is not going to get away with it; someday I'll get even with him.

I begin to think that my grandmother is hopelessly a Wop. She is a small, stocky peasant who walks with her wrists criss-crossed over her belly, a simple old lady fond of boys. She comes to the room and tries to talk to my friends. She speaks English with a bad accent, her vowels rolling out like hoops. When, in her simple way, she confronts a friend of mine and says, her old eyes smiling: "*You lika go the Seester scola?*" my heart roars. *Mannaggia!* I'm disgraced; now they all know that I am Italian.

My grandmother has taught me to speak her native tongue. By seven, I know it pretty well, and I always address her in it. But when friends are with me, when I am twelve and thirteen, I pretend ignorance of what she says, and smirk stiffly; my friends daren't know that I can speak any language but English. Sometimes this infuriates her. She bristles, the loose skin at her throat knits hard, and she blasphemes with a mighty blasphemy. (169-170)

One of the first books written in English by an Italian immigrant that came to the attention of American critics was *Son of Italy*, by Pascal D'Angelo. The book, which includes prose and poetry, is the extraordinary narration of the hardships he faced as a foreign worker in America and his passionate effort to achieve poetical expression. When it first came out it was welcome with great enthusiasm and it is, to this very day, a fundamental book for understanding the history

---

4   Most likely Vittorio Emanuele II, first king of unified Italy (1820-1878).

of immigration. Here is what it says about the difficulties of learning English:

> None of us, including myself, ever thought of a movement to broaden our knowledge of the English language. We soon learned a few words about the job, which was the preliminary creed; then came *bread, shirt, gloves* (no kid gloves), *milk*. And that is all. We formed our own little world —one of many in this country. And the other people around us who spoke in strange languages might have been phantoms for all the influence that they had upon us or for all we cared about them. (68)

And here it is, the creation of a "little world," a world separated from that of the others, as if they were ghosts. And here are also the first token words, without emotion or value, indispensible in the concrete world.

Francesco Ventresca[5] was a teacher. When he first arrived to these shores he was a pick-and-shovel worker and, in an extraordinary case of strong will, decided to start going to school at 21 years of age. He became so absorbed in studying that he eventually became chairperson of a foreign language department in a [non-specified] college. In his memoirs he wrote:

> From that moment on I started living with my fellow countrymen with my body only, but not with my heart and mind. While they were chatting, playing cards and cursing, I was busy reading out loud my English lessons and looking up word definitions in the dictionary. My companions would look at me strange and finally one of them said: "Cecco,[6] if you go on like this you are going to go crazy." The prophecy didn't scare me. And I kept reading, reading and reading.

This separation from his Italian companions in "heart" and "mind"

---

5   Francesco Ventresca (1872-1954). *Personal Reminiscences: Celebrating Sixty Years in America (1891-1951) and Fifty Years as a Teacher of Foreign languages.* New York, Ryerson, 1937. Ventresca was originally from Introdacqua (Molise), the same town as Pascal D'Angelo.

6   Cecco. Nickname for Francesco.

is noteworthy in that it is related directly to the notion of education. The hostility for and rejection of education is so strong that, to them, studying is the equivalent of madness. From their point of view, the necessity to adopt the new language is responsible for the shrinking of their native tongue and for the impoverishment of their emotional world. Often, it also pushed them to renegade their very names and to adopt English ones. At times this was the result of the immigrants' wish to become completely American and no longer be considered *wops* or *dagoes*; foreigners targeted by the antipathy of landlords, policemen and civil servants. Sometimes it was the Americans' difficulty in pronouncing their foreign names that suggested the change, informally at first, then officially. Changing names was very easy, requiring only the approval of a judge. In many cases the new last name was the English translation of the Italian family name, thus *Papa* became Pope; *Verdi* became Green; and *Ferraro* was translated with Smith. In other occasions the change was a pejorative, as was the story I read in the memoirs of Constantine Panunzio.[7]

> The first important incident in that American house was the change of name. George Annis, my landlord, who—as I discover later was almost illiterate—could not pronounce my Italian name. He thus suggested that I changed it. At first I was stunned and I thought how my parents [sic][8] would have reacted, since they gave me that name on purpose, to perpetuate my grandfather's. But I wanted to become as similar as possible to an American and it seemed there was no other way. I let George change my name into a genuine American name. This is not an uncommon experience for many immigrants to America. Even today, some change it out of expediency; others take the initiative to be American at least in their name. But in most cases the change is forced by the landlord. In some cases the changes are funny. The name I was given by George was over the top as far American origins are concerned. It

---

7   Constantine Panunzio (1884-1964). *The Soul of an Immigrant*. New York, Arno Press, 1969.

8   The original text by Panunzio is in English. Prezzolini translated *parents* with *parenti*. This is apparently an oversight. *Parenti* in Italian means relatives. From the context it is rather clear that it was the parents (*genitori*) not the relatives who named the author of the memoirs.

was American in its nature and it smelled of *Americanism*. For a period of three months I was called Mr. Beefsteak. When I found out about the real meaning of the word I rebelled. I didn't want to be known as a cut of meat. Then, George changed my name again into Frank Nardi, and Frank Nardi I was until I went to school and could return to my original name.[9] In the meantime with my relatives I felt the humiliation of having changed my name. I sent them a bunch of envelopes already addressed to Frank Nardi, telling them they should use them to send me their letters. I later found out that many other immigrants had done the same thing to hide the fact that they had changed their names.

Even in the larger picture painted by *The Grand Gennaro* by Garibaldi Lapolla—the story of the rise and fall of an Italian family—the problem of the split between the two languages appears:

The older son of the "great" Gennaro learned English incredibly fast and was proud of it. When mother spoke to him in Italian he would always answer in English. "Why in English, Roberto?" his father would ask. "Do you want to forget your sweet language?" His younger brothers were following his example. Then, Gennaro decided to follow in the steps of signor Monterano and bought an English grammar and started studying with his wife. But his accent made his children laugh despite the fact that his cadence was harmonious and full of sibilants.

Joe [sic] Pagano,[10] author of a series of sketches and vignettes titled *The Paesanos*,[11] in a short story describes a gathering of Italian Americans on the occasion of a baptism. Hanging on a tavern's walls are the portraits of Roosevelt[12] and Mussolini: the first with tired

---

9 Panunzio was born in Molfetta (Bari). In all likelihood his birth name was *Costantino*, later anglicized in *Constantine*. It is very common to run into Italian Americans whose last name is *Constantino*, spelled with an *n* in the first syllable but with the traditional Italian ending *o*. This is probably a transcription error on the part of an English-speaking clerk. The additional *n* allows the original name to conform partially to English orthography.

10 Jo Pagano (1906-1982).

11 *The Paesanos*. Boston, Little, Brown and Company, 1940.

12 Franklyn Delano Roosevelt (1882-1945). He served as the 32nd President of

eyes behind spectacles, the other with a black beret and a belligerent jaw. Also on the walls are the American and Italian flags, crossed like scissors. It's a rainy day, the tavern is filling up and soon the large room is crowded, with people gathered in small groups:

> (...) some sitting and some standing, chatting and laughing and bantering in Italian American lingo—*Yah, I sez him.... Woudn' tcha like ta know*—and other similar expressions.

The stories narrated in English by Italian American authors bring to light the pain, the poverty, the humiliations, the betrayals, the miscommunication and the confusion that are usually kept hidden during the official speeches, the banquets and social events that attract politicians, Chambers of Commerce functionaries, lawyers, travel agents, fraudulent bankers and other new rich. Those stories are really moving. And at the center is always the linguistic tragedy, the tragedy of impossible expressivity, the demolition of words and, therefore, thought. This tragedy devastated the Italian American psyche in two different ways. The first was the *impoverishment* of the lexicon. The immigrant *cafone*[13] picked up only the most mechanical and functional aspects of the linguistic mixture made of *jobba* [job] and *pezze* [pieces, dollars]. The other phenomenon was the schizophrenia, the split in the immigrant's soul between Italian and American identities, often represented by the conflict between two generations: fathers and mothers against their grandparents on one side; and against children, grandchildren and their friends on the other.

There were obviously several exceptions. For instance, people who ended up in the countryside were luckier than those who stayed in the cities. Those who went to California found better conditions than on the Atlantic coast; people with even minimal education resisted better than the illiterate. However, the general picture remains the same. The language and the lingo of Italian Americans reveal the crisis of the spirit and the customs.

---

the United States, from 1933 to 1945.

13   *Cafone*: southern Italian term used to designate farm laborers. The origin of the word is still disputed. It is now used as an insult, meaning crude, rude, ill mannered, crass. Italian Americans use the term with its vernacular pronunciation, *gavoon*.

Part Seven

Caricatures and Characters from the World of the Transplants

FARFARIELLO
THE *CAFONI* OBSERVED BY A BOURGEOIS

I don't know who the first writer was who jammed a word from the Italian American lingo into an Italian-language poem, but this I know for certain: he couldn't have cared less about art. The same must have felt those who came after him and created a genre that turned out to be a cross between a storytelling musical and a Vaudeville-like act, the kind of show that had great success in small theaters in all the Little Italies of the United States between 1890 and 1940. Farfariello, alias of Eduardo Migliaccio,[1] was the most important, original and popular interpreter of this genre. He had phenomenal success all over the United States and also in Italy. He succeeded in attracting a non-Italian public that nicknamed him "The Italian Harry Lauder."[2] For those who don't know Lauder, just as I didn't know before I began researching Farfariello, he was a Scottish baritone who became greatly popular in those times with a repertory of popular songs. Yet, Farfariello, as far as I am concerned, was something else. He was a critical and moralistic observer with a satirical vein. He was, in a sense, a historian of the curious characters that lived (and live) in the world of the Transplanted: on this side the *cafoni*; on the other side their exploiters. In order to portray them accurately, he used the lingo of Italian Americans because it was the most effective way to reproduce their identities. He created the caricature-characters of the *cafone scostumato* [offensively uncouth bore], *Pasquale Passaguai* [Pascal Always-in-Trouble], the *cafone risagliuto* [new-rich], the *cafone patriota* [patriot], the *cafone nervoso* [irritable, anxious], the *cafone sciampagnore* [squanderer], the *cafone cantante* [ever-singing], the *cafone 'ngannato* [gullible, deceived], the *cafone socialista* [socialist] and finally… *lu presidente dello globbo* [the president of the social

---

1   Eduardo Migliaccio (1882-1946). With the stage name *Farfariello* [Neapolitan dialect: Little Butterfly] he created dozens of characters, based on the satirical representations of *cafoni*. *Farfariello* is a vernacular term that indicates a vainglorious individual who talks incessantly saying all sorts of inane and absurd things, boastful and with no credibility.

2   Henry "Harry" Lauder (1870-1950). Songwriter, singer and entertainer.

club.] In total he created some five hundred characters that mirrored the sociological and anthropological types of Italian immigrants. The writers of satirical poems knew they were handling controversial material, and in fact on paper they used to underline with a red pen the words taken from the lingo to emphasize their provenance. To them this was not poetic material. In order to understand the difference, we should go back to the use of Italianized foreign words by other true artist-writers, such as Gioacchino Belli[3] and Giovanni Pascoli.[4] In one of his sonnets, Belli gives a cabinet maker the responsibility to explain the meaning of *gratis* and *picnic*, vulgarized and Italianized into *aggratis* and *picchenicche*. The first word is from Latin; the second from English by way of French:

> Sto *picchenicche* è una parola grega,
> Che vvo' di': *ppagà er pranzo a un tant'a testa*

> [This *picnic* is a Greek[5] word / that means: *each one pays for his own lunch.*]

The sonnet ends with these words:

> Be'… dunque… *aggratis* significa a *uffaggna*
> *Picchenicche* vo'ddi': *ppaghi* chi *mmaggna.*

> [Well, then, *gratis* means for free / *picnic* means: if you eat you'll pay.]

For Belli, foreign words adapted to the Italian ear are a local-color issue. His satire has to do with social classes: the man-of-the-people from low-class Rome explains with all sorts of errors the meaning

---

3   Gioachino Belli (1791–1863). Author of the most famous collection of sonnets in *romanesco*, the street dialect of Rome. Mostly composed between 1830 and 1839, a selection was first published in 1866.

4   Giovanni Pascoli (1855-1912). He is one of Italy's best-known poets. By training he was a scholar of classical languages, in particular Latin. His works were unconventionally anti-rhetorical and his style revolutionized Italian poetry.

5   "Greek" may be the metonym used in Roman dialect to indicate an incomprehensible language. Normally, Italians use "Arabic" instead of "Greek" for this purpose.

of new words used by the wealthy, adopted from a language he calls "Greek." English words underwent the same treatment by the writers of Little Italy (even if they didn't know Belli).

In Pascoli, the artistic use of English or Italian-English words gives a veneer of local color in the well-known poem *Italy*.[6] Here the touch of local color has a sentimental and patriotic value, tinged with nostalgia. No one else was able to bring the Italian American lingo to such a high level of cultural and emotional expression. Pascoli is also the only one, as far as I know, who was able to extract new effects from the rhyme of Italian words and words of the new lingo imported from America.

> Venne, sapendo della lor venuta,
> Gente, e qualcosa rispondeva a tutti
> *Joe*, grave: "*Oh, yes, è fiero*, vi saluta.
>
> *Molti bisini…* oh yes… No, tiene un *frutti-*
> *stendo……. Oh yes*, vende *checche, candi, scrima*.
> Conta *moneta*! Può comprar coi frutti.
>
> Il *baschetto* non rende come prima.
> *Yes, un salone* che ci ha tanti *bordi*.
> *Yes*, l'ho visto nel pigliar la *stima*.

> Hearing about their arrival,
> People came. Everyone got an answer from
> *Joe*, serious: "*Oh yes,* he is *fine* and says hello.
>
> *Lots of business…*oh yes… No, he owns a
> *fruitstand. O yes*, he sells *cakes candy icecream*.
> He makes *money*. He can buy with fruit.
>
> The *basket* is not as profitable as before.
> *Yes, a saloon* with many *boarders*.
> *Yes*, I saw him boarding the *steamer*.

I won't debate Livingston's analysis of those words and his claim that

---

6   Composed in 1904 it was published in the collection of poems *Primi poemetti* (Bologna, Zanichelli, 1905).

Pascoli used them incorrectly, perhaps because of his limited knowledge of English. The issue is not Pascoli's philological precision, rather his artistic ability to use new material. He understood both its validity and limits. Those words are like tiles introduced into a mosaic to give it a sense of primitivism, like Middle Ages paintings with the crown on the Madonna's head made of real gold with precious stones rather than painted.

Pascoli's smiles are unlike Belli's full-mouth laughs: they are hints of sweetness and understanding. Pascoli is taken by surprise by these new beings that appear unexpectedly in the middle of Tuscany—where he lived at the time—carrying the echo of a faraway experience, the resonance of money, customs and words. In the same way, French or Arabic words must have impressed thirteen century people who heard them in the mouth of other Italians; merchants and navigators who had traveled to foreign lands and were bringing back foreign smells, animals and rare specimens never seen before. In order for those words to become poetry, however, they require the magical touch of someone like Pascoli, curious like a smart peasant and sensitive like a girl.

The storytellers and Vaudeville artists—Farfariello first among them—were cut of a different cloth. They wrote thousands of poems with music performed in Italian theaters. Texts and scores were printed on thin sheets of paper with funny vignettes from woodcuts and sold everywhere in the stores and newsstands of the Little Italies. The authors used the lingo as an identification badge. Then, alas, when they tried to write serious poetry, they would switch back to the kind of Italian laden with clichés that schools had taught them. But, even in these songs one can still find an implicit attitude of superiority by the semi-educated class toward southern peasants. Yet, they left behind images of a *cafone* who, with his poor, limited and concrete language, could express his defiance, scorn and pain for the tribulations he had to endure in America. It is the kind of attitude and emotion that surfaced in all its clarity in the apologue regarding a no-nonsense female character who was reading a script, written in passable but stereotypical Italian by some know-it-all high-school dropout. The playwright insisted that she should use the word *palazzo* instead of the standard term *bildingo*. "What are you talking about?"

she asked. "You call this *bildingo* a *palazzo*?"[7] Under the pressure of capitalist exploitation; of racism from the Irish who were competing for the true profession of the Catholic faith; and the disdain of the Anglo-Saxon ruling class; the *cafoni* developed a language that was much livelier than the sausage-stuffed semi-official Italian made of dead expressions preserved under brine in a dictionary, and good only for patriotic rhetorical plays.

Eduardo Migliaccio was born in 1880 [sic] in Cava dei Tirreni[8] where his well-to-do Neapolitan family used to spend the summer. His grandfather migrated to the United States, invested his fortune in a Pennsylvania mine but—based on what I heard from the last descendants in the family—ended up losing everything. His grandson arrived here probably when he was eighteen years old. He found a job in a bank but didn't last long. That kind of work wasn't for him. According to an interview he gave to the periodical *Americolo*[9] (founded by Fiorello La Guardia), to make ends meet Farfariello started working as a scribe, writing letters under dictation for illiterate immigrants to their Italian relatives. He discovered feelings, expressions and personalities that made a deep impression on him. Like many Italians he could write rhymes with ease. In fact, he was only thirteen years old when he wrote his first sonnet (Apollo,[10] apparently, forgave him.) In his earlier years, in Naples he had admired the work of the "*grandissimo Maldacea.*"[11] In New York he hung out with Italians and started going

---

7 *Palazzo* is a polysemic word that means both "sumptuous palace" and "ordinary large building." Apparently, Italian Americans used the word *palazzo* to indicate an elegant and luxurious building; while a modest apartment building was called *bildingo*.

8 Cava dei Tirreni is in the province of Salerno, near the southern-most end of the Amalfi coast.

9 *Americolo*. Periodical founded by Fiorello La Guardia before he became mayor of New York. The venture ended in failure. The only references to the periodical are in the catalogs of the Library of Congress and the New York Public Library. It was published by La Guardia Publishing Co. in 1925. Editor F. H. La Guardia. NYPL has Volume 1,2; up to n. 48 (1925-1926).

10 Apollo was the Greek god of music and poetry.

11 Nicola Maldacèa (1870-1945). Neapolitan comedian, songwriter and performer. His satirical monologues made fun of the élite as well as the plebes.

to the local theaters where wannabe entertainers were performing. It didn't take long before he decided to try, confident that he could do better than them. His first gig was in a small variety theater where he was paid seven dollars a week. In a short time he became a success. Cleverly, he used the material he had learned working at the bank and as a scribe, and started with satirical portraits and caricatures of the people he had met. Later in his career, he said he had realized that "the Italian community was infested with all sorts of swindlers who devised every possible scheme in the world to scam and bleed the poor *cafoni*." Apparently, he was animated by the spirit of a reformer, something very rare in an Italian, and even more in a Neapolitan. And maybe he was sincere. Poor Italian immigrants were squeezed by their oppressive American bosses, but also by the more odious exploitation of small southern-Italian wheeler-dealers who could barely read and count, but knew how to take advantage of fellow countrymen, with the callousness of usurers and the avidity of merchants. Before legitimate Italian banks opened branches in New York, Chicago and San Francisco, the communities were dominated by so-called bankers, notaries or travel agents that took advantage in every way possible of the ignorance of the immigrants and who, systematically, would go bankrupt and flee back to Italy with bags full of money. Nothing in this world was as expensive as ignorance and Italian immigrants were the ideal victims predestined to pay the tribute that naïveté and ignorance have always paid to knowledge and cunning. Who knows? Maybe Farfariello's songs helped alerting the immigrants of the most obvious scams perpetrated by despicable shysters and crooks. Many of these were genuine criminals and convicted felons who had entered the United States at a time when no passport was required. Indeed, many were pushed to leave Italy by the local police, happy to see them go. Unfortunately, though, in the end, in artistic terms, Farfariello left us with a much stronger and vivid caricature of the gullible immigrant, rather than the satire of the scamming élite.

Descriptions portray Migliaccio's as tall and stocky, with gray, penetrating eyes and bushy eyebrows. His photos as a young man show a handsome adolescent with typical Neapolitan features, a pleasant smile, a vivacious spirit and luminous eyes. His grandfather was deeply disappointed when he decided to become an entertainer. For a solid, respectable bourgeois family it wasn't considered proper to have a child who worked as a clown. I was told that his grandfather never went to see him perform. Migliaccio, however, maintained a behavior in line with his social class. In his family he imposed very rigid morals, he was quiet and, if anything, private and somber. A person who did business with him told me that he behaved more like a funeral home director than a Vaudeville comedian. He always dressed impeccably in the fashion of the time, in spats, with a black jacket, striped pants, whirling a cane. He didn't like to travel. An American observer mentioned seeing him often alone, sitting at the table of a café in Little Italy, intent on observing clients and passers-by. From his own word we know that he was picking his caricatures from real life, trying to penetrate their thoughts. Like many artists, he took care of the most minute details of his characters. For instance, he made all his wigs by himself. He used fake beards and moustache or, sometimes, full-face masks. He had a mid-range voice, not too powerful but pleasant. He had a very wide repertoire, with an estimated five hundred characters. He also imitated famous personalities of his days. Among the most successful ones was Enrico Caruso. Often he impersonated women, or a Bowery bum,[12] or an Italian recruit in the American army. In the course of one show he would impersonate about five or six of them. At times he was doing four shows a day.

Farfariello's caricatures—as well as those of other performers— reveal the real problems and the emotional issues of the immigrants of the first generation. We see these poor people confronting the new circumstances of their lives, often unable to understand what was going on around them and constantly penalized because they could not make sense of reality. Thus, the general theme turns out to be their animosity toward the country that had lured them with the myth of easy wealth. Hopes and dreams crashed, followed by the teary or ridiculous stories of their tragedies; of the conflicts with the law; of the rejections by women; of the humiliations when they spoke English. The emblem of this whole world is the mythical figure

---

12   Reference to the famous New York skid row; location of flop houses and cheap taverns; patronized by alcoholics, vagrants and beggars.

of Pasquale Passaguai, who runs into every trouble imaginable (the name Pasquale in Neapolitan dialect already suggests a bumbling idiot.) At the same time, we see the re-evaluation of the motherland that slowly becomes a mythical entity thanks to her ancient glories and, most of all, for having given birth to Christopher Columbus, without whom America would not exist. Here is the origin of the consoling myth that for centuries has comforted Italians in all their defeats: "When today's oppressors were small barbaric tribes, Italians were already a great civilization." Typical of the first theme is the invective *America Sanemagogna*[13] [America son of a whore] that closes a sonnet by Carlo Ferrazzano.[14]

> Chi dice ca l'America è civile
> Nun tene lu cerviello sestimato:
> Questa è la terra de lu tradimento;
> Questa e' la terra de lu scustumato.
> Addò vedite a li paise nuoste
> Ca na figliiola quannu fa l'ammore
> Vene l' innamurate a qualunque ore
> S'a piglia e se la porta a divertì?
> E quannu se retira
> Si parla sulamente
> A pate o a mamma, siente:
> *No laiche? Mi go ve!*
> Chi nasce qua nasce senza vergogna:
> Questa e' la terra cchiù *sanemagogna.*

> Those who claim America is civilized
> Don't have a functioning brain:
> This is the land of betrayal;
> This is the land of the vulgar.
> Where do you see in our hometowns
> That when a girl is being courted
> Her lover comes at any hour
> And takes her out to have fun?

---

13   *Sanemagogna*: phonetic rendition of son of a gun.

14   Carlo Ferrazzano. *La Merica Sanemagogna* [America Son-of-a-Gun]. Quoted by Jerre Mangione and Ben Morreale in *La Storia: Five Centuries of the Italian American Experience*. New York, Harper Perennial, 1992.

And when she gets back
If she speaks at all
Her father or mother only hear
"No like? Me go away."
Those born here are born without shame:
This is the most *sanemagogna* land.

Typical of the second theme is the skit *Orrè Italy* [Hurrah Italy], in the style of the *Commedia dell'arte*.[1] Here is the text, by the same author:

Na serra dentro na *barra* Americana dove il patrone era americano, lo *visco* era americano, la birra era Americana, ce steva na *ghenga de loffari* tutti americani: solo io non era americano; quanno a tutto nu momento me mettono mmezzo e me dicettero: "Alò spaghetti; *iu* mericano *men*?" "No! no! Mi Italy *men*!" "*Iu blacco enze*?" "No, no!" "*Iu laico* chistu *contrì*?" "No, no! Mi *laico* mio *contrì*! Mi *laico* Italy!" A qusto punto me chiaviene lo primo *fait*! Dice: "*Orrè* for America!" Io tuosto: "*Orrè* for Italy." Un ato *fait*. Dice: "*Orrè* for America?" "*Orrè* for Italy." N'ato *fait* e n'ato *fait*, fino a che me facetteno addurmentare, ma però "*orrè* for America" non o dicette!

Quanno me scietaie, me trovaie ncoppo lu marciapiedi cu nu *pulizio* vicino che diceva: "*Ghiroppe bomma*!" Io ancora stunato *alluccaie*: "America nun *gudde*! for *orrè* Italy!" Sapete li *pulizio* che facete? Mi arrestò. Quanno fu la mattina lu *giorge* mi dicette: "*Wazzo maro laste naite?*" Io risponnette: "No *tocche* nglese!" "No? Tenne dollari?" E quello porco dello *giorge* nun scherzava, perchè le diece *pezze* se le pigliaie!...

[One evening in an American bar [*barra*], where the owner was American, whiskey [*visco*] was American, beer was American, there was a gang of loafers [*ghenga de loffari*], all American. I was the only non American. Suddenly they surrounded me and started talking: "Hello spaghetti, you [*iu*] American man [*men*]?" "No! No! Me Italy man [*men*]!" "You Black Hand [*Iu blacco enze*]?" "No, no!" "You like [*Iu laico*] this country [*contrì*]?" "No, no! I like [*laico*] my country [*contrì*]. I like [*laico*] Italy." At this point I took the

---

1 *Commedia dell'arte* is a genre of theater performance born in Italy in the sixteenth century. It spread to the rest of Europe with enormous success. It was based on improvisation and the use of masked characters. Each mask identified a type or personality that the audience immediately recognized.

first fight (punch) [*fait*]. He says: "Hurrah [*Orrè*] for America!" Me, tough guy: "Hurrah [*Orrè*] for Italy!" Another fight [*fait*]. He says: "Hurrah [*Orrè*] for America?" "Hurrah [*Orrè*] for Italy." Another fight [*fait*] and another fight [*fait*], until they knocked me out, but "hurrah [*Orrè*] for America" I didn't say it.

When I woke up I found myself on the sidewalk next to a policeman [*pulizio*] who was saying: "Get up, bum [*Ghiroppe bomma*]!" Still out of it, I looked at him [*alluccaie*]: "America no good [*gudde*]! Hurrah [*orrè*] for Italy!" You know what the policeman [*pulizio*] did? He arrested me. The following morning, the judge [*giorge*] asked me: "What's the matter last night [*Wazzo maro laste naite*]?" I answered: "No talk [*tocche*] English!" "No? You have dollars?" And that pig of a judge [*giorge*] wasn't kidding, because he took ten pieces [*pezze*].]

This is not high poetry. Actually, to be honest, it isn't even poetry. But at least it's alive. At the same time, the petty bourgeois that finished college in Italy, or at least high school or even vocational schools, were "making the presses squeal" as we used to say. Their poems were in correct Italian, a language with no contact with reality; full of clichés and bombastic images; teary or bleating; always false and rhetorical; leftovers of memories and rhyme repertories such as the literary pustules of Riccardo Cordiferro. Sometimes you could hear the effects of this rhetoric even in authors who were writing in English, like Arturo Giovannitti.

In comparison, these caricatures, created for commercial reasons (the ten *pezze* is the compensation Ferrazzano received for his pieces,) had a purpose and were welcome by a public that felt their sting and appreciated their satirical intent. Rough, uncouth, many times with *double entendres*, they were coming out of a historical necessity and, to this day, they are among the few genuine documents left of the first period of Italian immigration to America.

July 15, 1962

ALMERINI, SENECA, CASTELLUCCI: THE UPPER CLASS LOOKS (DOWN) AT THE IMMIGRANTS

Doctor Achille Almerini,[2] ear, nose and throat specialist, graduated from medical school in Italy and moved to New York where he opened a successful practice with mostly Italian clients. With a difficult personality, always complaining and grumpy, he left America three or four times and finally returned to Italy where he concluded his life. His was the typical example of the chronic unhappiness that grabs many immigrants who, while they are in America are nostalgic for Italy; but, as soon as they go back, they realize they can't do without America which, in the meantime, has become a sort of addiction.

Like most of the people in his social class he was not satisfied with *fare l'America*. He was struck by the coarseness and ignorance of the former *cafoni*, but mostly by their vanity after they had made money or achieved some measure of success.

The nationalist undertone of those times can be read in a couple of his sonnets.

L'ITALIANITÀ COLONIALE

È una cosa piuttosto complicata:
Consiste soprattutto nella pratica
Di porger l'altra guancia o l'altra natica
S'uno ti dà un ceffone o una pedata.
Non guasta aver la casa mobiliata
D'una *Victrola* o una pianola asmatica
Sui cui suonare, come di prammatica
L'inno fascista di qualche serenata.
Se un *giuda* purchessia torna d'Italia
Decantando il Vesuvio e i maccheroni
Fondigli un busto o almeno una medaglia.
Ma se chiede: "Perché non t'insaponi?
Perché mandate qui tanta canaglia?"
Digli che sei paesano di Marconi.

---

2   Achille Almerini (1881-1947).

II

Dante non serve: nessuno sa chi sia.
Cristoforo Colombo serve a poco,
Dopo ch'hanno scoperto in alto loco
Che un norvegese gli spianò la via.
Meglio Marconi! La radiofonia
È attaccaticcia come il vizio del gioco:
Con quella tu, sdraiato accanto al fuoco,
Ci hai gli sport, l'arte e la filosofia.
Ci hai tutto quel che vuoi. A udir Marconi
Resta di stucco il *giuda* purchessia:
Non basta più se tu non t'insaponi.
È convinto. Confonde i maccheroni,
Le vongole con la radiofonia;
Gee whiz! ma sono *smart* questi cafoni!

COLONIAL ITALIANNESS

The thing is complicated.
It consists mostly in offering
The other cheek or the other butt-cheek
When one slaps or kicks you.
It also helps to have a house furnished
With a *Victrola* or an asthmatic keyboard
So you can play, as one should,
A fascist hymn and serenades.
If a *giuda*,[3] whoever he is, returns from Italy
Praising Vesuvio and maccheroni
Cast a bronze statue or at least a medal for him.
But if he asks, "Why don't you wash?"[4]
Why do you send here so many criminals?"

---

3 Here *giuda* stands for *Giudeo* [Jew]. *Giuda* in Italian refers commonly to Judas Iscariot, the apostle who betrayed Jesus. The assonance between *Giudeo* [Jew] and *Giuda* makes the two terms almost interchangeable. *Giudeo*, in turn, was the common adjective for Jewish and Jew throughout the nineteenth century in Italian, later superseded by *Israelita* [Israelite] and, more recently, by *Ebreo*. The term *Giudeo*, with many phonetic variations, is still present in several dialects. In the context of this poem, the term *giuda* clearly conveys disdain and contempt.

4 Implying "Why don't Italians wash?"

Tell him that you and Marconi[5] are fellow countrymen.

II
Dante is useless, nobody knows who he is.
Christopher Columbus is of little help
After the higher-ups discovered that
A Norwegian opened the way for him.
Marconi is better! Radiophony
Is sticky like a gambling addiction:
With it, laying down by the fire,
You get sports, art and philosophy.
Everything you want. When he hears Marconi
Even the *giuda*, whoever he is, is stunned:
It no longer matters if you don't wash.
He is sold. He confuses maccheroni and
Clams with radiophony;
Gee whiz! Aren't they *smart*, these cafoni!"

In other compositions we can read the irritation toward Americans who keep foreigners at bay; the antipathy toward Jewish competitors (regularly called *giudei*);[6] or the protest against prohibition that prevented Italians from drinking wine, as in the following *Noah Got Drunk*.[7]

LA SBORNIA DI NOÈ

Well, fin d'allora un proibizionista
C'era e fu Cam, che visto il padre brillo

E sbottonato, *screamed*… cacciò uno strillo,
Da far invidia a un prete metodista.

Sem e Giaphet, che s'erano provvista
La cantina, gli disser: "Sta tranquillo!

5   Guglielmo Marconi (1874-1937). Winner of the Nobel Prize for Physics in 1909, he is attributed the invention of the radio.

6   As explained in a previous footnote, in this poem the author uses the much stronger *giuda* instead of *giudeo/giudei*.

7   The reference is to a less well-known biblical episode whose protagonist is a drunken Noah (Genesis 9:24).

Keep quiet!" e appuntarono uno spillo
Dove le brache facean brutta vista

Quando Noè lo seppe, il giorno poi,
Chiamò Giafet e Sem, e disse: Bravi!
Sia benedetto chi uscirà da voi!

Ma quanto a Cam, *sun of a gun*, se i suoi
Nipoti gli somigliano siano schiavi
Vostri: sian *waiters or elevator boys."*

NOAH GOT DRUNK

Well, since the beginning a prohibitionist
Existed and he was Ham, who, having seen his father drunk

And exposed, *screamed*…. He let out a scream
that could make a Methodist minister jealous.

Shem and Japheth who had filled up
The cellar, told him: "Calm down!
Keep quiet!" and with a pin closed his pants
Where they were showing an ugly sight.

When Noah found out the next day,
He called Japheth and Shem and said: "Good!
Blessed will your descendants be!"

About Ham, *sun of a gun*, if his descendants
Look like him, let them be your slaves:
Let them be *waiters or elevator boys."*

This piece is in standard Italian, not in lingo and not even *slang*.
The Italian American lingo appears instead in his most famous sonnets,
full of sarcasm, whose function is to ridicule the enriched *cafone*. Here
is one where such character speaks:

I
Tengo lo *storo* in basso di città,
E quando vuoi puoi farmi il *telefòno*:
Viemmi a trovare, ogni momento è buono:
Mattina e sera il *business* mi tien là.

Distante,? Eh! Cento *blocchi*, non canzono:
Ma la distanza a te che te ne fà?
Don chèr, con tutte le comodità
Di tutti i treni e i *carri* che ci sono.

Non è un gran *trubel*; basta che tu provi;
Alla terza *Avenù* c'è *l'oliveta*:
Prendi il treno e discendi in *Aussonstritto*,
Fai quattro *blocchi* a destra e vedi scritto
Fra *l'andetèca* e il *rialestèta*:
"Qui si parla italiano" e lì mi trovi.

II
Vedi all'Italia, se anche ci hai moneta,
Magari non ti stimano per niente:
Sono paesi piccoli e la gente
Sa le faccende tue dall'A alla Zeta.

Qui, più ci hai *morgheg* sul *rialestèta*
Più *isi* tu diventi *prominente*,
E più *isi* ti fanno presidente
Le società, più sei analfabeta.

Con l'amicizia poi d'un pezzo grosso
Politiscia, *bartenda* od avvocato
Da *Mistar so end so* diventi un *bosso*;
Poi ti fanno il banchetto, tal e quale
Come da noi lo fanno al deputato,
E ti mettono in coppa del giornale.

III
Ma *sciùa* che prende tempo, e te l'ho scritto
(È meglio certe cose dirle prima):
Non credere che sceso dalla *stima*
Trovi le *pezze* in mezzo dello *stritto*.

Non aver fretta d'arrivare in cima:
Chi troppo corre non cammina ritto,
Nel *bisiniss* si comincia zitto, zitto,
Dal poco e miete solo chi concima.

L'America non è come al paese:
Non esser *stingi*, perché *guarda male*,
Ma se puoi cerca di salvar moneta.

Eniuè, lascia che te lo ripeta,
Perché questa è la cosa più essenziale:
Prima di tutto imparati l'inglese.

IV
Difficile? Non tanto quanto credi:
Sei giovane e fai presto ad imparare:
Ollrait, detsoll, sciarap, go om, gherare!
(A un seccatore che ti vien fra i piedi).

E quando non ti puoi capacitare
Tu chiedi: *Uazz de matter?* Se mai vedi
Una guagliona ci si dice: *ledi*:
E dà del *Mistar* fino al tuo compare!

Ma imparati l'inglese, perchè se
Domandi la tua strada in italiano
A uno *sciainatore*, o a quel del *fruttistendo*
Quello, sia piemontese o siciliano,
Per far veder che ne sa più di te,
Sai che riponde?: *ai du not anderstendo*.

V
Vedi un po' gli altri: i *germanesi*, i *scini*
(Ma sì, i giuda!) se san l'american:
Tu contentati d'essere italiano
Ma *spicca* come *spiccano* i vicini.

Neviorca l'ha scoperta Verrazzano!
D'accordo, già lo sanno anche i bambini:
Per cui se senti mai gridarti *ghini!*
Non ci far caso, e' un *lofar* o un villano.

Non cercare di farlo persuaso!
È inutile! Finisce che quel là
Ti fa un *blecch'ài* o ti fracassa il naso.

E tieni a mente! quando si fa il *fait*
Chi le busca ci ha torto e chi le dà
È uno *smart fello end evritingsollrait.*

VI
Ormai è una leggenda vecchia e sciapa
Che noi qui siamo un branco di straccioni:
Gli *airisc*, si sa, che son loro i padroni
Ci soffian dentro per l'amor del Papa.

A quelli che ci togli dalla capa
Che a Roma c'è i briganti coi tromboni.
Bisogna compatirli ... son coloni
Anche loro e han le sue teste di rapa!

Che ce n'importa? Ne abbiam fatte tante
Per affermare l'italianità
E mò facciamo il monumento a Dante!

Me lo saluta lei? direbbe Oronzo[8]
Ma in colonia, nun te ne incaricà!
Se l'ideale è *cip*, più *cip* è il bronzo.

I
I have a *store* in the lower city
And when you want you can make me *telephone* call:
Come by, anytime is good:
Morning and evening the *business* keeps me there.

Far? Eh! One hundred *blocks*, no kidding:
But the distance, what's to you?
I don't care with all the conveniences,
With all the trains and *cars* running around.

---

8   The meaning is rather obscure, however, from the context it is probably similar
to "Yeah, sure, that will be the day." The reference is to erecting a monument to
Dante.

It's not a big *trouble*; just try;
On Third *Avenue* there is the *elevated track*:
Take the train and get off on *Houston Street*
Go four *blocks* to the right and you will see the sign
Between the *undertaker* and the *real estate*:
"Italian spoken here." That's where you'll find me.

II
You see, in Italy, even if you have money
Chances are they don't respect you at all:
In those small towns people
Know your business from A to Z.

Here, the more *mortgage* you have on your *real estate*
The *easier* it is to become *prominent*,
And more *easily* they make you president
Of the club, even if you are illiterate.

With the friendship of a big shot
Politician, *bartender* or lawyer
From *Mister So-and-So* you can become a *boss*;
Then they give you a banquet, the same way
In Italy they do for a senator
And they put you on the newspaper's front page.

III
But *sure*, it takes time, I wrote you about that
(It's better to say certain things up front):
Don't believe that as soon as you get off the *steamer*
You can find *pieces* [dollars] in the middle of the *street*.

Don't be in a hurry to climb to the top:
Those who run don't walk straight,
In *business* one starts quiet and slow,
From little, only those who fertilize will harvest.

America is not like back home:
Don't be *stingy* because it *looks bad*
But if you can, try to save money.

Anyway, let me repeat it
Because it's the most important thing:

First of all, learn English.
IV
Hard? Not as much as you believe:
You are young, you will learn quickly:
Alright, that's all, shut up, go home, get out of there!
(To a pest that gets in your way).

And when you can't make sense of things,
You ask: *What's the matter?* But if you see
A cute broad, you call her: *lady*:
And call *mister* even your best friend!

Learn you English, because if
You ask directions in Italian
To a *shoeshine* or at that *fruit stand*,
That guy, even if he is Piedmontese or Sicilian,
To show you he knows more than you,
He is going to answer: *I do not understand.*

V
Take a look at the others: the *Germans*, the *scini*
(Yes, the giuda!) they know American:
If you content yourself to be Italian
Then *speak* like your neighbors *speak.*

New York was discovered by Verrazzano!
True: even children know that;
So if you hear someone call you *guinea*!
Ignore it, it's a *loafer* or a boor.

Don't try to persuade him!
It's useless. It will finish with that guy
Gives you a *black eye* or smashes your nose.

And keep in mind! When you get into a *fight*
Who takes the beating is wrong and who gives it
Is a *smart fellow and everything is alright.*

VI
By now it is an old and trite legend
That here we are but a heard of bums:
The *Irish*, we know, they are the bosses,

They fan the flames out of their love for the pope.

You can't get it out of their heads
That in Rome[i] there are brigands with flint guns.
Pity on them… they are peasants too,
And among them there are blockheads!

What do we care? We worked so hard
To affirm our Italian-ness
So, now, let's make a monument to Dante!

"Say hi to him for me!" Oronzo[ii] would tell me.
But in the colony, don't volunteer for the job!
If ideals are *cheap*, bronze is even *cheaper*.

[i] Rome here stands for Italy (synecdoche).
[ii] Oronzo: generic name, needed for rhyming.

Pasquale Seneca's (1890-1952)[9] work was similar to Almerini's, but instead of satirical verses he preferred a sort of jocular narrative. He was a teacher of Italian at the University of Pennsylvania in Philadelphia. Seneca took aim at the president of a fictional Italian association, in one of those colonial events where the main attraction was the vanity and ignorance of the immigrants who were trying to imitate the rituals of American society. *Il Presidente Scoppetta*[10] *ovvero la Società della Madonna della Pace* [*The President Scoppetta or the Madonna of Peace Society*], printed at the author's expense, is a series of comical/satirical vignettes of Italian American customs, dedicated to Eduardo Migliaccio (Farfariello) and clearly inspired by his satirical works.

This is not exactly a work of art. The official events represented were taken from reports that appeared in the *Opinione*,[11] a Philadelphia newspaper. The humor is too facile and obvious and the narration has no depth. In Seneca's pamphlets the members of this fictional society fight with each other; beat each other up; stab one another; maneuver

---

9   Pasquale Seneca (1890-1952). Professor at the University of Pennsylvania, Philadelphia, PA.

10   *Scoppetta* in Sicilian means double-barrel shotgun.

11   *L'Opinione*. (1906-1935). Philadelphia, PA.

to steal each other's official position; deliver ungrammatical speeches similar to those in the *commedia dell'arte* and so forth. The goal is to induce laughter through verbal misunderstandings. The characters all are immigrants from the town of *Brigantello* [Little Brigandville] in southern Italy who settled in one of the major cities of the Union. The main character is Francesco Saverio Scoppetta, founder of the newspaper *La Calzetta d'Italia*[12] and owner of a *passage* agency. What kind of passages these were, it's left vague, although, some claimed it was the passage that money made from other people's pockets to his own. Obviously these people were mean spirited and were spreading gossips that the president had a rather dubious past, and that he had to flee his hometown to avoid being arrested by the authorities. In any case, he now was one of the richest members of the community and a very powerful *politiscia* [politician]. Of average stature, stocky; with small and lively eyes; a red and fleshy nose and thick moustache, he gave the impression of being smart and funny. This was Scoppetta. He would be everywhere and take care of everything by himself. Scoppetta here and Scoppetta there. He knew what wedding would take place even before the spouses themselves knew they were getting married. And there would be no shoot-out before he had determined who was going to be shot. He was much, much more involved than a Rossini's *factotum*.[13] His enemies had their work cut off for them in trying to denigrate him! Scoppetta was highly aware of the great services he had rendered to his fellow *paesani* and of the credit he had accumulated with the entire colony. "I, I" he used to say, "I *startated* (started) Italianism and analphabetism in this nationality." ["*Io ho startato l'italianismo e l'analfabetismo in questa nazionalità.*"]

Among the society's activities there are *picchinicchi* [picnics], banquets and weddings; schemes for a *cavaliere*[14] medal; rivalries

12   Pun. *Calzetta* plays on the phonetic similarity with *Gazzetta* (Gazette.) *Calzetta* in standard Italian means ankle sock. The expression *una mezza calzetta* (half a sock) is used to indicate a person of little consequence, worthy of little or no consideration.

13   Reference to Gioacchino Rossini's character of Figaro in the opera *Il barbiere di Siviglia*. *Factotum* is Latin for Jack-of-All-Trades.

14   *Cavaliere* literally means knight. It is an official title bestowed by the Italian government on individuals who have distinguished themselves in their fields of endeavor. The title is given both to Italians and foreigners and it is highly coveted especially abroad among descendants of Italian immigrants where it is a rarity.

among groups; patriotic parades; members' funerals... In short, every imaginable occasion for mooching food; making bombastic speeches; engaging in conflicts of vanity and interests; showing off recently acquired wealth that were—and still are—the *raison d'être* of Italian American associations.

Even with the exaggerations of caricature, President Scoppetta reflects the conditions of the community that existed, more or less with identical characteristics, in stagnant immigration centers on the outskirts of large American metropolitan centers. The sharp-eyed observation on the part of a few educated individuals, marked a conscious distance between the urban class and the peasants who had just undergone the process of urbanization. This is a distinction that is as old as Italian literature. Pretty similar is the inspiration (to use a term adopted by our local Italian poets) of *Dante's Adventures in America*,[1] by V.A. Castellucci, clearly the pseudonym of an author who could not use his name. I picked up some clues that lead me to believe it must be a Florentine, probably a priest. In one of his satirical poems, the protagonist, Virgilio F. Publius,[2] a colonist—that is a *cafone*—trudges through vernacular insecurities by mixing together languages and creating some kind of Italian American vocabulary.

Virgilio came to America before Dante and when the latter arrives, he welcomes him with his horrendous language:

> Finalmente Dante, ti hai diciso di[3] approdare su queste *sciore sarpando l'Attellante* con la stessa *stima* che trasportò *maiselfe lazz taim ego*. *L'appinessa* di questo momento mi fa dimenticare *evritinga*: dimenticar persino la *deprescion*, il *ripillo* del *diocettisimo mandamento* e la vittoria di La Guardia...

> [Finally, Dante, you decided to land on these *shores sailing the Atlantic* with the same *steamer* that carried *myself lots of time ago*. The *happiness* of this moment makes me forget *everything*: I even

---

1   Castellucci, V. A. *Le avventure di Dante in America; poemetto satirico umoristico.* New York, Italian Publishers, 1935.

2   The reference is to Publius Vergilius Maro, the Ancient Rome's poet author of the *Aeneid*, and Dante's guide through the Inferno.

3   Substandard Italian for *ti sei deciso a.*

forget the *depression*, the *repeal* of the *Eighteenth amendment*[4] and La Guardia's victory…]

This language is way overdone, too heavy-handed, and doesn't have the plebeian mocking value of popular songs. Here one can hear an educated person from a small town imagining how the *cafoni* speak Dante's language. Even the dialect words aren't real: they are artificial, created for comic effect like Pig Latin. I can't imagine any immigrant ever using the word *gretti* for great or *sciore* for beach. The theme, however, is similar to that of the other examples I mentioned.

---

4   The Eighteenth Amendment to the United States Constitution, promulgated in 1919, prohibited the manufacture, sale, transport, import, or export of alcoholic beverages. (It is not generally well known that the amendment did not prohibit the purchase or consumption of alcohol.)

PROFESSOR *SAUSAGE* BECOMES *COMMENDATORE*

A while ago a friend of mine from Australia told me the story of how Professor Salsiccia [sausage] was given the title of *Commendatore della Repubblica Italiana*.[5] Earlier, he had received the title of *Cavaliere* by the king during the Fascist regime. My friend thought I would get outraged, instead he only succeeded in making me laugh. I answered: "It fits perfectly." "Why?" he asked. "Because when I was younger—I explained—the title of *Commendatore* was used for mockery. And *Onorevole*[6] was an outright expression of scorn. These titles have been given to so many less-than-respectable individuals that young people considered them terms of ridicule, not as rewards to be aspired to as achievements in their future lives."

I met Professor Salsiccia the first time I was invited to teach a summer course at S. University, in Australia. In the suburbs of that city there lives an enterprising Italian community with its fruit-and-vegetables and fish markets. They had raised money and were able to endow a chair in Italian. The majority of the community did not speak Italian but mostly some dialects and broken English. Yet, they vaguely understood that, in this new country, their origins in a land known for arts, sciences and letters still had some cachet. On the occasion of great banquets, they would trade in Italian celebrities with the same ability reserved for selling fish in the market or get the general contract for a real estate venture. With absolute ease they could mix together Dante, Verdi, Puccini[7] and Marconi regardless of who they were and what they had done.

The students called him *Salsiccia* for the color of his skin, closer to the gray variety of Tuscan *cacciatora* than the pinkish *luganega* of Lombardy. The name referred also to his body, swollen with fat and overflowing with human odor; a body that he moved with great

---

5   *Commendatore della Repubblica* is an official title and honor bestowed by the Italian government. It has higher standing than the more common *Cavaliere*.

6   Title commonly given to the members of the *Camera dei Deputati* [House of Representatives].

7   Giacomo Puccini (1858-1924). One of Italy's most famous opera composers. His best-known works are *Tosca*, *Turandot* and *La Bohème*.

pump down the streets, advancing with a majestic posture and always admiring his own self-importance. He believed that people who had arrived at his level in life behaved in that manner. He wasn't smart about anything and his body represented his vision of the world. When I first arrived at the university, he made sure I understood I owed my appointment to him and him alone, that he was an important person at the university and that the Italian consul trusted him. About himself, he would say: "I follow my bosses' orders." His bosses were top university administrators to whom he would try to kiss up with regular Christmas and New Year's cards; with words of obsequy and servility; and with poorly chosen wine gifts. An expert in the *arte del porvenir*,[8] he even gave one of his superiors a *Borsalino*[9] hat as a gift. Unfortunately the hat did not become the face of the person whom he regaled: nature gave him a penchant for kissing up to his bosses but not the sharp eye of an artist.

From the very beginning of our conversation I was struck by the complete absence in him of taste and artistic sensibility, of subtlety and critical ability. He was a teacher of Italian, but he could not tell the difference in the sound of a verse by Petrarch and one by Dante. His knowledge of the language was atonal. He had learned the words but the words had no cultural or emotional resonance for him. When he spoke, the words were like metal pieces in a linotype machine, all melting at the same temperature. When I talked to his colleagues, they said the way to evaluate him was not by his intelligence or acuity, but by simple grammar and syntax. I happened to replace him once in a language class and I noticed he was using a twenty-year-old book. If anybody mentioned that the book was deficient in many ways, he would look at them askance, as if that were a personal insult. He had a total phobia of learning and changing what he had learned. Just the idea of changing the textbook to him felt like a criticism to his doctrine. Later, I also realized that he had no interest whatsoever in Australian literature. Whenever a contemporary author was mentioned, he would prick up his ears as if he smelled a trap and would only mumble some

---

8   *Arte del porvenir.* Spanish idiom: the art of seeing ahead; foresight.
9   Famous brand of Italian fedora-style hats.

294 • THE TRANSPLANTS

previously memorized trite clichés. Textbooks were the only source of his culture. His knowledge was based on anthologies; memorized passages; and critical essays published in some abridged version of a survey of Italian literature published for middle-school children. He never had a personal opinion and always found shelter behind somebody else's critical assessment. His publications were dry, bookish and boring. In general, they consisted of collections of documents bunched together without any critical consideration. Complex and intricate points were always left without footnotes or, at most, were basic repetitions of information found in encyclopedias or anthologies. Astounding was his inability to comprehend the value of different sources and their prestige. The *Peretola Review*[10] and the *Nuova Antologia* for him were at the same level. The historical contingencies didn't matter. Whether a particular statement was made during a banquet or in a private letter or published in a book, it was all the same to him. It was in the documents, thus, it was enough. The more pages he put together the greater his work appeared to him, because it seemed that his brain resided in his backside. He called this: *scholarship*. The sense of humor that abounds among Anglo-Saxons was completely missing in his conversation. He would take everything seriously, even himself and his degrees. He had learned nothing from the country that adopted him except self-delusion. He would look at me with apprehension because I didn't have a *laurea*.[11] Someone must have told him I had done a few decent things for Italian literature, otherwise I am sure I wouldn't have been allowed to join other *laureati* [college graduates] like him. At the graduation ceremony at the end of the academic year he would wear his gown with great pride; careful that his mortarboard fit perfectly; with honor cords and tassel perfectly straight and aligned. He took his task as usher very seriously: he would stand by the door collecting invitation cards or he would lead the participants to their seats. His face and gestures showed a profound sense of self satisfaction. One could find him inevitably at every sermon, academic function and funeral. On some of these occasions I noticed that in the days when he wore

10   Fictional. Peretola is a small, rural town near Florence.

11   Italian university degree, equivalent to a baccalaureate. With the degree comes the title of *dottore*.

cap and gown he would swell up. I mean it in real, physical terms. He was born to be an officer good for parades, but instead he had become a professor. Yet, his real nature would come through in those functions. He liked to project a sense of authority. Whenever he could, his girth would inflate, his face would expand and his words would become even more pompous and bombastic. Clichés and common places would reach incommensurable proportions. This was the moment when his only real passion revealed itself. This peculiar individual, insensitive to art; ignorant of philosophy; for whom religion meant only participation in Sunday social functions; would be moved to tears—literally—in front of the idea of power signified by a uniform, a beret, a cord or a little star. He would have done god-knows-what for an extra bar on the epaulets of the prison-guard uniform he was mentally wearing. I understood all this when I heard him deal with students who were taking one of his courses. He would literally sweat from the pleasure of having people under his power; people who, if they passed his course, one day would look back and know they owed to him the glory of wearing a mortarboard and golden honor cords.

I kept wondering how a person with no literary interest could end up occupying a position that was so diametrically opposed to his nature. Finally, I found an answer. One should never believe that in social life there is such a thing as unexplainable and unreasonable fortune. Those who climb high must have some kind of qualities. The only question is whether the qualities match the nature of their success. In his case, Professor Salsiccia advanced by *providing services.* First of all, he was a faithful executor. There are so many arrogant scholars who are too busy with supposedly serious work and would never lower themselves to taking care of administrative duties. Salsiccia was only too happy to comply. He kept a meticulous archive with a card for each student where he reported every grade with comments on their progress. He truly enjoyed this job. To him, teaching Italian meant to keep the archive up to date. He was also performing the same kind of services for the Italian consul. The overworked consul didn't have the time to take care of school diplomas for Italians or Australians. Whenever new immigrants arrived with school-related problems, he would ask Salsiccia to solve them, and he was as happy

296 • THE TRANSPLANTS

as a seal in a pool to show his worth. He would look at the new arrivals with condescension and with the promise that he would take care of the problem. At the end of the conversation he would dismiss them with a pat on the shoulder, the same pat he was glad to receive from the university's higher-ups. That's how such an egregious ignoramus managed to become someone in Australia and in Italy. Without any human interest and artistic taste, with no intellectual curiosity, he had plenty of the wisdom of the peasant who has to navigate between the avid landlord, the sly merchants and the stubborn animals. All his acumen was directed, day and night, at playing different human elements against each other. And he became very good at that. He convinced the consul that he was a powerful figure at the university, where his colleagues considered him a little more than a dunce. With the university administration, he looked like he was the representative of Italians in Australia, a group of people the administration wanted to tap for donations. The administration could not judge him as a teacher in a discipline of which they were ignorant. The consulate considered him an ignoramus but thought that if Australians were so dumb as to give him a professorial position there was no harm in maintaining the fiction. When he got any kind of recognition from the consulate, he would use it with the university with the result of added cachet and a small salary raise. When the consulate sent him to Italy, several Italian academics who were hoping to be invited to Australia welcomed him with open arms, befriended him and treated him with the same kind of flattery that he would use to endear himself to his superiors. These very academics are now trying to get him a chair in an Italian university after he retires from his position in Australia. In the meantime they gave him an honorary doctorate.

On some occasions, though, Professor Salsiccia got involved in situations that were beyond his abilities. In those cases, his retreats have become famous. When he hitched his cart to a powerful person and, as sometimes happens, this person didn't come out on top, Professor Salsiccia felt guilty, but only because he didn't play the right card. Then, he did an about face. And since he had no finesse, wisdom or cleverness, he did so in such a coarse and transparent way that he got caught. He had bet on Fascism. He associated himself with the regime because he was convinced it would last a long time and even published books with the support of pro-Fascist organizations active in Australia. When Australia entered WWII against Italy, he understood the game was over and the ground had shifted under his feet. Always accustomed to be on the side of the authorities—like a good, solid cop—he wrote a letter to the city's newspaper denouncing Mussolini. The newspaper published it immediately as a sign of genuine conversion.

This is not to say that he was evil. To be evil, one has to have some inner strength, and Salsiccia has none of it. I saw him try to destroy harmless, defenseless people. But he didn't do it out of evil. It was just due to his ambition and vanity, none of which was commensurate with his abilities and strengths. In one occasion, he wanted to tear down the dissertation of a poor devil, an Italian Australian who had slaved for years doing research and trying to collect hard-to-find sources. The candidate wasn't particularly bright but he could interpret those materials as well as Salsiccia. He also didn't speak very good English, but neither could Salsiccia. Salsiccia had the accent of the low class districts where he grew up. For instance, he would pronounce *foist* for *first* and similar amusing things. In any case, he took a position against the dissertation not out of meanness but because of his swollen ego and the need to exercise authority. I remember I defended the poor devil, that dissertation toiler: my argument was that at that same university there were several professors who wrote English as badly as the doctoral candidate. Also, since the university was forcing people to write a book, even those who never had any intention to write one; the university was bound to tolerate that its library shelves would fill up with such monstrosities. In conclusion, a bit deviously, I reminded him that the departments gave a hundred dollars to professors who needed an editor to improve their language. Why couldn't something similar be done for a student as well? My subtle ironies, more than the objective value of the dissertation, carried the day. The dissertation was approved, contrary to the opinion expressed with a chuckling voice by Professor Salsiccia.

A few years after my Australian visit, I heard he had been invited to give lectures at Italian universities. I also heard about the mockery he drew behind his back. Once, he sent a circular letter to Italian professors to inform them that he had been charged with an important responsibility and he could offer teaching positions to Italian students in Australia. This was immediately after WWII when jobs in Italy were extremely scarce. The hope to go to Australia triggered a great competition. Some professors took him seriously and many students believed in the scam. It never happened. Australia didn't need professors, and even less it needed students to teach Italian. Professor Salsiccia did these kinds of things out of sheer vanity. When I confronted him about it, I realized he had no idea how much hurt he had caused. His only motive was his desire to aggrandize himself.

To conclude: for all these reasons I believe it was a good idea to award to him the honor of *Commendatore* of the Italian Republic. This shows that the times haven't changed. In the eras of Prime Ministers Giolitti [1892-1921]; Mussolini [1922-1943]; and Scelba [1954-1955];[1] the orchestra conductor has changed, but the music has stayed the same.

New York, May 27, 1955

---

1   Mario Scelba (1901-1991). Italian politician, prime minister from 1954 to 1955. He is most famous for being *Ministro degli Interni* (Minister of Interior Affairs, a portfolio that includes the state police) from 1947 to 1955, when riot-control police often handled labor strikes and anti-government demonstrations with violent methods.

A SMARTO EDITOR

Era *smarto* il dabben uomo,
Conosceva il *bisinisse*,
Era amico del *polisse*
E in colleggio non andò.[2]

From an Italian American song

[He was *smart*, the good man,
He knew his *business*,
He was friends with the *police*
And he didn't go to college.]

I couldn't find the original text of the lecture given by Fortune Pope at the International University of Social Studies[3] on the occasion of the official inauguration of the Chair of Journalism. He was preceded by a speech titled "Italy's New Social Structure" given by the Italian minister Antonio Segni.[4] In the course of the ceremony Pope received an honorary degree and a gold medal from the university. I was only able to get a summary of a conversation he had with some students after the lecture. These curious young people wanted to find out more about the *Progresso Italo-Americano* and they asked if they could interview the speaker, as is common place in America. Here is the dialogue that ensued.

Student: Is it true that you have modified the Italian language used in your newspaper?

Pope: Of course, otherwise nobody would be able to understand it. A newspaper cannot reach out only to people who know the language or those who teach it. These were aristocratic ideas of the Fathers of Italian *Risorgimento*. We had to confront the real issues. I am going to

---

2   Colleggio. Misspelling for *collegio*. In standard Italian it properly means boarding school. In Italian American it has the same meaning as in English.

3   Our research on institutions with this name yielded no results.

4   Antonio Segni (1891-1972). He was prime minister in two occasions and president of Italy from 1962 to 1964 when he resigned after a stroke.

tell you the story of what really happened to a naive and clueless Italian who wanted to rent out his house. He placed a paid announcement in the newspaper with a text that sounded something like this: "For rent, masonry-built house, no heat, no super, long-term commitment, next to elevated railroad." He got no inquiries. After several tries, this clueless Italian went to the person in charge of classified ads to complain. The employee took a look and, as soon as he finished reading, he broke out laughing. "But of course" he said, "how can you think you can find anyone with this thing? Let me take care of it for you." So, he edited the texts as follows: "For rent house of *bricchi* [bricks (formal Italian: jugs)], no *stima* [steam (formal Italian: estimate, respect)], no *genitore* [janitor (formal Italian: parent)], long *lista* [lease (formal Italian: list)], next to *olivetta* [elevated railroad (formal Italian: small olive)]. The next day the house was gone.

Student: Did you make other changes besides including the lingo of Italian Americans?

Pope: Of course. Our newspaper is in Italian but we are trying to bring the language closer to the American language, that is, the language spoken by the majority of our readers.

Student: Can you give us some examples?

Pope: Sure. This is where you can see the fruits of our technique. Standard Italian says *rivolgere un invito*: we say *estendere un invito* [extend an invitation]. We don't write *stupro* for rape; for us it is *assalto* [military-style assault]. We use *Casa Comunale* [Town Hall] instead of *municipio*; *corte* [courtyard] not *tribunale*; *confrontare* [to compare] instead of *affrontare* [to face]. In our neighborhoods even Jesus speaks like us. In our language he teaches: "Date ai poveri le vostre *possessioni*" ["Give your possessions to the poor"] instead of "*quello che avete*" ["what you have"]. Don't you think this is a great innovation? If I donated 100,000 dollars to the Accademia della Crusca[5] to complete its dictionary project, it would certainly include me among the authors quoted with reverence by the institution.

Student: Say, do your innovations also include grammar and syntax?

5   Accademia della Crusca [Academy of Bran]. The oldest academy of linguistics in the world, founded around 1570 by Florentine scholars, philologists and writers. It is the most authoritative, albeit non-official, arbiter of proper Italian language.

Pope: Our readers don't really care much. Does it really matter if the singular word *vaglia* [postal money order] does not change in the plural and remains simply *vaglia*? We turn the plural into *vagli*, which is the inexistent form of the inexistent singular *vaglio*. Calling it an error is sophistry. Do you think anybody noticed that we announced that the book *Tractatus de instructione confessorum* [*Treatise on the Training of Confessors*][6] is a "theology treatise?" A bit of *latinorum*[7] gives us a good reputation even if we can't translate it. Sometimes we give ourselves a bit more latitude. For instance: we cannot allow the verb *partorire* [to deliver a child] to use the auxiliary verb *avere*. Therefore we say: "La signora *è partorita*" [the lady is delivered] instead of *ha partorito* [delivered].[8] For us the board of education *fa noto i nomi* [communicates the names; in correct Italian: *rende noti i nomi*] of the teachers suspected of being Communist Party members.

Student: Supposedly, you take a similar approach to other foreign languages as well.

Pope: Well, since we don't speak any, we rely on our fact-checker in chief. He is also in charge of the creative order of our *spellatura*[9] [spelling; in standard Italian *spellatura* means skinning or flaying], or, as you say in Italian, *ortografia* [orthography]. It looks good when you see in print words like *Gesammelle Reuden* [correct spelling: *Gesammelte Rüden*], a book by a respected prelate. The Library of Congress most likely must believe it is a totally new book.

Student: Did you also have a chance to change history or geography?

Pope: Certainly. Axel Munthe was a famous Swedish tenor, at least for the readers of our newspaper. Curzio Malaparte is a French journalist. The trade attachés in foreign embassies are "Jewish diplomats." The

---

6 Antoninus Archiepiscopus Florentinus. *Tractatus de instructione seu directione simplicium confessorum.* Köln, Zell, ca. 1468-1470.

7 The reference is to a famous episode in Manzoni's *I promessi sposi.* The illiterate protagonist, Renzo, argues with the priest don Abbondio, complaining that he uses *latinorum* to confuse and deceive. *Latinorum* is pig-Latin for *Latin*.

8 The incorrect use of the auxiliary verbs (*essere* and *avere*) in compound tenses is an immediate marker of lack of proper education and is highly stigmatized.

9 *Spellatura* in Italian means skinning, flaying. It is the operation to remove the skin (*pelle*) from an animal.

Università di Pavia owns an institute in Florence. In Buenos Aires, Argentina, on May 30, 1952, a strong wind, the *bora*, was blowing so hard it felt like Trieste. And Italian President Luigi Einaudi must have been surprised when he found himself opening a Catholic university in Piacenza. Guido d'Arezzo, thanks to our intervention, became the "regulator of music." And Lorenzo de' Medici must worry sick up in heaven at the thought that Florence will host a symposium on his "development and completion…"[10]

Student: This is really something. It is good that you finally introduced to Italy—that has such lousy newspapers—a renovated Italian language full of sharp and subtle innovations. And you also gave us the opportunity to learn it in your very publication.

Pope: This is nothing! Did you know I elevated Giotto's fame by announcing that in Pomposa some experts found a lost canvas[11] of his work? Isn't this a true revolution in the history of painting? In comparison this is going to blow away the studies of [Giovanni Battista] Cavalcaselle, Bernard Berenson, Emilio Cecchi, Mario Salmi, Roberto Longhi…[12] But this is not all. I even invented the modern

---

10   Axel Munthe (1857–949). Swedish psychiatrist and archeologist. A polymath and polyglot, he lived in Italy.
• Curzio Malaparte (1898–1957). Italian journalist and writer. His real name was Kurt Suckert. *Malaparte* means "the bad side."
• Università di Pavia, founded in 1361. Pavia, near Milan, was the capital of the Longobard kingdom from 568 to 774.
• *Bora* is the wind from the north-east that blows toward the Adriatic see, typical of the city of Trieste.
• Luigi Einaudi (1874-1961). Italian politician and economist. He was the first president of the Italian republic from 1948 to 1955.
• The city of Piacenza is indeed the seat of a branch of the *Università Cattolica del Sacro Cuore* [Catholic University of the Sacred Heart] with headquarters in Milan.
• Guido d'Arezzo (991/992– ca 1033). Musicologist. He is considered the inventor of modern musical notes and staff notation.

11   Giotto di Bondone (1266/7-1337). Painter and architect, he reintroduced perspective into western painting. His most famous works are the cycles of frescos respectively in the church of San Francis in Assisi and the Scrovegni chapel in Padua.
• Famous Benedictine abbey in northern Italy whose first traces go back to 874.
• There are no known paintings on canvas by Giotto.

12   Giovanni Battista Cavalcaselle (1819–1897). Writer and art critic.
• Bernard Berenson (1865–1959). Art critic and professor. His best known work

technique of journalism-as-riddle. People believe we print so many errors and outlandish stuff because we are slovenly scoundrels. Not true. Do you want to know the real secret? We want to sharpen our readers' minds. For instance, recently we published this news item, with no supporting context. In the middle of the paper, without particular emphasis, with the headline "Meeting between Dino Grandi and István Bethlen,"[1] we published the following article:

> The Italian minister of foreign affairs arrived today in Hungary from Poland. He was given a warm welcome by the local authorities, the population and the Italian colony. Minister Grandi immediately went to visit the Hungarian Minister of Foreign Affairs Bethlen. They examined a series of issues concerning Italian-Hungarian relations and the problems that are presently destabilizing Eastern Europe. After the conversation the ministers declared their satisfaction at the progress made.

Undoubtedly some of our readers must have been delighted. For us, instead, it was just sheer joy to realize that nobody caught on to our practical joke. At the top, above the headline, we didn't add the warning that this event took place thirty years ago. For a newspaper editor the best insurance against mistakes is that his readers will never be able to call him to task. When one realizes this, believe me, it inspires great confidence. At times we do the same with statistics we receive from Italy. They are totally useless. Just imagine: we once published an item stating that on such-and-such a day the port of Brindisi[2] had a total traffic of 600,000 passengers. I made Brindisi the first port in the world. Not even New York can compete with it. And, no need for corrections. This also is part of the journalistic technique I am teaching you now. A well made newspaper never admits its errors. Not only.

---

is *The Italian Painters of the Renaissance*. New York, Phaidon, 1952.
- Emilio Cecchi (1884–1966). Art and literary critic.
- Mario Salmi (1889–1980). Art critic and historian.
- Roberto Longhi (1890–1970). Art historian.

1   Dino Grandi (1895–1988). Minister of foreign affairs from 1929 to 1932.
- István Bethlen (1874-1946). Hungarian prime minister from 1921 to 1931.

2   Brindisi. City on the coast of Apulia. The port of Brindisi presently is an active naval passenger traffic hub, with service primarily to Greece.

Its readers should never become suspicious. I gave you examples that prove that it is possible to publish anything without consequences. For instance we wrote both that "Italy's southern regions have the highest suicide rate" and that "Italy's southern regions have the lowest suicide rate." You, Italian youngsters, should learn from those of us who live on the other side of the ocean that you can do anything you want. And if you do that, not only will you make money, but you will be asked to teach, and you will even be supported by the prestigious presence of the prime minister. Here are our recommendations for the new generations of Italians: follow the example of the journalists from the other side of the ocean; move the Italian language to tears; shake up syntax; correct history, orthography, data and dates. If you do so, you will receive praise by the new Italy, the new Italy born in the name of democracy....

[I could go on, if anybody wished.]

New York, November 25, 1955

FOUR DOGS FIGHTING FOR THE SAME BONE

On October 4, Professor Lustri-Pungiglioni[3] passed away. He taught language, literature and Italian civilization at Brander College.[4] For many years he went by the sole name Lustri [luster], a name that fit him perfectly, by the way. He fell in love with the historical figure of Princess Pungiglioni,[5] a star of Italian *Rinascimento* so important that to this very day scholars are tracking down the lists of her dirty laundry and the recipes of famous dishes prepared by her cook. Since he wrote a book about her, Professor Lustri convinced himself that he had become a member of the family. He thus appealed to a judge to have the name Pungiglioni added to his own, explaining that he could not live without it. He couldn't add the title of prince because American law does not recognize such titles. However, he could change his name. American law allows even a street sweeper to call himself Washington or Lincoln even though these names belong to the national patrimony. With foreign names they are even more lax, even if one chooses Bonaparte[6] or Pungiglioni. Back in Italy, the real Prince Pungiglioni protested but he could do nothing against an American decree that has validity only in America. There is no patent to protect the name Pungiglioni: his ancestors forgot to apply for one in Washington, D.C. And, incidentally, Washington, D.C. did not exist in those days.

The news of his impending demise leaked out of the family circle and trickled into the little world that occupies itself with Italian studies; and, most of all, occupies all the college teaching positions in Italian—which have not changed at all for the last twenty years. Here some curious phenomena begin to appear. Since there are no new university positions in Italian, whenever someone leaves by resignation, retirement or death, the event is immediately object of intense interest; like what happens in the army when a general retires. As the news of

---

3   Clearly a fictitious name. *Lustri* suggests *illustre* [illustrious]. *Pungiglioni* means bee stingers.

4   Fictitious.

5   Fictitious name.

6   Last name of Napoleon.

306 • THE TRANSPLANTS

his imminent demise spread, secret meetings were scheduled. Letters were written. Telephones rang off the hook. Discreet visits took place. Some individuals, who had not talked to each other in a long time, had lunch together. College presidents received as gifts volumes from people they had never heard from before. Even the cardinal was quietly told that, after a brief stop in purgatory, a new soul would be soon on his way to heaven; and that, in the meantime, a chair would be available right away for a Catholic professor.

Comforted by the fervid prayers of the aspiring candidates, wrapped in veils of sighs and sorrow, Professor Lustri-Pungiglioni finally became a "dear departed."

As soon as the city newspaper published the obituary with a biography prepared by the family, the phenomena increased in intensity and relevance.

Meanwhile, in Orlando, Florida, the author of the *History of Italian Teaching in the United States* and other Italophile essays, was counting the years before the age for a full pension after teaching Italian grammar without ever teaching his student to speak Italian. These students were the children of lucky farmers of orange groves. He taught them for more or less sixty semesters, always using the same identical textbook from the beginning of his academic career, which happened to be just after he dropped out of medical school in Naples. The news of Lustri-Pungiglioni's death arrived by means of the local Italian language newspaper he was using in class; despite the fact that the periodical is written in *lingua cafonica*,[7] namely a mixture of sentences in the dialect of Abruzzi translated into Italian and mixed together with local terms derived from English. The short news item was originally a wire sent from New York to Italy by the agency ANSA and published in an Italian newspaper. With a few translation mistakes and typos picked up along the way it finally landed in Florida. Here it sparked in him a sudden burst of enthusiasm, something that had never happened before. He decided that this time he would give it a shot. Up until now, he had never applied for a position that would finally reward his labor as historian of Italian culture. The position was

---

7 *Lingua cafonica*. Approximately "cafonic" language. Brilliant neologism that mixes *cafone* and *fonica* [phonic].

in New York, with those great libraries, archives, and the possibility to give lectures to a knowledgeable public. Finally he could get out of his *borgo selvaggio*[8] [hick hamlet]. (That's how, in his literary jargon, he would call that beautiful city nested among citrus groves—but only in the secrecy of his own mind, never in public, to avoid creating conflicts.) He could not miss the chance. So, certain of his entitlement he started gathering his credentials.

In Boston, on the eastern hill, where many unremarkable Italian families live, lights were shining in Ms. Bonuzzi's parlor. Her husband was a teacher of Italian in one of the city's middle schools. But because there were very few students of Italian, he had to refresh his Latin studies from the time when he was a young lad. He was also teaching Spanish, which he had learned in summer school in intensive programs administered with huge injections of forty-day courses. The lady of the house had always dreamed of living in New York where her family also lived and would scold her husband for not being smart enough to get a job there. When she heard the news on the radio, a torrent of images flooded her mind. Weekends with her family… Strolls along Fifth Avenue… As soon as her husband walked in the door with a bundle of papers to grade under his arm, she gave him one of her usual lectures. It was urgent for him to go to New York as soon as possible and see that college's president. But first he should ask his Boston colleagues for letters of recommendation; collect all the book reviews he had written for professional journals; all the radio interviews; and even that rare congratulation note from the Italian consul. He should wear his best winter coat, new shirt etc. etc. It was an endless flow of instructions, one on top of the other, so chaotic and rambling that if he had followed these he wouldn't be able to follow those and vice versa.

From a country in central Europe, where she was teaching in a finishing school for rich young ladies, a girl[9] sent a telegram to the college president: "Profoundly sorry death adored teacher, eager to continue splendid tradition." To tell the truth, to those of us who knew both the deceased and the candidate, that note sounded a bit off-key.

---

8 *Natio borgo selvaggio* [native uncivilized hamlet]. It is one of the most famous citations from the poem *Le Ricordanze* by Giacomo Leopardi, composed in 1829.

9 *Ragazza* in the original.

Many times we heard the young candidate wonder how such a vane individual, enamored only of himself and his own eloquence, ever managed to become a professor of Italian literature in a prestigious college. And, on the other hand, many times we heard the teacher joke about the critical theories of the girl he himself had promoted with top grades. To him her criticism was just a bunch of foolishness, typical of today's youth perverted by critics like Benedetto Croce[10] and De Sanctis about whom the only thing he knew were the names.

Marquise Boninsegni[11] had just disembarked from the ocean liner *Cristoforo Colombo* when, on the pier, she ran into a friend, a teacher, who was surprised to see her in New York. The first thing the teacher told her was that the professor had suddenly died and his position was vacant. Marquise Boninsegni wasn't really a marquise. She was the daughter of a marquis but she wasn't the oldest child.[12] Moreover, she was married to an American commoner whom she had met during WWII, stuffed in an U.S. Army officer's uniform, with an automobile, and tons of chocolates in his pockets. So, she married him. Once she got to New York she must have been a bit disappointed when she found herself doing house chores with her husband who had a modest job working in a bank. When she heard about the position she started hoping she could make use of the *laurea* she had been awarded in Italy several years earlier. It was a nice *laurea* that showed that the marquise, a beautiful lady who knew how to dress beautifully, had studied Latin and Ancient Greek with a final grade of 80/100.[13] Her thesis was on a *canzoniere*[14] of the 15th century. The marquis in all those years had not given a single thought to Italian literature. First it was because of the war; then the marriage; then the need to learn English so she could communicate with her husband's family that looked at her askance

---

10   Benedetto Croce (1866-1952). Philosopher, historian and literary critic. He was one of the most influential thinkers of twentieth century's Italy.

11   Fictitious.

12   Normally, aristocratic titles are inherited only by the first born, although different traditions exist in various parts of Europe, with numerous exceptions and special privileges.

13   Equivalent to a C average.

14   Collection of poems.

when she tried to pronounce the *th* sound that always came out like a *t* from her splendid set of teeth. All these things had kept her mental abilities and time totally busy. On top of this let's not forget to add that she had achieved a rather solid position thanks to her canasta-playing skills. Now, the idea that she could take advantage of the degree she had in the drawer went straight to her head. "An Italian *laurea*…. It must be worth a lot." When she realized that the marquise was interested in the position, her friend—who wouldn't have minded the position for herself—suddenly turned cold. Her friend told the marquise that in New York City only private schools can hire people with foreign degrees. Public schools demand an American degree, plus a dozen courses on pedagogy that teach people how to teach so that they end up knowing absolutely nothing about the subject they are going to teach. And, finally, she said, it was more important to have the correct English accent than a native Italian accent, even if the position was in Italian. The students, she hinted, would laugh at a teacher with an accent and the school's prestige would plummet. The marquise was crushed. At dinner that night she took it out on her husband: "What kind of country is this America of yours… A bunch of barbarians… They don't even recognize the value of an Italian *laurea*… Do they even know who Professor Vandàli was?"[1] To tell the truth, the marquise attended only two lectures by Vandàli, either because she skipped his classes or because Vandàli was always away on some kind of academic business and barely lectured at all. Her husband, who kept hearing that name, at a certain point sought out information whether the two of them had something going, but he got back excellent reassurance: Vandàli was an old, harmless man in a good state of preservation. No danger loomed.

In a university in a western state there was a young professor of Italian who never read Italian newspapers and knew he wouldn't learn a thing from the Italian-language newspaper published in his town. Indeed, he prohibited his students from reading it. He preferred reading the classics, critical essays and erudite journals. He was passionate about new studies that tried to reconstruct the context of literary works

---

1 Professor Vandàli (whatever his real name was) must have been the marquise's (whatever her real name was) thesis advisor.

through the investigation of paintings, sculptures and architectural works. He followed Berenson and Heinrich Wölflin.[2] For him Italian literature, even contemporary literature, was dead literature to be studied like those of the Aztecs and the Babylonians. Much of what he talked about was way over the heads of his students who, from previous studies, had learned about *heritage, environment, religion* and *race*. Some of them managed to learn the new language made of *structure, engagement, models* and *sensibility*. He would ask, for instance, if the *Divine Comedy* was a drama or a narrative. He was up-to-date with new critical trends and his writings were very involved, alluding to a profundity that wasn't there. He spoke agile words and conducted subtle analyses with a rich English vocabulary. His taste led him to poets of turbulent and dark periods, complicated and ambiguous. Here he could practice his critical skills that consisted more in inventions than discoveries. He too was caught by the frenzy to send his publications to the college president.

In a few days the table of the college president was flooded with dozens of diplomas, piles of books, newspaper clips, abstracts from academic journals, letters of support and recommendation. He received applications from two full professor, four assistant professors, some twenty lecturers, a couple of unemployed journalists and more. Suddenly a rumor started circulating from north to south and from east to west. The successor had already been selected. Before the search had even begun.

New York, December 23, 1956

---

2   Heinrich Wölflin (1864–1945). Swiss art historian.

THE FAKE AMERICAN

Ms. Sofia Chiochi, the daughter of Italian immigrants, was taught by her parents that in order to *fare l'americana* [look/act like an American] she always had to appear optimistic and happy with the world. And she learned her lesson well. Her mouth constantly sprays praise and enthusiasm, gushing sugared fluids and sticky jam. Saccharine pills tumble out of her lips in every occasion and in every moment of her life. Every single sermon she listens to in church is *magnificent*. The dances she attends are *splendid*. The lectures she goes to are *extraordinary*. Not to speak of the receptions! At the end she runs to the hostess, grabs her hand with both of hers, or, if she is closer, throws herself on her and kisses her on both cheeks: "Just *marvelous*"; "I have never had such a *great time*"; "It takes *you* to do things *that well*"; "A total *success.*" She rests her voice on "*wonderful*"; sings again and again "*Thank you*"; stretches on purpose "*how much I enjoyed it*" to make it last longer. Then she cocks her little cute head to the side, pouts her lips and appears to be in a constant state of exhilaration; like a child who was just given a piece of candy. Her face becomes even redder than the makeup she wears because her blood goes straight to her head when she slobbers that way.

In her family nobody is ever sick. Even if someone is delirious with fever, she would always say that everything is fine. She uses Italian suffixes for endearment to an excess and she revels in them, in a Tuscan accent that is completely unnatural in a woman from southern Italy. Often she asks one of the Italian teachers she knows if they are willing to go to her house to lead a conversation or to give a *conferenzina* [tiny little lecture] to a bunch of girls she is tutoring in Italian. I also was asked, and I accepted. As soon as I finished she jumped all over me and almost ate me alive with compliments. "Nobody, nobody has ever spoken so well…" "Your erudition is scary…" "I read all your works and I owe you everything I know in this life…"

In that moment of sullen depression, while I was keeping my glance low to avoid those ridiculous effusions, I noticed the big toe that was sticking out of her sandal, nail painted deep red, covered with the thin nylon net of modern stockings. I didn't say a word, but I placed my thick shoe sole on the toe and started pressing with deliberate cruelty, as if it were the button of the escape hatch of a submarine about to sink. I thought she would scream *"Murderer!"* and throw me out of her house. Nothing happened, except a terrifying smirk of pain that lowered my blood pressure. I had to stand there and listen that my conversation was the *nicest* she ever heard in her life....and that I was a real poet. Then, limping, she walked me to the door.

New York, April 13, 1956

PORTRAIT OF CARLO PATERNO

The majority of Italian immigrants who have achieved great success in America have been builders or contractors. This is what I evinced from thousands of obituaries I have been collecting for over fifteen years. These were people, Americans of Italian descent, whose names were sufficiently important at the time of their death to appear in the pages of the *New York Times* or the *Herald Tribune*. The data I collected is a very rich source of information that maybe some day will be useful to sociologists interested in a serious analysis of the power, wealth and determination of Italians in America—something more serious than the usual blather that is regularly published.

I got to know only one of these *contrattori* (the English word is contractor) from up close: Mr. Carlo Paterno.[1] He is the biggest of them all: the biggest by the size of the fortune he made, even in American terms; and the biggest in terms of personality. Whenever I think back about him, the first thing I remember are his lively eyes, sparkling with intelligence and energy. They flashed like beams of light and gave his Italian American and Anglo-Italian speech a deeper meaning, enriching his words with nuances and allusions. Under the lower lip there was a birthmark that matched the shape of his face with his curling Spanish-style mustache. I can still see him moving around with flair and a pleasant and willful smile. I always perceived in him a superior form of power that emanated not from money but from a faun-like vitality connected with the eminent functions of life. There was no conversation with him that didn't leave me with an internal tickle, like an electric charge; and the impulse to take some initiative, to do something. Paterno didn't trade in high concepts or moral exhortations; nor would he tell particularly compelling stories. It was something that came directly from his own persona. He was short, stocky, a bit plump, and would look at people straight in the eye. He had a slightly hoarse voice, probably his only annoying trait. I met him for business reasons. When I was director of *Casa Italiana*

1   Charles Paterno (1876-1946). He graduated from Cornell Medical School in 1899 but never practiced medicine. He became a very successful contractor with many large projects to his credit in New York.

he donated a library of twenty thousand volumes—a collection that by now has grown to approximately thirty thousand volumes. In addition to the classics, the most important texts of criticism and all the general reference works needed by scholars of Italian; the updated collection contains books and periodicals on modern Italy going back to 1861.

His brothers were also contractors, although they weren't as smart or as successful as he was. They also gave a great contribution to the library, donating the construction of the physical building; while he, with better insight, took upon himself the onus of financing the library. This, in the end, turned out to be actually less expensive than the contributions by his brothers and brother-in-law, and his name will also live for ever in the collection that was named in his honor. With this initiative he had become the perfect American-style patron of the arts.

I ran into him in several circumstances. He had the same great quality I noticed in most successful business people: he knew his own limits. Thus, for the selection of the books he trusted the advice of a competent person, Doctor Henry Furst[2] (at that time I was still living in Italy,) and never interfered or disagreed with him. He just wanted the budget to come out right with the books properly bound and correctly placed on the shelves. His great satisfaction came from the fact that the library was used by a growing number of grateful scholars. Whenever he came to visit he was always on time, dressed comfortably and appropriately, without ostentation, just as one would expect from a man his age and station. The flower in the lapel wasn't affectation. He genuinely loved flowers and for his entire life cultivated this passion. Once he had become wealthy, he scratched an itch he had since he was a boy and built for himself a manor on the left bank of the Hudson. This was a dream he had all his life, since the time when, as a young boy, he pushed his little rowboat upstream on the Hudson River, the river that Verrazzano thought was a sea channel.

In a castle's annex he built spacious green houses, each equipped for a specific purpose, with different levels of temperature and humidity for the various types of plants and flowers he was growing. He

---

2   Henry Furst (1893-1967). Polyglot and Italophile. He worked as correspondent for the *New York Times Book Review*.

employed several gardeners who took his orders and recommendations meticulously. He would talk with them for hours about his favorite subject and shared with them ideas about techniques and observations, always respectful of their knowledge and respected by them for his. It was a great pleasure to see him whirl from one plant to the next, from a seed bed to the next, looking around with his sparkly eyes and pointing to the successes and the progresses of this and that flower or plant. He created hybrids and tested grafts of all sorts. All the people who fall in love with nature end up playing with it, trying to compete with it and its creations. And so did he.

Doctor Paterno was born in Castelmezzano in the province of Potenza in 1878 [sic]. By chance events, he was pushed on the road that took him and his family this far. His father, a brick layer and small contractor in Naples, went bankrupt after the earthquake of 1883 and decided at that point to leave the city and emigrate to America. In New York he picked up the old profession but took care to develop a special expertise, as is basically required by the industrial production model of this country. His specialty was erecting foundations for buildings. After he finished building the underground perimeter walls of a building, he would leave the rest of the job to someone else and move on to the next contract. That's how he was described to me by an architect who got to know him: He was a tough man who used to slap around his children. Like all the old immigrants of that time, he was pressured by the need to earn money as fast as possible and to save every penny he could. He never turned down a job and, even after he could afford it, was never able to fully relax and enjoy life. Whoever will write the history of European immigration to America should bear in mind the pressure they felt and the effects of this mindset, even after they had achieved security and material comfort.

An anecdote of those days tells us about little Carlo on a Sunday, carrying a bunch of newspapers on his back, on his way to sell them. To save the price of the ticket he didn't use the tramway. At a certain point he stopped to rest on a bench in a park and fell soundly asleep. He was so tired that he didn't wake up even when someone stole all the newspapers—and even his shoes. When he woke up he was terrified. There was no way he could go home in that state, so he started

316 • THE TRANSPLANTS

wandering about. Suddenly in a flower shop he saw a help-wanted sign. He inquired and was hired immediately. As the day-salary could not cover the loss of the stolen newspapers and shoes, he decided to raise the price of each bouquet and pocket the difference. This way he was able to cover his losses.

His ambition was to be a doctor but he didn't have the money for the tuition. His creativity and business sense came to the rescue. When he was younger he had invented a tool to curve the tip of gas-light burners resulting in brighter light and lower consumption. He had tried without success to show his invention to the chairman of a gas company. One day he read in the newspaper that the company's chairman had died. He showed up at his office and, with an air of despair, he claimed he had an appointment with him, made by phone. He managed to be received by the vice-chairman who decided to give the invention a try and test it in the stations of a subway line for a month. Paterno was sure his contraption could save at least ten percent. However, to be sure, he had the ingenuity and the patience to go every day to the stations and turn down the valve of each lamp just a tiny bit, and then return in the morning to set them back so that nobody would discover his trick. At the end of the trial period he got a call from the now-chairman who informed him the savings were even higher than predicted and wanted to buy his patent. He received a sum of money (his son told me it was $500) that he used to pay for tuition at Cornell Medical School, one of the best in the country, thus achieving his goal.

Destiny interfered and steered him in the direction of the construction business. He wanted to practice as a doctor, but his father, who in the meantime had become a full-fledged general contractor, died suddenly while in the middle of a major project. Doctor Paterno and his brothers decided to take over and finish the job. At the end, he had enough money to finance the construction of a larger building. He soon realized that this activity was more remunerative than being a doctor and decided to invest in this industry and in real estate. In the first two years he was able to set aside $22,000. No doctor at the beginning of the career could ever make that kind of money. He never used his medical degree but he was very proud of it. When World

War II started, he was gratified when he received a draft card calling him up to serve as a *doctor*. He dusted off the briefcase with all the tools and reported to the recruitment center. Here it was discovered that there had been a mistake and that the draft card was destined to a different Doctor Paterno. This was a major disappointment for him.

At first he worked with his brothers. None of them was a creative architect: they didn't create new forms nor did they think too hard about the ancient ones. In their buildings nothing is reminiscent of Italy. They made American buildings typical of that particular era, which means functional structures with veneer facades slapped onto hard skeletons. They were the first to come up with the idea to build apartment buildings higher than six floors.[3] They were masters at juggling the building code with its more and more stringent regulations concerning elevators, furnaces, water heaters, trash compactors and running water in addition to the technical aspects of materials and building techniques. The times were also very favorable. Banks were eager to lend and the government threaded light on taxes. One of Dr. Paterno's suppliers, with a mixture of anger and admiration, once told me: "You see, that man can barely sign his own name (he was wrong about this) but if you ask him how much steel; how many miles of tubing; how many thousands of bricks you need to build a forty-two-storey building; he can tell you in a second." In his office I remember seeing autographed photos of some of America's most important steel tycoons with notes of friendship and admiration. The signature of this immigrant to them was as good as their own. The Paternos knew how to build, and he knew where to build. As New York kept growing, their imagination expanded ahead of the city. It was actually their imagination that guided the city expansion, along the Hudson River, for instance; where they built the first edifices at 280, 285, 290 Riverside Drive. Their company was called *Skybeam Realty Corporation*. They were Americanized and left it to Italian wine merchants to use evocative names of Italian cities or past glories. *Skybeam*, not *Roma*. They also speculated on land and buildings, and were relentless in their negotiations on the price of construction materials. Doctor

3 New York building code required residential buildings with more than six floors to be equipped with elevators.

Paterno built his castle on a piece of land valued at $200,000. He bought it for $50,000. When he thought that the real estate tax was too high, about $30,000 a year, he razed the castle and on the land built a garden city made of large buildings of various heights. Each apartment had at least one window overlooking the river. He rented them out at reasonable prices and filled them all up quickly, despite the hard times (1939).

The true sign of his personal greatness was his strategic thinking during the economic crisis of 1930. Here, Doctor Paterno rose above the other members of his family as well as the majority of builders and developers in New York. When the crisis hit, every single developer and builder was tangled up in land speculations, with dozens of new projects on the way. In order to sail upwind, he understood that it was necessary to change tack and he turned out to be the only one who knew how to do it. Instead of burning money to finish buildings that were destined to remain vacant, he had the intuition that it was crucial to save cash, as much cash as possible. To restore the confidence of small depositors, President Roosevelt had recently passed a law insuring bank deposits up to $5,000.[4] Paterno told me that he had all his relatives open small accounts in all the insured banks in the city, thus squirreling away the cash he had on hand. Instead of saying "This building is worth two million: I will invest half a million more and save it." He would sell it and lose money. In some cases he accepted to be foreclosed by his major lender, the Metropolitan Insurance Co. He lost a dozen buildings this way and abandoned several more halfway and paid contractual penalties. As he was telling me those stories, his eyes were shining with a certain kind of faun-like and Mephistophelian glee.

In those terrible days of fear and economic distress, our conversations always ended up on the only topic that mattered: the Great Depression and its effects on America. He mentioned he had liquidated loans worth five million at six percent interest for $30,000. He also sold 270 Park Avenue for half a million dollar, the same building he had refused to sell for nine million dollar just a few months earlier. At a certain point, after a moment of silence, he added: "Look, if I can get

---

4 Today's Federal Deposit Insurance Corporation.

out of this crisis still standing, I will be much richer than before." His relatives didn't take his advice and reacted differently. He had warned them: "Get out of it. Pay the penalties. It doesn't matter. Don't stay in. Sell everything." I still remember the enormity one of them told me while he was sitting, or, better, sinking, in an armchair, almost chocking on his words: "Can you imagine, Dr. Prezzolini? All I have left are two million…" A friend of mine who was also present and I exchanged glances, winking: "Maybe we should lend him a dime to take the subway home…"

I liked the attitude of the risk-taker in Dr. Paterno. He could handle a bad day with the same happy face as a good one. He would talk about liquidations as if he were talking about purchases. And, in fact, in the end, he was still standing and had enough time to build another city before dying. On another occasion he confessed: "I have brick fever. Even when I am in the country relaxing, I can't stop building walls…" He knew how to gain the affection of people who were working for him. An architect told me that the subcontractors that worked for him knew they could always get a loan without going to the banks. And his suppliers knew that while he wasn't generous, which would have been foolish, he was intelligent and understood difficult situations. He understood the world and knew how to take advantage of opportunities. Once he told me about a nit-picking inspector whose ruling could cost him several thousands of dollars without any real benefit to anybody. He understood that in order to get rid of him he had to give money to a third party. Unlike the majority of contractors and landlords, he never gave much fodder to lawyers and was never dragged into litigations and scandals by the local press. My relationship with him was cordial without being too close because I was really paranoid that he would think I was eyeing his money. I always treated him with the respect he deserved for the generous gift that is at the heart of *Casa Italiana*. But I never buttered him up, or, at least not too much. I was invited to his castle once and there I caught an aspect of his personality that I would have never imagined. I knew his love for flowers but I didn't know about his kindness toward animals. It was winter time and I noticed that in one of the castle's large, heated rooms, a little window, up high, was left open. He explained that on one occasion when the window was open two pigeons had flown in and nested on a ledge. He gave order to leave it open so that they could go in and out as they wished.

Some time later, spontaneously, he donated to the library of *Casa Italiana* a sum of money whose interest could be used for maintenance and other basic needs. It was a kind thought. To thank him for the gift we organized a nice ceremony with a speech by Columbia's president, Nicholas Butler.[1] The *Casa* that day was filled with rare plants and flowers brought in from his green houses. On that occasion I had a chance to speak with his gardeners. One of them told me: "You probably can't believe it, but for all his millions he is an unhappy man." The gardener ignored he was talking to a person who had no problem believing him. Every time I have been able to penetrate the intimate life of someone who appears to be fortunate, I have always discovered unhappiness. I don't think that even millions of dollars could change this rule. Paterno was a mixture of boldness, spirit of initiative and imagination. In 1922 he started planting one and a half million conifers in a large tract of land in Bedford Hills. He bought the saplings for a penny each and ten years later sold them as Christmas trees for a dollar and a half. Each little tree carried a note that more or less said: "Dear child, I am your Christmas tree. Take care of me because if you do, I will grow bigger and stronger, just like you." After selling thousands of them, many more were left because they were too big. He had the idea to transplant about 200,000 of them along the avenues of Windmill Manor, one of his properties, and a favorite location for horseback riders. He advertised the place exalting the clean air, the absence of mosquitoes, horse flies and gnats, repelled by the resins of the trees. He called it *The Sportsmen's Paradise*, with a great golf club, airplane hangars and a lake filled with 50,000 trout. He brought in deer to populate the woods that in winter could be visited on horse-drawn sleighs.

His first wife, Minnie Middaugh, a widow with a child, had died at age 74 in 1943. She was an educated woman, a college graduate, a musician and concert player. A member of the Christian Science

---

1 Nicholas Butler (1862-1947). Nobel Peace Prize laureate of 1931. He was Columbia's president from 1902 to 1947.

sect, she loved horses and horseback riding. In October of the same year he married his second wife, Anna Blome of White Plains. Death took him by surprise on the golf course on May 31, 1946. His son, Carlo M. Paterno, took over his business and in 1947 opened a new garden-city with luxury houses immersed in the woods.

I don't think he ever participated in political activities, or that he belonged to any political party. I never saw his name in the events of the Italian American community. Fiorello La Guardia was not fond of him. However, being the mayor of New York, he had to be present when he inaugurated Castle City at its opening in 1939.

From the magazine "L'Europeo," 1955

THE CORSI AFFAIR

This case has become a sore spot in the relations between the United States and Italy. Unintentionally, John Foster Dulles[2] acted in a way that Italians consider offensive. In truth, it is just a blunder, a foolish act, but in politics appearances count more than reality. Edward Corsi is one of today's most respected Italian Americans. He was born in Italy to a well-to-do family, the son of a far-left party congressman from Abruzzi. He was still a child when his father died and his widowed mother married a man of modest means. Due to financial difficulties, the family left Italy for the United States and settled in the same district where Fiorello La Guardia and Vito Marcantonio[3] also lived. Here, little Edward had to start from the bottom, both in terms of education and social status. Corsi is a simple and quiet man, with common sense and good judgment. He is very honest, highly educated, with an artistic talent as a painter. He is also a realist when it comes to confronting political problems; but, despite this, he never cynically accepted the status quo and corruption of our times; and always stayed true to a deep compassion for the human condition. Thanks to this combination of sensibilities, he never took on airs of importance and arrogance, something that many Italian Americans typically do as soon as they achieve success in business or in politics. I have often said that Corsi is one of the best products of American influence on the Italian character: when an Italian immigrant manages to avoid becoming a criminal; ending up in an insane asylum; or swelling up into a *prominent*, that means he really is a good man. There are many of them, but unfortunately Italy doesn't know they exist: Italian authorities who visit the United States—the likes of Mario Scelba, Gaetano Martino, Pietro Parini or, as happened most recently, Amintore Fanfani;[4] never

---

2   John Foster Dulles (1888 1959). Secretary of state in the Eisenhower administration from 1953 to 1959.

3   Vito Marcantonio (1902–1954). Lawyer and politician. He replaced Fiorello La Guardia when he resigned his position as House representative to run for mayor of New York City.

4   Gaetano Martino (1900-1967). Statesman and politician. He was Minister of Foreign affairs from 1954 to 1957.

THE TRANSPLANTS • 323

get the chance to meet any of them (they always end up meeting with Fortune Pope instead).

Social solidarity is not particularly strong among Italians or Italian Americans, as demonstrated, for instance, by the fact that they contribute very little to public charities. It is thus rather impressive to see how Corsi became involved in public life; working with the activists who were helping new immigrants who had recently settled in the tuberculosis-infested, dirt-poor and very dangerous East Harlem neighborhood; in the same hovels where Italians used to live before Blacks and Puerto Ricans moved in.[5]

The first time we met he was still a modest social worker who toiled around the clock for a meager salary in a social welfare center located in a predominantly Italian neighborhood. The former Harlem House, now called La Guardia House,[6] is an institution devoted to assisting new immigrants in need of basic guidance and support. It is not a charity like a soup kitchen for the unemployed; rather it is a community center where newly arrived immigrants, especially those who do not speak English, can find intelligent and generous advice and aid, free of charge. Today, it organizes sports activities for youngsters, tours for the elderly and support groups for young mothers. The center also offers art courses, lectures and other events that keep children off the streets where they could get involved in racial confrontations and fights. The old economic problems of yore have been replaced by new social conflicts and crises. At the time when I first met him, Corsi had to fulfill the roles of lawyer, adviser, peacemaker and judge. He knew everybody by name and attended every baptism and wedding. These are not easy tasks, and the only compensation he received was respect and some influence. Corsi was well known but he was too

---

• Pietro Parini (1894- 1993). Navy officer, government functionary and diplomat.

• Amintore Fanfani (1908-1999). He was prime minister of Italy five times between 1954 and 1987. He was also minister of foreign affairs from 1958-1959.

5 East Harlem was the largest Italian neighborhood in New York for two decades around 1930. What is now Spanish Harlem in those days was called *Italian Harlem*.

6 Located on 116th Street, between First and Second Avenue in Manhattan, it was established as Haarlem [sic] House in 1919 and renamed La Guardia Memorial House in 1956.

honest and too non-political to take advantage of his popularity. He never enjoyed great name recognition beyond his circle. He also had too much integrity to compete with demagogues and wheeler-dealers who only knew how to promote themselves. When he entered political contests, he didn't get as many votes as other colorful characters who had much less substance but were much more brazen with promises. Moreover, he was a member of the Republican Party, a party that in New York never had a majority. He started his political journey with La Guardia, and then became a trusted adviser to Dewey for labor relations in the state of New York. In the last elections the Republicans lost the governorship of the state and Corsi left his position as labor commissary.

His golden period, in the moral, not financial sense, was the time when President Herbert Hoover[7] appointed him commissary of Ellis Island. The institution closed down in 1954, but in its heydays that name meant sheer terror for millions of people. It was the entry gate for immigrants and those who were refused entrance would end up spending weeks or months in those sad rooms, like in a prison. It really struck a chord when the son of immigrants was chosen to run the place. Corsi acquitted himself with humanity and firmness in this job and wrote a book about his experience: *In the Shadow of Liberty.*[8] The book is full of episodes, portraits, anecdotes and observations packed with color and humanity. It's too bad a book like this was never translated into Italian, instead of all the junk from America that is treated as if it were the apotheosis of the human spirit.

After he left his position as labor commissary for the state of New York, the Republican Party, to express its appreciation for his work, sent him to Washington as assistant for immigration affairs in Dulles's department. Here he was put in charge of a delicate and complex issue. In 1953 President Eisenhower had signed into law a bill sponsored by House Representative Francis Walter and Senator

---

7   Herbert Hoover (1874–1964). President of the United States from 1929 to 1933.

8   *In the shadow of liberty: The Chronicle of Ellis Island.* New York, Macmillan, 1935.

Patrick McCarran[1] giving special immigration rights to a group of about 240,000 displaced Europeans who, after World War II, had been persecuted for political reasons and were practically without a country.[2] About sixty thousand of them were Italians, mostly from the north eastern regions that had been lost to the Yugoslavian forces.[3] This humanitarian initiative was meant to show to the world the generosity of the United States. Instead, it turned out to be a bureaucratic farce and an exercise in hypocrisy. From the very beginning I predicted that it would be impossible to reach the preordained quota by the stated deadline of 1956. The number of applicants processed by the United States immigration authorities in those countries turned out to be so low that it caused the indignation of European politicians who were concerned with the presence of large groups of displaced persons, housed in temporary camps, in their countries. Appointed and welcomed by Dulles as a personal friend, Corsi was sent to Italy and Germany to try to figure out first-hand why there had been such long delays in processing the applications. When he returned to Washington and outlined a number of proposals to solve the logjam, he ran into opposition inside the state department and Congress. One of the co-sponsors of the law, Walter, denounced him for having been

---

1   *Immigration and Nationality Act* (Pub.L. 82–414, 66 Stat. 163, enacted June 27, 1952); also known as the *McCarran-Walter Act* from the names of the two congressional sponsors.
   • Francis Walter (1894-1963). House representative from Pennsylvania. He was the sponsor of the bill in the House. From 1951 through 1963 he served as chair of the House Un-American Activities Committee.
   • Patrick McCarran (1876-1954). Senator from Nevada from 1933 to 1954. He was a staunch anti-communist.

2   The problem of displaced people was still very acute in Europe in the aftermath of WWII, due to the new borders that forced entire populations from native regions into refugee camps or areas under U.S. military administration. In some cases, this situation lasted for decades after the war.

3   The area involved the city of Trieste and neighboring territory in what today are the border areas of Slovenia and Croatia. As per international law, Trieste legally was a Free Territory divided into two areas, named respectively Zone A and B. Officially under military administration by the Allied Forces, they were de-facto annexed respectively by Italy and Yugoslavia. This temporary situation lasted until 1975 when the Italian and Yugoslavian governments signed the Osimo Treaty accepting a partition that reflected the state-of-fact on the ground.

326 • THE TRANSPLANTS

a member of associations that the attorney general[4] had labeled as subversive. Corsi denied any involvement. On one occasion Walter was forced to recognize that his accusation against Corsi was wrong. In another case, Corsi stated he never allowed his signature to be used.[5] It is notorious that pro-communist groups in those days often arbitrarily used the names of people who were considered sympathizers. Corsi was a life-long Republican but belonged to the liberal wing of the party and had good relations with the labor unions. Most likely he had frequent contacts with people who were secretly communist. The state department understood this was a pretext and, at first, it looked as if it did not consider Corsi to be a traveling salesman of subversion. The investigation was not yet complete when suddenly rumors started circulating that Corsi's position was not a permanent one but, rather, a ninety-day temporary assignment. After three months in this post, Corsi was offered a different position, a rather vague one, in charge of recruiting immigrants for South American countries. It was a nasty trick. Maybe another man would have accepted the gold-coated poison pill, but Corsi resented this treatment. He spoke with Dulles and the truth came out: the state department didn't want any trouble with Congress and decided to throw Corsi overboard. Later, when asked, Dulles denied it was true, although Corsi still confirms everything and calls him a liar to this day. In truth, Corsi is simply guilty of having tried to make a hypocritical law work, a law nobody wants to implement and that was scheduled to expire in 1956 anyway.

Dulles's trick was so transparently obvious that the press unanimously sided with Corsi. Even some Democrats jumped on it with the goal of embarrassing Dulles. Republican organizations of New York state even requested that the president fix Dulles's error and honor the commitment the president himself had made to the law that was supposed to show the world how generous the United States is toward the unfortunates without a country...

New York, April 22, 1955

---

4   It isn't clear if by *procuratore generale dello stato* the author meant the United States attorney general or the attorney general of New York State.

5   Presumably the reference is to some kind of petition or open letter.

COMMENDATORE NACCHERINO[1]

This little man is everywhere. Thanks to his pint-size body, he squeezes into tight spots; slides under tables to emerge the other side; filters into any room; jumps out from a corridor without warnings and manages to get everybody's attention. He is a propaganda master of Italian culture abroad. He is the champion of winning causes and conquered admiration. He always travels first class, for free, and sits at the captain's table where he charms everyone with his conversation, literary or legal, depending on the circumstances. He is always busy arguing the thesis that Beatrice was a virgin, that Amerigo Vespucci[2] was a man of impeccable honor and he has an at-the-ready list of initiatives: a Dante theater; a Petrarch library; a new monument to commemorate Garibaldi or another statue to Christopher Columbus who, as he claims, based on the documents in his possession, was certainly Italian. All he asks for himself, besides the monuments, is a little office with a tiny room to sleep in and some travel funds. He is not asking too much. His self-appointed missions are vacuous but studded with speeches. He is only happy when he is sent on a mission somewhere in the world, preferably America. He tries to become member of executive committees only in order to fulfill this ambition. He brags about his friends in high places in Italy, his many acquaintances abroad, his commemorative publications and the number of languages he claims he can speak (approximately). He is the bane of consuls who are sick and tired of being forced to give him a room and find him a public for his lectures who put everyone to sleep, even those most used to these kinds of official tortures. Italian Americans got to know him well and they are less concerned because they can make him happy with a meal, a cigar and a few promises that everybody knows will

---

1   Most likely this is the caricature portrayal of a real person whose name has been changed. In Tuscan dialect *naccherino* means cute and lively boy.

2   Dante's muse.

   • Amerigo Vespucci (1454-1512). Navigator and cartographer. He was the first explorer to recognize that the Americas are a distinct and separate continent, a fact that he first represented in his maps. Consequently, as a shorthand convention, the "new continent" was named after him.

not be kept. From the time he graduated from university in Italy he hasn't studied anything anymore. He believes in the authenticity of Dante's house in Florence and Torquato Tasso's prison in Ferrara; in Francesco Ferrucci's patriotism and in Fabrizio Maramaldo's betrayal; and that Flavio Gioia invented the compass. Moreover, he is willing to be held personally accountable for the claims of Italianness of William Paca, one of the signers of the Declaration of Independence, and Francesco Vigo,[3] the alleged (by him) discoverer of the headwaters of the Mississippi river. He gets all flustered when people express doubts or questions about his claims and calls them "melancholic souls." He believes he has a constructive temperament and in fact some of his expeditions as missionary of Italian culture leave behind in the square those excrescences commonly called monuments.

New York, January 27, 1956

---

3   Francesco Ferrucci (1489-1530). Captain in the Florentine army.
   • Fabrizio Maramaldo (1494-1552). Italian *condottiero* (leader of a mercenary army). Legend has it that, contrary to every rule of chivalry, Maramaldo killed Ferrucci in cold blood after disarming him. Ferrucci's last alleged words were: "Coward, you are killing a dead man." *Maramaldo* in Italian is metonym for treachery and infamy.
   • Flavio Gioia da Amalfi is a purely fictional thirteenth century navigator and explorer. He is the mythical inventor of the compass, which, in reality, was invented by the Chinese; and whose principles, according to some, may have been introduced to Europe by Marco Polo.
   • William Paca (1740–1799). Signatory of the Declaration of Independence as representative of Maryland.
   • Francis Vigo born Francesco (1747-1836). Founder of a public university in Vincennes, Indiana.

TONY LOFURBO

On a train approaching Chicago, in one of the many suburbs that surround the city, travelers can notice a tower as high as the YMCA or the buildings of local banks. On the tower a sign glows: *Tony Lofurbo Ware House* [sic]. Lofurbo[1] arrived here when he was three years old. Thanks to his father's hard work and the help of the American system, he received the kind of education that in Italy he couldn't have even dreamt about. His natural intelligence allowed him to discover that without an education in America one cannot go very far. He also understood that Americans have a migratory instinct and move easily from place to place, from neighborhood to neighborhood, chasing opportunities. He thus concluded that a warehouse where people could store their stuff temporarily would be a good way to make money. He did it the right way because he also understood that in this country, in order to make money, you have to do things well. And, in fact, his warehouse can store anything safely and is well protected from humidity and thieves: from furniture to merchandise to a grandmother's jewels to a wardrobe. He has a fleet of vans to move all the various items in and out; and a small army of certified, experienced movers that can be trusted with anything; all with a clean record.

Never has one of his trucks been hijacked and the merchandise stolen. Lofurbo is a really talented man, with lots of nice relationships with organized-crime figures. To use an American expression, *he is worth a million dollars*. Often, it happens that people who move away stop paying rent or don't retrieve their stuff from the warehouse when the contract expires. Then, thanks to a contract clause prepared by his astute lawyers, all the abandoned goods become his possession. Tony Lofurbo has a good reputation: he befriended a local senator; congressmen visit with him and he has lunch with the mayor once a week. He is strong and stocky, with oily skin and pale lips. In his dark eyes lurks the mark of a tremendous will that knows how to command respect and fear. Yet, he is always happy to help whenever he can. Indeed, the greatest pleasure of his life is to show and use his

---

1   Lofurbo literally means The Sly-One.

influence and power. If you got a ticket and want to have it fixed, most likely he can take care of it. And if he can do it, he will show that he is happy to do it and he will love you more after he took care of it for you.

Since he has become a rich person he has learned that in America a prominent social position comes with obligations toward society. He supports Catholic charities at the direction of the bishop who honors him with spiritual guidance and who celebrated his daughter's marriage in the biggest Madonna-of-Pompeii-style church in town. He also founded a small *Casa della Cultura Italiana* in a building in his neighborhood with a large room for parties and gatherings. He is always invited to baptisms, weddings, twenty-five-year wedding anniversaries or birthdays by barbers, contractors, restaurant owners, shipping agents, bankers, storekeepers, doctors, lawyers and other people from all professions that distinguish the Italian community. In the main room of the *Casa* are the portraits of Dante, Puccini, Marconi and Lofurbo. Sometimes the *Casa* organizes cultural meetings, sandwiched between a girl who sings Neapolitan and Hollywood songs, and a pianist who takes a chance with Béla Bartók.[2]

Two forces exist in Tony Lofurbo's mind: great gratitude for America for the opportunity it gave him to become what he has become; and great admiration for Italy, about which he ignores practically everything but that, as he sort of understands, represents something honorable in America. For people like him, it is like a certificate of noble origins.

New York, January 27, 1956.

---

2   Béla Bartók (1881–1945). Hungarian composer and pianist, he is considered one of the founders of ethnomusicology.

A TUSCAN IMMIGRANT
BUILDS A CITY IN ARIZONA

I spent so little time in the gorgeous state of Arizona that my memories only consist of a few, memorable images. The first is that of a church I saw emerging from the desert in the morning light and I admired for two hours until the sun was high in the sky. Dedicated to San Xavier del Bac, it is Arizona's most important and certainly most ancient church. It was conceived by the Italian Jesuit Eusebio Kino[3] and materially built by Spanish Franciscan friars with the labor of Indians. I also admired another kind of monument: this is not a church but a shopping center, namely the central market of a new city near Tucson. The builder is Sam Nannini [sic]. Everybody in Tucson, in Arizona and in Montecatini[4] knows him. It began at the local post office where I went to mail a certified letter. "Are you from Italy? Do you know Sam Nanini?" Then I went to the bank to cash a check: "Do you know Sam Nanini?" Even the barber who gave me a shave, a Mexican, asked me: "*Usted es italiano*.... Do you know Sam Nanini?" By the end, I was ashamed I didn't know him. So I asked a common acquaintance if he could try to contact him at my behest. I found out there had been some miscommunication: he had invited me to lunch for the day before but somehow the message hadn't reached me. "We waited for you for three hours yesterday," said his wife. "And it took me three hours to find you," I replied. Everybody knows him but finding him is a different story...

He owns enough land to build an entire city, land he bought when the desert still cost peanuts. He is now building houses on it, two to three thousand feet from each other, all clustered along Nanini Street or something else named Nanini. In each one of these neighborhoods

---

3 Saint Francis Xavier (1506-1552). Spanish Catholic priest and missionary. He was one of the co-founders of the Jesuit order.
• Father Eusebio Kino (1645-1711). He was the founder of the San Xavier del Bac Mission in 1692. The mission is located ten miles south of Tucson, Az.

4 Sam Nanini (1889-1978). Real estate developer and builder.
• Montecatini Terme. Italian town in the province of Pistoia in Tuscany. It is famous for its spa and mineral waters.

(or maybe they should be called *farborhoods*) things are named after him. After we entered the development my driver, who, he had assured me, knew Nanini, could not find his house. Finally, after knocking on several doors of houses built by him and sold by him, we arrived at the shopping center. Right across the street, in a cute, nice, super-modern doll's house we found him by the main door. He looked like a tenant more than the landlord. When we asked where Mr. Nanini lived, he answered with great simplicity that it was he, *the* Nanini, as if he were standing in front of a house in some small town in Italy. Nanini is a bit like those Tuscan farmers I used to see in Piazza della Signoria[5] in Florence on market days. The same sun-baked face, a little hat cocked to one side, a simple but good-quality suit, the same calm demeanor. I wasn't there to negotiate a deal with him and maybe when it comes to business he is a different person, but, all in all, America has such a sedative influence on businesspeople that even a Tuscan must subject himself to it. After lunch he took his wife's car and drove me around to visit "his town," despite the fact that we could have walked, for it was so close.

This man, who, I guess, must have left Montecatini, or more precisely Borgo a Buggiano, some forty years ago in search for a better life, must have a lot of money and a wealth of perspectives. For sure he owes something to luck (after all, he could have died as soon as he arrived.) But when one thinks of the vastness of the country where he landed penniless; of the vastness of forces that must have opposed him, including the competition of people like him from every corner of the globe motivated by the same drive and goals; of the huge efforts and caution and patience needed to succeed; then Nanini's life is definitely something to be saluted tipping one's hat. I didn't tell him that and maybe he will be surprised when he reads it, but the more I think about it, the more extraordinary this seems. Apparently, he made money in Chicago building houses, god-only-knows how many and how horrible. But here, in Arizona, the local traditions and the freedom afforded to him by his wealth generated in him the ambition to create something more graceful or, as he says, more intimate. I didn't challenge him on this word: Nanini is a cautious man, and

5   The main square in the center of Florence, where Palazzo Vecchio is located.

understood that before you can build houses you need stores. This is the latest trend in America: those who can afford it are fleeing the cities, in a phenomenon called *suburbanization*.[1] Now, all *suburbia* [sic] are clustered around a *shopping center*. He just finished building one that already houses a bank, a beauty salon, a *market*,[2] a jeweler that sells junk and a restaurant with a room for banquets. In short, all the amenities that American middle class expects are there. At that time, construction was under way for a huge parking lot. I imagine the entire area will be lined with palm trees. I was particularly struck by two factors: the gorgeous location, with mountain views in the day, and, at night the view of city lights; and the happiness of the people he was running into. His workers came up to him with questions about a lock or a window or whatever: he knew everything and was an expert at everything, implicitly sending out the message that nobody could fool him. A real Tuscan-farm foreman, I can assure you, not just with four pairs of oxen and a tractor, but in a city that was growing under his eyes. A city. Now his ambition is to be a Florentine (and, to an extent, he is succeeding): from the corners of his buildings hang street lights in the shape of those that adorn Palazzo Strozzi.[3] The overall style, though, has gone through the treatment of local architects and reflects a Spanish or Mexican influence. I liked the low walls of bare bricks without plaster, the low roofs on the low slung houses—although I just don't think it is either intimate or particularly Florentine. The worst are the sculptures spread here and there, reminiscent of Via dei Fossi.[4] I don't think he was aware of it and I fear that this man, so much on the defensive against the dangers of America, left himself vulnerable to those of Lucca and Florence. But maybe I am wrong. I am not an art expert and maybe these are authentic sculptures that go

---

1   In the original the word is *suburbanismo*, a neologism created ad-hoc but never recorded in Italian dictionaries.

2   Shopping center; market: in English in the original.

3   One of the most magnificent palaces in Florence, build by the Strozzi family, fierce adversary of the Medici. Construction started in 1489 and was completed in 1538.

4   Via dei Fossi is a narrow street near the center of Florence where a large number of antique stores, dealers and restoration shops are (still) located.

back to the time of the war of Pisa against Lucca. In Tucson Nanini is unanimously considered an honest man and, obviously, a pleasant man. It is a pleasure to find this kind of Italian.

Tucson, January 29, 1961

AN UNHAPPY IMMIGRANT

When he was still a boy, Angelo M. Pellegrini[5] emigrated with his family from the province of Lucca, in Tuscany, and settled in a remote part of the northern United States, the state of Washington, by the Pacific Ocean. He did a variety of jobs and thanks to his intelligence, his family's sacrifices and the opportunities afforded to him by the American educational system, he pursued his studies until he became professor of English literature at the University of Washington in Seattle. In 1949-1950 he won the prestigious scholarship awarded by the Guggenheim Foundation. His project was to study "the contribution of Italian immigration" to the United States. Once he arrived in Italy he decided, instead, to focus on something different. The book he wrote, *Immigrant's Return*[6] was accepted for publication by the publisher Macmillan, one of the major American houses. It was received with positive reviews and, I imagine, good success. The theme of the book is the disappointment suffered by an American of Italian origin who returns to his ancestral homeland. Here, he realizes that he is not at all Italian: he understands he is fully American. Italy was not a good fit for him. We are not talking about the Italy of arts, literature and landscape, and in fact the book has very few references to these aspects. It's the Italy of Italians, the Italy of the public habits and the Italy of politics. This immigrant returned believing he would feel in himself a surge of his Italian soul. Yet, he was taken aback by everything, or almost everything, he saw. Everything seemed foreign to his cultural and personal structure. What he missed most of all in Italy was the sense of *democracy*. This may displease my readers and trigger irritation, condescending smiles and objections. However, it is an important testimony: based on my experience, many of the observations are common to many Italian Americans who may not express them out of reticence; or because they don't have the stomach; or the guts or the possibility to talk openly about their feelings. Pellegrini's book may displease and certainly will displease many; however, his testimony is

---

5   Angelo Pellegrini (1904–1991). Author.

6   *Immigrant's Return*. New York, Macmillan, 1951.

a reality that we must take into account. We could analyze what the book misses and I am sure we would find lots of things. However, his perspective is sincere (maybe a bit narrow); his words are fluid albeit not artistic; and facts appear to be true or verisimilar, even when they are stripped of their historical and concrete context. Now let's see what he has to say.

Pellegrini's book is an autobiography, therefore a rare and important document. The overwhelming majority of Italians who immigrated to the United States never had the time to write true autobiographies. The only traces they left were dry statistics: how many came; how many children they had; how many died; how many ended up in prison; how many ended up in insane asylums; how many went back to Italy in defeat; how many became rich. The reality of their sufferings and triumphs remains, however, without history. The few narrative works produced by their descendants, written in a new language, never succeeded in creating an artistic rendition of those lives. Those truly are *lost generations*.

Pellegrini had the good luck of positive circumstances. His family migrated to a state far from the big cities; in the middle of the woods; with lots of space and surrounded almost exclusively by Americans. He didn't end up in the Little Italies where vice and crimes festered and where the immigrants got stuck, kept there by the contemptuous attitude of the Anglo-Saxon ruling class. The Pellegrini family, instead, lived among simple lumberjacks, and the dominant impressions he recorded as a boy were two: abundance and equality. When Pellegrini writes lyrically about the American breakfast and or about mass education, it is easy to understand that he did not live like the great majority of Italian immigrants. This is enough to shift the entire paradigm of comparisons in the rest of his book for the simple reason that he does not take into account that his is an almost unique perspective and definitely a relative one. His book would have been profoundly different had he lived on MacDougal Street[7] in New York; or in the neighborhoods on the other side of the tracks in Chicago; or in any other American city populated mostly by poor people. Edward

---

7   McDougal Street is located in Greenwich Village. This neighborhood at the time of Prezzolini's writing still had a large population of Italians.

Corsi, who came to America in the same period, around 1915, in his autobiography wrote about boys who scavenged along the railroads, picking up pieces of coal that fell off the trains to heat their houses in winter.[8] This American professor doesn't look like much of a professor. By that I mean that he doesn't seem to have much critical spirit: the first condition to validate an experience is to distinguish between personal facts and general facts.

When Professor Pellegrini, educated in America, went to Italy, his mind was stuffed with a bunch of clichés about the differences between Americans and Italians. Among them, for instance, was the cliché whereby Americans chase dollars while Italians are idealist; that Italian cuisine is better than the American; that Italian films are better and so forth. Step after step, all these delusions fell apart in his mind. In his journey though Italy, Pellegrini discovered a country he didn't know.

He begins the story with the ship that should have maintained a certain speed but couldn't because of problems with a piston. In every trip a piston breaks down. And if one piston does not break down, it is because three or four pistons break down. Food on board is decent but not as good as often described by other accounts. Wine is fake, "phony." The waiters are helpful but they gather around the table "like chickens" and don't give him enough space to enjoy peace and quiet. Once he arrives in Italy, the vaunted Italian slow-going for Pellegrini is one of the worst disappointments, in comparison to the stigmatized American frenzy. The Italians he sees are breakneck nuts who drive cars and motorcycles faster than Americans; and everybody is rushing trying to grab public transportation with a kind of ferociousness that amply surpasses the Americans'. When he goes to the movies, he doesn't find films by Roberto Rossellini and Vittorio De Sica but *Forever Amber*.[9] Every theater screens American movies. He looks for wine and finds that Italians drink Coca-Cola. He thinks he will be able to smell the aroma of oleanders, but he only picks up the stench of public urinals. Obviously, he is scammed in a restaurant where a soup he did not

8   Coincidentally, this very activity is described in most vivid terms by Mario Puzo in the novel *The Fortunate Pilgrim* (New York, Lancer Books, 1964).

9   *Forever Amber*. Dir. Otto Preminger. Distr. 20th Century Fox, 1947.

order nor eat was added to the check. About money: his travel mate, the typical representative of a particular segment of the crass Italian middle class, arrogant and full of itself, tells him that "Americans are only about business and dollars." However, Pellegrini's "first and last" impression is that "Italians are even crazier than Americans about money."

When he arrives to his native hamlet, Casabianca,[10] near Montecatini, nothing has changed in the last forty years: same poverty; same resignations to calamities; same passive acceptance of fecal filth and related flies that inevitably come with it. With it, he also sees their fears: fear of losing whatever little they have; fear of hunger; of being swindled by their neighbors; the kind of fear that makes people harvest grapes before they are ripe, so that the wine in the end will end up lousy. They dress in rags, they age prematurely, and they are envious. Later, in Montecatini, Pellegrini encounters maids and waiters: they are the best in this world, but they are servile. And, as a counterpoint, he depicts the clients of the famous spa with swollen bellies; who demand to be addressed as *cavaliere* and *commendatore*. The portraits of resignation are immediately followed by those of cynicism.

It doesn't seem that Professor Pellegrini is particularly well prepared to express a judgment on whether "spiritual values" are stronger in Italy than in America or, as he decides at the end of the book, stronger in America than in Italy. His artistic taste, just to mention one aspect, is defined by a belief he shares with the American philosopher John Dewey.[11] His thesis is that the value of a work of art is determined by the *ideas* it presents. It is a fairly clear criterion. However, the direct consequence would be that *Cabiria* is D'Annunzio's best work and that *Uncle Tom's Cabin* is one of the most important texts of the nineteenth century; that the *Canzoniere* by Petrarch is no big deal; and that Victor Hugo is more artistic than Guy de Maupassant.[12] Pellegrini

---

10   Small town in the province of Pistoia, in Tuscany.

11   John Dewey (1859-1952). Philosopher, psychologist, and educational reformer.

12   *Cabiria*. Silent movie directed by Giovanni Pastrone, screenplay by Gabriele D'Annunzio (1914).

  • Harriet Beecher Stowe. *Uncle Tom's Cabin; or, Life Among the Lowly*. Boston, J.P.

apparently does not know Italian writers other than Carlo Levi and Ignazio Silone. And he is really stunned when some critics tell him that Silone is a bad writer. After all, how could it be, since he is one of the only four foreign members of the American Academy? To him this is sufficient proof. In Italy he talked to people from different social strata. However, it seems that the only group of intellectuals he has had exchanges with is the group of Carlo Levi, Gaetano Salvemini and Pietro Calamandrei.[13] The only Italian writer from the past he quotes is Giuseppe Giusti,[14] maybe because the peasants from Montecatini and surrounding areas are familiar with him.

Now, someone should submit to Professor Pellegrini a few issues he has not thought about. First of all, he didn't ask himself why that land full of poverty and degradation, "where no man or woman in America would accept to live," has generated for centuries so much intellectual and artistic light; and, in the broadest terms, has created an organization like Catholicism that has been sufficient to respond to the spiritual needs of millions of people, good Americans included. He didn't ask himself whether the social life of peoples, over the centuries, isn't like that of human organisms; where you can change a part without destroying the whole; and if in history we aren't forced to accept some accidents in exchange for certain kinds of benefits. In Italy, the result of these socio-historical factors resulted in the formation of an aristocratic civilization. Pellegrini protests against this in the name of America's democratic civilization. By the same token, an Italian professor could go to America and protest against democracy, which was the initial

---

Jewett and company; Cleveland, Jewett, Proctor, and Worthington, 1853.

• Victor Hugo (1802-1885). French novelist and poet. His most famous work is *Les Misérables* (1862).

• Guy de Maupassant (1850-1893). French writer and one of the fathers of the modern short story.

• Carlo Levi (1902-1975). Painter, writer, anti-Fascist activist. His most famous book is *Christ Stopped in Eboli*. Torino, Einaudi, 1945.

• Ignazio Silone (1900). Writer and public intellectual.

13   Piero Calamandrei (1889-1956). Writer and jurist. The list contains only the names of notorious pro-socialist anti-Fascists, representing an ideological bent very much in contrast with Prezzolini's inclinations.

14   Giuseppe Giusti (1809-1850). Satirical poet who targeted tyranny.

and heroic feat that created America, imposed by a minority. By the same token one could complain that girls in certain countries have blue eyes instead of dark; or blonde hair instead of black.

Pellegrini tells the truth when he acknowledges that he is American. He is American particularly in the characteristic way of the majority of American tourists and scholars who have *no sense of historical depth.* Suffice it to say that they have actually looked for "spiritual values" as if they could find them. And it doesn't matter whether they looked in Italy or in America. These are questions for American professors. Italian spiritual values are in Italy, American spiritual values are in America.

One more question, more embarrassing, would be: why is it that many Americans, who are not dumb and ignorant; indeed some of whom are highly educated while others are natural and simplistic but intuitive, such as the majority of artists and American writers whose list would be too long; why, I was asking, did they feel relieved in going from America to Italy? This has happened not just at the time of Horatio Greenough and Samuel Morse, but it is still happening today, at the time of Alfred Hayes, Truman Capote and Ernest Hemingway. [15]

Take Samuel Morse. Before inventing the telegraph, he was an accomplished painter. He went to Italy to study and lamented that Americans don't care about art the same way Italians do. He wrote: "I, in general proud of my compatriots' spirit, recognize that they care little about fine arts and about men of taste and science. Here [in America] men are judged by their wallets.... A beautiful painting or a marble statue is very rare in the houses of the rich people of this city...." Thusly wrote Morse, who was a ferociously anti-Catholic Anglo-Saxon.

---

15   Horatio Greenough (1805-1852). Sculptor. He lived in Florence.

• Samuel Morse (1791-1872). Painter turned inventor. He invented the telegraph and co-developed the Morse code.

• Alfred Hayes (1911-1985). Writer and novelist, he wrote screenplays for Italian Neo-Realism films.

• Truman Capote, born Truman Streckfus Persons (1924-1984). One of the greatest 20th century's American writers, inventor of the genre known as "nonfiction novel."

• Ernest Hemingway (1899-1961). Novelist and Nobel Prize for Literature in 1954.

Professor Pellegrini did not invent the telegraph, as we would say in Italy. He discovered that there is no democracy in Italy. It isn't a discovery. It's old hat, at least if by democracy he means the American kind. If he means something else, I can assure Professor Pellegrini that in the region where he was born, and where I was educated, there is a much more natural and humane form of democracy than in the Deep South of the United States.

New York, January 16, 1952

Part Eight

Witnesses of Italian Immigration

Adolfo Rossi

Mayor Des Planches

Dario Papa and Ferdinando Fontana

Giuseppe Giacosa

Amy. A. Bernardy

Irene di Robilant

THE HUMANIST WHO SOLD FANS

We have only few testimonies on the Great Migration, one of the great tragedies of modern times but a silent one. Its protagonists and victims could not write and could barely express themselves: today, the survivors do not want to remember. When someone tries to interview them, they hide behind a wall of reticence often covered with a plaster coat of pride or shame. The success that some of them finally achieved, has become a screen for all the others, a screen behind which so many heart-wrenching stories are hidden away. This situation makes my recent discovery of a precious and rare little book even more important. On a library's shelf I found the story written by a certain Adolfo Rossi[1] about his adventure in the United States. Rossi was from Lendinara, a small town in the province of Rovigo, a place where he felt unhappy and irritable "like a caged bird." Entrepreneurial, full of dreams and eager to discover new things, he boarded a ship in 1870 with 400 lira[2] in his pocket. The money didn't last long. One night, on the ship, soon after the journey had started, his money was stolen and he arrived in New York with only three and a half lira for himself and his companion. Rossi had attended high school, which in those days was considered a high level of education. His first job in Italy was as a postal clerk but he was too smart to stop there and ventured further, eventually becoming the author of some novellas that were published in literary journals. He even founded a periodical, *Il grillo del focolare*.[3] In the course of years of traveling to many countries, he published several books, some of which are still precious testimonies of the emigrant conditions. In 1906 he was appointed emigration inspector with the unanimous vote of a commission composed of notable members of the Italian parliament, among which were Senator

---

1   Adolfo Rossi (1857-1921). Journalist, writer and diplomat from the town of Lendinara in the province of Rovigo. He died in Buenos Aires.

2   Approximately $3,000 in today's money.

3   The English translation means *The Hearth's Cricket*, which is reminiscent of Dicken's Christmas novella *The Cricket on the Hearth* (1845).

Giorgio Arcoleo and Representative Francesco Saverio Nitti.[4] He later became vice-commissioner.

Rossi's personality is optimistic, creative and good natured. He writes in a style similar to Edmondo De Amicis's: simple, direct, cordially open, with little depth, with the ability to observe a situation with clarity, but always skimming the surface. It's the style of a person without preconceived ideas, without vanity, without deep passions but with a vague desire to experience the world. He didn't leave Italy with his heart full of rancor toward the motherland, unlike the subversives of those days (who were actually quite right in their feelings); nor with total ignorance about Italian history and what it had taken to unify the country (unlike the majority of the unschooled emigrants). He didn't even feel the contempt for manual labor typical of the Italian bourgeoisie of those times. He wasn't a genius: his cultural horizon wasn't particularly broad and his style doesn't have much color or warmth, yet it is captivating. At least he hadn't been spoiled and corrupted by D'Annunzio's style,[5] a fate that plagued many journalists that came after him. He was kind-hearted but wasn't aware he was an amiable person, and wasn't a show off. His cultural limitations and these other qualities made him an unbiased, humane and honest observer and, therefore, a reliable and uncommon witness. When I first read his book, a long time ago, I wasn't able to compare his work to those of immigrants that left Italy after World War II, but now I have a more solid and better defined understanding of this kind of literature and, therefore, I have a more precise impression.

It would be impossible to find a man like him today because he would be tainted by bitter disillusionment hidden under humanitarian sugar coating. Rossi was a natural as a man and as a writer. He didn't write for sensationalism. He was just looking for a place bigger than Lendinara and for a horizon wider than the one offered by a post office window in a small town in the Veneto region. He read Jules Verne,

---

4   Giorgio Arcoleo (1848-1914). He was elected to the Camera dei Deputati and later appointed to the senate by the king in 1902.

   • Francesco Saverio Nitti (1868-1953). Prime minister in 1919-1920.

5   D'Annunzio was targeted by detractors, among which Prezzolini, for his decadent aesthetics and turgid prose.

not Emilio Salgari. He read *Gil Blas*,[6] and remembered well the hero who "arrived to a new city penniless, knowing no one, knowing not what he would do." His adventures have a bit the same flavor and humanitarian tone of *Gil Blas*.

When he first arrived in New York, Rossi didn't know English. On the ship, even before being robbed, he realized he had already been scammed by the travel agency that put him on a much worse vessel than he had paid for. In those days, immigrants were at the mercy of scammers, thieves and swindlers who latched on any prey like bloodsucking leeches. His passage took place in a huge room where he slept on the bare floor without even a mattress (cautious travelers knew better to bring their own.) There was no point in protesting as there was no one to protest with. Indeed, if someone became too strident in his protests, he would run the risk of being thrown overboard. As soon as he landed in America, Rossi was cheated once again, this time not by an Italian shipping agent but by leeches hanging out at the port. He ended up sleeping on park benches where he was robbed again. Everything would cost him ten times more than the fair price because he could not argue and didn't know how to bargain. But he never lost his optimism and confidence. In New York he was endlessly amused by the traffic of people coming and going; by the kaleidoscope of peoples; by the stupendous panorama of the bay crisscrossed by white steam ships with counterweights; by the elevated railroads and the views from their windows; by the jungle of spears and tall buildings. Even the sun seemed new every day and every beautiful day made him forget the fog of the day before. With determination he focused on learning the language of the new country because he realized how important that was. He was living on bread, cheese and water but with the first money earned at his first job he bought a grammar book. Like all other adventurers, sometimes he had to resort

---

6   Jules Verne (1828-1905). French author considered to be one of the fathers of modern science fiction.

• Emilio Salgari (1862-1911). Writer of adventure novels for young people, taking place mostly in Asia or other exotic locations. Apparently he was not one of Prezzolini's favorites.

• *Gil Blas de Santillana*. Published in 1715-1735, written by French author Alain-René Lesage (1668-1747). Picaresque novel narrated in the first person.

to audacity rather than sincerity. When he was offered a position as ice cream maker in a big hotel he accepted, despite the fact he had only a few days of experience on a similar job. I was really pleased to see how the son of petty bourgeoisie didn't put up airs and, despite his high school diploma, took various menial jobs where physical strength counted more than smarts and culture. He sold Japanese fans on Coney Island in the summer; worked as a waiter in a hotel; tried to open a boarding house; became a servant in the house of rich Americans; and finally the destiny brought him into the orbit of Carlo Barsotti,[7] another adventurer with a broader reach and fewer scruples who, despite the fact that he could barely write anything beyond his signature, had founded a little Italian newspaper. That newspaper is still alive today and is called the *Progresso Italo-Americano*. All the details of his story are true and demonstrable, at least based on what I can surmise from comparing Rossi's to other testimonies and with reports about people and places.

In his book he talks about meeting rich Americans and their stunned reactions at discovering an Italian who didn't play mandolin, didn't sing and was properly mannered (probably even more than they were). He tells stories of usurers with a sign with three balls hanging above the door (they can still be seen in New York, although they no longer strangle people); of work-shifts of twelve-plus hours a day; of prices that compared to those of today seem incredible (one could eat for 25 cents); of the simple life of a president of the United States whom Rossi waited on in the hotel where he was working; where that personage would stay without a personal servant; eating alone and perfectly content with a steak, a glass of milk and coffee. All these brushstrokes paint a large canvas of the customs of those days, a time that few can recall now due to the incredibly rapid transformation of the United States in the past century.

Rossi met personally Antonio Meucci,[8] the inventor of the

---

7 Carlo Barsotti (1850-1927). Founder and first editor of *Il Progresso Italo-Americano*; founder of the *Italian American Bank* in 1882.

8 Antonio Meucci (1808-1889). Inventor and a friend Giuseppe Garibaldi. Meucci invented the first telephone but could not afford to pay the fees for a patent. He died in poverty.

telephone and a personal friend of General Giuseppe Garibaldi. He even devoted a chapter to the general's memories. There is nothing new or particularly fancy in it, but it helps get closer to that heroic figure. Rossi, propelled by his crave for discovering new worlds, took a trip to the interior of the United States, in the regions recently abandoned by Indians and, even more recently, colonized by pioneers. These were the areas that attracted adventurers in search of gold and silver in the Rocky Mountains. With just a verbal contract as assurance, Rossi with some other twenty Italian workers found himself traveling for days by train until they reached a most remote mountainous area at more than 6,000 feet in altitude. Here there was absolutely nothing to house them: they had to build a shelter and he ended up doing pick-and-shovel manual labor and work in the kitchen. Often poor European immigrants ended up in situations similar to slavery: they didn't know the language and could not rely on help from American authorities or from consular representatives of their native countries, too distant from those desolate areas and most likely ineffective and uninterested in the fate of manual laborers. These were truly circumstances where only the strongest in body and, above all, in spirit would be able to survive over time; save a bit of money and eventually run away to start a new life elsewhere. Confronted with the same dire choices, while other Italians workers became discouraged and prone to rebellion or flight; he acted pragmatically and with political savvy: he understood perfectly well what kind of injustice he was victim to, but also understood how self-damaging it would be to react or run away. Despite all these terrible experiences of hardship, Rossi never lost faith in and admiration for the United States.

The description he left about the neighborhood where many Italian immigrants first settled in New York (a place that no longer exists) is a classic.

> Murders and assaults are unfortunately rather frequent in the Italian neighborhood, first of all because it is infested with lots of criminals escaped from justice in their country after they had killed, stolen and committed all sorts of crimes; and also because even the honest peasant-worker, born in a peaceful village who decided to migrate to flee hunger and lured by the mirage of money or influenced

by the example of other people, once he arrives in America often becomes morally worse. Nostalgia; the longing for his relatives so far away; life in a filthy neighborhood; the greed of the boss who cheats him out of his salary; crime gangs that dominate among and extort from the workers from the south, all this embitters the character of the poor devil. Add to all this a lifestyle that is completely different; the change in climate; the population density; the difficulties posed by the foreign language; the greed; the envy he feels toward the paesani who stroke it rich. In these conditions the immigrant becomes irritable, irascible; lives in constant fear of being cheated, swindled, betrayed; and, even if he never did before, he starts carrying some kind of weapon. A large part of the sad scenes of blood are caused by alcohol and cheating among spouses. It's strange: the peasants who live in *tenement houses* [sic] are mostly illiterate; uncouth; thrown off- balance by hunger; bled to death by bosses; exhausted by work. However, passion is always burning in their chest. They live horrible lives; endure physical efforts so hard it stuns their brains; in jobs like cleaning sewers… They live in dark and black rooms, filthy, unhealthy, where it seems impossible the ray of love could penetrate. Women are often ugly, with busted shoes and dirty clothes: it seems that males and females should vegetate insensitive to anything that concerns the heart; but, to the contrary, those unfortunate people love with incredible intensity and when they are betrayed they become savagely vindictive and blood-thirsty.

I could go on for ever with passages like this that show the author's uncanny ability to analyze customs and social dynamics. I will confine my comment to saying that in this book we find one of the very first descriptions of the Italian American lingo, preceding by at least ten years the observations by Livingston's little study *America Sanemagogna* [America Son-of-a-gun].[1] Some of the expressions reported by Rossi must have disappeared, such as *friloncio* [free lunch]. This was a marketing technique of the time when the patrons of a bar who ordered a beer would also get all-you-can-eat sandwiches. Today no bar or restaurant offers the same deal and pretty soon, I am afraid, we will have to pay for peanuts and potato chips that some bars still have on the counter. And soon bars and restaurants will also charge for the air we breathe.

---

1   "La Merica Sanemagogna." *Romanic Review* 9 (1918): 214.

Besides the historical relevance of Rossi's memoirs, I confess that the reason I was so captured by this book was the author's personality. It was as if I could hear him talk, with a kind tone full of common sense. I wish all Italian politicians who visited immigrants in those days had the same insight. Instead, they did not have a clue about the real circumstance of those lives, and they started worrying about the best way to assist those poor people only after the phenomenon was already receding and was nearing its end. We are not talking about the end of the emigration era, rather the end of the kind of emigrant described by Rossi: a man capable of enduring the abandonment *of* the motherland and the abandonment *by* the motherland. I couldn't put down this book for it describes the true tragedies of emigration; so unlike the stories filtered through the rose-tinted glasses of the *search for freedom* and success; celebrated in today's official banquets in honor of high ranking politicians from Italy; senator or ministers who have the same understanding of this phenomenon as those of 1880—meaning, no understanding at all.

Emigration was a *national failure* along a road strewn with dead bodies, tragedies, destitution, madness and enslavement. The survivors and their children deserve our admiration, but not those who want to transform it into a *triumph* by means of cheap and schlocky rhetoric. Their words inevitably sound like the *communiqués* of the supreme commands of armed forces when they want to hide a rout.

New York, January 17, 1960

A PIEDMONTESE IN THE FAR WEST

Emigration was, without a doubt, the most important demographic phenomenon in Italy after unification on the wake of *Risorgimento*; and yet personal accounts of their experience remain rare and mostly indirect. The emigrants' sweat and tears left no memoirs and their fate was ignored because *nobody wanted to look*. In short, it was a mass escape of rural masses from Italy. In the previous chapter I examined the testimony of Adolfo Rossi, a middle-class man from the Veneto region who became an emigrant and took a hard look at the phenomenon of emigration, *looking from down up*.

I would like to examine now the work of another person whose perspective was *from high up looking down*. Edmondo Mayor des Planches[2] was the first Italian ambassador ever to tour the United States, fully aware of the national and international problems created by migrations. He was of aristocratic origin; with a profound sense of duty; cultivated and well endowed with common sense; inimical to rhetoric and knowledgeable about the history of the United States. He spoke English and was a fearless observer, capable of understanding the phenomena of the social and political world without biases, tears and false outrage. His is a first-rate testimony by a first-rate observer. Born in Savoy,[3] I presume his family had followed the fortunes of the royal house of Italy first to Turin then to Rome. He was one thousand percent Piedmontese. I didn't spend time researching his personal history because his writings speak for themselves. His travelogue was first published in the *Nuova Antologia* and later reprinted in the volume *Attraverso gli Stati Uniti per l'emigrazione italiana* published in 1912 [sic].[4] It is an important document. Mayor des Planches journeyed through the United States, from New York to New Orleans, on to Texas and California and returned East through Chicago and Detroit.

---

2 Edmondo Mayor Des Planches (1851–1920). Born in Lyon, France. Diplomat and politician. From 1901 to 1910 he was Ambassador of Italy in Washington.

3 Western-most region of Piedmont, now part of France, and ancestral fief of the Savoy dynasty that unified Italy.

4 *Attraverso gli Stati Uniti per l'emigrazione italiana*. Torino: Unione tipografico-editrice torinese, 1913.

In the course of his journey he ventured into side trips, particularly in the southern states. He wrote a direct, precise and incisive prose without wasting words: he truly belonged to the Italy that existed before D'Annunzio (whose great success spoiled the modest but honest language of Italian newspapers). Upon visiting a new city or locality, he would report tersely what he could observe directly, describing houses and people; taking notes on the cost of rent and other basic necessities, including salaries, social behaviors and on the relations among races and classes. He also wrote succinct biographies of individual Italian immigrants thus creating a small gallery of portraits made of the humble stories of people nobody else had bothered to notice. He did not penetrate too deeply, he didn't take a chance with hypotheses and he totally lacked in empathy and poetry. His ambition was to be like a camera, not a probe, with a style more like Julius Caesar's than Cicero's.[5] That's why I like his book so much. His best pieces describe American trains, cars, churches and the meeting places of Italian Americans. Anecdotes are very rare; however, I found a very good one about how clueless many immigrants were in those days.

> A functionary of the Italian consulate in New York finds in the elevator of the consular house, on Broadway, a fellow Italian crouching on the floor in a corner. The elevator operator, an English speaker, says: "They found him in the street and they brought him here to be taken in by the consulate. But now he doesn't want to get off. He has been going up and down for an hour." The poor man doesn't understand and doesn't respond. What to do? The functionary asks him questions. The poor devil was on his way to Philadelphia to visit some relatives. He had no idea what an elevator was and believed he was in a special kind of train that was supposed to take him to destination.

I believe this is the only anecdote told by Des Planches. Humor wasn't his strong suit: his best quality was his imperturbability in front of different customs and emotions. A major example of this is his coolness

---

5   Marcus Tullius Cicero (106-43 B.C.E). Writer and orator in Ancient Rome. His style, extremely elaborate and intricate, is the bane of students of Latin. The *periodo ciceroniano* [Cicero-style clause] became the model of Italian official documents starting in the sixteenth century.

about lynching (it should be noticed that he visited several localities where Italians had been lynched.)

> Lynchings in general are acts of summary and exemplary justice executed—either with cool determination or under an emotional surge—by the masses against individuals who are either factually or presumably guilty of crimes. They follow certain procedures that by now have become ritualized: hanging, shooting the hanging bodies etc. Lynchings are ordinarily carried out against Blacks with the goal of an immediate exemplarity, either as punishment or vengeance for the rape of white women. In the lands on the frontier and in remote areas lynching is practiced to this very day also against white people as punishment for serious crimes.

One can sense that behind these words is a man with great legal education and training who knows how to describe a phenomenon with precision but without indignation, not even repressed, as we would expect in a person educated in a society with the moral cult of the law. To him lynching was a natural fact that in certain conditions was bound to happen, like a solar eclipse or a flooding. There is beauty in this kind of style.

I should also add that when he had to deal with cases of lynching of Italians, he was relieved he didn't have to shake hands with the authorities of the localities where those events took place. At the same time, when he tells those stories and recounts how the events developed, he clearly signals that the Italian victims had some degree of responsibility; at least to the extent that they used threats of violence or otherwise violated local norms. At the same time we have beautiful descriptions of the towns where these crimes took place. They are a pleasure to read, after seeing so many fake western movies. Here is a piece about the boomtown of MacGehee [sic] in its boom years.[6]

> For the time being, the population is a mix of males from every corner of the world and from every walk of life. There are manual laborers who work for the railroad and the repair shops for two dollars a day, a few storekeepers, railroad clerks; and then land speculators,

6   McGehee is located in Desha County, Arkansas. Its establishment is tied to the construction of a railroad line in 1878.

adventurers, gamblers and worse. It is sunset: they hang out along the soft, muddy street with deep tracks made by car wheels, the only street in town; or on the sidewalks made with wobbly wooden planks, in shirt sleeves, with dirty hats, smoking, chewing, spitting large wads, somber, angry. The majority looks tough, suspicious. Some talk softly with one another like conspirators. This is social anarchy. Everyone does whatever he pleases. There is only one right that is recognized and respected: personal and private property. It is in the common interest to respect it. Every other aspect of life is dominated by unrestrained freedom, lack of laws and the rule of force.

In this portrait all that's missing is the image of some Loretta Young[7] strolling along, with a long skirt, a hat with improbable white feathers and incredible lace on the protruding breast. Add that and we would be straight inside a movie. However, women barely appear in Mayor des Planches's reports. In his relations with American authorities and the clergy he was affable and friendly, but he became inflexible when the rights of Italians were at stake. He denied that Italians were brought to the south to replace Black labor, but when he reflected on the subject, he recognized that unfortunately southern Italians did not have the kind of sense of dignity that would prevent them from mixing with Blacks. He felt very proud when he heard from local authorities and the clergy that Italians were honest, hard-working and thrifty. Almost all the biographies he left us described Italians who brought honor to themselves, were successful and ended up with important positions in society (more in California than anywhere else).

The central goal of his book was to convince Italian immigrants not to get stuck in the big cities of the Atlantic coast and the industrial north. He thought they should spread out to the countryside in the west and most of all in the south where land was cheap and where Black labor was not very productive. (He described Blacks as lazy, hand-to-mouth and easy prey of vice: a rather traditional albeit correct perspective.) In these regions the climate is also closer to that of southern Italy. Here is, in his own words, his *dream*:

---

7 Loretta Young (1913-2000). Actor. Screen name of Gretchen Young.

My goal is to favor the settlement on the entire territory of the United States of Italians that are now concentrated in the large Eastern cities, particularly New York, Boston and Philadelphia; where the majority lives in segregated neighborhoods in conditions that are morally unhealthy, physically unsanitary and economically depressed. Too many of them share very limited space in a state of promiscuity; always among themselves; isolated from the society that surrounds them. Here they hang on tight to the habits, traditions and superstitions of their native towns. They give a dismal spectacle of themselves, taking care only of the most basic needs with the lowest salaries. They cause damage to themselves and others with cheap competition and criminality; and they look like parasites living off the American society of which they are not an organic part, and which is tempted to reject them as it cannot absorb them. In the meantime, they are treated like alien beings, inferior, often object of disdain and condescendence, of hatred and ridicule; like the Jews in their medieval ghettos, or like the pariah cast in Indian cities. For many of those who end up living in those cities, city life is not a normal condition. It has been calculated that forty eight percent of Italians who migrated to the United States were originally peasants. They adapt to the cities with too much ease because they can get some material things they never had before; because other folks from their hometowns live there and they cling to them to feel less lost; because they don't know where else to go; because in order to get here they spent all the money and all the emotional energy they could muster and now they are overwhelmed by inertia. They happen to end up in a certain place and they stay put. They crowd the places, on top of each other like sheep in a sheepfold; the newcomers are jammed into the small space already occupied by those who arrived earlier, dozens per room, hundreds per floor, thousand per building; in dangerous agglomerations where the human ferments of destitution, vice, disease and crime develop.

Isn't this a beautiful piece? After reading this, I thought that he could have been a great journalist, had he not been a diplomat. Not even the pages written by Rossi, who was a professional journalist, reached this level of clarity. Italian immigrants, as Mayor des Planches says, were illiterate. They followed what relatives told them (in the best case) or what they were told by immigration agents (the slave drivers of the new era, who would deliver the bodies to the masters). As to the problem of *directing* Italian immigration, Mayor des Planches had moderate ideas. Like everyone else, he thought it made sense to have more consuls with smaller areas of jurisdiction and more resources to assist the needy. At the same time, he proposed to develop welfare agencies that combined joint initiatives of Italians and Americans: a very smart idea that went nowhere. He also reports the failure of some colonies organized for Italian farmers, such as Sunny Side, Del Rio[1] etc. He probably did not understand that nobody could be better at figuring out the best place to settle than the immigrants themselves. After all, their motivation was self interest and they knew what they were good at. It is also rather dubious that if Italy had sent more immigration agents, even if more capable and less corrupt (where could they be found in those days?), they would have changed the situation. One of the forces that kept Italian immigrants inside the cities was their sheer hatred for farming, and it would have been very difficult to convince them otherwise. Despite the fact that this pragmatic gentleman, Piedmontese bureaucrat, faithful servant of the house of Savoy, was sometimes a dreamer and was looking down from up high, he left us a prime collection of observations and data and a very precious testimony. We can see this, for instance, when we compare his observations with the attention Rossi gave to certain phenomena, thus revealing different experiences. Rossi was the first one (as far as I know) to annotate with precision the new words that immigrants created by fusing Italian and English together. Des Planches, instead, didn't even register the phenomenon. Yet some of the immigrants he interviewed (and indeed did he interview them…) must have answered with the new lingo. Only once, in the south, where he found Italians who had replaced Blacks as cotton pickers, he noticed that cotton processing was called *ginnatura* (from *gin*, namely the operation of extracting seeds from the cotton). Nothing else grabbed his attention.

I have always maintained that the witnesses to history have only seen, heard and noticed what they could. Mayor des Planches was a scrupulous writer who never failed to use double *ii* as a plural for the word *studio* and to mark with an accent the word *sèguito* [continuation]

---

1   Most likely the reference is to Del Rio, Texas, where Italians settled in the late 1880s.

to avoid confusion with *seguìto* [followed: past participle of *seguire*]. But the Italian American language was not important to him, nor was it worthy of his attention.

New York, March 27, 1960

TWO GREAT JOURNALISTS WITNESSED THE TERRIFYING BEGINNNINGS OF ITALIAN IMMIGRATION

Two Italian journalists were able to observe from the very beginning the effects of the sudden, improvised, unplanned collective migration of peasant masses from southern Italy to an English-speaking world that was undergoing rapid industrialization whose consequences fell both on the migrants themselves and on the American people. Their names are Dario Papa and Ferdinando Fontana.[2] The first one occupies a position of great relevance in the history of Italian journalism. The journey to America marked an important moment in his life as he was prompted to change his political ideas from pro-monarchy to pro-republic. The second one, Fontana, was a well-regarded poet of the *Scapigliatura*[3] movement. Both were fluid and transparent writers with the sharp eye and the good memory of good reporters. Their journey through the country from New York to San Francisco took place around 1881 and lasted two years. Both were struck by the most obvious aspects of American life and many of their observations would be worth quoting, if this were the object of my interest. But I am interested instead in their insight into the lives of Italian immigrants. Fontana devoted two long chapters to the conditions of immigrants in New York.[4] The first chapter concerns the facilities they found when they first arrived. This was before the world-famous Ellis Island. The entry point was Castle-Garden, "a huge building where all immigrants are gathered as soon as they disembark in New York. The majority of the building is occupied by an immense hall that can easily accommodate a thousand people. Along its perimeter runs a ledge, about thirty feet up." From that ledge Fontana was able to look down into the hall. The

---

2   Ferdinando Fontana (1850-1919). Poet, playwright and librettist of Puccini's first two operas: the long-forgotten *Le Villi* (1884) and *Edgar* (1889).

3   *Scapigliatura*. Literary and artistic movement centered in Milan in the second half of the nineteenth century. It was influenced by the Paris *bohèmian* movement that advocated anti-conformism and originality.

4   Dario Papa, Ferdinando Fontana. *New York*. Milano, G. Galli, 1884.
   • *Viaggi*. Lecco, Rota, 1893.

impression was so strong that he stated: "I will never forget it, should I live as long as Methuselah."[5] In that hall the immigrants were sleeping all together, men and women, old and young, healthy and sick, living and moribund. And they were all cooking their national dishes.

> When I climbed up on the ledge the hall was half empty. It was around nine in the morning. A few small groups of immigrants that had arrived a few days earlier were gathering near the heaters in the corners. Some were sleeping on mattresses lain on the floor, wrapped in raggedy blankets. They were speaking softly; once in awhile I could hear someone cough, or a child's cry followed by the monotonous sound of peasant baby cribs rocking on the floor. Together with the noises, a dull and nauseating smell was wafting upwards toward me. It's the typical smell of hospitals, insane asylums, prisons and all those places where people are segregated in large numbers. It's a smell like a miasma; of stagnant air; of foul breath and putrefying organic substances; rendered sharper by a faint odor of dust (...) Slowly, the huge hall filled up. Some ships had docked. A crowd, a true crowd of people from all nations, squeezed in. A noise like the flux of a tide was rising, followed by wafts of hot and miasmatic air. I could feel it on my face. A thin fog was condensing above the crowd. In the middle of the noise, at intervals, the voice of a young man with an official hat with golden insignia would shout. He was an interpreter who repeated in all the European languages: "We are looking for Such-and-Such from Such-and-Such country."

Scenes like these don't exist anymore, but we certainly remember seeing them during and after World War II. Isn't what Fontana described in 1881 the atmosphere of concentration camps and prison camps? Isn't this proof that emigration was born in poverty, despair, torment and anguish? This must be what was left in the adults and even more in the children: a sense of fear and anxiety that would last their entire life and would be passed on to the next generation. Isn't this the atmosphere of a catastrophic *rout*?

Fontana observed all the various groups, from Jews to Germans to Irish. The biggest and most destitute were the Irish and the Italians. Fontana noticed that, unlike the Irish, even the most brutish Italians,

---

5   Methuselah. Biblical patriarch reported to have lived 969 years.

even the filthiest among them, at least were not victim to the curse of alcoholism. He noticed a swift Italian man trying to hide from view of the police, with whom probably he had some pending business. He saw a little old lady from Calabria who could not explain why she was there and whom she had come to visit. He heard the bad-grammar propaganda of Protestant charitable societies. Some immigrants who heard Fontana speak Italian asked him to read a letter they were carrying. It turned out they had been swindled by a hustler who had promised them jobs as soon as they landed, working for some person who had no idea what they were talking about. In a few lines there he collected a sample of the garden variety of indignities endured by the immigrants, abandoned to themselves, ignorant, surrounded by a swarm of hustlers and swindlers from their own country. Another chapter is devoted to the shame for the jobs they had to take, first of all, shoeshine. Fontana, a bit rhetorically, describes the tears of wounded pride from the eyes of the scion of a noble family in whose veins "ran the most gentile blood, the purest, the most generous that a human creature could vaunt," and who had to kneel in front of a... Black person, "in front of the representative of the lowest of all races." Fontana describes him in realistic terms:

> This guy (...) with his large chest pushed up high, in a pose of cloying arrogance, dressed charlatan-esquely *à la fashionable* [sic], with his ramshackle mouth open in a wide smile to display to the passersby two thick rows of milky white teeth that held a big Avana cigar; that Black guy was there, stretching his neck, with his smug face, triumphant; puffing out clouds of aromatic smoke; twirling a walking cane of rare wood with gold inlays in his right hand gloved in a yellow glove, paradoxically yellow.

Luckily, Fontana wrote this racial [sic] passage fifty years before Fascism caved into Nazism: I reported it here (only a small part of it, as it goes on and on!) only because I thought that it represents the attitude of Italians. I can only imagine what would have been the attitude of a rich American, someone who made his own fortune; or maybe a former slave owner from the south; or even an American from the north that did free Black people from slavery but would never allow them into his house. The direct effect of the docility of Italians in taking those vile jobs was the contemptuous opinion that Americans in general harbored towards them. Fontana moves from the analysis of this particular job to garbage pickers.

> To see hundreds of Italians prostrated at the feet of people to shine their shoes is cause for heartbreak. But to see thousands of them bending their backs in front of mountains of garbage; rummaging through it like famished dogs; that really hurts deeply. In New York garbage is collected in busted barrels placed on the sidewalk in front of every house (...) Next to the barrels, full to the brim with all sorts of filth, there is always some bum picking through them. If he is not Irish, the bum is Italian, but not some old Italian man in poor health who could justify that vile activity with the excuse of old age and his unsuitability to a less humiliating job. No: a young Italian, strong and healthy, sometimes even with a spark of intelligence that transpires from behind the brutishness that covers him from head to toes.

Today the patriotic Fontana would be happier: Italians don't pick up garbage anymore; it is mostly Black people. Indeed, Italians own many of those companies and they hire Blacks for these jobs; and, as if this weren't enough, this industry is involved in a *racket* [sic] that is, at least according the local press, primarily Italian. They are probably the grandsons of the people that Fontana saw sifting through the garbage and that Giacosa, later, will see do the same in Chicago. Fontana continues:

> The rag traders in New York receive their supplies almost exclusively from the Italian colony that lives in the Five Points[6] section of town, a neighborhood in a very central location in the city; not far from the *down town* [sic] and with a very sad reputation. Here the houses are only three-storey high; with walls dripping with

---

6 The neighborhood of Five Points was in Manhattan, in the section that later became Little Italy, and now is extension of Chinatown. Its boundaries were Centre Street to the west, the Bowery to the east, Canal Street to the north and Park Row to the south. The name derived from the intersection of five city streets. It was considered the worst of all slums, infested with disease and dominated by criminal gangs.

humidity and the plaster disintegrating; with busted windows and no glass panes. The narrow streets are in horrendous conditions, paved and perennially covered with layers of muck and trash. To walk through Five Points at night, they say, is an act of courage (…) Almost every week some kind of bloody incident or aggression or street fight ends up in the newspapers and focuses the attention of the city on the terrible Five Points. It is true that the most horrendous crimes in New York are caused with the same frequency by people of other groups. However, the desperate and deranged look of our co-nationals; their miserable and despicable jobs; the quickness in pulling a knife; the filth where they live; plus the aggravating factor of legendary, melodramatic brigandage; all contribute to placing them, for the right or the wrong reasons, among the most likely to commit crimes; and, therefore, to being always the first suspects when crime is an issue.

Fontana also noticed the merciless attitude against Italian immigrants, from the American press to street urchins. But, intelligently, he understands that part of the blame goes to the motherland that allowed the peasant masses to languish in a state of brutishness; and part of the blame also goes to America that let the landlords of those hovels make gigantic amounts of money by allowing the buildings to decay into the state of primitive caves. Even today, despite the fact that the conditions are better, the same complaints are raised against the owners of *slums*. Today, Italians don't live there anymore; now it's the turn of Blacks and Puerto Ricans. Fontana was also one of the first ones, in the face of the hostility of the press and the public opinion, to take the risk of declaring that one could understand, albeit not justify, the use of knives by Italians; the only weapons they could use against aggressive and threatening mobs.

How can the poor Italians defend themselves against this huge enemy mob; without deadly weapons; and, moreover, with their hot temper rendered even harsher by centuries of suffering? The only defense they have is terror: the knife… And they use knives the way the meekest animal would use its teeth when pushed to the extreme limit.

At the end Fontana goes through the Italians who managed to climb into relevant positions in business; the owner of luxury restaurants or the celebrities of the cultivated society. He observed that the conditions of the Italian community were already improving, and he had words of praise for the Italian consul and for a journalist named Adolfo Rossi. I noticed that none of the names of the prominent Italians was known to me, and neither were their restaurants. None of them, it seems, was able to get established long enough to be passed on to the next generation and stay in business for at least thirty years. Maybe many went back to Italy after making their fortune. Maybe their children, educated in American schools, didn't want to or didn't know how to continue. Maybe their descendants were chewed up by American life. Fontana's reportage is an important document. It is a pleasant reading even to this day. And it shows that Italian immigration began in the midst of fear, anguish and contempt.

HE PREFERRED HAPPY ITALIAN DRINKERS TO THE LONELY NEW YORK DRUNK

In 1891 Giuseppe Giacosa wrote *La Dame de Challant* for Sarah Bernhardt's upcoming debut in North America. For the occasion he traveled to the United States where he resided for few months during which he took notes for what would later become a volume titled *Impressioni d'America*.[1] Seventy years after its publication I doubt it would be worth publishing a new edition; but at least it is a book worth reading. Giacosa's testimony is more relevant than his theories, just the same way as his eyes are more valuable than his brain. In his prose, I sense quite clearly the intention to emulate Edmondo De Amicis. At least, the literary model that inspired this book is better than the models he followed in his production as a playwright. The choice of materials, the framing of the scenes, the rhythm of time, the moderate tone, the lexicon taken from everyday's language; they all take us back to that *respect for the public* that later D'Annunzio-inspired journalism would eventually discard and ignore, with the excuse of ennobling the columns of periodicals. This book contains a message that the author wants to communicate; thus, in order to help his readers, he writes in a way that makes sure they will understand; with his own ego kept under tight control. He also avoids the facile parochialism of exalting our co-nationals and putting down foreigners. The light of the author's intelligence and culture are focused on understanding and interpreting with impartiality; to the point that I would call this one of the most honest products of bourgeois literature of the period. Literally, Giacosa resists the temptation to write about Niagara Falls or the abattoirs in Chicago; the topics of *beautiful prose* that in those days, for foreign correspondents in America, were the equivalent of

---

1   Giuseppe Giacosa (1847–1906). Playwright and librettist. He wrote the librettos for some of Puccini's most famous operas: *La bohème*, *Tosca* and *Madama Butterfly*.
   • *La Dame de Challant*. New York, Rullman, 1891. Based on a short story by Matteo Bandello (c. 1480-1562), it was first produced in New York in 1891.
   • Sarah Bernhardt (1844-1923). French stage and early film actor, nicknamed "The Divine Sarah."
   • *Impressioni d'America*. Milano, Cogliati, 1898.

Niccolò Paganini's sonatas.[2] He was saved from the typical traps where many others, with more talent but a larger ego, would fall; probably because he was already accomplished and also knew how far he could stretch the strings of his violin. His tone is never too high and this allows him to avoid playing out of tune.

There is an aspect that should and could attract the attention of today's readers, namely the comparison between America then and America today. This is not what the author planned, obviously, but it has the positive effects of giving us contrasting snapshots. We can find this contrast even in the lexicon, with words like *moro* [Moor][3] instead of *negro* [Black person]; or *viale* instead of avenue. This latter one is a word we don't translate anymore knowing full well that, in Italian, *viale* stands for a tree-lined double-wide street, while American avenues rarely have trees. The snapshot quality of his observations also appears in the description of things he saw and that are now obsolete. It is sort of pleasurable reading about them; the same way it is pleasurable to look at a fifty year old photograph.

The chapter on bars is definitely the most successful in the entire book. Giacosa caught immediately the difference between Italian-style drunkenness and the American version.

> In Italy drinkers reveal their vice even in the moments when they are trying to control themselves. The moment he pours the only drink he will allow himself; and the moment he brings the glass to the lips; his eyes shine full of anticipation. It is a glance like a caress, full of tenderness, ready for joy; a bit constrained and contained by the heroic resolution not to exceed. When he puts back on the table the empty glass after a few delicious sips, one understands that temptation and resistance hang on the wire of his willpower

---

2 Niccolò Paganini (1782-1840). Composer and one of the greatest violin virtuosos of all times. His *Capricci* are some of the most technically challenging pieces ever composed.

3 *Moro* is the adjective used to indicate people of dark complexion in ancient Italian. It was also used for Africans. As an example, Shakespeare's character Othello in Verdi's opera *Otello* is described as *il Moro di Venezia*. *Negro* came into use in the colonial period (late 1800s) and became the default term for Black person. Different and evolving sensibilities now prefer the use of *nero*, while *negro* has taken a negative, quasi-racist, connotation.

in an unstable balance. He dodges the glances of the bartender to avoid the temptation of sin. He places the little chalice on the edge of the counter without pulling back his hand, as if hesitant about the decision. Nobody can guess whether he wants a refill or if he is putting it down, satiated. He leaves it up to the intuition of the bartender or to the supreme god of all drinkers and gamblers: chance.

In comparison, American drinkers are gloomy and dominated by the will to drink.

If one enters a bar around ten in the evening he will find more or less the same crowd that was there in the afternoon... Same men, tall, lanky, elegant and royally posturing. Yet, to a keen observer it will be obvious that their composure is due to an effort of volition rather than natural grace. They are no longer straight but rigid and stiff, their faces with a violent expression. One would guess that they are drinking with disgust, as if they were forced; for most of the time they stand there in a state of inertia; surrounded by a crowd; in total loneliness; unaware of what surrounds them. Nobody talks with the person next to him, not even in a whisper. Those brightly lit places, full of taciturn people, are more sinister than our dives.

Beautiful description, isn't it? And just as valid today, despite the fact that New Yorkers were different back then. The kind of Anglo-Saxons Giacosa met in those places in those days, today are aristocratic exceptions hidden behind the doors of exclusive clubs. However, as often happens with Giacosa, he didn't dig deeper into the subject. He had the right intuition but he missed that Italian drunks in general drink wine, while Americans drink whisky. There is a huge difference in terms of time, quantity, quality, measure and character in these two kinds of drunkenness. Generally, wine drunkenness is slower and convivial. With whisky, it's quicker and lonely. Should we say that whisky is Protestant and wine Catholic? The Irish would complain...

A couple of chapters in Giacosa's volume (a total of 285 pages in small format) are dedicated to Italians. Giacosa's testimony here is even more valuable. He could access direct sources of information since he knew both languages, Italian and English. He immediately understood the difference between the Italian immigrants who had the foresight, or the good luck, to settle in the countryside and those who got stuck in the cities without professional skills.

> In Texas, Italians are held in great esteem, contrary to what happens in the rest of the United States; possibly with the exception of California (...) The most serious issue Americans raise with Italian immigrants is the sordid, degrading and incurable passivity and resignation to the worst activities, to the lowest and worst-paying jobs. The Italian plebes in New York and Chicago give a spectacle of supine resignation to poverty and cynical indifference to the pleasures of life. This shows in their dresses, their abodes and their food. The only ones who are in worse shape perhaps are the Chinese.

Giacosa's initial conclusion was that hostility toward Italians was caused by the fact that Italians were content with low-level lifestyle; but then he examined other possible reasons for the alleged antipathy. A co-national explained to him that "Yankees resent the money that Italians send back to Italy." Another, an educated American, enamored of Italy, found a reason in the fact that, of all foreigners, Italians were the slowest to become Americanized. Giacosa concluded by blaming the American ruling class that taught Italian immigrants that "votes are merchandise that can be traded"; and that by trading them they could improve their station in society, get higher salaries, obtain expedite and righteous justice. I wonder: in Giacosa's times, weren't votes also bought and sold in elections in Italy? Anyway, I don't believe anyone left a better description of the debasement of Italian immigrants than the page he devoted to Italian women working in the garbage industry in Chicago.

> As far as I know Chicago does not have neighborhoods that are exclusively Italian. Therefore, the spectacle of our miserable condition can be found everywhere and in particular in activities in the lowest industries where only our co-nationals end up working. The most common is rummaging through the garbage accumulated near huge grain depots, leather-tanning shops, railroad stations and piers. This is the activity of old women from southern Italy who came to America with a husband and children. While the men tend to their professions or jobs, the women spend the whole day with garbage, in any kind of weather: rain, snow or wind. If they are lucky at the

end of the day they bring home a few cents. Paper, leather waste, rags, nails, metal sheets, rivets and metal wires: these are the final discards, the vilest refuse of the wasteful industrial-mechanical civilization. They pick everything and put it in sacks. A pair of slippers; a ripped blouse; a small bottle with the remains of some unknown medication: to their eyes these are true treasures. Who can draw the line between the usable and the unusable? They will probably put on those slippers and wear that blouse. The eternal feminine in them has no fashion demands. Aren't they also nourished by the dumpsters?

Giacosa also saw American filthiness. When he visited the world-famous Chicago slaughterhouses, he protested against their reputation for cleanliness and order.

Blood vapors impregnate all the pores of walls and ceilings. Sprays and rivulets of blood infiltrate troughs, barrels, counters, columns and floor boards where they are converted into brownish, evil-smelling mud, slimy and sticky, that frequent washes cannot dissolve and cannot sweep away; and instead push even further into wood fibers until it penetrates them completely. The rooms are low-ceiling and crammed, thus the workers always bump into each other and visitors must suffer stomach-churning contacts. There are few windows. A faint light comes from them onto the dark walls obscured by the vapors exhaled from water-boiling cauldrons and pulsating cuts of meat. In this environment hundreds of workers move around; each assigned to a particular function and forced by the mechanical rhythm of the operations to a furious pace without pause. Those unfortunate don't have faces and bodies of men. The faces are congested into an expression of overwhelming disgust by a determined stiffness of will; and by the bloody inebriation that bites them. Their eyes are constantly forced open by the greasy and shiny redness that birdlimes forehead and cheeks; by the coagulated blood that hardens beard and hair; in the visual effort to discern in the shadow the precise point where to land the hatchet's blow. All this gives them appearances that have nothing to do with those of human beings; that are below the very ferine animality they butcher in such formidable carnage.

We are not yet where Upton Sinclair[1] would take us in 1906 but we are pretty close. Giacosa in these circumstances isn't the romantic poet or the pathetic realist who portrays the joys and sorrows of northern Italian bourgeoisie. He is a good reporter. He left us a testimony of America in those days that has only one defect: it's short, quick and without the foundation of historical culture. His opinions, in general, drift toward the adoration for the United States, almost in anticipation of what will soon become the general tone of reportages by Europeans in that period (for instance Albert Houtin's);[2] and that will reach a peak after World War I (*Amica America* by Jean Giraudoux, 1918).

In Giacosa, for instance, we can see the beginning of the idealization of American women. "American women, the young ones, are more full-of-life than ours. They are in better health, taller, skinnier. From their brisk stride and diffused cheerfulness transpires a *joie de vivre* that pervades the face and the entire body." At that time Europe had not yet discovered the *mammismo* and *piovrismo*[3] of American women (or, to be fair, of *many* American women.) This discovery, moreover, will be made by Americans, not European writers.

New York, August 1, 1960

---

1 Upton Sinclair, Jr. (1878-1968). Novelist and essayist. He achieved great notoriety with the book *The Jungle* (New York, Doubleday, Page & company, 1906) that denounced the working conditions in the Chicago stockyards.

2 Albert Houtin (1867-1926). French priest and philosopher. He was excommunicated for his positions in favor of modernism. He is the author of *L'Américanisme* (Paris, Librairie Émile Nourry, 1904).
 • Jean Giraudoux (1882-1944). French writer and diplomat. Author of *Amica America* (Paris, Émile-Paul Frères, 1918).

3 *Mammismo* [mama boy-ism]: excessive attachment to one's mother in adult age. *Piovrismo* [octopus-ism] is a neologism not reported by Italian dictionaries.

AN ITALIAN WOMAN IN AMERICA
AN EDUCATED NATIONALIST

Since I started reading and re-reading books about the United States written sixty, seventy or eighty years ago by Italians, I have had the impression I am leafing through a family album full of daguerreotypes and old, faded photographs; but also the collection of a photo magazine, with sharp snapshots of old and obsolete customs. Since the United States was born after a revolution against England—indeed, against Europe—it has attracted the attention of many observers and millions of readers. There are now hundreds of books about this nation, and the crescendo of publications is not abating. Books are available in all languages. There are reports, investigations, impressions, studies, paeans, criticisms, invectives, diaries, memoires; with illustrations, drawings, photographs in black and white and in color; statistics; books sporting a white beard and books that contain poison ivy. Books by Italian writers are not very numerous and none of them achieved world fame like the essays by Alexis De Tocqueville.[4] Most recently I re-read a book published just before World War I. This event marked America's entry into European politics and a fatal milestone in the relations between America and Italy. It was also the sign that modern communication technology had shrunk the distance between the two continents, with the result that Europe's war and peace now also concern America. It was a fatal date for Europe and also for the United States in that it marked the end of the American period of isolationism from the European world. The author of this book, *America vissuta*,[5] was Amy A. Bernardy. I normally don't pay much attention to the biographies of individuals. Italy does not have a very good library reference system for biographical and bibliographical information; thus, I could only surmise that the author was probably a student of

---

4 Alexis de Tocqueville (1805-1859). French historian and political thinker. His most famous book is *De la démocratie en Amerique*, published in two volumes in 1835 and 1840.

5 Amy A. Bernardy (1879-1959). Journalist and historian.
  • *America vissuta*. Torino, Bocca, 1911.

Pasquale Villari,[6] in love with classical studies and with the nationalist ideology that had sprung up around that time. It was published under the aegis of the Florence Institute of Higher Studies.[7] If we go by her last name, we can also guess that she was a foreigner, an impression confirmed by the first name. None of this matters much. Apparently she was well off and could count on solid introductions as shown by the fact that she was received by the Italian ambassador and by President Theodore Roosevelt.[8] She collaborated with the journal *Il Marzocco*[9] and authored books on the history of the relations between Venice and the Turkish empire and other powers in the seventeenth century. I bet my head (metaphorically) that she was wearing eyeglasses. (See note at the end of the chapter.) She wasn't a very compelling writer, although she was a rather apt observer and an eager researcher. She also enjoyed hyperboles. Here is the portrait of the United States found in the opening pages:

> [T]his great Republic is like a Harlequin costume in the positive sense of the term: thousands of pieces are stitched together into a dress; fraying and patched up; in bits and pieces; and yet able to endear itself to the public more than old clunky armors of antique paladins. Beautiful and horrible; infantile and generous; skeptical with a tragic and scary cynicism; obsessed with a grotesque fanaticism worse than the medieval kind; the result of mixing heroic and rebellious bloodlines; depraved and chaste; uncontaminated and filthy; descendant from puritanical ancestors and daughter of outlaw fathers. This bastard, cosmopolitan race is the American race, the race that more than any other one should have in itself the seeds— and more than just the seeds—of all the virtues and all the vices from the North and the South; from the Orient and the Occident;

---

6   Pasquale Villari (1827-1917). Historian and politician. He taught at the *Reale Istituto di Studi Superiori Pratici e di Perfezionamento* in Florence from 1870 to 1876. He was also president of *Società Dante Alighieri* from 1896 to 1903.

7   Most likely the *Reale Istituto di Studi Superiori Pratici e di Perfezionamento*. Founded in 1859, it was a post-graduate research institute. It was the original nucleus that later became the *Università degli Studi di Firenze*.

8   Theodore Roosevelt (1858-1919). He served as the 26th President of the United States from 1901 to 1909.

9   *Il Marzocco* (1896-1932). Cultural and literary journal.

all gathered here by ways of immigration; transmitted by foreign medleys; generated by indigenous hybridization; determined by hereditary tendencies; excited by climate and nature. All this could turn this race into the only race in the world from which we could expect all that the world can give, magnificent or unbearable. "*Nisi imperasset*" [If it didn't already rule the world].[10]

I reported this short passage because it is a nice piece. We can see here the culture and taste of those days; and we can see the watermark of the author's erudition that, as she does frequently in the book, culminates in a Latin quotation. It also illustrates a sententious spirit that shows no shame in proffering moral judgments that are tautologically indisputable. However, this nice piece is based on the wrong presupposition that in those times an American race actually existed (it doesn't exist even in the present); and that it was the result of many European, Asian and African races. This is not the case today and was even less so back then.

In America there are certainly offsprings of the mixture of different races, generally northern races, because they were the first ones to colonize this country. Yet, a true *American race* does not exist. In its place we have the Anglo-Saxon concept of social life, that is, the social model that all the other races adopt and that constitutes the form, the *structure* of this country. This country is not dominated by an Anglo-Saxon race; rather by Anglo-Saxon concepts. The constitution, with its preoccupation for individual liberty, state rights and private education, is Anglo-Saxon. The justice system, based on open debate in court, is based on the criterion of *case by case* jurisprudence and not that of statutes. The role of police; and the freedom of assembly and freedom of the press are Anglo-Saxon. The form of marriage and divorce; and the position of women in society are of Anglo-Saxon origin. Even non-Protestant religions conform to the criteria of Anglo-Saxon churches. Any Catholic who seriously analyzes the structure of his Church in the United States will agree that, in many respects,

---

10 "*Omnium consensu capax imperii nisi imperasset*" ["If he wasn't already ruling the world, everyone would have pronounced him worthy of heading an empire,"] Tacitus, *Historiae*, 1,17. The comment refers to Emperor Galbia who reigned for only one year after the death of Nero.

it resembles Protestant churches more than the southern European Catholic churches that were not directly influenced by Protestantism.

This book was composed in a rather uninhibited way and without an agenda (which makes for captivating reading); mixing together interviews with presidents, personal diaries, gossip columns, art notes, discussions on theories, quick sketches about Greek and Chinese communities etc. At the foundation is the concept of *race*. Ms. Bernardy maintains that Americans and Italians had nothing in common and, therefore, there was no chance they could fuse into one entity. This is rather questionable if one takes the word *fuse* literally: of the two elements required for a fusion, the Italian supplied the moldable matter; while the Anglo-Saxon provided the die. One gave it the body; the other, the soul. Up until now America is an operation performed by the Anglo-Saxon race on the masses that did not have a distinct national identity. And here we come to the other mistake made by Ms. Bernardy. She believes that Italian *paesani* from the south were *Italian*. At most, if they had a collective identity at all, this was the *Catholic* identity; but they lacked a national consciousness, education, language and affection (they loved their little native hamlets, but not Italy as a nation and state.) On the good side, Ms. Bernardy shows she had a very sharp eye and independent judgment toward our co-nationals who, she believed, could never become *fused* with America. (Indeed they *fused*, did they ever! In general they were reduced to the bare minimum, like a denominator.) Her book contains two chapters on Boston's Little Italy that constitute one of the most important testimonies on the quality of life of Italian immigrants in America.

Here is a passage about two characters of the colonial world that have disappeared: the *paesano* and the *banchista* [banker] of our Little Italies.

> In this Little Italy we basically find a series of small villages, gathered around a couple of bell towers. The immigrant mass at this time is all concentrated around different nuclei; polarized around as many leaders as there are villages, bell towers and small churches in Italy. They came from places identifiable by those landmarks and—on the other side of the Atlantic—*paesani* and *compari* rebuilt the same places repeating the echo of the names. The concept of *paesano* is

the fertile creator of colonial nuclei. Any attempt to embrace wider concepts and ideas of renewal and moral changes among the masses fails against this bastion. An example comes from the banking business. Immigrants blindly trust only the *paesani* and for this reason they end up losing everything to the bankruptcies—alas, real ones—of so many apocryphal banks that exist only because the *paesani* trust and support them. And, for the same reason, larger impersonal institutions encounter resistance and distrust when they try to open up branches in Little Italy. If you ask an immigrant where he keeps his money, he will tell you that *lu paesano* has it. Try to persuade him there is a better way: impossible. The *paesano* who keeps his money is also his confidant, his lawyer, his personal adviser, his protector, his federal agent. When *lu paesano* goes belly up or runs away with the money, the poor victim cries, curses or resigns, depending on the individual personality. Then, he goes back to working and saving. And he hands his savings to the next *paesano*. If this one happens to be honest, all is well. If not... This explains the tremendous power of the little retail banks in comparison to institutional banks; and the enormous difficulty in the form of passive resistance encountered by the *Banco di Napoli* [11] with immigrants who do not want to use its services for commercial operations. In effect the *Banco di Napoli* is an impersonal financial institution. That's it. For the cosmopolitans among us that is enough: indeed, that's what makes it more secure. But for the immigrant it is unquestionably inferior to the typical traditional bank which, like at the time of Dante, is located in the neighborhood's drug store; the emporium *de omnibus rebus* [of all possible things] and related *quibusdam aliis* [and all kinds of other things]. Sure, it is more than a bank. It is a bookstore, a newsstand; often with a printing shop (culture and finance are fused in one civilizing *trust* [sic]). The colonial bank is also notary office, travel agency, shipping company, navigation, *express* agency, pharmacy and employment bureau. Often it includes a *grosseria* [grocery store], a warehouse for imported foodstuff, even a pasta factory and sometimes a bakery oven. The banker is also a landlord who owns lots of buildings rented to great profit thanks to his extensive connections. His name, in the colony, is *banchista*. All this is traditional, legitimate, familiar, smart, profitable, very respectable and honest... when it is an honest arrangement. When

---

11   *Banco di Napoli*. One of the oldest banking institutions in Italy. It was founded in 1539 as a *banco di carità* [charitable bank], namely, a pawn shop that made loans without interests.

it is not honest, he uses his client's money to buy foodstuff for his own *grosseria* and will sell at double the price to the flattered client. Not only, but he sells to him on credit with an interest; or he mortgages the salary that the client earns working for an allied contractor, from whom he has already received a percentage that is inversely proportional to the wage the client is earning after the *banchista* himself convinced him to take a job at a lower pay. This way the *banchista* receives a cut from everyone he has helped earn money by using his clients. He also lends money to show off how his generosity; but he will do so only when he is already sure he has under his nails enough profit generated by the employment of his client; and enough profit to cover possible losses. In the financial contracts with his employees, he inserts a clause requiring that they drag into his net all the *paesani*. He is also involved in murky deals about putting up bail money for people in trouble with the law. He rents or sublets homes that he reports as assets worth $10,000 in real estate, while in reality 70 or 80% of it is mortgaged. He accepts deposits of $10,000 although he knows full well that he only has reserves to cover a minimal part of it. And nobody will be surprised if the home sublet to a boarder is put to a different use by an entrepreneurial Madame... It is a fatal closed circle, a diabolical net that imprisons the immigrant who cannot rebel. If he rebels, the organization comes down on him and he ends up being blacklisted. The blacklisting of workers reaches the level of atrocity. It is painful to admit it, but the worst enemy of an Italian is usually another Italian.

I would also like to quote another nice passage by Bernardy, full of interesting observations and passion:

> To be happy in America one needs an aptitude for mechanical things; an opportunistic and entrepreneurial spirit, sharp about business and dull and primitive in everything else. One needs to be conventional and follow all *approved standards* like a sheep. One must show great interest for everything American and superior contempt for everything Latin, even the things that made Latin life great and beautiful. The Italian immigrant, to the contrary, is full of rural vitality, individualism and regionalism. His business sense is rudimentary. Although he doesn't know and cannot express it, his soul is burdened by the ancestral traditions of his bloodline. This soul, tenacious and constantly challenged, impalpable but omnipresent,

is what we feel in Little Italy (the nickname given by Americans to the neighborhoods where Italian immigrants live). You are moving across American life and then, suddenly, you feel that something is going through your spirit, and penetrates it, and bares it under the attacks of hyper-civilized barbarism. You feel a little tear in the fabric of your being: a regret, a longing for everything that was, for everything that is and that maybe will be. It is the waft of exile, cold and thin; it is a moment of void, loneliness and pain. Everything around you seems to break up into smithereens, collapse, suddenly fall down, in the incurable nostalgia of your lonely heart. Then, with its boredom, with its travails, American life takes over again. What was it? It is the soul of Italy that passed you by.

This piece describes both a period and a woman writer with her illusions and her acute perceptions. But also with blind spots. Forty years later I visited the same neighborhood in Boston. There is no longer any trace of the Italy she describes, except for a few faded restaurants. All the Italians who found success adapting to industrial society and the opportunistic and entrepreneurial spirit; to the business acumen, limitations, conventionalism and acceptance of approved Americans standards; they all fled to try to make a *new face* for themselves in upper-middle-class suburbs. In general they are caught in mid-air, no longer Italian and not yet American: "*Color che son sospesi.*"[12]

Bernardy didn't see the responsibility of the Italian ruling class for this state of affairs. Italian leadership gave to these *adaptable* neither a national consciousness nor a technical education. Undoubtedly, these were wonderful people: suffice it to say that they survived and solved their economical problems. Here the original stock helped: by that I mean the southern peasant stock that for centuries fought against an impoverished land, against an unfertile soil and the *barons*.[13] Perhaps,

12 Dante, *Inferno*, Canto II, 52. "*Io era tra color che son sospesi.*" ["I was among those who are suspended [in mid air]."] Vergil describes this way his personal condition in the *Limbo*, the anti-chamber of Inferno, where worthy souls that died without baptism are relegated without hope of ascending to heaven.

13 The reference is to the aristocrats that owned immense tracts of land, the *latifondo*, that constituted the majority of estates in the south. These were almost always absentee landlords who lived around the royal court, either in Naples or Palermo, extracting wealth from their possessions in a merely parasitical way.

despite her ideas about race and stock, Ms. Bernardy didn't realize that there were differences in the patterns of Italian immigration to America. Maybe these were due to race and stock, or maybe to history. Let's take Tuscans and Ligurians on one side and southern Italians on the other. The Tuscan-Ligurian immigration to California created different outcomes than that of southerners to Boston. Tuscans emerged as *contractors*, builders and entrepreneurs (though not architects); Ligurians as bankers and wine makers.

It would be unreasonable to expect correct prophesies from a writer motivated by a patriotic spirit with great observation skills and style—a bit frondose, yes, but still a *style*. She left us a couple of books that are important testimonies. Due to the unusual circumstances of her life, she was one of the few Italians, and certainly the only Italian woman of her time; who understood the phenomenon of Italian immigration, unknown and ignored by all with the exception of a handful of politicians and journalists of that period. The visits of politicians to the United States began when the immigration phenomenon was about to end. Today lots and lots of them, now that immigration is over, keep coming. The Italian ruling class is always late.

New York, September 4, 1960

[Endnote in the original] Amy A. Bernardy, a valiant scholar of popular traditions, died quietly in Rome on October 25, 1959. She was born in Florence where her family, originally from Savoy, had moved. She graduated from the University of Florence in the Faculty of Letters with a thesis on Venetian–Turkish relations in the XVII and XVII centuries.[1] The thesis was published with an introduction by Pasquale Villari.

A very erudite woman with a vast culture and a polyglot with a reserved but enthusiastic personality, she traveled frequently in particular to North America where for several years she was a lecturer at Smith College in North Hampton [sic], Massachusetts. She became interested in Italian immigrants and produced investigations, reports,

---

1   Amy A. Bernardy. *Venezia e il Turco nella seconda metà del secolo XVII*. Firenze: Civelli, 1902.

publications and broadcasts. She was particularly interested in women and children living in industrial centers, and participated actively to the activities of the Dante Alighieri Society and other similar institutions that tried to assert the values of Italianness.

Giovanna Dompè, Commemoration of Amy. A. Bernardy
June 15, 1960, Università di Roma

AMERICA AT THE TIME OF CHARLESTON
AS SEEN FROM A EUROPEAN FEMALE ARISTOCRAT

Approximately twenty years after Amy A. Bernardy wrote two passionate books, full of direct impressions, on the United States, another woman, Irene di Robilant,[2] a descendent from an ancient Piedmontese family, published a volume about life in America. It was not a book of memoirs, impressions, observations or portraits of things seen, despite the fact that she had seen a lot in her position of secretary (in reality, founder) of the *Italy-America Society*.[3] Her book was full of information, notions, facts, figures and quotations. It was the first book of its kind meant for the general public; with a wide panorama on many aspects of American civilization and complete with a bibliography after each chapter; witnessing the author's impartiality and seriousness. It was a survey on the economic situation, the educational system, the primitive peoples of North America and other practical issues. It included accounts by other competent Italians who had traveled through the continent and saw it useful to report back what they had learned. Nothing similar had ever been published in Italy before: di Robilant was the first and she did a great job. Let's begin with an important fact that until today could be easily missed, namely the evolution of approaches in the books by European travelers to America in the decades straddling the last two centuries. Between 1880 and 1900, the main purpose appeared to be the need to report about this very distant land, a semi-barbaric country with plenty of unusual things that, to the observers, stood out as oddities. In di Robilant's book we see the tendency to discover patterns of similarities and differences between Europe and America, even in terms of culture. For instance, in a little book with impressions of America published in 1897 [sic], the famous composer Jacques Offenbach focused on the strident differences between the two cultures

---

2   Irene di Robilant (1895-?). Author, economist and translator. *Vita americana* (*Stati Uniti del Nord-America*). Torino, Fratelli Bocca, 1929.

3   The *Italy-America Society* was founded in New York in 1918 by a group of prominent Americans from the fields of finance, media and politics. Coincidentally (?), it was housed in the same building at 25 West 43rd Street in New York where the John D. Calandra Italian American Institute is presently located.

in the volume *Orpheus in America*.[4] He mentioned, for instance, the fact that orchestra members in America would rehearse in shirt sleeves. It isn't my intention to compare the two books: their goals are completely different, but I must add that they are both completely different *and* diametrically opposed. Di Robilant took pleasure in discussing the state of higher education; the press and journalism; publishers and magazines; music and the art scene; novelists, short-story writers and playwrights. Additionally, she wrote about *cultural* America, something that must have surprised many Italians (and Europeans); revealing for the first time the force, progress and successes of this country in fields where many would not have expected to find anything valuable. The *many* who didn't know about the American cultural scene, by the way, also included people of higher status who had just immigrated to America but had no idea what was going on. Thus, despite the fact that most of the information is now obsolete, this *catalog* is a good document of those times. The other observation I want to make is di Robilant's generally optimistic tone, and her favorable disposition toward America. This could be a consequence of the new relations that Europe and American developed after World War I in 1918. (In the same period, the genius of Giraudoux published a book whose title aptly expressed the mood of the time: *Amica America*.)

Di Robilant's book belongs in the honeymoon-like atmosphere created by American intervention against Germany (1917). Unlike Giraudoux's, though, her feelings are not expressed in dewy and mythical terms but rather with the lucidity and accuracy of a report. This intelligent, highly educated, curious and dedicated woman was a rare case in the Italy of old. Today, after World War II, things are different, but back then it was really unusual for the daughter of an aristocratic family to leave her home and country to end up working abroad as a secretary. This position put her in contact with the rich, sophisticated, artistic and powerful New York society: from Otto Kahn, protector of the Metropolitan Museum, to the Morgan family—the

---

4   Jacques Offenbach (1819 -1880). German composer and cellist, naturalized French citizen.

   • *Orpheus in America: Notes of a Traveling Musician*. New York, G. W. Carleton & Co.; Paris, Calmann Lévy, 1877.

top international bankers—and their lawyer, Paul Cravath,[5] whose Wall Street office was open day and night. She considered herself a bit like an unofficial ambassador of the newer and better post-war [WWI] Italy and she conceived her book as part of her responsibilities and duties as an Italian abroad. Who knows how many times, hanging out with Italian diplomats or with *nouveau-riche* Italian immigrants, in her humble position of secretary of an organization—small compared to the greatness of the official and social New York—she felt a revulsion against the superficiality of the former and the vanity of the latter? But her book gives no hints of this. As a woman, she must have had strong inclinations for some of those people and personalities, but not for others. However, she controlled her pen very tightly to the point where her impartiality is almost excessive; at the cost of reducing essential differences to naught; swallowed by a sense of fairness that becomes injustice when she put on the same level both the great and the mediocre. She was a keen observer of reality and always referred to it in the background. After World War I, American democracy, maybe for the first time since 1779, became the inspirational model for European masses (while the harsher realities were hidden away).

This book also examined the problem of the historical experiences stored inside the various racial groups. In particular it examines the vicissitudes of people of color, of Jews and Irish; explaining what kind of treatment they had received upon arrival; always keeping the tone of an impartial observer. One chapter, of course, is devoted to Italian immigration, without the enthusiasms or the despair of Bernardy. She fully understood that the so-called inassimilable foreigners that Bernardy observed as prisoners of the ghettos—Chinatowns or Little Italies—would be replaced by a second generation that would be fully American and often even more patriotic than the descendants of the Mayflower.[6] Here we don't run into visions of shantytowns, miserable

---

5   Otto Kahn (1867-1934). Banker, philanthropist and patron of the arts.

    • Descendants of the financier, banker and philanthropist John Pierpont Morgan (1837-1913).

    • Paul Cravath (1861-1940). New York lawyer and founding partner of the law firm known today as Cravath, Swaine & Moore.

6   In the original (p. 444) a footnote explains: "The first ship that in 1620 brought Anglo Saxons to North America."

jobs, horrible cohabitation with other races, cruel labor conditions and contagious diseases, as told in the stories by other visitors, from Adolfo Rossi to Giuseppe Giacosa. What she offered, instead, is a short chapter that defined the framework and guidelines for an analysis of the place of Italian immigration in the context of American history. It's like focusing the lens of a camera and the perspective, in its general outline, is still valid today.

Thirty years later, after World War II, the ties between the United States and Europe have been strengthened. The third generation of Italian Americans is now coming to age and a new chapter needs to be added. However, in terms of an analysis of Italian immigration within the context of American history, the book maintains its validity. The chapter in question does not indulge in useless national pride or acrimony toward America. Here and in other parts of the book, di Robilant ignored or omitted the tragic aspects of the conflicts in a nation that was formed artificially from powerful but abstract ideals, born from and reflected in the hopes of the ruling class. These were also ideals that derived from social, racial and economic realities in conflict with one another that often ended up squeezing out and mutilating those who got caught in the middle, whether they wanted or not, whether they knew it or not.

Since the end of World War II America has been the subject of many books. These are generally lively portraits and snapshots, colorful, impressionistic and full of anecdotes. However, none of them is grounded in the perspective of America's history like this one. Rather than *Vita Americana*[1] the title should have been *La cultura Americana*. At the time of her writing, in 1929, the author of the introduction already noticed the *Americanization* of European culture, a phenomenon that involved customs, mentality, and forms of industrial and political organization; a phenomenon that has continued to grow to the point that it is now one of the essential traits of our time. One of the least predictable developments of this process is American influence on European literature and philosophy. One of the merits of the book I just described is the chapter on American Philosophy, which is certainly one of the first times American philosophy is even mentioned at all.

---

1   *Vita americana (Stati Uniti del Nord-America)*. Torino, Fratelli Bocca, 1929.

The author did not foresee the popularity that pragmatism and John Dewey's pedagogy would eventually reach in Europe, although some hints had already begun to appear. This is a typical example of the merits and demerits of this book: sensibility about new things but not always a good judgment about them.

New York, October 23, 1960

AFTERWORD
Why Italian Americans Are Touchy

It was no surprise that an article I wrote about *Mafia mentality* among Italian Americans, (something different from Mafia proper), caused a reaction by one of the surviving tabloids still published in semi-Italian in the United States. The comments to my piece are a fabric woven with insults and falsities. The majority of Italian American press still has learned nothing from America; namely that public disputes require the precise, verbatim citation of words actually uttered by the antagonist. In abiding to this commandment, I would like to explain now why Italian Americans are so touchy as not to be able to argue without getting angry. And I will show how it is done with facts and arguments, without nasty words.

Emigration was an enormous tragedy for all the peoples that were forced to solve their economic problems by moving to a foreign country with a foreign language and foreign traditions. All experts in psychology recognize that uprooting human beings from the society where they grew up is one of the greatest hindrances to normal development. In one of the most recent books about the foundation of American civilization, I read the following statements about immigrants and the process of adaptation, here called *alienation*.[2] "In the transition between the old abode and the new, the immigrant always had a period of time of waiting patiently. There were long wakes in flophouses by the European peers until the ocean crossing could be secured by a travel agent and the ship's time of departure. In third class, always overcrowded for the sake of profit, were cold, dirty, fetid and often rat-infested. The long dark nights and daytime differ little from one another. Scarcity of food, unsanitary water, scurvy, dysentery and typhus caused death. When the ship finally arrived at destination, the immigrant found himself stunned and disoriented, in a world where the traditional skills and knowledge of his peasant heritage could not compete. In order to survive, he had to find immediately a job, any job, accepting any working conditions and number of hours,

---

2   A footnote contains the following information: Max Lerner. *America as a civilization*, pp. 86-87. (New York, Simon and Schuster, 1957).

thus becoming an easy prey for the *padroni* who exploited him, for scamming countrymen and bloodsucking usurers. Often, he would remain in the first large city where he had arrived, stuffed in a ghetto with others from the same home country. At times, he managed to go inland, hire a parcel of land or work as a salaryman, always with people of his same ethnic group. In either case, first he had to convert his abilities into capital; therefore, for many many years, he had to scrape by to save, living on nothing, until he could open a tiny shop or a diner; a small vegetable farm or a puny construction company.

I found the following description in the volume *The Uprooted*, by Oscar Handling:

> For years and years, often for their entire lives, many of these immigrants were kept in a condition of estrangement, alienated both from the culture they left and the culture that had not accepted them yet and that they did not want to accept, ending up alienated from themselves. The old customs of the village communities, despite their many faults, give people a stable direction in life. Here a man knows what others expect from him. However, the new lifestyle in large cities and the rapid-growing towns of America were disorienting in that he was forced to convert his energy into dollars for every single thing he needed to survive. Even more tragically, immigrants discovered that their own children adapted easily to the new rhythm of life, accepted the same ideals and were eager to mix in with the new environment. From the immigrant's point of view, the children were drifting away and becoming foreigners to their own parents. In order to eliminate the distance between themselves and their friends, the new generations started seeing their fathers and mothers with American eyes, representing them as strangers and foreigners, like objects. The circle of alienation was thus complete.[3]

In other words, with the exception of those whose upbringing was founded and educated in the same language and civilization as that of the host nation, all immigrants suffered to some extent a psychic trauma, as if they were the survivors or a shipwreck or a blaze.

---

3   Oscar Handling (1915-2011). Historian. He is credited with inventing the field of immigration history in the 1950s. *The Uprooted*. New York, Grosset & Dunlap, 1951.

* * *

No immigrant can be said to be a normal person. America was first made by immigrants and later filled with other immigrants who did not speak the language of the first ones, who did not share their religion, political practices, tastes and social games; and as a consequence of that, it is full of abnormal people. The nervousness we perceive in the political sphere, similarly to what we see in literature, derives from this fact. This is what lead D. H. Lawrence to begin his *Studies in Classical American Literature*[4] with the observation that the first Americans were all "fugitives," and deriving from this principle important conclusions on its fundamental character.

One should also consider that the distance in terms of customs was further increased by the educational level of the immigrants. Thus, the traumatic effects of immigration were felt more severely by those with lesser ability to comprehend the new reality. The immigrant who arrives in an unknown country must lose the deepest of his own self in order to adapt, and this is much worse than losing a part of one's body in an accident.

* * *

These spiritual mutilations can still be seen and heard in the language, or dialect, of Italian Americans, that is the series of broken words that are often ridiculed by peninsular Italians when they hear them. It is a language made mostly of nouns; a nomenclature that misses social and human values; a list of tokens; a few hundred English terms, distorted, and with a vowel attached at the end to imitate Italian: *giobba, polizzo, ghella, fattoria* (meaning, factory), *bosso, moneta* (money), *stima* (heating.)[5] This vocabulary of brutal and transactional words was the confine within which the lives and expression of millions of Italians were constrained.

---

4   David Herbert Lawrence (1885-1930). Writer and poet. *Studies in Classical American Literature*. New York, Thomas Selzer Inc., 1923.

5   In standard Italian *fattoria, moneta, stima* mean respectively: farm, coin, estimate or reputation.

* * *

Had Italian emigration been assisted and protected by the Italian government; and if Italian immigration had been welcomed by the American government during those tragic years (from 1880 to 1910) with a sense of respect for the personality of the immigrants, with schools and a safety net of social services (as it is today with the Puerto Rican immigration), the process of integration would have been less taxing, thus avoiding spiritual mutilation and degradation.

However, everyone knows how the great migration happened, although few in America care to remember, in a combination of pain, privation, hardship, scams (by Americans but also by fellow countrymen) and the complete abandonment by the state.

That's why I wrote and repeated many times in my reports from the United States that the Italian immigrants who didn't go crazy or became criminals must all be saints. I should have been more precise, including the Prominent with the criminals and the insane. The Prominent class, in fact, represent one of the most conspicuous products of the new barbarism of Italian Americans. Their lack of culture, together with the exalted vanity for their economic success tends to hide from the observer a history of struggles, dangers and cunnings, by virtue of which they attained the position they now occupy, surrounded by the glacial silence of the dominant Anglo-Saxon society. These stories of success tend to erase from the picture even the fundamental values of a civilization that were preserved through the destruction of their entire past existence: the strength and cohesion of the family.

Nobody can accuse Italian Americans of being responsible for their own degradation. The indictments should be directed to the governments of those days, Italian and American, who allowed the law of the jungle to rule over the masses of adults looking for work in the new continent, abandoned at the mercy of exploiters without scruples; and who abandoned the youth to be educated only schools by the streets and the gangs.

* * *

A tally of the dead, insane, suicide, prisoners, destitute has never been attempted. Only the strongest and the lucky survived the mass human sacrifice of bodies and spirit and reached economic success. That's what they were looking for, and that's what they achieved.

Only a few works of art and literature by Italian Americans left a documentation of this tragedy. Those were the few who learned the language of the ruling class, their *padroni*: Pascal d'Angelo, Pietro di Donato, Garibaldi Lapolla, Emanuele Carnevali, Guido d'Agostino,[6] Arturo Giovannitti, Jerre Mangione and few others. This is where we can find the truth; not in the speeches by diplomats; or the orations by Italian American politicians during patriotic banquets; or the articles by visiting journalists. Scraps of the truth are hidden in secret diplomatic correspondence, maybe in the notes of independent writers such as Giuseppe Giacosa, Amy Bernardy and Alberto Pecorini.

* * *

The survivors grew up in an expanding America that was getting richer and powerful and that took advantage of their work, ignoring them socially and pandering to them only when their children had become an electoral mass to be seduced immediately before elections. Like America and along with America, they grew and became richer and, in a sense, even powerful (at least, numerically). A small group of people who were able to mobilize their innate Italian sharpness and individualism, with a desire to live like the *padroni*, began to grow inside the communities. Left to their own devices to learn how to survive in the streets, they learned from the streets. They looked around and realized that in America what matters is wealth, and that all the *padroni* set the dollar as their main ambition, the yardstick by which men were measured and ranked. So, they pursued the dollar too, with even less scruples and a lot of determination, organizing some of the best (but not the first) criminal associations of America. Here they operated with the savvy of finance ministers and the gall

---

6   Guido d'Agostino (1910-2009). Writer, novelist.

of storm troops leaders. They understood and took advantage of the vices of the ruling class, providing the pleasures that their hypocrisy condemned, namely women, alcohol and gambling.

* * *

The majority of Italian Americans was not on their side but was not against them either. They didn't have the savvy to understand that the negative reputation of the big crime entrepreneurs and dealers of social contraband would have tarnished even those who were working eighteen hours a day to secure even minimal education for their children, to lift them out of the abject yoke of poverty as soon as possible.

The majority of Italian Americans did not react the same way the dominant constituencies of society did. With speeches by politicians; sermons from the pulpits; denunciation by newspapers; and finally – when needed – with the Lynch law and vigilantes squads (organized in murderous gangs and mobs that got rid of criminals), Americans worked to prevent the formation of a state within the state.

The greater mass of Italians was apathetic and complied with the demands of small-time extortionists in their neighborhoods; and turned a blind eye to illicit traffic, the same as they had done back in Italy. None of them dared testifying in court because they did not trust the police. This silence was observed by almost all the journalists working for Italian language publications and, because of this silence, the reputation of *mafioso* fell on every one of those humble, kind, peaceful Italian immigrants who repaired and shone the shoes of the *padroni*; and who were content slicing salami in the *grosserie*; or, with their arms were building railroads and skyscrapers designed by English-speaking engineers.

* * *

The *mentalità mafiosa* continues today among the residues of those communities that contributed to Italian reputation in America. But if anyone dares saying that the cause of this public relation disaster were weakness and reluctance to react; the collusion by the prominent and their colonial banquets; and the acquiescence by Italian diplomats, rather than an innate criminal disposition, whoever says that is accused of defaming and persecuting Italian Americans.

As far as I am concerned, I openly maintained that I prefer Al Capone to the Italian American cobbler who became famous in the press for crafting a pair of slippers for General Eisenhower. And, about the insults of those who accuse me of being an enemy of Italian Americans, I regard them as a badge of honor.

* * *

I wanted to make the point that Italian Americans are thin skinned. And here is the reason. Italian Americans suffer the trauma of emigration, a trauma consisting in uncertainty of language, and condition. As they did not feel certain they were fully Italian or fully American, the result is an overhyped sensitivity about the opinions of others.

Mafia no longer exist among Italian Americans, or at least not the kind of Mafia that typical Americans think of: a secret organization so powerful as to control and dominate the entire criminal enterprise in the United States, with tentacles abroad. Italian criminals in America may have been people of great ingenuity but they never reached that level of power.

Every time the subject comes up, Italian Americans immediately react as if they were being accused; and they react with apologies that go overboard, denying that Mafia exists at all and that there are no criminals among Italians. Thus, these defenders, claiming implicitly that all Italian immigrants were angels, lose any credibility with their potential audience and their complaints against films and books with criminal characters with Italian last names can be easily ignored.

It would be expedient to acknowledge that there was a number of Italians, or descendants of Italians, who, as a reaction to the false morality of the new country, after learning how to navigate the system, managed to get ahead in the only way they knew how. At least, in this respect, they managed to be feared, if not respected. By excusing them, they only end up not being feared and still not being respected.

WORKS CITED

Alighieri, Dante. *Divina Commedia*. 1308-1320.

Almerini, Achille. "L'italianità coloniale."

_____. "La sbornia di Noè."

Antoninus, Archiepiscopus Florentinus. *Tractatus de instructione seu directione simplicium confessorum*. Köln, Zell, ca. 1468-1470.

Ariosto, Ludovico (1954) *Orlando furioso*. Translated by Allan H Gilbert. New York, S.F. Vanni.

_____. *Satira II*. 1517.

Belli, Gioacchino. *Sonetti romaneschi*. 1864-1865.

Bernardy, Amy. *America vissuta*. Torino, Bocca, 1911.

Blue Book. New Orleans, Thomas C. Anderson, ca.1911.

Botta, Carlo. Historian. *Storia della guerra dell'indipendenza degli Stati Uniti d'America*. Paris, D. Colas, 1809.

Cabiria. Directed by Giovanni Pastrone. Screenplay by Gabriele D'Annunzio. Itala-Film, Torino, 1914.

Carducci Giosuè (1950) *Odi barbare*. Translated by William Fletcher Smith. New York, S.F. Vanni.

Carnevali, Emanuele. *Tales of a Hurried Man*. Paris, Contact Éditions, 1925.

Castellucci, V.A. *Le avventure di Dante in America*. New York, Italian Publishers,1935.

Chamberlain Lawrence, Alberta. *Who's Who Among Living Authors of Older Nations*. Los Angeles, Golden Syndicate Publishing Company, 1931.

Compagni, Dino. *Cronica delle cose occorrenti ne' tempi suoi*. 1310-1312.

Cordiferro Riccardo."T'ho troppo amata."

_____. "Perché?"

Corsi, Edward. *In the shadow of liberty: The Chronicle of Ellis Island.* New York, Macmillan, 1935.

D'Angelo, Pascal. *Son of Italy.* New York, McMillan, 1924.

D'Azeglio, Massimo. *I miei ricordi.* Firenze, Andrea Croci Editore, 1881.

De Amicis, Edmondo. *Sull'oceano.* Milano, Treves, 1889.

De Capite, Michael. *Maria.* New York, The John Day Company, 1943.

De Montaigne, Michel. *Les Essais.* 1595.

De Tocqueville, Alexis. *De la démocratie en Amerique.* 1835-1840.

Des Planches, Edmondo Mayor. *Attraverso gli Stati Uniti per l'emigrazione italiana.* Torino, Unione tipografico-editrice torinese, 1913.

Di Robilant, Irene. *Vita americana (Stati Uniti del Nord-America).* Torino, Fratelli Bocca, 1929.

Enciclopedia Italiana. Istituto dell'Enciclopedia Italiana, Roma, 1929-.

Fante, John. *Dago Red.* New York, The Viking press, 1940.

Feder, Sid, and Joensten, Joachim. *The Luciano Story.* David McKay, New York, 1955.

Ferrazzano, Carlo. "La Merica Sanemagogna."

Fontana, Ferdinando, and Papa, Dario. *Viaggi, Volume 2.* Lecco, Rota, 1893.

Forever Amber. Directed by Otto Preminger. 20th Century Fox, 1947.

Four Centuries of Italian Influence in New York. Museum of the City of New York. New York, 1955.

Giacosa, Giuseppe. *La Dame de Challant.* New York, Rullman, 1891.

_____. *Impressioni d'America.* Milano, Cogliati, 1898.

Gil Blas de Santillana. Published in 1715-1735, Lesage, Alain-René

Giovannitti, Arturo. *Arrows in the Gale.* Riverside, Hillacre Bookhouse, 1914.

Giraudoux, Jean. *Amica America.* Paris, Émile-Paul Frères, 1918.

Gregorovius, Ferdinand. *History of the City of Rome in the Middle Ages.* London, G. Bell, 1909-1912.

Guicciardini Francesco (1949) *Ricordi*. Translated by Ninian Hill Thomson. New York, S.F. Vanni.

Houtin, Albert. *L'Américanisme*. Paris, Librairie Émile Nourry, 1904.

Incalicchio, Giuseppe. "Comparison."

Kunitz, Stanley, et al. *Authors Today and Yesterday. A Companion Volume to Living Authors*. New York, The H. W. Wilson Company, 1933.

La Wally. Music by Alfredo Catalani. 1892.

Lapolla, Garibaldi. *The Grand Gennaro*. New York, Vanguard Press, 1935.

Leo XIII. *Rerum Novarum*. 1891.

Leopardi, Giacomo. "A Silvia." 1828.

Lerner, Max. *America as a Civilization*. New York, Simon and Schuster, 1957.

Little Caesar. Directed by Mervyn LeRoy. Warner Brothers, 1931.

Livingston Arthur "La Merica Sanemagogna." *Romanic Review*, vol. 9, 1918.

Mangione, Jerre. *Mount Allegro*. Boston, Houghton Mifflin, 1943.

Manzoni, Alessandro. *I promessi sposi*. Guglielmini e Radaelli, Milan, 1840.

Mercantini, Luigi. "La spigolatrice di Sapri." 1858.

New York Confidential. Directed by Rouse, Roussel. Warner Brothers, 1955.

Offenbach, Jacques. *Orpheus in America. Notes of a Traveling Musician*. New York, G. W. Carleton & Co.; Paris, Calmann Lévy, 1877.

On the Waterfront. Directed by Elia Kazan. Columbia Pictures, 1954.

Papa, Dario, and Fontana, Ferdinando. *New York*. Milano, G. Galli, 1884.

Parini, Giuseppe. *Il giorno*. 1763-1765.

Pascoli, Giovanni. "Italy." *Primi poemetti*. Bologna, Zanichelli, 1907.

Pecorini, Alberto. *Gli americani nella vita moderna osservati da un italiano*. Milano, Treves, 1909.

Pellegrini, Angelo. *An Immigrant's Return*. New York, Macmillan, 1951.

Petrarca, Francesco. "La gola e 'l sonno e l'oziose piume." *Canzoniere*. 1336- 1374.

Pisani, Lawrence Frank. *The Italian in America. A Social Study and History*. New York, Exposition Press, 1957.

Poliziano, Angelo. *Orfeo*. 1479-1480.

Prezzolini, Giuseppe, et al. *Repertorio bibliografico della storia e della critica della letteratura italiana dal 1902 al 1932*. Roma, Edizioni Roma, 1937-1939.

Pulci, Luigi. *Morgante*. 1478.

Scarface. Directed by Howard Hawks. Universal, 1932.

Seneca, Pasquale. *Il presidente Scoppetta, ovvero La Società della Madonna della pace (dalla sua fondazione al suo scioglimento)*. Philadelphia, 1927.

_____. "Orrè Italy"

Sinclair, Upton, Jr. *The Jungle*. New York, Doubleday, Page & Company, 1906.

Some Like it Hot. Directed by Billy Wilder. United Artists, 1959.

Sondern, Frederic. *Brotherhood of Evil, The Mafia*. New York, Farrar, Straus, and Cudahy, 1959.

Stowe, Harriet Beecher. *Uncle Tom's Cabin; or, Life Among the Lowly*. Boston, J.P. Jewett and Company; Cleveland, Jewett, Proctor, and Worthington, 1853.

The Opening of a Window. Gene Radanò, 1961.

The Untouchables. Produced by Martin Quinn. ABC, New York, 1959-1963.

West Side Story. Music by Bernstein, Leonard, lyrics by Stephen Sondheim, 1957.

Who's Who in America. Chicago, Marquis Who's Who Ventures, 1899-.

CITED ITALIAN AMERICAN
NEWSPAPERS AND PERIODICALS

L'Adunata dei refrattari. New York, 1922-1971.

Americolo. New York, 1925-1926.

Il Bollettino della sera. New York, 1898-193?.

Il Borghese. Roma, 1950-2001.

The Boston Free Press. Boston, 1960-1967.

La Calzetta d'Italia.

Il Carroccio. New York, 1915-?

Il Cittadino. 1910-1919.

Colombo. Houston, TX.

Controcorrente.

Controvento.

Il Corriere d'America. New York, 1922-194?

The Delaware Valley Italian American News Herald. Philadelphia, 1961-present.

La Follia di New York. New York, 1893-1966.

La Gazzetta del Massachusetts. Boston, 1903-1944.

Il Grillo del focolare.

Italamerican.

L'Italia. Chicago, 1886-?

Italian Quarterly. 1957-present.

Italian Review. Providence, RI, 1924-?

Italica. 1926-present.

Italo-American News.

Il Mondo libero. Dearborn, MI, 1963-?

La Notizia. Boston, 1916-?

L' Opinione. Philadelphia 1906-1935.

La Parola del popolo. Chicago, 1922-1963

Post-Gazette. Previous name *La Gazzetta del Massachusetts*. Boston, 1944-present.

Il Progresso Italo-Americano. New York, 1880-1988.

La Sentinella. Bridgeport, CT. 191?-1948.

Sons of Italy Times. Philadelphia, 1959-.

Italian News.

La Tribuna italiana. Tucson, AZ.

La Voce. Firenze, 1908-1916.

La Voce d'Italia. Brooklyn, NY, 1947-?

CITED ITALIAN NEWSPAPERS AND PERIODICALS

ANSA. Roma, 1945-present.

Il Corriere della Sera. Milano,1876-present.

L'Europeo. Milano, 1945-2013.

Le Farfalle. Firenze, 1921-1929.

Le Forche Caudine. 1884-1885.

L' Illustrazione italiana. Milano, 1873-1962.

Lacerba. Firenze, 1913-1915.

Il Marzocco. Firenze, 1896 1932.

La Nazione. Firenze, 1859-present.

Nuova Antologia. Firenze, 1866-present.

Piccolo Giornale d'Italia [sic].Trieste, 1881-present.

Il Pungolo verde. Campobasso.

La Rassegna letteraria. Palmi, Reggio Calabria.

Il Resto del Carlino. Bologna,1885-present.

La Voce. Firenze, 1908-1916.

LIST OF REAL PERSONS

LIST OF FICTIONAL CHARACTERS
AND PSEUDONYMS OF UNIDENTIFIED PERSONS

ABOUT THE AUTHOR

GIUSEPPE PREZZOLINI (27 January 1882 – 16 January 1982) was an Italian literary critic, journalist, editor, and writer. He served as the Head of Columbia University's Casa Italiana and was the founder of the cultural and literary journal *La Voce*.

ABOUT THE EDITOR AND TRANSLATOR

FABIO GIRELLI CARASI is professor in the department of Modern Languages and Literatures at Brooklyn College. In the course of his career he has been active both in the fields of academia and journalism, having worked as regular contributor for several Italian publications, among which *Airone, Management* and *La Repubblica.* His academic interests include educational technology and 20th century Italian literature, with several publication on the poetics of Cesare Pavese and Guido Gozzano, and particularly on the work of Primo Levi. He has participated in international conferences in Europe on the topic of "multiculturalism" and the ideology of identity in minority groups. Recently, he has turned his attention to Italian American studies and the history of Italian immigrants to the United States as exemplary of the process of integration impose on all immigrants; the role of institutional violence (incarceration, capital punishment, segregation, discrimination and – in its extreme form – lynching) in achieving that goal; and the price paid by both individually and collectively by immigrant minorities.

He is currently engaged in a research on the printed media of the period 1880-1920 in the areas where episodes of lynching of Italians took place, predominantly in the Deep South; in an attempt to establish comparative criteria for the analysis of the various manifestations of racism suffered by Italian in America and other minority communities.

CROSSINGS
AN INTERSECTION OF CULTURES

Crossings is dedicated to the publication of Italian-language literature and translations from Italian to English.

Rodolfo Di Biasio. *Wayfarers Four*. Translated by Justin Vitello.
    1998. ISBN 1-88419-17-9. Vol 1.

Isabella Morra. *Canzoniere: A Bilingual Edition*. Translated by Irene
    Musillo Mitchell. 1998. ISBN 1-88419-18-6. Vol 2.

Nevio Spadone. *Lus*. Translated by Teresa Picarazzi.
    1999. ISBN 1-88419-22-4. Vol 3.

Flavia Pankiewicz. *American Eclipses*. Translated by Peter Carravetta.
    Introduction by Joseph Tusiani. 1999. ISBN 1-88419-23-2. Vol 4.

Dacia Maraini. *Stowaway on Board*. Translated by Giovanna Bellesia and
    Victoria Offredi Poletto. 2000. ISBN 1-88419-24-0. Vol 5.

Walter Valeri, editor. *Franca Rame: Woman on Stage*.
    2000. ISBN 1-88419-25-9. Vol 6.

Carmine Biagio Iannace. *The Discovery of America*. Translated by William
    Boelhower. 2000. ISBN 1-88419-26-7. Vol 7.

Romeo Musa da Calice. *Luna sul salice*. Translated by Adelia V. Williams.
    2000. ISBN 1-88419-39-9. Vol 8.

Marco Paolini & Gabriele Vacis. *The Story of Vajont*. Translated by Thomas
    Simpson. 2000. ISBN 1-88419-41-0. Vol 9.

Silvio Ramat. *Sharing A Trip: Selected Poems*. Translated by Emanuel di
    Pasquale. 2001. ISBN 1-88419-43-7. Vol 10.

Raffaello Baldini. *Page Proof*. Edited by Daniele Benati. Translated by
    Adria Bernardi. 2001. ISBN 1-88419-47-X. Vol 11.

Maura Del Serra. *Infinite Present*. Translated by Emanuel di Pasquale and
    Michael Palma. 2002. ISBN 1-88419-52-6. Vol 12.

Dino Campana. *Canti Orfici*. Translated and Notes by Luigi Bonaffini.
    2003. ISBN 1-88419-56-9. Vol 13.

Roberto Bertoldo. *The Calvary of the Cranes*. Translated by Emanuel di Pasquale. 2003. ISBN 1-88419-59-3. Vol 14.

Paolo Ruffilli. *Like It or Not*. Translated by Ruth Feldman and James Laughlin. 2007. ISBN 1-88419-75-5. Vol 15.

Giuseppe Bonaviri. *Saracen Tales*. Translated Barbara De Marco. 2006. ISBN 1-88419-76-3. Vol 16.

Leonilde Frieri Ruberto. *Such Is Life*. Translated Laura Ruberto. Introduction by Ilaria Serra. 2010. ISBN 978-1-59954-004-7. Vol 17.

Gina Lagorio. *Tosca the Cat Lady*. Translated by Martha King. 2009. ISBN 978-1-59954-002-3. Vol 18.

Marco Martinelli. *Rumore di acque*. Translated and edited by Thomas Simpson. 2014. ISBN 978-1-59954-066-5. Vol 19.

Emanuele Pettener. *A Season in Florida*. Translated by Thomas De Angelis. 2014. ISBN 978-1-59954-052-2. Vol 20.

Angelo Spina. *Il cucchiaio trafugato*. 2017. ISBN 978-1-59954-112-9. Vol 21.

Michela Zanarella. *Meditations in the Feminine*. Translated by Leanne Hoppe. 2017. ISBN 978-1-59954-110-5. Vol 22.

Francesco "Kento" Carlo. *Resistenza Rap*. Translated by Emma Gainsforth and Siân Gibby. 2017. ISBN 978-1-59954-112-9. Volume 23.

Kossi Komla-Ebri. *EMBAR-RACE-MENTS*. Translated by Marie Orton. 2019. ISBN 978-1-59954-124-2. Volume 24.

Angelo Spina. *Immagina la prossima mossa*. 2019. ISBN 978-1-59954-153-2. Volume 25.

Luigi Lo Cascio. *Othello*. Translated by Gloria Pastorino. 2020. ISBN 978-1-59954-158-7. Vol 26.

Sante Candeloro. *Puzzle*. Translated by Fred L. Gardaphe. 2020. ISBN 978-1-59954-165-5. Vol 27.

Amerigo Ruggiero. *Italians in America*. Translated by Mark Pietralunga. 2020. ISBN 978-1-59954-169-3. Vol 28.

CPSIA information can be obtained
at www.ICGtesting.com
Printed in the USA
BVHW071516260421
605863BV00005B/848